CALL OF DUTY® BLACK OPS II

Call of Duty: Black Ops II, like all other games in the *Call of Duty* series, is a first-person shooter (FPS). This means you play most of the game looking through the eyes of the main character as he fights his way through the campaign's many scenarios.

This section of the guide is for users new to first-person shooters, or those who haven't played an FPS in a few years.

GAME DIFFICULTY

In Campaign mode, you can choose from four difficulties:

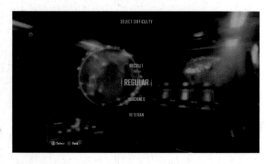

> **Recruit:** For players who are new to first-person shooter games.

> **Regular:** This is the default difficulty. It does not present anything too difficult.

> **Hardened:** Enemies are tougher and more likely to throw grenades. Taking cover to avoid damage is crucial.

> **Veteran:** This is extremely difficult and challenging for even the most experienced *Call of Duty* veterans.

You can lower this at any time, by pausing and selecting a lower difficulty. Remember, you cannot raise the difficulty.

HEALTH

There is no health meter or number to represent how much health you have. Your well-being is represented by blood splatter on the screen. A red arc shows up when you are hit. This arc represents the direction from which the attack originates. Take cover and the screen clears, showing that you are recovering.

TAKING COVER

In *Call of Duty: Black Ops II*, it's very important to take cover to avoid taking too much damage. Crouch down and move behind a wall, a counter, some rubble, or any object that can give some level of protection from incoming fire.

Most weapon fire penetrates softer objects such as wood, plaster walls, and cubicle walls. Use this to your advantage when enemies employ these as cover. But beware: their bullets penetrate these substances, too.

LOADOUT

At the start of each campaign level, you are given a particular weapon loadout. You are given two guns and two types of grenades. Press Y/Triangle to customize your loadout. You can choose two weapons to carry with up to three Attachments for each. Select the two types of grenades and up to three Perks. These weapons, Attachments, and Perks need to be unlocked before selecting them. Refer to our Arsenal chapter for more information.

Enemies drop their weapons when they're killed, giving you the opportunity to switch your guns often.

SHOOT FROM THE HIP

Whenever your weapon is ready to fire, a crosshair appears in the middle of the screen. This represents the spread of your weapon when you fire it from the hip or fire without targeting.

Firing in this manner is less accurate than aiming down the sight (ADS), so it's better to limit hipfiring to close-range weapons such as shotguns and machine pistols. This method is also a quicker way to fire. Long-range weapons, such as the sniper rifle, are very inaccurate when fired this way.

AIM DOWN THE SIGHT (ADS)

Aiming down the sight greatly improves the accuracy of your shots. It's the preferred way to fire your gun. It gives you a view of your weapon as you line up the shot with its sight.

 If a scope is attached to the weapon, then you only see through those optics. It may offer you the ability to zoom in on your target, giving you even better accuracy from long distances.

RELOADING

In the lower-right corner of your Heads-Up Display (HUD), two numbers are separated by a slash. The first number represents the ammo remaining in the clip and the second shows how much of that ammo you have in total. Below these numbers, two sets of icons represent the type of grenades you carry and how many. Your weapons can be reloaded at ammo crates throughout the levels.

To reload your weapon, press the Use button. Depending on which weapon is selected, the time required to reload can vary. It's always a good idea to duck behind cover when you reload, and sometimes it's better to switch to your other weapon if it reloads faster.

ACCESS KIT

Throughout the campaign, as long as you carry the Access Kit Perk, the word Access will appear on locations that can be opened with this kit. This nets you an extra weapon of some sort, protection, or tactical improvements. Often, this is required in completing challenges.

ALTERNATE MODES

If your weapon has an alternate mode, such as a grenade launcher, or you have picked up a special weapon with the Access Kit, such as mortar rounds, a graphic appears to the right of your ammo count. It is separated into four sections. The left represents Left on the D-pad, the top is Up, and so on. To use these modes or weapons, press in that direction. Around the outside of this graphic is your compass.

OPTICAL CAMOUFLAGE SUIT AND TARGETING FOR DRONES

In the future, an Optical camo suit can be found in an Access crate. This is used to blend in to the background. If this is available, an icon is shown above your ammo count. The words Camouflage Enabled are shown on the right side of your HUD when it is turned on.

Inside some Access locations, you gain the ability to target enemies with supporting drones. This is also represented by an icon above the ammo count that represents the type of drone. Press the direction shown and place the reticle on the desired target. Then press Fire to have the quad drone, CLAW, or ASD fire at that location.

MELEE

You always have a combat knife equipped. If you can get close to an enemy, press in on the Right Analog Stick to knife the foe. To stay undetected, move behind a hostile target and melee him. Inside Access locations, you find more melee weapons. After picking one up, you automatically use it when you melee attack.

GRENADES

Two grenades are carried with you at all times. Press Left Bumper/L2 to toss the left one and Right Bumper/R2 to toss the other. Damage grenades, such as Frag grenades, cause an explosion. Tactical grenades can stun, blind, or disable an enemy.

Grenade Danger Indicator

The Grenade Danger Indicator pops up when a grenade lands near your location. A small arrow points to where it sits. Move away from it to avoid taking too much damage. If you're quick, move over to it, pick it up, and toss it back at the sender. Be careful though, as it can go off in your hands.

USE BUTTON

You employ the Use button (X/Square) when you perform many actions in the campaign. This includes using a turret and picking up Intel. Text appears onscreen when an item can be used.

If you're against a strong barrier, such as concrete, and the icon indicates that the grenade is on the other side, duck behind cover to safely avoid the blast.

DOWNED BUT NOT OUT ENEMIES

If you knock down an enemy and he doesn't die, he may try to crawl away or pull out his handgun. Be sure enemies are completely out before you change targets.

SPRINT

Pushing in on the Left Analog Stick causes your character to run faster. Sprint between pieces of cover to become a tougher target to hit.

BRANCHING STORYLINES

Several times during the campaign, there are choices or actions that affect the story and even make one mission unavailable. For example, wounding or killing someone changes what happens later in the campaign.

REWIND STORY

Sometimes, you may make a decision in the campaign that you regret and wish to try a different way. For example, maybe you killed Defalco in the Karma mission and rescued Chloe. Later, perhaps you find out this has consequences that you may not like. In Replay Mission, when selecting a mission, you can press Right Bumper/R1 to reset the storyline to the mission that you're looking at. Now, when you continue the story, you pick up at this point in the campaign.

STRIKE FORCE MISSIONS

Up to five Strike Force missions open up at different times during the campaign. Your gameplay in the campaign affects how many Strike Force missions become available. Completing them is optional and you have a limited number of attempts to do so. They can be replayed outside of the story at any time by selecting Replay Mission.

SINGLE-PLAYER CHALLENGES

Each mission in the campaign has 10 challenges that can be accomplished to unlock weaponry. These include eliminating enemy personnel in certain ways, performing tasks, collecting intelligence, and finishing a level without dying. The

10 challenges are listed at the beginning of each level. We also show what is unlocked by completing two and five challenges in each mission.

SCORE

After completing a mission, you are scored based on kills, types of skills, challenges completed, and difficulty. You can then compare your score with others at the Leaderboard.

CAREER RECORD

In between missions in Campaign mode, you can view which challenges you have completed, what has happened in the story, and your best score by selecting Career Record from the loadout screen.

This section lists all the weapons, their Attachments, grenades, Equipment, and camo. In these tables we detail all relevant stats and what is required to unlock each particular piece of Equipment. While most of these items are unlocked while just completing missions, some can only be accomplished by succeeding at challenges. To see all available challenges, refer to the Single Player Walkthrough where each challenge is listed and covered throughout each mission.

WEAPONS

While every mission has a recommended loadout for your soldier, all missions can be accomplished using any weapon you have unlocked. All weapons can be allocated to either the primary or secondary weapon slots. Each weapon also has a list of Attachments, which can be applied to the weapons once they are unlocked to further customize your choices.

SUBMACHINE GUNS

Submachine guns are great for mobility, have the highest rate of fire, and are extremely deadly at close to short range. These weapons become inaccurate at medium to long range, but you can compensate for this with the right Attachments.

Weapon	Mobility	Damage	Range	Accuracy	Ammo	Description	Attachments	Unlock Requirement
MP5					30-270 Standard 40-360 Ext. Attach. 30-300 Ext. Perk 40-400 Both	Fully automatic with good accuracy. Effective at close to medium range.	Reflex Sight, Suppressor, Long Barrel, Extended Clip, Fast Mag, FMJ, Rapid Fire, Fore Grip	None
Chicom CQB					36-324 Standard 48-432 Ext. Attach. 36-360 Ext. Perk 48-480 Both	Fully automatic submachine gun. High rate of fire with a large magazine.	Reflex Sight, EOTech Sight, Millimeter Scanner, Suppressor, Long Barrel, Extended Clip, Fast Mag, Rapid Fire, Fore Grip, Laser Sight, Target Finder, Select Fire	Complete Pyrrhic Victory mission.
Uzi					32-288 Standard 43-387 Ext. Attach. 32-320 Ext. Perk 43-430 Both	Fully automatic with high rate of fire. Effective at close range.	Reflex Sight, Suppressor, Long Barrel, Extended Clip, Fast Mag, FMJ, Rapid Fire, Fore Grip	Complete Celerium mission.
MSMC					30-270 Standard 40-360 Ext. Attach. 30-300 Ext. Perk 40-400 Both	Fully automatic submachine gun. Increased ranged and reduced recoil.	Reflex Sight, EOTech Sight, Millimeter Scanner, Suppressor, Long Barrel, Extended Clip, Fast Mag, Rapid Fire, Fore Grip, Laser Sight, Target Finder, Select Fire	Complete Time and Fate mission.
PDW-57					50-450 Standard 67-603 Ext. Attach. 50-500 Ext. Perk 67-670 Both	Fully automatic personal defense weapon. Increased range and largest ammo capacity in its class.	Reflex Sight, EOTech Sight, Millimeter Scanner, Suppressor, Long Barrel, Extended Clip, Fast Mag, Rapid Fire, Fore Grip, Laser Sight, Target Finder, Select Fire	Complete Fallen Angel mission.
AK74u					30-270 Standard 40-360 Ext. Attach. 30-300 Ext. Perk 40-400 Both	Fully automatic with high power. Effective at short to medium range.	Reflex Sight, Suppressor, Long Barrel, Extended Clip, Fast Mag, FMJ, Rapid Fire, Fore Grip	Complete Karma mission.
Skorpion EVO					32-288 Standard 43-387 Ext. Attach. 32-320 Ext. Perk 43-400 Both	Fully automatic submachine gun. Highest rate of fire in class.	Reflex Sight, EOTech Sight, Millimeter Scanner, Suppressor, Long Barrel, Extended Clip, Fast Mag, Rapid Fire, Fore Grip, Laser Sight, Target Finder, Select Fire	Complete Suffer With Me mission.
MP7					40-360 Standard 54-486 Ext. Attach. 40-400 Ext. Perk 54-540 Both	Fully automatic personal defense weapon. Versatile and strong overall.	Reflex Sight, EOTech Sight, Millimeter Scanner, Suppressor, Long Barrel, Extended Clip, Fast Mag, Rapid Fire, Fore Grip, Laser Sight, Target Finder, Select Fire	Complete Achilles' Veil mission.
Vector K10					36-324 Standard 48-432 Ext. Attach. 36-360 Ext. Perk 48-480 Both	Fully automatic submachine gun. Contains recoil mitigation technology.	Reflex Sight, EOTech Sight, Millimeter Scanner, Suppressor, Long Barrel, Extended Clip, Fast Mag, Rapid Fire, Fore Grip, Laser Sight, Target Finder, Select Fire	Complete Odysseus mission.

ASSAULT RIFLES

Assault rifles are the most versatile of all the weapons. They are effective at all ranges, but are typically good in close to medium range. While their rate of fire varies significantly between each different model, their damage is consistent and the Attachments you choose can easily tailor the assault rifle of your choice to handle any situation.

Weapon	Mobility	Damage	Range	Accuracy	Ammo	Description	Attachments	Unlock Requirement
FAL					20-180 Standard 27-243 Ext. Attach. 20-200 Ext. Perk 27-270 Both	Fully automatic assault rifle with high damage. Effective at medium to long range.	Reflex Sight, ACOG Sight, Grenade Launcher, Select Fire, Suppressor, Extended Clip, Fast Mag	None
AK47					30-270 Standard 40-360 Ext. Attach. 30-300 Ext. Perk 40-400 Both	Fully automatic with high power. Effective at medium range.	Reflex Sight, ACOG Sight, Grenade Launcher, Select Fire, Suppressor, Extended Clip, Fast Mag	None
M27					30-270 Standard 40-360 Ext. Attach. 30-300 Ext. Perk 40-400 Both	Fully automatic assault rifle. Higher mobility and reduced recoil.	Reflex Sight, EOTech Sight, Target Finder, Hybrid Optic, Suppressor, Fast Mag, Fore Grip, Laser Sight, Millimeter Scanner, Grenade Launcher, ACOG Sight, Extended Clip, Select Fire	Complete Pyrrhic Victory mission.
SMR					20-180 Standard 27-243 Ext. Attach. 20-200 Ext. Perk 27-270 Both	Fully automatic assault rifle. High damage with a low rate of fire.	Reflex Sight, EOTech Sight, Target Finder, Hybrid Optic, Suppressor, Fast Mag, Fore Grip, Laser Sight, Millimeter Scanner, Grenade Launcher, ACOG Sight, Extended Clip, Select Fire	Complete Pyrrhic Victory mission.
Galil					35-315 Standard 47-423 Ext. Attach. 35-350 Ext. Perk 47-470 Both	Fully automatic assault rifle. Effective at medium to long range.	Reflex Sight, ACOG Sight, Grenade Launcher, Select Fire, Suppressor, Extended Clip, Fast Mag	Complete Celerium mission.
MTAR					30-270 Standard 40-360 Ext. Attach. 30-300 Ext. Perk 40-400 Both	Fully automatic assault rifle. Versatile and strong overall.	Reflex Sight, EOTech Sight, Target Finder, Hybrid Optic, Suppressor, Fast Mag, Fore Grip, Laser Sight, Millimeter Scanner, Grenade Launcher, ACOG Sight, Extended Clip, Select Fire	Complete Time and Fate mission.

Weapon	Mobility	Damage	Range	Accuracy	Ammo	Description	Attachments	Unlock Requirement
SWAT-556			15 / 10 / 5		30-270 Standard 40-360 Ext. Attach. 30-300 Ext. Perk 40-400 Both	Fully automatic assault rifle. High rate of fire with moderate recoil.	Reflex Sight, EOTech Sight, Target Finder, Hybrid Optic, Suppressor, Fast Mag, Fore Grip, Laser Sight, Millimeter Scanner, Grenade Launcher, ACOG Sight, Extended Clip, Select Fire	Complete Fallen Angel mission.
FAL OSW			15 / 10 / 5		25-225 Standard 34-306 Ext. Attach. 25-250 Ext. Perk 34-340 Both	Fully automatic assault rifle. Slow rate of fire with high damage output.	Reflex Sight, EOTech Sight, Target Finder, Hybrid Optic, Suppressor, Fast Mag, Fore Grip, Laser Sight, Millimeter Scanner, Grenade Launcher, ACOG Sight, Extended Clip, Select Fire	Complete Suffer With Me mission.
Colt M16A1			15 / 10 / 5		30-270 Standard 40-360 Ext. Attach. 30-300 Ext. Perk 40-400 Both	Fully automatic assault rifle. Effective at medium to long range.	Reflex Sight, ACOG Sight, Grenade Launcher, Select Fire, Suppressor, Extended Clip, Fast Mag	Complete Karma mission.
SCAR-H			15 / 10 / 5		30-270 Standard 40-360 Ext. Attach. 30-300 Ext. Perk 40-400 Both	Fully automatic assault rifle. Increased damage and range.	Reflex Sight, EOTech Sight, Target Finder, Hybrid Optic, Suppressor, Fast Mag, Fore Grip, Laser Sight, Millimeter Scanner, Grenade Launcher, ACOG Sight, Extended Clip, Select Fire	Complete Suffer With Me mission.
AN-94			15 / 10 / 5		30-270 Standard 40-360 Ext. Attach. 30-300 Ext. Perk 40-400 Both	Fully automatic assault rifle. The first two rounds of each burst are fired at a faster rate.	Reflex Sight, EOTech Sight, Target Finder, Hybrid Optic, Suppressor, Fast Mag, Fore Grip, Laser Sight, Millimeter Scanner, Grenade Launcher, ACOG Sight, Extended Clip, Select Fire	Complete Suffer With Me mission.
M8A1			15 / 10 / 5		36-324 Standard 48-432 Ext. Attach. 36-360 Ext. Perk 48-480 Both	Fully automatic assault rifle. High rate of fire with moderate recoil.	Reflex Sight, EOTech Sight, Target Finder, Hybrid Optic, Suppressor, Fast Mag, Fore Grip, Laser Sight, Millimeter Scanner, Grenade Launcher, ACOG Sight, Extended Clip, Select Fire	Complete Achilles' Veil mission.
Type 25			15 / 10 / 5		30-270 Standard 40-360 Ext. Attach. 30-300 Ext. Perk 40-400 Both	Fully automatic assault rifle. High rate of fire with moderate recoil.	Reflex Sight, EOTech Sight, Target Finder, Hybrid Optic, Suppressor, Fast Mag, Fore Grip, Laser Sight, Millimeter Scanner, Grenade Launcher, ACOG Sight, Extended Clip, Select Fire	Complete Odysseus mission.

SHOTGUNS

Shotguns are extremely deadly at close to short range. They are usually very inaccurate and benefit greatly from Attachments that provide range and accuracy. Even though their accuracy suffers, you can easily take out multiple enemies with one blast of your shotgun if they are grouped together. These weapons also have a very limited ammo capacity, so be sure to make each shot count, as reloads take a significant amount of time.

Weapon	Mobility	Damage	Range	Accuracy	Ammo	Description	Attachments	Unlock Requirement
Olympia					2-48 Standard N/A Ext. Attach. 2-50 Ext. Perk N/A Both	Double-barrel over/under shotgun. Effective at medium to close range.	Long Barrel, Fast Mag	None
S12					10-90 Standard 13-117 Ext. Attach. 10-100 Ext. Perk 13-130 Both	Semi-automatic shotgun. Deadly at short range.	Reflex Sight, Suppressor, Long Barrel, Extended Clip, Fast Mag, Laser Sight, Millimeter Scanner	Complete Pyrrhic Victory mission.
SPAS-12					8-56 Standard 11-77 Ext. Attach. 8-64 Ext. Perk 11-88 Both	Semi-automatic combat shotgun. Effective at close range.	Suppressor, Long Barrel, Extended Clip, Fast Mag	Complete Old Wounds mission.
R-870 MCS					8-72 Standard 11-99 Ext. Attach. 8-80 Ext. Perk 11-110 Both	Pump action shotgun. Strong damage and range.	Reflex Sight, Suppressor, Long Barrel, Extended Clip, Fast Mag, Laser Sight, Millimeter Scanner	Complete Fallen Angel mission.
M1216					16-144 Standard 22-198 Ext. Attach. 16-160 Ext. Perk 22-220 Both	Fully automatic shotgun with a rechamber every four rounds.	Reflex Sight, Suppressor, Long Barrel, Extended Clip, Fast Mag, Laser Sight, Millimeter Scanner	Complete Achilles' Veil mission.
KSG					14-126 Standard 19-171 Ext. Attach. 14-140 Ext. Perk 19-190 Both	Pump action slug shotgun. Fires a single slug for high damage at longer ranges.	Reflex Sight, Suppressor, Long Barrel, Extended Clip, Fast Mag, Laser Sight, Millimeter Scanner	Complete Odysseus mission.

LIGHT MACHINE GUNS

Light machine guns, or LMGs, are perfect for medium to long range. They deliver high damage and penetration and have the advantage of the largest amount of ammo per reload. While they are highly inaccurate, the sheer amount of bullets you can throw down the field makes up for this inaccuracy. This devastating firepower is balanced with the longest reload times of any weapon and a movement speed penalty. Due to the lengthy reload times, it is often best to switch to your other weapon if you find yourself running low on bullets and in a bad situation.

Weapon	Mobility	Damage	Range	Accuracy	Ammo	Description	Attachments	Unlock Requirement
RPD			15 / 10 / 5		100-500 Standard 135-675 Ext. Attach. 100-600 Ext. Perk 135-810 Both	Fully automatic with good power and quick fire rate. Effective at medium to long range.	Reflex Sight, ACOG Sight, Suppressor, Extended Clip, Rapid Fire, Fore Grip	None
QBB LSW			15 / 10 / 5		75-375 Standard 101-505 Ext. Attach. 75-450 Ext. Perk 101-606 Both	Fully automatic LMG. Highest rate of fire in class.	Reflex Sight, ACOG Sight, EOTech Sight, Target Finder, Hybrid Optic, Dual Band, Suppressor, Rapid Fire, Fore Grip, Extended Clip, Variable Zoom, Laser Sight	Complete Pyrrhic Victory mission.
M60			15 / 10 / 5		100-500 Standard 125-675 Ext. Attach. 100-600 Ext. Perk 135-810 Both	Fully automatic with high power. Effective at medium to long range.	Reflex Sight, ACOG Sight, Suppressor, Extended Clip, Rapid Fire, Fore Grip	Complete Old Wounds mission.
Mk 48			15 / 10 / 5		100-500 Standard 135-675 Ext. Attach. 100-600 Ext. Perk 135-810 Both	Fully automatic LMG. Increased damage and range.	Reflex Sight, ACOG Sight, EOTech Sight, Target Finder, Hybrid Optic, Dual Band, Suppressor, Rapid Fire, Fore Grip, Extended Clip, Variable Zoom, Laser Sight	Complete Time and Fate mission.
LSAT			15 / 10 / 5		100-500 Standard 135-675 Ext. Attach. 100-600 Ext. Perk 135-810 Both	Fully automatic LMG. Versatile and strong overall.	Reflex Sight, ACOG Sight, EOTech Sight, Target Finder, Hybrid Optic, Dual Band, Suppressor, Rapid Fire, Fore Grip, Extended Clip, Variable Zoom, Laser Sight	Complete Odysseus mission.
HAMR			15 / 10 / 5		75-375 Standard 101-505 Ext. Attach. 75-450 Ext. Perk 101-606 Both	Fully automatic LMG. Reduces fire rate over time, becoming more accurate.	Reflex Sight, ACOG Sight, EOTech Sight, Target Finder, Hybrid Optic, Dual Band, Suppressor, Rapid Fire, Fore Grip, Extended Clip, Variable Zoom, Laser Sight	Complete Cordis Die mission.

SNIPER RIFLES

Extremely deadly at long range, sniper rifles are the choice of patient marksmen. Many scope Attachments are available, which can further enhance the rifle's accuracy, as well as enable the marksman to see targets behind obstacles. Sniper rifles are great for taking out enemies in strong cover or elevated positions that you normally can't reach with other weapons. When using a sniper rifle, be sure to periodically check your surroundings to confirm enemies aren't sneaking up on you while you're focused on your target. Staying aware of your surroundings is often the difference between life and death for a sniper.

Weapon	Mobility	Damage	Range	Accuracy	Ammo	Description	Attachments	Unlock Requirement
SVU-AS					10-90 Standard 13-117 Ext. Attach. 10-100 Ext. Perk 13-130 Both	Semi-automatic sniper rifle. High fire rate with recoil.	ACOG Sight, Variable Zoom, Dual Band, Ballistics CPU, Suppressor, Extended Clip, Fast Mag, Laser Sight	Complete Pyrrhic Victory mission.
Dragunov					10-90 Standard 13-117 Ext. Attach. 10-100 Ext. Perk 13-130 Both	Semi-automatic sniper rifle. Effective at long range.	ACOG Sight, Variable Zoom, Suppressor, Extended Clip, Fast Mag	Complete Celerium mission.
Barrett M82A1					10-90 Standard 13-117 Ext. Attach. 10-100 Ext. Perk 13-130 Both	Semi-automatic, high caliber sniper rifle. Effective at long range.	ACOG Sight, Variable Zoom, Suppressor, Extended Clip, Fast Mag	Complete Old Wounds mission.
Ballista					7-63 Standard 9-81 Ext. Attach. 7-70 Ext. Perk 9-90 Both	Bolt-action sniper rifle. Deadly from the chest up, with faster handling speeds.	ACOG Sight, Variable Zoom, Dual Band, Ballistics CPU, Suppressor, Extended Clip, Fast Mag, Laser Sight, Iron Sights	Complete Time and Fate mission.
XPR-50					8-72 Standard 10-99 Ext. Attach. 8-80 Ext. Perk 11-110 Both	Semi-automatic sniper rifle. Deadly from the chest up, with moderate recoil.	ACOG Sight, Variable Zoom, Dual Band, Ballistics CPU, Suppressor, Extended Clip, Fast Mag, Laser Sight	Complete Suffer With Me mission.
DSR-50					5-45 Standard 7-63 Ext. Attach. 5-50 Ext. Perk 7-70 Both	Bolt-action sniper rifle. Deadly from the waist up.	ACOG Sight, Variable Zoom, Dual Band, Ballistics CPU, Suppressor, Extended Clip, Fast Mag, Laser Sight	Complete any two challenges on the Achilles' Veil mission.

< 14 15 >

PISTOLS

These weapons are typically employed as a secondary or backup weapon to whatever gun you are carrying as your primary weapon. While pistols can be deadly at short to medium range, they should usually only be used when your primary weapon is out of ammo or takes too long to reload, and when you are still surrounded by enemies. When using the pistol, you have greater mobility and, with Attachments, can silently take out unsuspecting enemies.

Weapon	Mobility	Damage	Range	Accuracy	Ammo	Description	Attachments	Unlock Requirement
M1911					7-63 Standard 9-81 Ext. Attach. 7-70 Ext. Perk 9-90 Both	Semi-automatic with medium capacity and power. Effective at close range.	Suppressor, Extended Clip	None
Five-Seven					20-180 Standard 27-243 Ext. Attach. 20-200 Ext. Perk 27-270 Both	Semi-automatic pistol. Versatile and strong overall with a large magazine.	Tactical Knife, Laser Sight, Suppressor, Reflex Sight, Extended Clip, Fast Mag, Long Barrel	Complete Pyrrhic Victory mission.
Makarov					8-72 Standard 11-99 Ext. Attach. 8-80 Ext. Perk 11-110 Both	Semi-automatic with medium capacity and power. Effective at close range.	Suppressor, Extended Clip	Complete Celerium mission.
Executioner					5-45 Standard N/A Ext. Attach. 5-50 Ext. Perk N/A Both	Double-action revolver pistol. Fires 28-gauge shotgun shells.	Tactical Knife, Laser Sight, Suppressor, Reflex Sight, Fast Mag, Long Barrel	Complete any five challenges on the Celerium mission.
Browning HP					10-30 Standard 13-39 Ext. Attach. 10-80 Ext. Perk 13-104 Both	Semi-automatic with medium capacity and power. Effective at close range.	Suppressor, Extended Clip	Complete Old Wounds mission.
Tac-45					10-90 Standard 13-117 Ext. Attach. 10-100 Ext. Perk 13-130 Both	Semi-automatic pistol. High damage at close range.	Tactical Knife, Laser Sight, Suppressor, Reflex Sight, Extended Clip, Fast Mag, Long Barrel	Complete Time and Fate mission.
KAP-40					15-135 Standard 20-180 Ext. Attach. 15-150 Ext. Perk 20-200 Both	Fully automatic pistol. Incorporates recoil-mitigation technology.	Tactical Knife, Laser Sight, Suppressor, Reflex Sight, Extended Clip, Fast Mag, Long Barrel	Complete Fallen Angel mission.
B23R					15-135 Standard 20-180 Ext. Attach. 15-150 Ext. Perk 20-200 Both	Three round burst pistol. High rate of fire with moderate recoil.	Tactical Knife, Laser Sight, Suppressor, Reflex Sight, Extended Clip, Fast Mag, Long Barrel	Complete Suffer With Me mission.

LAUNCHERS

Launchers are great for taking out heavily-armored targets like helicopters, tanks, and other armored vehicles. These powerful weapons only hold one projectile and must be reloaded after every shot. This makes them impractical for eliminating enemy personnel, but perfect for taking out hard targets. Some launchers have an alternate firing mode which allows them to automatically lock onto vehicles or helicopters.

Weapon	Mobility	Damage	Range	Accuracy	Ammo	Description	Attachments	Unlock Requirement
RPG-7					1-9 Standard N/A Ext. Attach. 1-10 Ext. Perk N/A Both	Rocket Launcher.	N/A	Complete Karma mission.
FHJ-18 AA					1-3 Standard N/A Ext. Attach. 1-4 Ext. Perk N/A Both	Guided shoulder-fired rocket launcher that can lock onto vehicles and turrets.	N/A	Complete any five challenges on Achilles' Veil mission.
RPG					1-9 Standard N/A Ext. Attach. 1-10 Ext. Perk N/A Both	Free-fire shoulder-mounted rocket launcher.	N/A	Complete Suffer With Me mission.
FIM-92 Stinger					1-19 Standard N/A Ext. Attach. 1-20 Ext. Perk N/A Both	Free fire rocket launcher that can be detonated mid-flight by pressing the Right Trigger. Toggle lock-on mode by pressing Left on the D-pad.	N/A	Complete any five challenges on the Suffer With Me mission.
SMAW					1-3 Standard N/A Ext. Attach. 1-4 Ext. Perk N/A Both	Free fire shoulder-fired rocket launcher. Can lock onto vehicles and turrets.	N/A	Complete Judgment Day mission.

SPECIALS

This category contains several unique weapons which usually have an extreme amount of firepower or special features, setting them apart from ordinary weapons. This diverse set of weapons includes everything from modern crossbows to ultra-powerful Gatling guns. These weapons are so powerful they have no need for Attachments. All of these weapons have special unlock requirements, which are detailed in the following table.

Weapon	Mobility	Damage	Range	Accuracy	Ammo	Description	Attachments	Unlock Requirement
Titus 6					10-45 Standard N/A Ext. Attach. 10-45 Ext. Perk N/A Both	Intelligent airburst grenade launcher that detonates after detecting nearby enemies.	N/A	Complete Pyrrhic Victory mission.

SPECIALS (CONTINUED)

Weapon	Mobility	Damage	Range	Accuracy	Ammo	Description	Attachments	Unlock Requirement
MM1 Grenade Launcher					24-0 Standard N/A Ext. Attach. 24-48 Ext. Perk N/A Both	Drum loaded semi-automatic grenade launcher.	N/A	Complete any five challenges on Old Wounds mission.
War Machine					6-24 Standard N/A Ext. Attach. 6-24 Ext. Perk N/A Both	Drum loaded semi-automatic grenade launcher.	N/A	Complete any five challenges on Old Wounds mission.
Ballistic Knife					1-1 Standard N/A Ext. Attach. N/A Ext. Perk N/A Both	Spring-action knife launcher. Increases melee speed and can fire blade as a projectile.	N/A	Complete any five challenges on Fallen Angel mission.
Spring Knife					1-1 Standard N/A Ext. Attach. N/A Ext. Perk N/A Both	Spring-action knife launcher. Increases melee speed and can fire blade as a projectile.	N/A	Complete any five challenges on Fallen Angel mission.
Manual Crossbow					1-15 Standard N/A Ext. Attach. 1-32 Ext. Perk N/A Both	Bow-action bolt launcher. Fires explosive bolts that detonate a short time after impact.	N/A	Complete any five challenges on Karma mission.
Crossbow					10-6 Standard N/A Ext. Attach. 10-32 Ext. Perk N/A Both	Bow-action bolt launcher. Fires explosive bolts that detonate a short time after impact.	N/A	Complete any five challenges on Karma mission.
Storm PSR					30-90 Standard N/A Ext. Attach. 30-240 Ext. Perk N/A Both	See enemies through walls, hold the trigger to queue bullets and release for extreme material penetration.	N/A	Complete Odysseus mission.
Assault Shield					N/A Standard N/A Ext. Attach. N/A Ext. Perk N/A Both	Ballistic-proof blunt shield weapon. Can be deployed on the ground as cover.	N/A	Complete any five challenges on Odysseus mission.
Death Machine					999-0 Standard N/A Ext. Attach. N/A Ext. Perk N/A Both	Six barreled Gatling gun. Possesses an extremely high rate of fire at the cost of mobility.	N/A	Complete any five challenges on Judgment Day mission.
Minigun					999-0 Standard N/A Ext. Attach. N/A Ext. Perk N/A Both	Six barreled Gatling gun. Possesses an extremely high rate of fire at the cost of mobility.	N/A	Complete any five challenges on Judgment Day mission.

GRENADES & EQUIPMENT

The Grenades & Equipment section lists all the Tactical items that can be equipped during a mission. You are allowed to take two of these items while setting up your current loadout. These items are very limited and you start each mission with three to use. Even though you only carry a small amount of these items, you can replenish your supply by visiting ammo boxes throughout each mission.

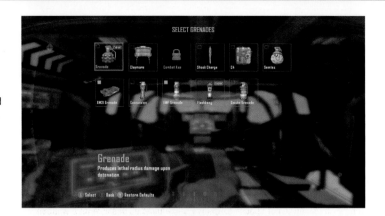

Equipment	Description	Unlock Requirement
Grenade	Produces lethal radius damage upon detonation.	None
Claymore	Directional anti-personnel mine that triggers a proximity-based explosion. Can be picked back up.	Complete Karma mission.
Combat Axe	Retrievable axe that causes instant death on impact.	Complete any five challenges on Pyrrhic Victory mission.
Shock Charge	Electrocutes and stuns nearby enemies.	Complete Suffer With Me mission.
C4	A plastic explosive device that is detonated remotely with the clacker or by double-tapping the X button.	Complete Celerium mission.
Semtex	Grenade that sticks to surfaces before detonating.	Complete Time and Fate mission.
XM31 Grenade	Wrist-fired grenade that will detonate on target.	Complete Pyrrhic Victory mission.
Concussion	Slows movement, disorients targets, and temporarily disables enemy equipment and turrets.	Complete Fallen Angel mission.
EMP Grenade	Disables nearby enemy electronic systems.	Complete Pyrrhic Victory mission.
Flashbang	Blinds targets, impairs hearing, and temporarily disables enemy equipment and turrets. Can be picked back up.	None
Smoke Grenade	Produces a smoke screen immediately upon impact.	Complete Old Wounds mission.

ATTACHMENTS

Attachments are special enhancements available for your weapons. You can only have three Attachments per primary and secondary weapon. When choosing Attachments, take into consideration the strengths and weaknesses of your weapon to compensate for any lack and to enhance its strengths. When you equip certain Attachments, it immediately locks out others of that type and displays a warning over Attachments that interfere with the one you chose. This means you cannot have more than one of that particular type. Choosing one of the Attachment types displaying the warning replaces your previous choice. There is never a reason to not choose as many Attachments as possible on a weapon. Select the three Attachments for each weapon which will be most useful to your current mission.

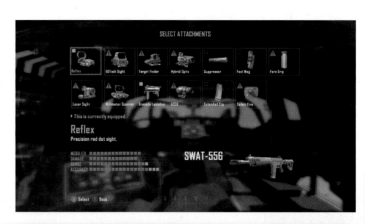

Attachment	Modifiers	Description	Unlock Requirement
ACOG Sight	Increases Range and Accuracy	Enhanced zoom sight.	None
Ballistics CPU	Increases Range and Accuracy	Reduced weapon sway when aiming.	Complete Pyrrhic Victory mission.
Dual Band	Increases Range and Accuracy	Nightvision scope with interlaced thermal overlay.	Complete Time and Fate mission.
EOTech Sight	Increases Range and Accuracy	Holographic sight. Provides a clearer view of the target than a red dot, but with less peripheral vision.	Complete Pyrrhic Victory mission.
Extended Clip	N/A	More ammo in each clip.	Complete Time and Fate mission.
Fast Mag	N/A	Reload faster.	None
FMJ	Increases Damage	Increased material penetration.	Complete Old Wounds mission.
Fore Grip	Increases Accuracy	Reduced recoil when aiming down the sights.	Complete Pyrrhic Victory mission.
Grenade Launcher	Increases Damage (only applies to launched grenade)	Switch to an under-barrel grenade launcher by pressing Left on the D-pad.	Complete Celerium mission.
Hybrid Optic	Increases Range and Accuracy	ACOG Sight with Reflex Sight attached on top. Press the Left Stick while aiming down the sight to switch between optics.	Complete Time and Fate mission.

ATTACHMENTS (CONTINUED)

Attachment	Modifiers	Description	Unlock Requirement
Iron Sights	N/A	Rail-mounted tritium iron sights.	Complete Time and Fate mission.
Laser Sight	Increases Mobility and Accuracy	Increases hipfire accuracy.	Complete Suffer With Me mission.
Long Barrel	Increases Damage and Range	Increases range.	Complete Karma mission.
Millimeter Scanner	Increases Mobility and Lowers Accuracy	Detects lingering heat signatures from stationary enemies through materials at up to 25 meters.	Complete Pyrrhic Victory mission.
Rapid Fire	Increases Damage and Lowers Accuracy	Increased rate of fire.	Complete Karma mission.
Reflex Sight	Increases Range and Accuracy	Precision red dot sight.	Complete Celerium mission.
Select Fire	Increases Range and Accuracy	Switch to burst or automatic fire by pressing Left on the D-pad. Automatic fire will always have more recoil.	None
Suppressor	Lowers Damage and Range	Invisible from radar when firing, reduced muzzle flash, but less range.	Complete Fallen Angel mission.
Tactical Knife	Increases Mobility	Carry a tactical knife in your off hand for faster melee attacks.	Complete Time and Fate mission.
Target Finder	Increases Range and Accuracy	Identifies enemies and notifies when an enemy is in the crosshair.	Complete Suffer With Me mission.
Variable Zoom	Increases Range and Accuracy	While scoped in, press the Left Stick to adjust between two different zoom levels.	Complete Old Wounds mission.

PERKS

In addition to your weapons, you should always select Perks to round out your loadout or fit your particular playstyle. Perks typically improve your character or your weapons. You unlock them by completing missions or challenges.

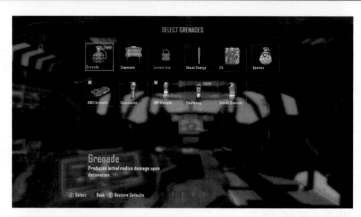

> Your First Perk

Access Kit is the first Perk you start with and perhaps the most important. This Perk is often necessary to complete missions and challenges, and, even when not required for completion, makes it much easier to survive each mission.

Perk	Unlocks	Description
Access Kit	Immediately available at the start of the game.	Your Access Kit gives you access to otherwise inaccessible parts of the map.
Adjustable Stock	Complete two challenges in Celerium.	Walk faster while aiming down the sight.
Ammo Pickup	Complete five challenges in Cordis Die.	Replenish ammo and grenades from all fallen enemies.
Climber	Complete two challenges in Karma.	Move faster when mantling.
Fast Hands	Complete two challenges in Pyrrhic Victory.	Switch weapons more quickly.
Fast Mag	Complete two challenges in Judgment Day.	Reload weapons faster.
FMJ	Complete two challenges in Suffer With Me.	You do more damage with all bullet weapons.

Perk	Unlocks	Description
Hardness	Complete two challenges in Odysseus.	Flinch less when damaged.
Hip Accuracy	Complete two challenges in Old Wounds.	Better accuracy when firing from the hip.
Hold Breath	Complete two challenges in Fallen Angel.	Hold breath longer when using sniper rifles.
Longer Sprint	Complete five challenges in Time and Fate.	Sprint for a longer duration.
Quickdraw	Complete two challenges in Time and Fate.	Aim down the sight faster.
Throwback	Complete two challenges in Cordis Die.	Reset the timer when throwing back a grenade.

CAMO

When you complete missions, you can customize the look of your weapons. As the following table illustrates, there are many different looks. These camos have no effect on gameplay and are purely an aesthetic choice, so have fun customizing your favorite weapon with your favorite camo.

CAMO	NAME	UNLOCK REQUIREMENT	CAMO	NAME	UNLOCK REQUIREMENT
	Devgru	Cordis Die		Nevada	Old Wounds
	A-TACS AU	Fallen Angel		Sahara	Celerium
	ERDL	Odysseus		Russia	FOB Spectre
	Choco	Judgment Day		Flecktarn	Second Chance
	Blue Tiger	Achilles' Veil		Flora	Default
	Bloodshot	Suffer With Me		Tiger	Karma
	Ghostex: Delta 6	Time and Fate		Carbon Fiber	Judgment Day
	Kryptek: Typhon	Pyrrhic Victory		Gold	Dispatch

BATTLEFIELD ACQUISITIONS

In addition to the weapons available in your loadout, you often find useful items in the field. These items are critical for completing many mission challenges.

ACQUISITION	DESCRIPTION
Mortar	Powerful explosive that can be thrown or set in animal traps.
Animal Trap	Can be set as a trap to lock down enemies.
Machete	Deadly melee weapon.
Knife	Melee weapon that you start with.
Pulwar	Deadly one-handed curved sword.
Anti-Tank Mine	Deployable mine that takes out armored units.
Combatant Suppression Knuckles	Melee taser.
Molotov Cocktail	Small AoE flame-improvised grenade.
Combat Axe	Throwable axe.
Nightingale Grenade	Distracts enemies.
IR Strobe	Marks an area for an air strike.
Mounted Machine Gun	Powerful machine gun that shoots lots of bullets at the cost of accuracy.
Sentry Turret	Used in Strike Force missions and can be picked up and redeployed. Also can be used against you in single player campaign.
SAM Turret	Locks on to aerial targets and once launched tracks its targets until they're destroyed.
MQ-27 Dragonfire	Miniature remote-controlled quad rotor hover units that have lightweight machine guns mounted on them. Highly maneuverable but easily destroyed.
CLAW	Extremely tough and heavily equipped walking tank. Can fire a minigun or launch grenades.
ASD	Small robots with treads that have burst-fire machine guns and rockets.
HAMP	Satellite that launches powerful kinetic strikes on painted targets.

OPERATIVE:
Alex Mason, CIA
Special Activities
Division

ID#: 5814700

HEIGHT: 5'11"

WEIGHT: 190 lbs.

○ **SUPPORT:**

Jason Hudson

○ **SUPPORT:**

Jonas Savimbi

MISSION DETAILS

Alex Mason steps out of retirement to rescue his old friend Sgt. Frank Woods, held captive in Angola by narco terrorist Raul Menendez.

PRIMARY OBJECTIVE
Rescue Woods

LEVEL OBJECTIVES

Ⓐ Prepare for incoming MPLA attack.

Ⓑ Push forward with the convoy.

Ⓒ Eliminate the mortar crews.

Ⓓ Destroy tanks.

Ⓔ Eliminate the mounted gunners.

Ⓕ Destroy the second wave of tanks.

Ⓖ Mount the Buffel to lead the final push.

Ⓗ Secure the barge and rescue Woods.

Ⓘ Search the container for Woods.

Ⓙ Use the Valkyrie launcher to destroy the Hind.

Ⓚ Escape into the jungle.

Ⓛ Get to the village and radio Savimbi for extraction.

Ⓜ Do not get discovered.

Ⓝ Enter village and find radio.

Ⓞ Approach and overpower Menendez.

Ⓟ Fall back to the river.

Ⓠ Defend position.

INTEL ———— ③

RECOMMENDED LOADOUT

PRIMARY

> FAL with ACOG, Select Fire, Fast Mag

SECONDARY

> M1911

GRENADES & EQUIPMENT

> Grenade
> Flashbang

PERKS

> Access Kit

CHALLENGES

> Eliminate enemy personnel (x15) with machete.

> Destroy all MPLA tanks.

> Eliminate enemy personnel (x5) with one mortar explosion.

> Sink enemy vessels (x5).

> Dive to prone on an enemy grenade and survive.

> Eliminate enemy personnel (x10) with animal traps.

> Kill (x4) enemies with one mortar primed animal trap.

> Use elevated improvised positions for confirmed sniper kills (x20).

> Collect Intel (x3).

> 100% survivability rating.

WEAPON/ATTACHMENT UNLOCKS

COMPLETE CHALLENGES	UNLOCK...
2	FAST HANDS PERK
5	COMBAT AXE MELEE WEAPON

"YOU BOYS BETTER GET YOUR S*#T TOGETHER…HE'S GONNA ATTACK!"

Agents David Mason and Mike Harper are on the hunt for Raul Menendez, who was rumored to have visited Frank Woods. They just miss Menendez, but Frank shares the story of how he and Alex Mason got acquainted with Menendez.

"IT'S UNCLE WOODS, SON. HE'D DO IT FOR ME."

Spending some quality time with his son in Alaska, Alex gets a visit from Lt. Col. Oliver North and Jason Hudson. They inform him that Frank is stranded in Angola, where he was sent to uncover an arms-smuggling ring. Alex can't let his partner down, so he and Hudson go in on the covert mission to recover Frank.

A OBJECTIVE
Prepare for Incoming MPLA Attack

Jonas Savimbi, leader of UNITA in Angola and ally to the United States, can help pinpoint the exact location of Woods and his team. However, Mason has to help him counter the incoming attack from their rivals, the MPLA. With Hudson supporting from the air, you pick up the story as Alex, riding into battle with the supercharged Savimbi.

B OBJECTIVE
Push Forward with the Convoy

As soon as your feet touch the ground, run for the MPLA soldiers heading your way. Take down as many as you can with your automatic weapon and machete. Use the advancing UNITA vehicles as cover.

"HERE THEY COME, MY BROTHERS!
FIGHT, MY BROTHERS!"

ELIMINATE ENEMY PERSONNEL (X15) WITH MACHETE

CHALLENGE

Taking out 15 enemies in this level with your machete completes a challenge. In the lower two difficulties, this is as simple as sprinting at the MPLA soldiers and hacking as you get close enough.
Hardened and Veteran requires a more covert approach. Take cover and then melee attack when you get close.

JUST GETTING STARTED

ACHIEVEMENT/TROPHY

Complete any challenge to earn this Achievement/Trophy.

OBJECTIVE
Eliminate the Mortar Crews

You must stay relatively close to the convoy, or you risk leaving the area and restarting from the last checkpoint. Weave through the convoy to the right side to find an Access door on the back of a truck.

ACCESS KIT

Throughout the campaign, as long as you carry the Access Kit Perk, the word Access will appear on locations that can be opened with this kit. This nets you an extra weapon of some sort, protection, or tactical improvements. Often, this is required in completing the challenges.

TACTICS

ACCESS ①

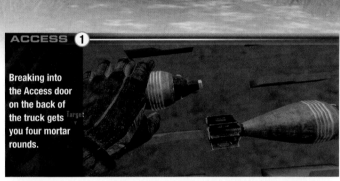

Breaking into the Access door on the back of the truck gets you four mortar rounds.

INTEL ①

Search the crater just to the right of this vehicle, where the first piece of Intelligence lies on the ground.

Four enemies manning mortars are further down the field. Pull out your gun and take out the right one first. Carefully advance toward the other three, who are protected by a boulder. Toss a mortar round or grenade their way to eliminate the threat.

OBJECTIVE
Destroy Tanks

"DAMMIT, HUDSON. THEY'VE GOT T-62 TANKS IN SUPPORT. WE NEED YOU TO TAKE THE HEAT OFF."

Once you get the ability to call for air support, press Up on the D-pad. This gives you a view from the helicopter as it flies over four tanks. Take them out with some well-placed rockets.

AIR SUPPORT

When you are in control of the chopper, press Right Trigger/R2 to fire the machine gun and press Left Trigger/L2 to fire rockets. You can use the machine gun to make aiming the rockets easier. Use the analog sticks to aim the reticle.

TACTICS

Press ✛ to call air support

OBJECTIVE
Eliminate the Mounted Gunners

Once you take care of the first wave of tanks, two trucks drive in with mounted machine guns. Quickly take out the left one, and then dive behind cover. Make your way around to the right and duck behind the big rock. Peek out and eliminate the second gunner to allow Savimbi's men to advance.

Target

FAL
20 / 160

OBJECTIVE
Destroy the Second Wave of Tanks

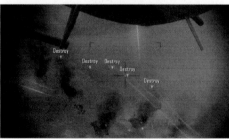

At this point, a second wave of tanks impedes any progress. Press Up again to resume control of the air support. Take out the four tanks as you sweep from the right to left. As you swing around to the left, five more tanks come into view. Quickly take them out, as you do not have much time.

CHALLENGE
> ## DESTROY ALL MPLA TANKS

If you successfully take out all 13 tanks in the two waves, another challenge is completed.

G OBJECTIVE
Mount the Buffel to Lead the Final Push

"THEY ARE WEAK. WE MUST FINISH THEM."

Continue fighting the enemy until Savimbi tells you to join him. Fight your way to the Buffel, and Mason climbs aboard. Continue to fight the MPLA as you hang off the APC. Be sure to take out the MG on the back of the truck.

> ### ELIMINATE ENEMY PERSONNEL (X5) WITH ONE MORTAR EXPLOSION
CHALLENGE

This is a good opportunity to get this challenge. Wait for a couple more enemies to approach the three mortars and toss your own mortar in to get all five guys in one shot.

H OBJECTIVE
Secure the Barge and Rescue Woods

"HE IS BEING HELD CAPTIVE BY A NICARAGUAN GUN RUNNER. A VERY DANGEROUS MAN."

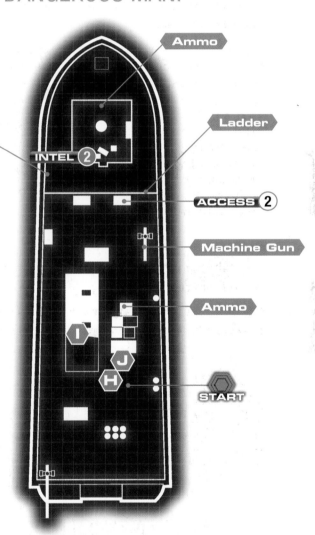

Ammo

Machine Gun Ladder

INTEL 2

Ladder

ACCESS 2

Machine Gun

Ammo

I

J

H

START

After the APC comes to a stop, Mason climbs onto Hudson's helicopter. They take off for the Cubango River, where Savimbi's men have pinpointed Woods on a barge. As the helicopter approaches its destination, it is shot down, but Hudson and Mason both manage to get aboard the ship.

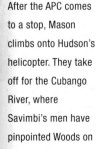

Once you're on the barge, take cover behind the container. Pick off the MPLA soldiers on the upper level and those who hide on the other side of the cargo. Sneak around the left side and take out any remaining enemies. An Access crate sits on the far side of the main deck.

SINK ENEMY VESSELS (X5)

When the first enemy boat approaches the right side of the barge, move to the mounted gun on that side and mow it down. Take out any others you can reach from that location before you jump onto the gun on the upper platform. Eliminate any boats on that side. Continue in this manner until all boats are gone, which should easily complete this challenge.

ACCESS ②

Cut open the lock on the crate to find a Flak Jacket inside. This protects against explosive damage.

INTEL ②

Search near the upper MG next to the bridge to find the second piece of Intelligence.

Enemy vessels start to approach from behind. They come up on either side of the barge. Some drop off men if they make it in time. Man the starboard-side machine gun and sink the ship that approaches. Move back and forth between this gun and a port-side MG that sits on the upper deck—destroy any boats within reach.

OBJECTIVE
Search the Container for Woods

Once you take care of the enemy vessels, join Hudson on the back side of the big container to find Woods inside.

< 30 31 >

J **OBJECTIVE**
Use the Valkyrie Launcher to Destroy the Hind

"YOU GOT TO KNOCK OUT THAT HIND, MASON."

As you head back out, a Hind helicopter bent on taking down the barge waits for you. Look to the left to find a Valkyrie launcher sitting on the ground. Grab it and find the chopper in the sky.

Wait for it to slow down, aim the launcher in its direction, and fire a rocket. Steer it into the helicopter. Repeat this until it falls to the ground.

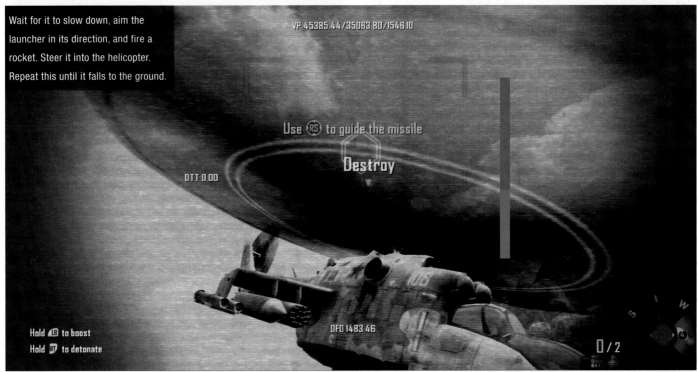

VALKYRIE LAUNCHER

The Valkyrie rockets are guided. Aim the weapon, put the chopper in the middle of the screen, and fire. Use the Right Stick to steer the explosive into the aircraft. A vertical bar on the right shows how long until it explodes—when the bar fully depletes. If you are lined up with your target, hold Left Bumper/L1 to boost, which gets the rocket there before your target has a chance to dodge. If you are close but a little off target, press Right Trigger/R2 to detonate the rocket nearby.

OBJECTIVE
Escape into the Jungle

Radio

Poachers'
Platforms

O

N

P

ACCESS 3

Ammo

Q

M

L

INTEL 3

Ammo

K

START

END

The barge runs aground and Hudson loses Woods in the water. After Alex grabs him, move backward until you reach the shore. Follow Hudson into the jungle until he stops. You can see a radio tower in the distance, which means there must be a radio. You can use this radio to call for an extraction.

OBJECTIVE
Get to the Village and Radio Savimbi for Extraction

"WHAT THE HELL ARE CUBANS DOING HERE?"

Cubans are just ahead, so step up to the log and take cover. Step out from behind the log and crouch behind Hudson until the coast is clear. When he gets up to

move, stand up and stick as close to him as you can. When he stops in the building, again crouch right behind him to stay out of sight.

OBJECTIVE
Do Not Get Discovered

When Hudson moves again, stand up, quickly move up behind him in the grass, and crouch down. Follow him until he stops to let some enemy patrols move past. Once again, wait for him to move and follow him out of the grass to some rocks ahead, where you set Frank down.

Follow

OBJECTIVE
Enter Village and Find Radio

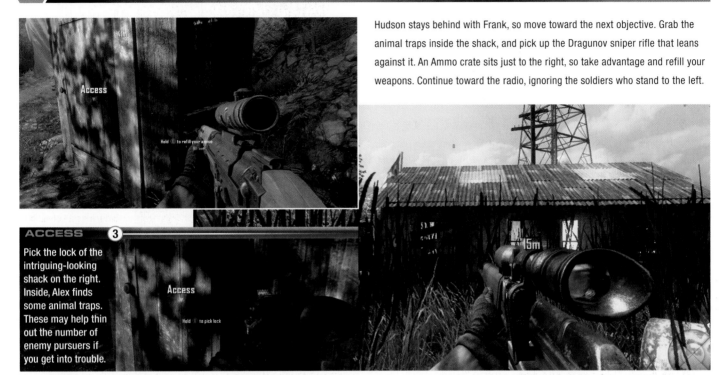

Hudson stays behind with Frank, so move toward the next objective. Grab the animal traps inside the shack, and pick up the Dragunov sniper rifle that leans against it. An Ammo crate sits just to the right, so take advantage and refill your weapons. Continue toward the radio, ignoring the soldiers who stand to the left.

ACCESS ③

Pick the lock of the intriguing-looking shack on the right. Inside, Alex finds some animal traps. These may help thin out the number of enemy pursuers if you get into trouble.

OBJECTIVE
Approach and Overpower the Radio Operator

Jump through the open window and approach the guy at the radio ahead. He isn't exactly the pushover that Mason was hoping for. A struggle ensues and you are knocked back outside—without radioing for any help.

"YOU'RE A DEAD MAN UNLESS YOU DO EXACTLY AS I SAY."

OBJECTIVE
Fall Back to the River

"WE GOT CUBAN REGULARS ON OUR ASS! LOOKS LIKE HALF A DAMN REGIMENT!"

Now you have an army hot on your tail. Hustle into the jungle. Lay down a few animal traps along the path, and then climb up one of the poachers' platforms. From here, pull out the Dragunov and snipe any enemies who enter the area.

ANIMAL TRAPS

Press Up on the D-pad to select the animal trap. Use them in narrow spaces or obvious trails. This can take out an enemy here and there, increasing your chances of survival. If you have mortar rounds, press X/Square once a trap is set to add an explosive to the mix. This causes a big explosion when someone gets stuck in the trap, taking out anyone nearby.

—— TACTICS

> **USE ELEVATED IMPROVISED POSITIONS FOR CONFIRMED SNIPER KILLS (X20)** CHALLENGE

Use the sniper posts scattered around the jungle to get a good position on the enemies. Take down twenty from these locations to complete this challenge.

OBJECTIVE
Defend Position

Continue to defend Hudson's position here until he tosses a smoke grenade. Jump down and follow him into the next area. As you pass through the narrow path, lay down a few animal traps to slow down the enemy.

"RIG SOME BOOBY TRAPS. WE NEED TO KEEP THEM OFF OUR TAIL."

> **ELIMINATE ENEMY PERSONNEL (X10) WITH ANIMAL TRAPS** CHALLENGE

> **KILL (X4) ENEMIES WITH ONE MORTAR PRIMED ANIMAL TRAP**

In the narrow path between the two jungle areas, place an animal trap and then arm it with a mortar. If you have time, place another nearby. If you take down four enemies with this trap, you'll complete one of these challenges. Continue eliminating MPLA soldiers with the traps to get the other.

Climb onto one of the sniper posts to get a position against the foe. The enemy tosses a grenade from time to time. If you are on the ground when one is tossed your way, return it in their direction or run to escape the blast radius. Continue picking off the Cubans from afar until Mason says to make a run for it.

INTEL (3)

After you enter the second jungle area, climb the first poachers' stand to find the third Intel.

> ### DIVE TO PRONE ON AN ENEMY GRENADE AND SURVIVE
CHALLENGE

The MPLA occasionally toss grenades at your position. Sprint toward a grenade and hold the Crouch button to dive on it. If you land directly on it and survive, you complete this challenge.

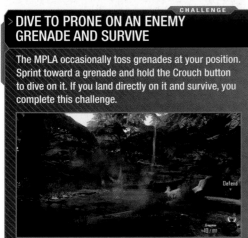

"WE GOTTA MAKE A RUN FOR THE RIVER, HUDSON!"

Follow Hudson to the final defensive position, and keep taking out the enemies. A couple MG trucks need your attention first, one on the waterfall and another to the left. Eliminate them with your sniper rifle, and then continue the assault on the other soldiers. An Ammo dump sits next to Woods if you're running low.

When Hudson mentions falling back to the beach where a boat sits, follow him. Place traps to slow down the pursuers. Approach Woods to help Hudson get him to the boat when a helicopter approaches. No need to worry—it's Savimbi, who has come to your rescue.

"YOU CAN'T KILL ME."

> ### NO MAN LEFT BEHIND
ACHIEVEMENT/TROPHY

Rescue Woods by completing Pyrrhic Victory.

02_CELERIUM

OPERATIVE:
David "Section" Mason, JSOC Counter Terrorist Force

ID#: 86900711

HEIGHT: 6'1"

WEIGHT: 200 lbs.

SUPPORT:
Mike Harper

SUPPORT:
Javier Salazar

SUPPORT:
Crosby

MISSION DETAILS

Mason's son David leads JSOC's elite counter terrorist force investigating Menendez's links to a revolutionary new microchip made from Rare Earth Element Celerium.

PRIMARY OBJECTIVE

Recover Celerium

LEVEL OBJECTIVES

- **A** Rendezvous with Salazar and Crosby.
- **B** Jump from the cliff to start your descent.
- **C** Reach the LZ.
- **D** Investigate the base.
- **E** Destroy the temple door.
- **F** Infiltrate the research facility.
- **G** Infiltrate the lower labs.
- **H** Open container.
- **I** Obtain the Celerium drive.
- **J** Rendezvous with extraction team.

INTEL ———— ③

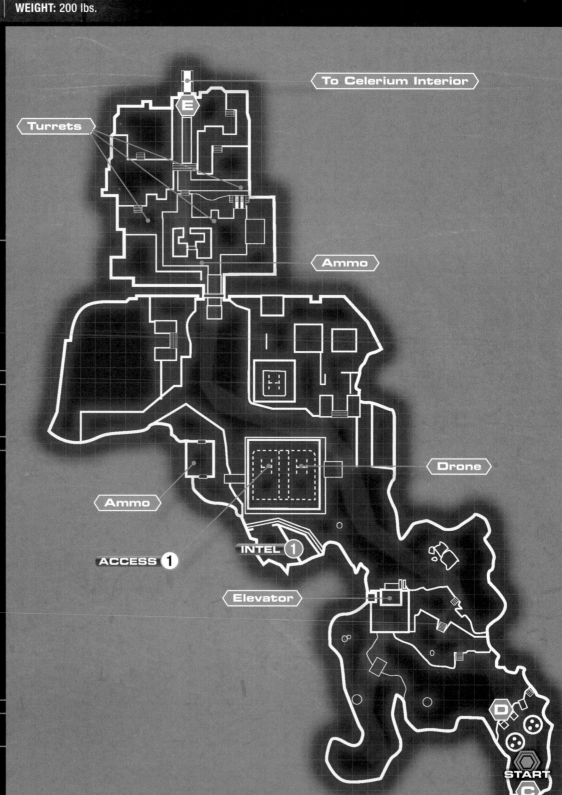

To Celerium Interior

Turrets

E

Ammo

Ammo

Drone

ACCESS ①

INTEL ①

Elevator

D

START

C

< 36   37 >

RECOMMENDED LOADOUT

PRIMARY

> M27 with
Millimeter Scanner,
Fast Mag,
Fore Grip

SECONDARY

> Titus 6 AB

GRENADES & EQUIPMENT

> XM31 Grenade
> EMP Grenade

PERKS

> Access Kit
> Fast Hands

CHALLENGES

> Eliminate enemy helicopter before liftoff.

> Destroy sentry turret (x2) while disabled.

> Eliminate enemy personnel (x4) with one round from Titus weapon.

> Eliminate enemy personnel (x10) with helicopter turret.

> Eliminate enemy personnel (x30) while using Optical camo.

> Destroy enemy ASDs (x2) by exploding nitrogen tanks.

> Eliminate enemy personnel (x10) with the Assault Shield.

> Protect ASD resource from destruction.

> Collect Intel (x3).

> 100% survivability rating.

WEAPON/ATTACHMENT UNLOCKS

COMPLETE CHALLENGES	UNLOCK...
2	ADJUSTABLE STOCK PERK
5	EXECUTIONER HANDGUN

"RARE EARTH ELEMENTS!"
"WHO CONTROLS ALL OF IT? CHINA!"

Woods continues to give his thoughts on Raul Menendez and the Chinese, who own almost all of the world's supply of Rare Earth Elements—an extremely valuable resource in 2025. A revolutionary new microchip has been created with one of these elements, Celerium, in a facility linked to Raul Menendez. Alex Mason's son David leads a counter terrorist force to the Hkakabo Razi Mountains in Myanmar where the facility resides.

A   OBJECTIVE
Rendezvous with Salazar and Crosby

"CUBANS. ELITE RANK.
STATE OF THE ART TECH."

Section and Mike Harper are on their way to meet up with Salazar and Crosby, using special gloves and bungee cord to scale the side of the mountain. Press the buttons that appear on screen to signal Harper and then swing him from your fulcrum point. Press the next button that appears to swing from Harper and then the two given buttons to attach to the rock.

Continue this routine until you reach a platform. A fallen tree attempts to take you two with it until Salazar steps in and saves the day. Follow the guys to the edge and press the two Shoulder buttons to deploy your wingsuit. They have all kinds of cool gadgets in 2025.

OBJECTIVE B
Jump from the Cliff to Start Your Descent

Jump off the cliff and use the Right Analog Stick to control your flight. Steer through the objective markers, staying in the middle of the cliffs. You take damage if you brush against the terrain, and you start over if you crash, so be careful as you descend.

OBJECTIVE C
Reach the LZ

Continue through the narrow pass and press the given button to deploy your chute. Aim toward the landing zone, indicated by the objective marker.

OBJECTIVE D
Investigate the Base

After surveying what lies ahead and getting the order to engage, take out the nearby enemies and drop down to their location.

OPTICAL CAMO SUIT

The enemies that you face in 2025 have Optical camouflage suits that allow them to blend in to their surroundings. Their outlines can still be seen, but you will have to be more watchful to spot them.

TACTICS

Move around the left side of the tree and fight your way to the elevator. Use the panel and ride it to the level above. Spot the enemies outside and take them down. Peek out to the right and take out more. Then turn around and eliminate another enemy on an upper level.

Run up the ramp to find a chopper attempting to take off. Blow it up before it gets airborne and then look to the left. Wait for a soldier to duck behind the cover ahead. Fire a bullet at the nearby red barrel to take him down.

CHALLENGE
ELIMINATE ENEMY HELICOPTER BEFORE LIFTOFF

Pull out the Titus-6 and fire a couple shots at the drone attempting to take off. These explosives will keep it grounded for good and earn you a challenge.

ACCESS ①

After destroying the drone, find an Access point on the bottom of another airship ahead. This gives you control of its turret.

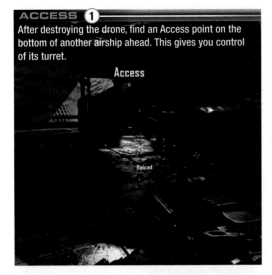

ELIMINATE ENEMY PERSONNEL (X10) WITH HELICOPTER TURRET

There are plenty of enemies scattered around, so getting 10 should not be a problem. Take out the two vehicles first, and then mow down any remaining personnel.

ELIMINATE ENEMY PERSONNEL (X4) WITH ONE ROUND FROM TITUS WEAPON

Your second weapon is the Titus 6 AB and it fires flechette explosives. You need to find a location with four enemies in close proximity to each other and fire a flechette in the middle of them. There are many enemies around these helipads. Before accessing the helicopter turret, find four together and take them all out with a single flechette.

INTEL ①

After using the drone's weapon to eliminate the surrounding guards, search the room behind you for the first Intel.

Cut through the building on the left and refill your ammo. Run through the arch ahead and take cover behind the ruins on the left. Tossing an EMP grenade at the sentry turrets disables them for a short while. Take that opportunity to destroy it.

DESTROY SENTRY TURRET (X2) WHILE DISABLED

Taking out at least two of the three turrets while they are disabled completes a challenge.

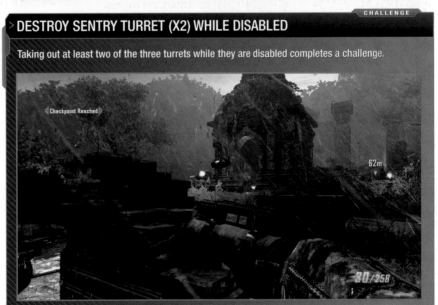

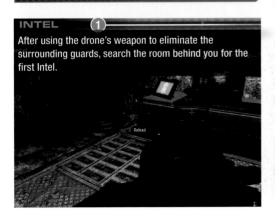

Eliminate the two turrets on the right and then head up the ramp. Ease your way out of cover as you shoot down the soldiers to the left. Join your crew behind the crates ahead and fire on more troops to the right.

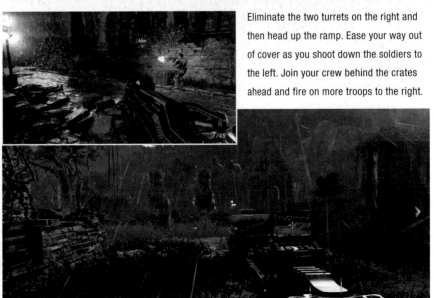

E Destroy the Temple Door

"SURFACE INSTALLATION IS NEUTRALIZED.
MOVING TO INVESTIGATE SECONDARY STRUCTURE."

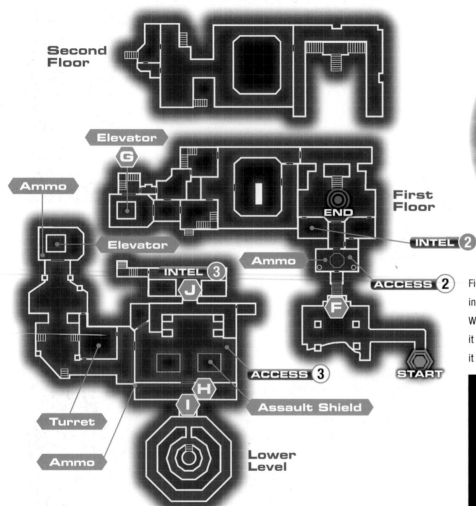

Second Floor

Elevator G

Ammo

Elevator

INTEL 3

J

ACCESS 3

Turret

Ammo

I H

Assault Shield

Lower Level

First Floor

END

INTEL 2

Ammo

ACCESS 2

F

START

Fight your way to the northeast, taking cover every once in awhile to scan for enemies with your Millimeter Scanner. When you reach the locked door, launch a flechette at it to blow it open. If you wait long enough, Harper does it for you.

F Infiltrate the Research Facility

Follow the corridor to a more modern-looking door and wait for Salazar to get it open. Step into the entryway and reload your weapon at the ammo crate.

ACCESS 2
Enter the research facility and move into the entryway. On the right side is an Access crate. Hack into it to find your own Optical camo suit. Press Down to activate the camouflage. Don't get carried away—you aren't invisible with this suit. It makes you less noticeable.

Toss an EMP grenade at the ASDs who show up in the lab ahead and finish them off with some gunfire. Eliminate the remaining soldiers before moving too far inside.

Follow Harper to the second floor and take cover behind the wall. Kill anyone you can target from there, and then fight your way through the lab. Once the floor is cleared, run down the southwest steps and take down the enemies inside the elevator.

INTEL ②

After grabbing the camo suit and taking out the ASDs and enemy soldiers, enter the office on the left. The second Intel sits on a desk inside.

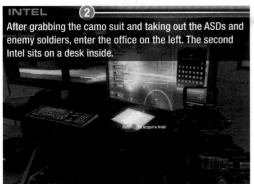

MILLIMETER SCANNER

With the Millimeter Scanner Attachment on your assault rifle, lingering heat signatures from stationary enemies can be detected through materials at up to 25 meters. This is great for this office building. Aim down the rifle and enemies hiding behind a wall show up as an outline. The penetration of the M27 allows you to take out a guy on the other side of an office wall.

────────── TACTICS

G OBJECTIVE
Infiltrate the Lower Labs

"TARGET THE NITROGEN TANK."

Join the rest of the team on the elevator and use the panel to proceed to the lower labs. Just as the doors open, an ASD attacks from the next room. Immediately shoot at the nitrogen tanks that sit a little left of center. This will freeze any nearby enemies, including this drone.

CHALLENGE
> DESTROY ENEMY ASDs (X2) BY EXPLODING NITROGEN TANKS

Take out two ASDs by shooting a nearby nitrogen tank to get this challenge. You get another opportunity shortly.

Fight your way to the doorway on the left, using your scanner to see where the enemies are hiding. Watch out as you turn the next corner, as an armored turret is mounted to the ceiling. Toss an EMP grenade to knock it out, and then finish it off with some gunfire. Once you get the "We're clear," move into the next lab.

ACCESS ③

Enter the room labeled P-54 to spot an Access door on the opposite wall. As you may decipher from the writing on the wall, an ASD is found inside. It will help out later in the mission.

H OBJECTIVE
Open Container

"MENENDEZ IS ARMING HIMSELF FOR WAR."

Take the opportunity while the guys marvel over Menendez's wealth to reload your weapons in the small room to the south. A noise is heard from somewhere in this room. Approach the panel on the side of the container and open it up to find Erik, who claims he will give up everything he knows if JSOC gets him out safely.

Enemies bust through the far wall and drop in from the ceiling, along with another ASD. Wait for the ASD to get close to the nitrogen tanks and blow them up to take it down, along with any nearby soldiers.

CHALLENGE
> ELIMINATE ENEMY PERSONNEL (X10) WITH THE ASSAULT SHIELD

Harper grabs an Assault Shield from one of the manufacturing units. Wait for another to appear from the second unit and grab it. By pressing the Fire button, you can bash an enemy with the Assault Shield. Take out 10 guys with it to get this challenge done.

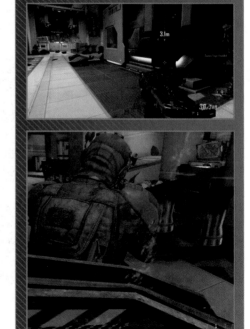

Two turrets are also lowered from the ceiling. Toss an EMP grenade their way and destroy them. Eliminate any remaining enemies in the lab.

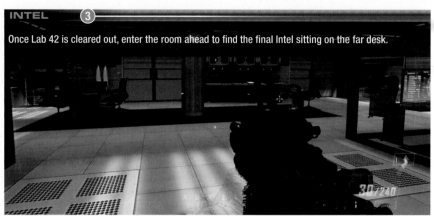

INTEL ③

Once Lab 42 is cleared out, enter the room ahead to find the final Intel sitting on the far desk.

OBJECTIVE I
Obtain the Celerium Drive

"THIS SINGLE DEVICE HAS MORE PROCESSING POWER THAN YOUR ENTIRE MILITARY INFRASTRUCTURE."

Return to the south side of the room and step up to the left panel. With Erik's help, the door opens to reveal where the Celerium is being kept. Before entering the room, place the Assault Shield at the doorway. Wait for the scientist to grab the drive and hand it over to Section.

OBJECTIVE J
Rendezvous with Extraction Team

After learning about a powerful weapon called Karma, more guards show up in the previous room. Grab the shield and bash your way through the ranks of enemies. Go up the stairs and continue to fight your way to the lab where you first entered the facility. Here Admiral Briggs and the extraction team wait for your arrival.

> PROTECT ASD RESOURCE FROM DESTRUCTION
CHALLENGE

If the friendly ASD survives until the end, this challenge is completed.

> GATHERING STORM
ACHIEVEMENT/TROPHY

Investigate the jungle facility to complete Celerium and earn this award.

03_OLD WOUNDS

OPERATIVE:
Alex Mason, CIA
Special Activities
Division

ID#: 5814700
HEIGHT: 5'11"
WEIGHT: 190 lbs.

○ **SUPPORT:**
Frank Woods

○ **SUPPORT:**
Tian Zhao

MISSION DETAILS

Mason re-enlists with the CIA and joins Woods in Afghanistan, supplying weapons to the Mujahideen in exchange for vital intel on Menendez's whereabouts.

PRIMARY OBJECTIVE

Gather Intel on Menendez Cartel

LEVEL OBJECTIVES

- **A** Investigate Menendez's connection with the Soviets.
- **B** Follow Zhao to the Mujahideen base.
- **C** Defend the West Blocking Point.
- **D** Destroy the Soviet BTRs.
- **E** Block the entrance to the village.
- **F** Defend the base from being destroyed.
- **G** Retake the weapons cache.
- **H** Return to Mujahideen base.
- **I** Interrogate Kravchenko.

INTEL ──────── ③

RECOMMENDED LOADOUT

PRIMARY

> M27 AK47 with ACOG, Grenade Launcher, Fast Mag

SECONDARY

> Makarov

GRENADES & EQUIPMENT

> Grenade
> C4
> Flashbang

PERKS

> Access Kit
> Fast Hands
> Adjustable Stock

CHALLENGES

> Eliminate enemy personnel (x15) with pulwar sword.
> Destroy enemy helicopter with a mortar.
> Destroy tank with anti-tank mine.
> Run down enemy personnel (x10) on horseback.
> Destroy enemy helicopter with truck mounted MG.
> Destroy enemy helicopter (x4) at North Pass.
> Utilize Stinger (without aircraft lock-on) to destroy enemy helicopter.
> Eliminate enemy personnel (x25) using alternate fire mode on Stinger.
> Collect Intel (x3).
> 100% survivability rating.

WEAPON/ATTACHMENT UNLOCKS

COMPLETE CHALLENGES	UNLOCK...
2	HIP ACCURACY PERK
5	WAR MACHINE SPECIAL WEAPON

"I CAN'T FIGURE OUT MENENDEZ WITHOUT GETTING INSIDE HIS ******* HEAD."

Section cannot understand how someone can have so much hatred toward the U.S., so he elicits the opinion of Javier Salazar, who is familiar with the Nicaraguan area in which Menendez began his rise to power. A series of misfortunes put Raul in command of his father's cartel and he cultivated a distaste for America.

Menendez started running guns in Afghanistan and the CIA caught wind of it. This is where Woods picks up the story— when he and Alex Mason meet up with the Mujahideen, a group of guerrilla rebels who were fighting against the pro-Soviet government. The CIA is here to exchange weapons for information on Menendez.

A OBJECTIVE
Investigate Menendez's Connection with the Soviets

"YOU KNOW ME. I DON'T LIKE ANYONE."

Frank and Alex travel to the desert to meet up with Hudson's contact, Tian Zhao. After Zhao's grand entrance and exchanging pleasantries, mount your horse.

ACCESS ①

Before following Zhao, run past your horse and approach the Access point. Use your crowbar to loosen up the pulwar sword.

Access

INTEL ①

After meeting with Rahmaan in the Mujahideen base, grab Intel off the gun crates in the corner of the same room.

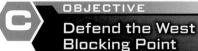

Hold X to acquire Intel

OBJECTIVE
B — Follow Zhao to the Mujahideen Base

"THE ONLY WAY THEY'LL FIND OUT IS IF THEY TAKE US DOWN."

Follow Woods and Zhao through the pass and to the Mujahideen base camp. A Russian attack is imminent, so you must hurry. Pressing in on the Left Stick makes the horse sprint just as it does when you are on foot.

Dismount the horse when you reach your destination and join Zhao and Woods. You are led into the map room where Rahmaan, the leader of the Mujahideen, and Hudson wait. The meeting is broken up by an attack outside.

OBJECTIVE
C — Defend the West Blocking Point

ACCESS ②

After the meeting, break into the room on the left as you leave the cave. Inside you find mortar rounds.

Access

Head for the exit, and jump on your horse. Head straight out of the base along with Zhao and Frank. Continue to follow behind them as you take down any Russian soldiers along the way.

Follow

< 46   47 >

DESTROY ENEMY HELICOPTER WITH A MORTAR
CHALLENGE

Quickly exit the base, trot directly at the landing helicopter, and switch to your mortar rounds. When you get close enough, toss the explosive to take it out and score a challenge.

RUN DOWN ENEMY PERSONNEL (X10) ON HORSEBACK
CHALLENGE

Sprint right at an enemy soldier and run him over for an easy kill. Do this against 10 enemies for this challenge. Be careful not to run over your allies, the Mujahideen.

D OBJECTIVE
Destroy the Soviet BTRs

After dismounting your horse, you find a group of Russians held up amongst some rubble. Take cover behind the rubble and start picking them off with well-aimed shots.

ELIMINATE ENEMY PERSONNEL (X15) WITH PULWAR SWORD
CHALLENGE

Take advantage of this area to get in some kills with the pulwar sword. Sneak around the outside and take the Russians down one at a time with a melee attack.

As you make your way to the south, two Soviet BTRs show up. Fight your way to a platform on the far side where a Stinger launcher weapon rests on a weapons cache. Look for the word "Weapons" to direct you there. Climb the steps carefully, as two Russians may be waiting if you didn't already take care of them.

Pick up the Stinger and use it on the far BTR. Move to the right and hit the near one with another rocket. This takes care of the current objective. Finish off any remaining enemies in the area.

ACCESS 3

On the opposite side of the platform where you found the weapons cache, find some anti-tank mines in an Access crate. These will come in handy later on.

OBJECTIVE
Block the Entrance to the Village

"LET'S MAKE DAMN SURE NO MORE VEHICLES MAKE IT THROUGH HERE."

It's time to block this way in and head back to the base. Place a demolition charge under the archway and then take cover straight ahead behind the short wall. Wait for your comrades to get close to you before pressing the Fire button and detonating the explosives.

OBJECTIVE
Defend the Base from being Destroyed

Jump on your horse and follow the path ahead, trampling any enemy soldiers that get in your way. Tanks roll in from the north; get in front of them and head toward the base to the south.

Pull out your Stinger and take out the two tanks that head your way. A couple ammo crates sit just to the north of the base. Visit one if you run low on rockets.

CHALLENGE
▶ DESTROY TANK WITH ANTI-TANK MINE

Get in front of the incoming tanks and hop off your horse. Place an anti-tank mine somewhere in line with the tanks. Place more than one to be extra sure you get the challenge.

INTEL ②

Look for the red flag near an ammo crate located northwest of the base entrance. Resting next to the flag is the second Intel.

Press Left on the D-pad to switch to aircraft lock-on mode and aim at the incoming chopper. Keep it in your sights, listen for a high-pitched sound, and let a rocket fly. Eliminate two aircraft, and tanks roll in again.

CHALLENGE

▶ DESTROY ENEMY HELICOPTER WITH TRUCK-MOUNTED MG

Look for an overturned jeep near the red flag northeast from the base entrance. Behind that flag is a truck with a mounted MG. Take out any enemies around it and then use the MG to take down a chopper.

CHALLENGE

▶ ELIMINATE ENEMY PERSONNEL (X25) USING ALTERNATE FIRE MODE ON STINGER

The Stinger's alternate fire mode allows you to manually detonate the rocket when you free-fire it without locking onto an aircraft. Use this capability to manually detonate the Stinger missile when it's over a group of enemies. This causes a "rain of fire" effect, killing enemies below the blast. Complete this challenge by killing 25 foes in this manner.

CHALLENGE

▶ UTILIZE STINGER TO DESTROY ENEMY HELICOPTER (WITHOUT AIRCRAFT LOCK-ON)

Wait for a helicopter to slow down as it turns or fires on a target. At that point, fire a rocket from the Stinger without the aircraft lock-on mode.

Switch off the aircraft lock-on and gallop right at the incoming tanks. Once you can see them in the distance, stop and take them out with some well-placed rockets.

OBJECTIVE

G Retake the Weapons Cache

"THE RUSSIANS HAVE OVERRUN THE MUJAHIDEEN AMMO CACHE TO THE EAST."

Use the ammo crate northeast of the base to refill your weapons. Then continue to the pass in the east. When you reach the first bridge, run up the right side.

Once you are on the other side, carefully approach the weapons cache as Russians are dropped just in front of it from a helicopter. Take them out as they descend and then pick off any remaining enemies inside the shelter.

CHALLENGE
DESTROY ENEMY HELICOPTER (X4) AT NORTH PASS

Use the Stinger to take down four helicopters in the North Pass, the area around the three wood bridges.

The weapons cache is on the opposite side of the canyon, but the bridges can be shot down. Quickly cross the nearby bridge if available or cross the ravine to a ladder on the other side. Be careful as soldiers surround this area. Stay on the move and continually scan the area—each side of the pass and up on the bridges.

OBJECTIVE
H Return to Mujahideen Base

Once the area is cleared, you radio in to Hudson to let him know the weapons are secure. The Mujahideen base is in trouble; jump back on your horse and head that way with Zhao and Woods.

< 50   51 >

"THE RUSSIANS WANT TO GIVE US ONE LAST DISPLAY OF BRUTE FORCE. LET'S GIVE THEM ONE LAST DISPLAY OF COURAGE."

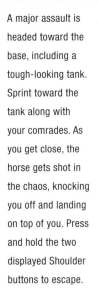

A major assault is headed toward the base, including a tough-looking tank. Sprint toward the tank along with your comrades. As you get close, the horse gets shot in the chaos, knocking you off and landing on top of you. Press and hold the two displayed Shoulder buttons to escape.

Woods helps you get onto the tank, where a fight is played out between Mason and a Russian who emerges from inside. After successfully taking out the tank, Alex Mason's nemesis is captured.

OBJECTIVE
Interrogate Kravchenko

"KRAVCHENKO MUST DIE!"

During the interrogation of Kravchenko, you are faced with a decision. You can resist the need to kill him and gather important information or allow Mason to shoot him. For the best result, rapidly tap the given button to put the gun down. Each time you do this, more information is learned.

DECISIONS

There are several times during the *Black Ops II* campaign where you are faced with a tough decision, such as killing Kravchenko or getting valuable information. These decisions will affect the story later on or even change the game.

———— TACTICS

ACHIEVEMENT/TROPHY

> SHIFTING SANDS

Gather intel on Raul Menendez from Mullah Rahmaan. Complete Old Wounds on any difficulty to earn this award.

STRIKE FORCE

After completing Old Wounds, the first Strike Force mission becomes available. It starts out with a tutorial and then goes into FOB Spectre. Whether you succeed or fail in that mission, the fourth campaign mission, Time and Fate, becomes available.

———— TACTICS

OPERATIVE:
Alex Mason, CIA
Special Activities
Division

ID#: 5814700
HEIGHT: 5'11"
WEIGHT: 190 lbs.

○ **SUPPORT:**
Frank Woods

○ **SUPPORT:**
Jason Hudson

MISSION DETAILS
The President of Panama
(Manuel Noriega) lends his
PDF armed forces to help
the CIA capture Menendez
at his drug cartel
compound in Nicaragua.

PRIMARY OBJECTIVE
Secure Raul Menendez

LEVEL OBJECTIVES

(A) Rescue Josefina.

(B) Observe Menendez.

(C) Clear the cartel village.

(D) Assault the mission.

(E) Clear the cocaine bunker.

(F) Find and capture Menendez.

INTEL ————— (3)

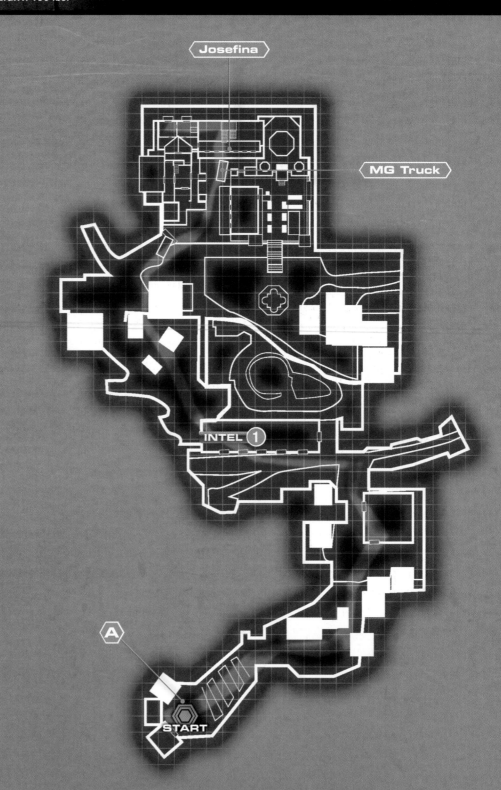

RECOMMENDED LOADOUT

PRIMARY

> Galil with Reflex, Select Fire, Fast Mag

SECONDARY

> M82A1 with Variable Zoom, Fast Mag

GRENADES & EQUIPMENT

> Grenade
> Smoke Grenade

PERKS

> Access Kit
> Fast Hands
> Hip Accuracy

CHALLENGES

> Eliminate PDF enemies (x7) with shotguns in under 10 seconds.

> Eliminate PDF enemies (x8) with truck mounted MG.

> Rendezvous with Josefina in under 140 seconds.

> Eliminate cartel enemy personnel with Molotovs (x12).

> Crash an enemy truck.

> Eliminate cartel enemy personnel with mortars (x10).

> Eliminate cartel enemy personnel with machete (x10).

> Locate evidence of CIA presence.

> Collect Intel (x3).

> 100% survivability rating.

WEAPON/ATTACHMENT UNLOCKS

COMPLETE CHALLENGES	UNLOCK...
2	QUICKDRAW PERK
5	LONGER SPRINT PERK

"HE IS BEING OFFERED UP ON A SILVER PLATTER BY OLD PINEAPPLE FACE HIMSELF, MANUEL NORIEGA."

Frank Woods has given Section a lot of information about Menendez's past. Now they just have to piece it together to try and make sense of it all. One such piece is a mission in Nicaragua, where Manuel Noriega is willing to help the CIA capture Menendez.

A OBJECTIVE
Rescue Josefina

PDF armed forces kidnap Menendez right from his sister's side. When they bring him back to their leader, the trustworthy Noriega kills his own men and sets Raul free. Menendez is irate about the treatment of his sister and takes it out on the man who saved his life.

Now you control Menendez, who is hell bent on rescuing Josefina. Armed with a shotgun and machete, charge down the hill, taking out any PDF soldiers that get in your way. Raul is pretty tough in this state of rage, but you can still be killed. Pause and let your health come back if you take a lot of damage.

Sprint between the buildings and up the steps to the left. Grab the combat axe to throw it at one of the soldiers ahead. Fight your way through the rest of the enemies and run up the hill.

ELIMINATE PDF ENEMIES (X7) WITH SHOTGUNS IN UNDER 10 SECONDS

Take out the guy at the top of the stairs with your shotgun and ignore the axe. Continue to take out the next six PDF soldiers with your gun to complete this challenge.

MAN OF THE PEOPLE

Stop the brutality inflicted by the PDF. As Menendez, protect the civilians by taking out the soldiers at the bottom of the hill, just before the barn, and inside the barn. If the civilians are saved, this award is earned.

Keep laying waste to any bad guys who get in Raul's way and approach the barn. Open the door and dodge side to side to avoid being trampled by the horses. Eliminate the two soldiers who harass the civilians before exiting the building.

Before leaving the barn, search the back of the wagon on the right to find the first Intel.

Fight your way through the village until you see the mission gate at the top of a hill. A truck crashes through the gate and comes to a stop inside the compound.

ELIMINATE PDF ENEMIES (X8) WITH TRUCK-MOUNTED MG

Mount the machine gun on the back of the truck and mow down 8 PDF enemies to get this challenge.

Fight your way through the courtyard and into the house. Run up the stairs and bust through the door to reach your destination.

OBJECTIVE
Clear the Cocaine Bunker

"CLEAR IT OUT. GRAB ANY INTEL RELATING TO THE MENENDEZ CARTEL."

The cartel's cocaine bunker is below the house. Wait for your comrades to open the Access door and follow them down the ladder.

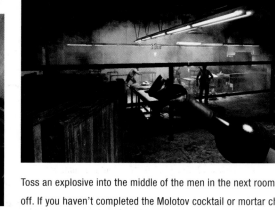

Toss an explosive into the middle of the men in the next room to start things off. If you haven't completed the Molotov cocktail or mortar challenges, use this opportunity to do so.

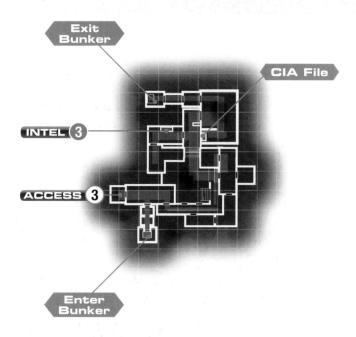

CHALLENGE
> ELIMINATE CARTEL ENEMY PERSONNEL WITH MACHETE (X10)

Melee attack 10 of the cartel personnel in the bunker to get another challenge.

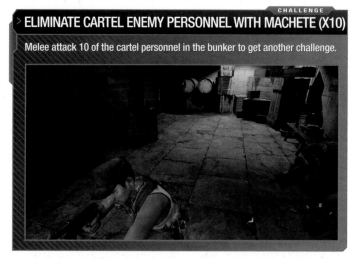

Make your way around the perimeter of the room, taking cover behind walls and crates. Use your whole arsenal to take them all down as you join Woods on the west side.

ACCESS ③

After dropping into the bunker, pick the lock to the Access door on the left. Grab the machete and look over the many options of weaponry inside.

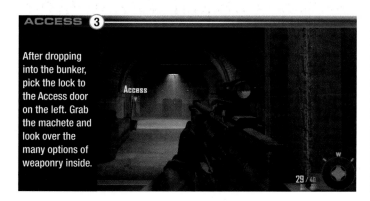

"HIS MEN WERE SUPPOSED TO SECURE MENENDEZ."

OBJECTIVE
Assault the Mission

Hudson figures Menendez is heading to the house, so that is your next stop. Take cover behind the fountain and pull out your sniper rifle. Take out the RPGs on the house balcony in the distance.

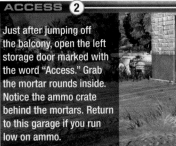

ACCESS ②

Just after jumping off the balcony, open the left storage door marked with the word "Access." Grab the mortar rounds inside. Notice the ammo crate behind the mortars. Return to this garage if you run low on ammo.

After cutting their numbers down a bit, run up the right side and climb the bell tower. Go to the top and use this advantageous position to snipe the cartel in the courtyard and on the balconies.

CHALLENGE

> ELIMINATE CARTEL ENEMY PERSONNEL WITH MORTARS (X10)

When fighting the cartel outside the house, toss mortar rounds into big groups of them. Once you take out 10 men with the explosives, this challenge is complete. You can also complete this in the cocaine bunker later on.

INTEL ②

Inside the bell tower, step off the ladder at the middle floor. The third Intel sits on a crate.

Run up the steps through the wooden structure and into the next house. Watch out, as more enemies hide behind nearly every wall. The penetration of the Galil assault rifle easily goes through the wooden walls of the house, so let them have it before they get a chance to fire.

Check the second room of this house for an Access crate. Inside you find eight Molotov cocktails.

Lob a Molotov cocktail toward the next house and then pull out your sniper rifle and eliminate another MG in the window. Continue up the steps to the right and fight through another building.

> ELIMINATE CARTEL ENEMY PERSONNEL WITH MOLOTOVS (X12)

CHALLENGE

Use Molotov cocktails to take down at least 12 cartel enemies to complete this challenge. Use them to clear out buildings and in the middle of groups.

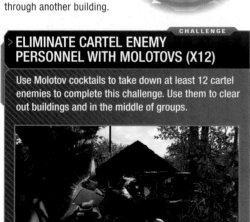

"LIKE OLD TIMES! HUH, MASON?"

Across the street, cartel members fire from the roof and balcony. Target the red barrel on the left to blow them to smithereens. Continue to fight your way down the street.

> CRASH AN ENEMY TRUCK

CHALLENGE

As a truck with a mounted machine gun charges your way, Woods says to take out the driver. Lay down fire on the cab of the truck from the first moment you see it to cause it to crash and earn this challenge.

Take out the enemies in the local area and then dash to the left side of the cart at the corner. Look to the right to spot many loyal men of Menendez. Snipers occupy the three second-story windows and the balcony. More guys hide behind everything down the street. Take out the snipers first and then eliminate anyone who peeks out from behind cover.

Fight your way up the hill and quickly take out the cartel member on the truck-mounted MG. Proceed into the house on the left and run up the stairs. Wait for Woods and Hudson to exit to the balcony, where you spot Menendez going into the barn.

< 54   55 >

RENDEZVOUS WITH JOSEFINA IN UNDER 140 SECONDS

CHALLENGE

Hightail it to the mission and up the stairs to get this challenge. There isn't a lot of time to aim down the shotgun barrel and take out enemies. Blind fire on the run or hack your way through to get there in time.

OBJECTIVE
B Observe Menendez (Mason's Perspective)

"NORIEGA'S MEN ARE MOVING IN. LET'S GO."

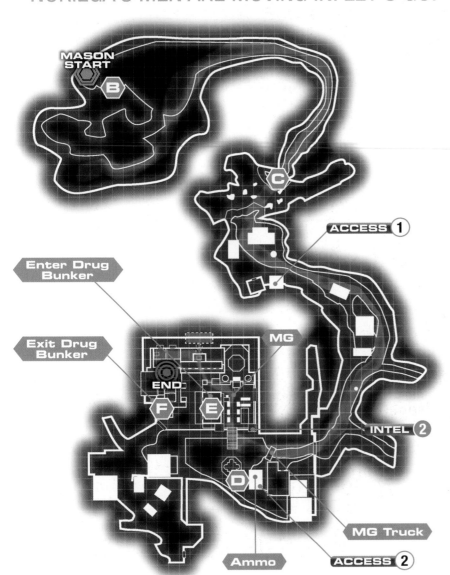

MASON START

B

C

ACCESS 1

Enter Drug Bunker

Exit Drug Bunker

END

MG

F

E

INTEL 2

MG Truck

D

Ammo

ACCESS 2

OBJECTIVE
C Clear the Cartel Village

Run down the hill and join up with some of Noriega's PDF troops. Look out for the enemies to appear in windows and on rooftops and take them out—especially the MG in the window in the right building.

Cross the river and fight your way up the embankment, keeping an eye out for civilians who flee the village. Take cover inside the right building and take out the cartel on the roof ahead and those who hide below.

Meanwhile, agent Hudson and operators Mason and Woods observe Menendez being kidnapped from the other side of the village. Now it is time to clear out the village.

INTEL ③

Search the small storage room on the southwest side of the first area—just before you reach the furnace room. The final Intel sits on a bench.

In the next room, you find cartel loyalists destroying documents in the furnace. If available, toss a couple mortar rounds into the room to thin out the numbers.

> LOCATE EVIDENCE OF CIA PRESENCE

At the furnace, turn right and continue until you reach a dead end. A CIA memo sits on the desk, barely avoiding the fire.

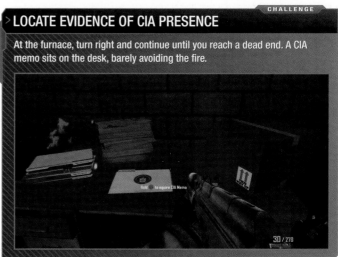

OBJECTIVE
F Find and Capture Menendez

"HE'S INSIDE THE HOUSE. WE ARE MOVING ON HIM NOW."

Take cover behind the desks on the west side of the room and eliminate the few remaining enemies at the doorway. Exit out the door and follow Woods up the ladder.

Despite Hudson's plea for Woods to stay away, follow Frank through a few more cartel men and up the steps. Enter the house to complete the mission.

> DRIVEN BY RAGE

Take down Menendez and his operation. Complete Time and Fate to get an Achievement/Trophy.

OPERATIVE:
David "Section" Mason, JSOC Counter Terrorist Force

ID#: 86900711
HEIGHT: 6'1"
WEIGHT: 200 lbs.

SUPPORT:
Mike Harper

SUPPORT:
Javier Salazar

SUPPORT:
Crosby

MISSION DETAILS
David Mason's team heads to Pakistan to spy on Menendez, who has co-opted rogue ISI leaders to reverse engineer a downed US drone.

PRIMARY OBJECTIVE
Gather Intel on Menendez

LEVEL OBJECTIVES
Ⓐ Gain access to Anthem Compound.
Ⓑ Avoid being spotted by drones.
Ⓒ Gain access to Anthem Compound.
Ⓓ Get to observation point.
Ⓔ Identify Menendez.
Ⓕ Record Menendez's conversation.
Ⓖ Rendezvous with Salazar.
Ⓗ Clear the rail yard.
Ⓘ Escape Anthem Compound.

INTEL ———————— ③

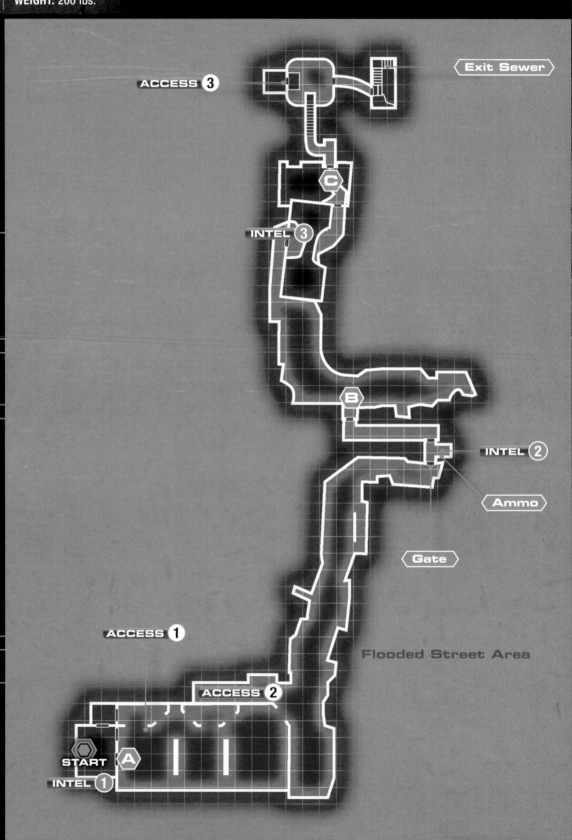

< 60 61 >

"THIS DEFALCO GUY COULD BE FAIRLY ENTERTAINING."

Defalco, Menendez's #2, has been spotted at an abandoned prison in Lahore, Pakistan. There is word that Menendez is meeting him there, giving Mason a good opportunity to spy on him.

RECOMMENDED LOADOUT

PRIMARY

> MTAR with Millimeter Scanner, Fore Grip, Extended Clip

SECONDARY

> Tac-45 with Tactical Knife, Fast Mag, Laser Sight

GRENADES & EQUIPMENT

> Semtex
> Concussion

PERKS

> Access Kit
> Fast Hands
> Quickdraw

CHALLENGES

> Avoid damage from large debris in streets.

> Direct CLAWs to eliminate enemy personnel (x8) in the flooded street.

> Record 400 TB of data from Menendez surveillance.

> Incinerate enemy personnel (x10) with Flamethrower Attachment.

> Protect CLAWs (x2) from destruction.

> Deploy SOC-T boost to find alternate routes (x2).

> Destroy enemy vehicles (x20) with drone missiles.

> Destroy enemy vehicles (x8) with the SOC-T.

> Collect Intel (x3).

> 100% survivability rating.

WEAPON/ATTACHMENT UNLOCKS

COMPLETE CHALLENGES	UNLOCK...
2	HOLD BREATH PERK
5	BALLISTIC KNIFE MELEE WEAPON

A OBJECTIVE
Gain Access to Anthem Compound

Section, Harper, Salazar, and Crosby break into a storage room at the end of a flooded street. They are joined by two CLAWs, Maximus and Brutus. Once Harper's magic touch gets Maximus going again, the CLAW clears out the area just outside the room.

INTEL 1
Before following the CLAWs, search the shelves on the west side of the storage room to find the first Intel.

ACCESS 1
Approach Brutus as soon as you leave the storage room and use your Access Kit on it to enable a Flamethrower Attachment.

COMMANDING THE CLAWs

You have the ability to direct the CLAWs to attack a specific location. Press Up to access a blue aiming reticle. Place it on the location you want the CLAWs to attack and press the Fire button to confirm. It takes a short while for the CLAW to get ready after firing. When the icon appears above your ammo count, you know it is ready again.

ISI soldiers roam the flooded street and keep watch from the balconies above. Scan the area and use the CLAWs' firepower to eliminate them. Take cover on the sides of the street and fight your way to a small tunnel on the right.

────── T A C T I C S

Let the CLAWs lead the way as you pick off enemies from afar. Follow them through the market as you target enemies with your data glove. Allow them to take out the security drone that shows up outside. Wait for the bus to crash into the outer wall and then head out to the street.

CHALLENGE
DIRECT CLAWs TO ELIMINATE ENEMY PERSONNEL (X8) IN THE FLOODED STREET

After giving the CLAWs access to the roof, you once again have the ability to direct them to attack a specific location. Have the drones take out eight enemies on the street and balconies to complete this challenge.

"THE CLAWs ARE BUGGING OUT IN THE DEEP WATER."

ACCESS ②

Once out on the street, look for an Access panel on the left. Force it open and press the button. This allows the CLAWs and Salazar to enter the building and reach the roof above, where they can provide support. Without the Access Kit, you do not have this extra help.

CHALLENGE
AVOID DAMAGE FROM LARGE DEBRIS IN STREETS

As you proceed, watch out for big debris (such as cars and buses) washing down the street. Avoid taking any damage from this debris.

You are now out of the CLAWs' line of sight, so you cannot rely on them anymore. Eliminate the soldiers at the street corner and quickly proceed. Up ahead you notice a bus being whisked down the street by the rushing water.

Run up to the gate and help Harper break through by rapidly tapping the button that appears on screen—just in time, too, as the bus pushes some debris into the entrance.

INTEL ②

After breaking through the gate and avoiding the bus, enter the alley on the right. The second Intel lies on the ground.

B OBJECTIVE
Avoid Being Spotted by Drones

"THOSE DRONES ARE ACTING AS DEATH SQUADS—EXECUTING LOOTERS."

Follow the path to some sandbags and observe the patrolling drone. Be careful not to be spotted by the drones, as they will shoot on sight. Avoid entering their spotlight and do not make too much noise.

Hop over the barricade and kneel behind Harper to avoid the drone. When it turns away, follow your partner to the wall ahead and duck behind him.

Continue this pattern through the building and past the trucks, stopping when he stops and crouching behind him. Finally, you reach a fallen building at the end of the street.

OBJECTIVE C

Gain Access to Anthem Compound

Follow Harper through a couple small openings on the right and duck behind a small piece of debris. ISI is posted outside the sewer entrance. Quickly take out the one on the right or else Harper will make a sarcastic remark.

Cross the boards and stop behind Harper while he cuts through the gate. Follow the sewer to the left and up the stairs.

23/228

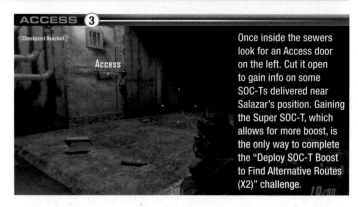

Once inside the sewers look for an Access door on the left. Cut it open to gain info on some SOC-Ts delivered near Salazar's position. Gaining the Super SOC-T, which allows for more boost, is the only way to complete the "Deploy SOC-T Boost to Find Alternative Routes (X2)" challenge.

10/30

OBJECTIVE D

Get to Observation Point

"MENENDEZ IS HERE—MAIN COURTYARD WITH ISI LEADER."

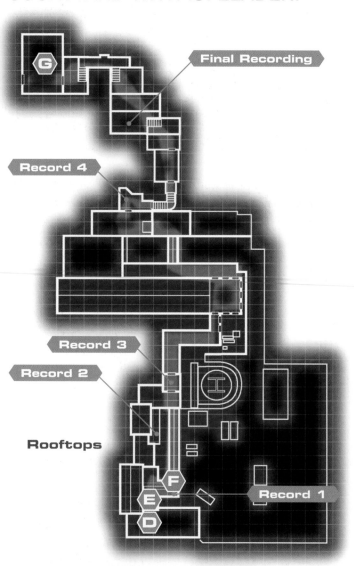

G

Final Recording

Record 4

Record 3

Record 2

Rooftops

Record 1

F

E

D

Target

Get to observation point

Climb another set of stairs and Briggs briefs you on where you can get the best vantage point. Use your rope to grapple to the rooftop. Hold the shown button to lock onto the edge; release the button to ascend to the roof.

Approach the soldier on the right and use a melee attack to take him down and move him out of sight. Harper eliminates the left guard. Be careful as you move across the rooftops, as more drones patrol the area.

OBJECTIVE
E Identify Menendez

USING THE SCANNER

Press Up on the D-pad to use the scanner, though the first time it will automatically come up. A small screen appears in the middle of your view. Hold Left Trigger/L2 to zoom in and get a better view if desired. Place the scanner on someone and keep it on him until the scanner identifies the person.

──────────────── TACTICS

Look around for Menendez's white suit as he walks with the ISI leader. Place the scanner on the man in the white outfit and let it recognize him as Raul Menendez. Stay on him to record their conversation.

OBJECTIVE
F Record Menendez's Conversation

Keep the scanner on them until they move out of range. Follow Harper to the next rooftop, being sure to stay out of sight of the drone. Once it is gone, continue down to a walkway below.

Immediately face the right corner and hold the crouch button to go prone and avoid another drone. Bring up the scanner and

continue to record the conversation as the pair walks in from the right. Keep the scanner on them as they pass, moving along with them to complete the first mission critical info.

"HERE COMES MENENDEZ. YEAH, LOOKS LIKE HE'S MEETING WITH SOMEONE ELSE."

When they again move out of range, follow Harper into a small room and wait for him to take out the operator inside. Pull up the scanner and spot Menendez as he enters from the right. Keep Menendez in the screen as you move the scanner to the left person and identify him as Defalco. Keep recording as they talk about their plans.

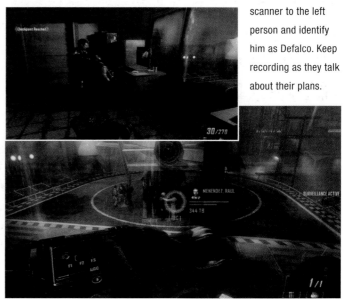

Once again, follow Harper out of the control room and duck behind him when he stops. Once it is clear, quickly move south. Unfortunately, it's too late, as Menendez is lost.

Follow Harper along more rooftops until he pauses at a railing. Hop over and drop to the ground right behind an ISI guard. Hit the guard with a melee attack while Harper secures the driver.

Enter the next building when Harper opens the door and look out the far window. Use the scanner again to pick up Menendez's conversation to record the third mission critical info. It is interrupted as a train passes in front of the target. If all of the key conversations have been recorded, unlimited units are available for the Dispatch Strike Force mission.

> ### RECORD 400 TB FROM MENENDEZ SURVEILLANCE
> CHALLENGE
>
> Keep the scanner on Menendez every chance you get to maximize the amount of data you record. This should easily net you the required 400 TB.

Follow Harper under water and into another room, where you end up right under Menendez. When a grenade is dropped right next to you and Harper, you both dive back into the water and then emerge to see what kind of damage was done.

OBJECTIVE G
Rendezvous with Salazar

Quickly get back under water or you will burn to death. Follow Harper back under water and up a set of steps. Take out the two enemies in the next hall along with more enemies in the garage ahead. The two CLAWs are now in position to aid your escape. Continue to clear out any enemies you can in the rail yard until you gain control of the drones.

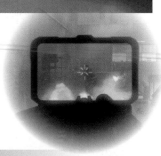

OBJECTIVE H
Clear the Rail Yard

While Section and Harper are held up in the garage, press Left on the D-pad to switch to Brutus. Fry the curious soldiers with the flamethrower and then turn to the right. Eliminate more ISI troops and the truck in which they arrived.

> INCINERATE ENEMY PERSONNEL (X10) WITH FLAMETHROWER ATTACHMENT

With the Flamethrower Attachment on Brutus, press Left Trigger/L2 to fry enemies in front of the CLAW. This means in front of its body, not the turret, so you have to turn the drone to aim in a different direction. Kill 10 enemies with this Attachment.

> PROTECT CLAWs (X2) FROM DESTRUCTION

If both Brutus and Maximus survive until the SOC-Ts show up, then you can check another challenge off of the list.

OBJECTIVE
Escape Anthem Compound

"SALAZAR! AIN'T YOU A SIGHT FOR SORE EYES."

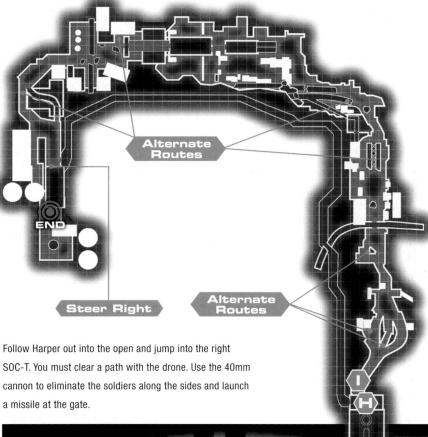

Once you clear out the area, press Right to take control of Maximus. First, eliminate the RPGs on the roof to the right. Once they are cleared, send some grenades at the two trucks and helicopter. Then overpower the RPGs on the street.

Control switches back to Brutus, so take this opportunity to fry more foes with the flamethrower. Once the area is clear, Salazar and Crosby show up with the SOC-Ts.

Follow Harper out into the open and jump into the right SOC-T. You must clear a path with the drone. Use the 40mm cannon to eliminate the soldiers along the sides and launch a missile at the gate.

06_KARMA

OPERATIVE:
David "Section" Mason, JSOC Counter Terrorist Force

ID#: 86900711
HEIGHT: 6'1"
WEIGHT: 200 lbs.

○ **SUPPORT:**
Mike Harper

○ **SUPPORT:**
Javier Salazar

○ **SUPPORT:**
Farid

MISSION DETAILS

JSOC learns from the surveillance gathered in Pakistan that Menendez has hidden a Celerium based cyber weapon called "Karma" on the floating city Colossus.

PRIMARY OBJECTIVE
Secure Karma

LEVEL OBJECTIVES

Ⓐ Get through security checkpoint.

Ⓑ Head to the CRC.

Ⓒ Infiltrate the CRC room.

Ⓓ Disable the electro-static filter.

Ⓔ Access CRC computer and search for Karma.

Ⓕ Rendezvous inside Club Solar.

Ⓖ Stop Defalco from escaping with Karma.

Ⓗ Open the mall door.

INTEL ————③

"IT'S COLOSSUS. KARMA WEAPONS ON A FLOATING CITY."

RECOMMENDED LOADOUT

PRIMARY
> PDW-57 with EOTech Sight, Suppressor, Extended Clip

SECONDARY
> KAP-40 with Tactical Knife, Suppressor, Extended Clip

GRENADES & EQUIPMENT
> XM31 Grenade
> Concussion

PERKS
> Access Kit
> Adjustable Stock
> Quickdraw

CHALLENGES

> Obtain retina scan in less than 60 seconds.

> Retrieve precious cargo (Ziggy).

> Kill enemy personnel with headshots (x5) in Club Solar.

> Ensure zero non-combatant casualties.

> Eliminate rappelling enemies (x5).

> Eliminate enemy personnel (x25) in the outdoor area.

> Incapacitate enemy personnel (x20) using Combatant Suppression Knuckles.

> Protect ASD resource from destruction.

> Collect Intel (x3).

> 100% survivability rating.

WEAPON/ATTACHMENT UNLOCKS

COMPLETE CHALLENGES	UNLOCK...
2	CLIMBER PERK
5	CROSSBOW SPECIAL WEAPON

JSOC uses the recordings from Pakistan to decipher that the Karma weapon is on the floating city of Colossus. That makes the resort the next destination.

OBJECTIVE
A   Get through Security Checkpoint

As the Icarus 9 lands at the Colossus Resort, Section, Harper, and Salazar step out and head for the checkpoint. With Farid's help, they are disguised as union inspectors. Walk through the left door and stop in front of the security guard. After some confusion in the other security lane, you are allowed to pass.

B OBJECTIVE
Head to the CRC

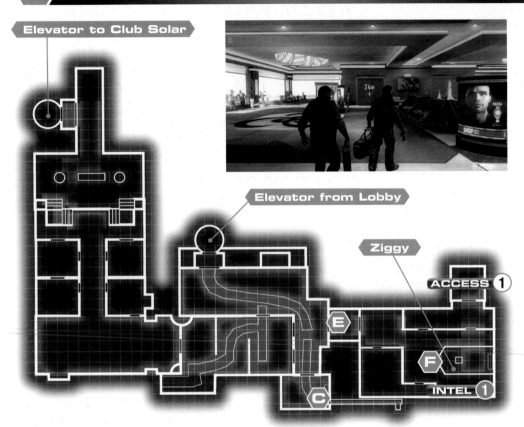

Elevator to Club Solar

Elevator from Lobby

Ziggy

ACCESS ①

E

F

C

INTEL ①

Central Records Computing is JSOC's best shot at locating Karma in the vast resort. The trick is finding a way in. Move past the ID check and step inside the elevator at the back of the room. After dropping Harper off on a separate floor, ride the elevator down to a floor still under construction.

As Salazar takes out the right guard, shoot the left. Follow the blue path to the far room and approach the table with the blueprints. Section removes Ziggy from the briefcase and places it in the open vent.

C OBJECTIVE
Infiltrate the CRC Room

"COLOSSUS RECENTLY EMPLOYED PRIVATE MILITARY CONTRACTORS TO AUGMENT ITS REGULAR SECURITY TEAM."

Ziggy Finish

Ziggy Start

D

CONTROLLING ZIGGY

Ziggy is a high-tech, remote-controlled spider that can climb most walls. Just move into the side of the vent and the camera will rotate as the robot clings to the new surface. Right Trigger/R2 fires his zapper. Press A/X to make him jump. This also gives him a little boost. Be careful not to jump when you are scaling a wall, as gravity will cause Ziggy to drop to the floor.

Now you control Ziggy with the tablet. Move through the vent, up the incline, and jump over the gap. If you don't make it, simply climb up the other side.

OBJECTIVE
Disable the Electro-Static Filter

Turn left at the pipes and continue to follow the path until you reach a panel on the wall. Approach it and fry it with the zapper. Now turn left and keep moving through the small hole.

Rotate between the vent covers and then climb up the left wall. Squeeze through the small opening. Then move

to the right surface, so that you can go through another hole.

Follow the pipes in the next room up to the right, jump over to more pipes on the left, and then climb up to another vent on the wall. Jump into the hole and follow it to a red button.

Use the zapper to open the vent and jump onto an unsuspecting guy below. Quickly zap the man a couple times to take him down, and Ziggy performs a retina scan.

CHALLENGE
OBTAIN RETINA SCAN IN LESS THAN 60 SECONDS

One of the challenges is to get Ziggy through the vents and perform the retina scan in less than 60 seconds. You can see what your mission time is in the bottom left corner. Any time you are on a flat surface, jump to make up time. Be ready with the zapper, and when you are navigating the holes in the vent, rotate to the correct side ahead of time.

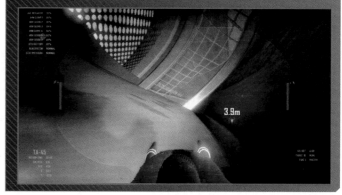

OBJECTIVE
Access CRC Computer and Search for Karma

After gaining access to the next area, immediately take out the two enemies ahead and take cover in the entryway. More enemies surround the room. Eliminate them from there, or from behind the desk, until you hear "clear."

ACCESS ①

Enter the northwest room and spot the Access on the computer. Hack the computer to get a biometric scanner that provides an enemy signature on Section's HUD, giving all of the guards a red glow for easy recognition.

INTEL ①

The first Intel sits on a desk along the east wall.

Join Salazar in the small room on the north side. Step up to the computer to establish an uplink to the central database.

› RETRIEVE PRECIOUS CARGO (ZIGGY)

Before accessing the computer, search the floor for Ziggy. Pick it up to complete a challenge.

"PLACING THE UPLINK."

Section attempts three searches while on the computer, with each one requiring you to press the Analog Sticks in different directions. For most difficulties, the directions are given, so just do as it says. For Veteran difficulty, they are not shown. Here are the four commands you need to enter:

ACTION	CONTROLLER COMMANDS
Search manifest for Karma	Press both sticks Right
Search automated security systems for Karma	Press Left Stick Right and Right Stick Left
Search security cameras for keyword Karma	Press Left Stick Right and Right Stick Left
Once Karma is identified, confirm	Press both sticks Up

The security cameras find Karma and it's actually a person, identified as Chloe Lynch, a former employee of Tacitus. She is located upstairs in Club Solar.

OBJECTIVE
Rendezvous Inside Club Solar

Follow Salazar to the CRC room entrance where Farid opens the door. This puts you back out in the remodeling area from before. Take out the PMC guards

hiding behind the construction equipment. Proceed ahead where enemies break through the previously locked door.

Remain at the doorway and pick off the guards who enter from the hallway on the right. When that room is clear, move up and take cover behind the wall. Climb into the right office and carefully make your way down the hall.

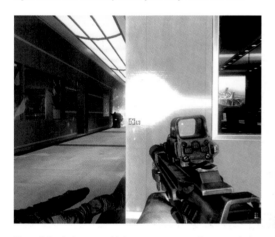

Stop at the balcony and take cover as a smoke grenade is deployed on the floor below. Four guards emerge, so take them out before moving down the steps and entering the open elevator. Salazar splits off and heads upstairs, while Section heads for Club Solar where he will meet up with Harper and Chloe.

"SECURE HER, HARPER. WE'RE ON OUR WAY."

Elevator

START

Club Entrance

Use your VIP status to make your way through the club. Weave in and around the people until you find Chloe and Harper on the dance floor. After mayhem ensues, you and Harper end up behind the bar.

As the civilians scatter off the dance floor, several PMC guards remain. Time is slowed down as you circle around the floor, stopping at four locations until you reach the DJ stand. At each stop, take out as many enemies as you can.

CHALLENGE

> KILL ENEMY PERSONNEL WITH HEADSHOTS (X5) IN CLUB SOLAR

Aim for the PMC soldiers' heads during the slow motion sequence on the dance floor. Taking out at least five with headshots completes another challenge.

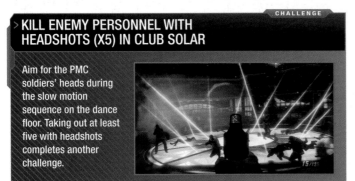

OBJECTIVE

G > Stop Defalco from Escaping with Karma

Defalco has Karma and is escaping through the mall, but before you pursue him, stop off at the armory once it is open.

Top Floor

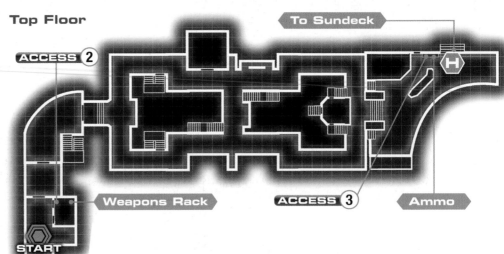

ACCESS 2

Inside the armory, Access the locker on the left by cutting the lock. This gets you Combatant Suppression Knuckles, a weapon that adds a little jolt to your melee attack. You also have several weapons to choose from if you wish for a change.

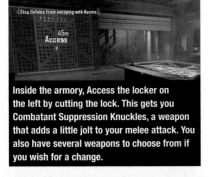

Bottom Floor

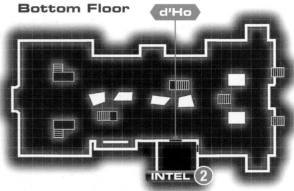

CHALLENGE

> INCAPACITATE ENEMY PERSONNEL (X20) USING COMBATANT SUPPRESSION KNUCKLES

Melee attack the PMC soldiers whenever you get the chance. Taking out 20 in this way will earn you a challenge.

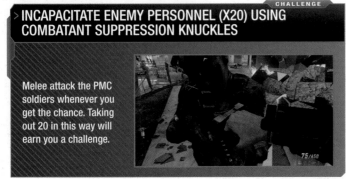

"FARID, DEFALCO IS BLOWING THE SHIP."

Enter the mall and duck behind cover. Before making your way downstairs, take out several guards on the walkway ahead.

INTEL (2)

Search the clothing store d'Ho on the first floor of the mall. The second Intel sits on the back counter behind the register.

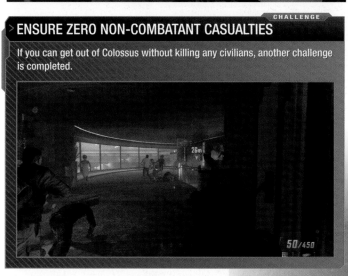

CHALLENGE

> ENSURE ZERO NON-COMBATANT CASUALTIES

If you can get out of Colossus without killing any civilians, another challenge is completed.

OBJECTIVE
H Open the Mall Door

Use the many pillars and advertisements as cover as you fight your way through the mall. Up ahead you find Salazar trying to open the mall door next to an info booth.

CHALLENGE

> ELIMINATE RAPPELLING ENEMIES (X5)

Watch for the PMC soldiers who rappel into the mall from above. Kill five of them before they reach the ground.

ACCESS (3)

Look for the Access point to the left of the info counter. Force it open to find Buster, an ASD unit. Farid hacks it to give you a friendly drone to help out.

CHALLENGE

> PROTECT ASD RESOURCE FROM DESTRUCTION

If this friendly ASD survives until the end of the mission, a challenge is complete.

Reload at the ammo crate. Then help Salazar get the door open. Exit down the steps and out to the sundeck. Be careful as the security ASDs will target anyone who is armed—including friendlies. Use EMP grenades to stun them and quickly move past.

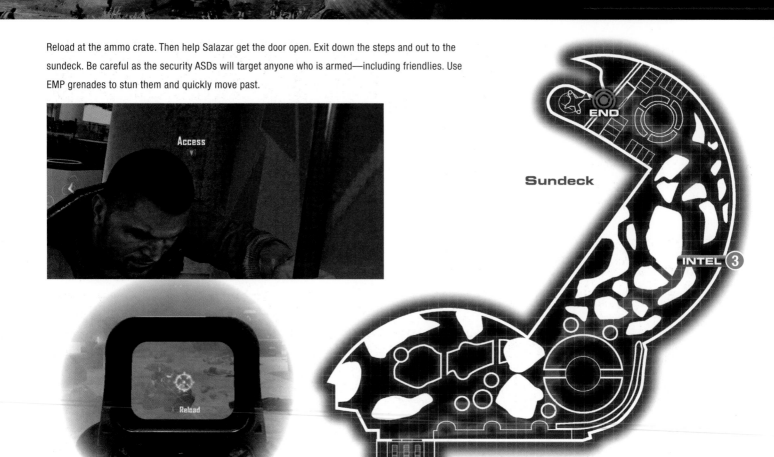

Sundeck

INTEL 3

From Mall

Many more PMC soldiers rappel in to the outdoor area, so take cover whenever possible. Fight your way across the bridge ahead and up to the balcony. Use grenades to thin out the groups of enemies.

CHALLENGE

> ELIMINATE ENEMY PERSONNEL (X25) IN THE OUTDOOR AREA

Take out as many enemies as you can at the start of the outdoor area to get the 25 required for this challenge.

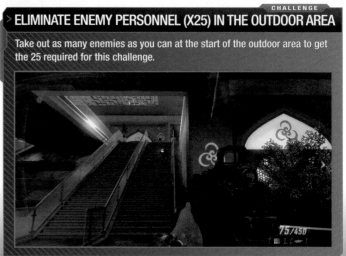

"BRIGGS AIN'T GOING TO BE HAPPY IF DEFALCO GETS CHLOE OFF THE SHIP."

Once Farid tracks down Defalco, you need to step it up or he will escape. Head toward the objective marker, descend to the lower level, and run to the right side of the mall.

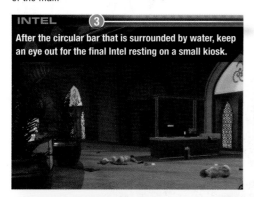

INTEL ③
After the circular bar that is surrounded by water, keep an eye out for the final Intel resting on a small kiosk.

Quickly make your way along the right side of the sundeck and up the steps. If you move too slow, Defalco escapes with Karma. But if you reach him before he exits, he looks back and fires at you. Take cover and eliminate him and his two guards.

SAVING KARMA MEANS NO SECOND CHANCE NEEDED

Killing Defalco and rescuing Karma causes the Strike Force mission Second Chance to not be available during the campaign, since you already have Karma. Otherwise, you can still save her by completing that mission.

——— TACTICS

ACHIEVEMENT/TROPHY

> **WHAT HAPPENS IN COLOSSUS**

Find the Karma Weapon by completing the Karma mission.

OPERATIVE:
Sgt. Frank Woods, CIA

ID#: 19680517
HEIGHT: 6'
WEIGHT: 190 lbs.

SUPPORT:
Alex Mason

SUPPORT:
McKnight

SUPPORT:
Jason Hudson

MISSION DETAILS
Mason and Woods join US Navy SEALs in the invasion of Panama, on a mission to capture Manuel Noriega.

PRIMARY OBJECTIVE
Capture Manuel Noriega

LEVEL OBJECTIVES
A Meet up with Mason and McKnight.
B Retrieve bag from shed.
C Get to Wood's vehicle.
D Capture Noriega.
E Assist SEALs.
F Escort Noriega to Army checkpoint.
G Kill Menendez.

INTEL ———— **3**

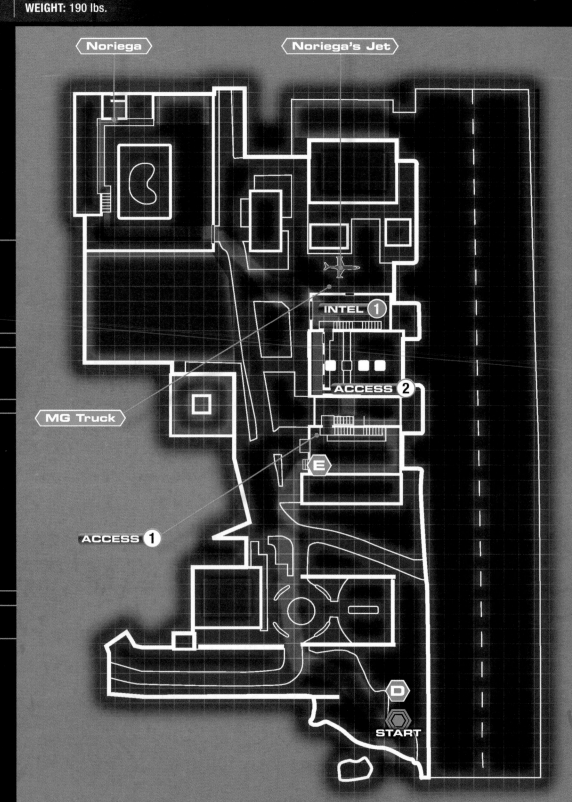

"LOOK, THE DEAD DON'T SUFFER.
THAT'S WHY YOU AND I ARE STILL HERE."

David Mason demands to know what happened to his father, so Frank obliges him with the story. Menendez was spotted meeting up with Noriega, so Alex Mason and Woods joined US Navy SEALs in the invasion of Panama.

RECOMMENDED LOADOUT

PRIMARY

> MP5 with Reflex, FMJ, Rapid Fire

SECONDARY

> M16A1 with ACOG, Grenade Launcher, Extended Clip

GRENADES & EQUIPMENT

> Grenade
> Flashbang

PERKS

> Access Kit
> Fast Hands
> Adjustable Stock

CHALLENGES

> Perform a knife throw at enemy guard post.

> Survive an enemy RPG blast which causes enemy collateral damage.

> Destroy Noriega's private jet.

> Eliminate enemy personnel (x10) with truck mounted MG.

> Destroy enemy ZPU (x1).

> Distract enemy personnel (x8) with Nightingale grenades at the same time.

> Eliminate enemy personnel (x15) with IR strobe.

> Eliminate enemy personnel (x8) in the clinic.

> Collect Intel (x3).

> 100% survivability rating.

WEAPON/ATTACHMENT UNLOCKS

COMPLETE CHALLENGES	UNLOCK...
2	FMJ PERK
5	FIM-92 STINGER LAUNCHER WEAPON

A OBJECTIVE
Meet up with Mason and McKnight

After pulling up to McKnight's house, walk up the driveway and then follow Alex to the backyard.

B OBJECTIVE
Retrieve Bag from Shed

After meeting up with McKnight, go to the shed to grab the duffel bag. Approach the picnic table to discuss mission details with McKnight and Mason.

OBJECTIVE C
Get to Woods' Vehicle

Afterward, follow them back to the front of the house to find a kid vandalizing Mason's vehicle.

OBJECTIVE D
Capture Noriega

"HUDSON, IT'S MASON. THE BOMBING'S BEGUN AHEAD OF SCHEDULE. SOMETHING YOU WANT TO TELL US?"

After dropping out of the zodiac boat, head up the beach and climb the ladder. At the top, let Mason take out the first guard. Then throw a knife at the next guy.

CHALLENGE
> PERFORM A KNIFE THROW AT ENEMY GUARD POST

As soon as the second guard appears, press the Fire button to throw a knife at him.

Take cover behind the sandbags and eliminate the threats who enter from all sides. Use grenades to blow up the surrounding vehicles, taking out anyone nearby.

Move up the left and kill any soldiers who remain. Head down the steps and then toward the building on the right.

ACCESS 1

On the left of the ramp, find an Access crate and cut open the box to find Nightingale grenades.

OBJECTIVE E
Assist SEALs

"CHECK YOUR FIRE. WE ARE ENTERING THROUGH THE SKYLIGHT."

Follow Mason up the steps to the roof of the hangar. Take down any PDF soldiers there and then follow Mason through the skylight. Take down a few enemies below before dropping down to the walkway.

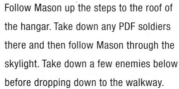

DISTRACT ENEMY PERSONNEL (X8) WITH NIGHTINGALE GRENADES AT THE SAME TIME

CHALLENGE

While on the catwalk, press Up on the D-pad to select your Nightingale grenades and toss one down below. Kill eight enemies in total who are distracted by these grenades.

ACCESS ②

Before following Mason to the right, pick the lock on the door to the left to enter the Access area. Here you find a flak jacket, which will help complete a challenge just ahead.

Follow Mason into the office and turn to the right to spot an RPG in the opposite corner. Take out the soldiers who enter the hall. If you do not have an RPG, switch your secondary weapon for the one on the floor and follow Mason to the stairs.

SURVIVE AN ENEMY RPG BLAST THAT CAUSES ENEMY COLLATERAL DAMAGE

CHALLENGE

Move into the middle of the office area and let the rocket launcher fire at you. Another enemy should be approaching on the catwalk outside the office. Step to the left to survive the blast and score the challenge.

INTEL ①

Before going downstairs, search the shelves on the left for an Intel.

Once downstairs, take cover as you take down the enemies outside, including the guy manning the machine gun. Sprint out to that truck and take control of the weapon to eliminate several more enemies in the far corner, including someone inside the window and on the roof.

ELIMINATE ENEMY PERSONNEL (X10) WITH TRUCK MOUNTED MG

CHALLENGE

To get this challenge, sprint out to the truck as soon as you get downstairs and man the machine gun. Mow down everyone you can find to get the challenge. You will have to be quick, as Mason is also targeting these same guys.

DESTROY NORIEGA'S PRIVATE JET

Pull out your RPG and launch a rocket at the private jet that sits next to the MG. Take that, Noriega.

Follow Mason through the building and pause at the next door. Take down a couple soldiers near the Adelina Motel. Next, meet Mason on the second floor walkway just outside room 225.

"WE HAVE CONFIRMATION ON THE LOCATION OF FALSE PROPHET."

DIRTY BUSINESS

Listen and think before you shoot. If you listened to the full interrogation of Kravchenko in Old Wounds (resisted shooting him) and found the CIA file in the drug bunker in Time and Fate, this award is earned as you are reminded of what you learned.

F ▸ Escort Noriega to Army Checkpoint

"I'LL KEEP THE GARBAGE IN CHECK."

The mission has been changed. Now you and Mason must escort Noriega to a prisoner swap checkpoint. Three officers abuse civilians just ahead. Take them down and then join Mason and Noriega in the hallway to the left.

Breach the door and then move outside. Take out any enemies you see before moving down the street to the left and into the alley. Be careful as civilians also populate the streets. Meet up with Mason and take cover behind the refrigerator.

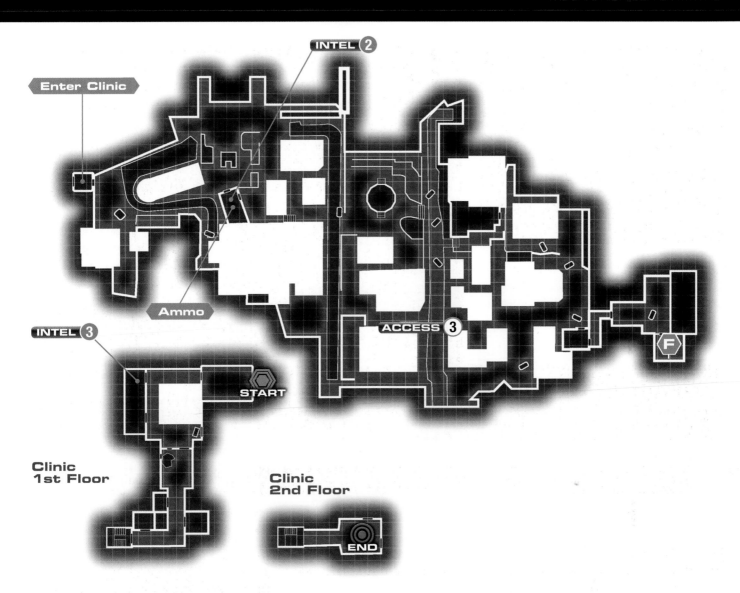

Enter Clinic

INTEL 2

INTEL 3

Ammo

ACCESS 3

F

START

Clinic
1st Floor

Clinic
2nd Floor

END

ACCESS 3

Access

Force open
the fence gate
at the Access
point ahead.
Inside you find
IR strobes on a
fallen soldier.

"I SWEAR IF THAT GUY BREAKS
COVER ONE MORE TIME, I'LL
SHOOT HIM MYSELF."

CHALLENGE

ELIMINATE ENEMY PERSONNEL (X15) WITH IR STROBE

Toss an IR strobe in the middle of some enemies to call down gunship fire
on that position. Be careful to steer clear of that area for a while. Use this on
the street next to where you found the strobes and anywhere else you find a
group of bad guys.

Watch out for incoming grenades as you fight your way down the street to the right. Pause at the second opening and wait for your helicopter to destroy the gazebo.

Duck behind the rubble and look up to the roof on the right. Eliminate the two RPGs and the soldier manning the anti-aircraft gun.

> DESTROY ENEMY ZPU (X1)   CHALLENGE

Pull out your RPG and destroy the anti-aircraft gun on top of the roof to score another challenge.

Meet back up with Mason to the north and clear out the nearby street. Climb up the left steps and take down more soldiers in the next area.

INTEL ②

Move into the open door on the left that leads into the back of an Electronica store. Look on the counter for the second Intel.

Refill your ammo and take cover at the north exit. Toss an IR strobe into the courtyard and wait for the gunfire to stop. Carefully move down the street, keeping an eye peeled for machine guns and enemies above.

"NORIEGA'S A PUPPET. WE'RE ALL JUST PUPPETS."

Move to the Centro Medico building to the west where Noriega and Mason wait for you. Breach the door and follow the hall around to the left.

INTEL ③

From the clinic entrance, move down the hall and enter the open doorway ahead. The final Intel is sitting next to the sink.

< 88 89 >

Continue through the building and approach the nurse who is hurt in the next room. At this time, you are ambushed. Mason takes one guy out, but more rush in from ahead. Kill them all before following after Noriega.

An IR strobe is tossed into the room, so immediately turn around and hightail it out of there. Follow Noriega down the hall and jump into the window ahead. Drop into the next hole and out to the street. This leads directly to the checkpoint.

OBJECTIVE
G Kill Menendez

> **ELIMINATE ENEMY PERSONNEL (X8) IN THE CLINIC** CHALLENGE

Quickly take out as many enemies as you can inside the clinic. Kill eight to complete the challenge.

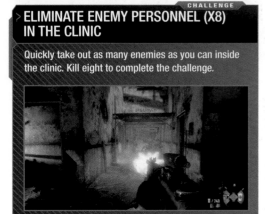

Follow Mason up the stairs to the second floor and wait at the doorway. Once Noriega falls into the next room, approach and help him up.

"I'M A SOLDIER. I TAKE ORDERS AND I GET **** DONE."

As you exit the elevator, follow behind Noriega as he moves through the door. At the balcony, you are given a sniper rifle to take out Menendez, who is brought out by a couple soldiers on the road below. You have a choice here to either kill Menendez by shooting him in the head or wound him with a shot to the leg.

> **FAMILY REUNION** ACHIEVEMENT/TROPHY

There are two futures. Earn this award by wounding the target instead of killing him.

> **FALSE PROPHET** ACHIEVEMENT/TROPHY

Capture Manuel Noriega and bring him to justice by completing Suffer With Me on any difficulty.

08_ACHILLES' VEIL

OPERATIVE:
"Farid," Undercover CIA Asset

ID#: 10081967
HEIGHT: 5'10"
WEIGHT: 180 lbs.

○ **SUPPORT:**
David Mason

○ **SUPPORT:**
Mike Harper

○ **SUPPORT:**
Javier Salazar

MISSION DETAILS

Deep cover CIA operative Farid has penetrated Menendez's inner circle and is poised to capture him during a JSOC assault on Menendez's HQ in Yemen.

PRIMARY OBJECTIVE

Capture Raul Menendez

LEVEL OBJECTIVES

Ⓐ Join Menendez on stage.

Ⓑ Rendezvous with Menendez at the Citadel.

Ⓒ Clear the LZ.

Ⓓ Pursue and capture Menendez.

Ⓔ Capture Menendez.

INTEL ——————— ③

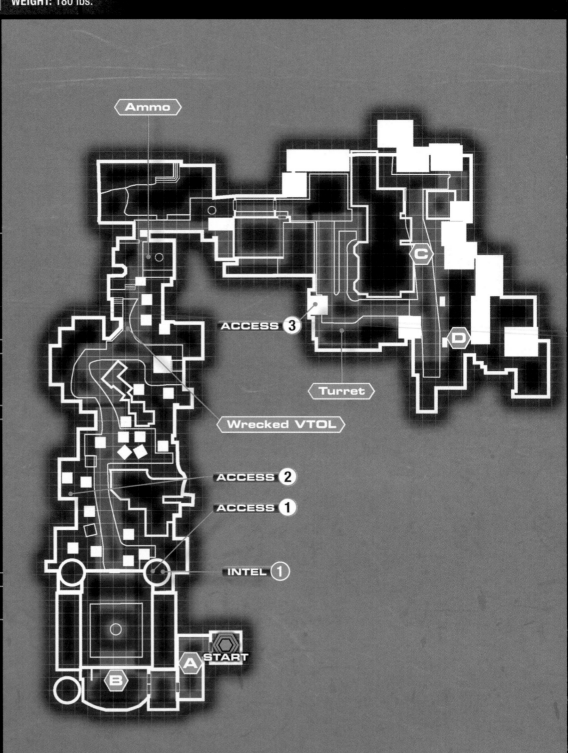

"WE HAVE TO MOVE ON YEMEN RIGHT AWAY."

RECOMMENDED LOADOUT

PRIMARY

> Skorpion EVO with Laser Sight, Long Barrel, Target Finder

SECONDARY

> B23R with Laser Sight, Reflex, Long Barrel

GRENADES & EQUIPMENT

> XM31 Grenade
> EMP Grenade

PERKS

> Access Kit
> FMJ
> Hip Accuracy

CHALLENGES

> Destroy enemy quad drones (x20).
> Eliminate enemy personnel (x20) with sword.
> Melee enemy personnel (x20) while using Optical camo.
> Destroy enemy quad drones (x8) with turret.
> Eliminate enemy personnel (x5) by exploding vehicles.
> Destroy enemy ASD (x4) while disabled.
> Eliminate enemy personnel (x5) as VTOL gunner.
> Direct quad drones to eliminate enemy personnel (x25).
> Collect Intel (x3).
> 100% survivability rating.

WEAPON/ATTACHMENT UNLOCKS

COMPLETE CHALLENGES	UNLOCK...
2	DSR 50
5	FHJ-18AA LAUNCHER WEAPON

CIA operative Farid has worked his way into Menendez's inner circle, and JSOC plans an immediate assault on Yemen to capture him. Menendez always seems to be one step ahead. Are they just falling into his trap?

A OBJECTIVE
Join Menendez on Stage

Despite any doubts you may have, follow Menendez down the hallway and onto the stage outside, where a crowd of his supporters have gathered. Shortly, the JSOC assault begins, but Menendez is ready for it.

OBJECTIVE
Rendezvous with Menendez at the Citadel

"MENENDEZ KNOWS. I AM SURE OF IT."

Menendez informs Farid to meet him at the Citadel. Immediately start gunning down the American quad drones that swarm the courtyard as you make your way down the right side.

ACCESS ②

Move up the left side of the market and through a couple open doors. Cut open the Access safe to find a sword.

INTEL ①

From the start, run to the right tower and enter the open doorway. The first Intel lies on the floor just up the stairs.

CHALLENGE

> ### MELEE ENEMY PERSONNEL (X20) WHILE USING OPTICAL CAMO

> ### ELIMINATE ENEMY PERSONNEL (X20) WITH SWORD

These two challenges go hand-in-hand. Enable the Optical camouflage suit found in the Access crate and hack away at the American soldiers with the sword found in the Access safe.

ACCESS ①

After collecting the first Intel, climb up to the upper floor to find an Access crate. An Optical camouflage suit is found inside. Use this immediately to make it harder for the Americans to see you.

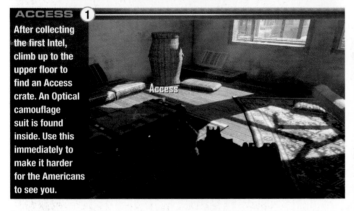

CHALLENGE

> ### DESTROY ENEMY QUAD DRONES (X20)

As Farid, take down 20 drones in total to complete this challenge. Use the turret beyond the Access gate to build up your count.

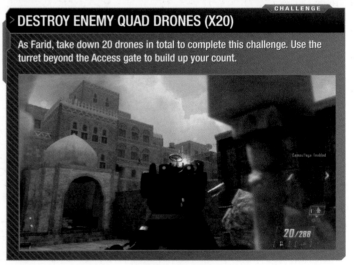

Jump out of the second story window to some scaffolding outside, continuing to fight off the MQ-27 Dragonfires. Follow this to the left and hop off.

Fight your way through the market, keeping these challenges in mind as you do so. Watch out for grenades and cars on fire. Cut through buildings for extra protection. And take cover behind a wall, when heavily damaged.

"YOU STAY STRONG, MY FRIEND. I PROMISE YOU, I'LL GET YOU THROUGH THIS."

An aircraft comes crashing down at your next objective marker. Cut through the nearby door and help Menendez's followers destroy more drones.

Quickly run through the tunnel, across the next balcony, and refill your weapons at the ammo crate. Move through the doorways ahead to find another courtyard. Run around the perimeter to the right, using the crates and debris as cover. ASDs join the American assault.

> DESTROY ENEMY ASD (X4) WHILE DISABLED

CHALLENGE

Toss EMP grenades at the ASDs to stun them, and then finish them off. Three ASDs are in this general area and the fourth can be found on the other side of the road ahead. An extra one can be found after the balcony turret. If you run out of EMP grenades, hit an ammo crate to restock.

Take cover at the archway in the southwest corner as you eliminate the American soldiers and ASDs. Fight your way along the right side through a couple doorways to a locked gate.

When you reach the Access gate, break in and follow the path to a balcony where a turret can be used. Take advantage of this high-powered weapon and eliminate anyone you can see. Be quick about getting to the turret and using it, as the Americans will try to destroy it.

CHALLENGE

DESTROY ENEMY QUAD DRONES (X8) WITH TURRET

Quickly man the turret, found beyond the Access gate, and shoot down all of the quad drones that populate the area.

CHALLENGE

> ELIMINATE ENEMY PERSONNEL (X5) BY EXPLODING VEHICLES

Toss grenades near the vehicles in the market and use the turret on the vehicles below to rack up the needed 5 kills.

"AMERICAN BLOOD ON YOUR HANDS, FARID."

Once the area is clear, head to the right and down the stairs. Fight your way to the south and move through the doorway. Open the next door to find Menendez. He ultimately gives you a choice: shoot at your comrade or Menendez.

ACHIEVEMENT/TROPHY

> ULTIMATE SACRIFICE

Only one can survive. Choose to shoot Menendez to earn this award.

OBJECTIVE
C Clear the LZ

OPERATIVE:
David "Section"
Mason, JSOC Counter
Terrorist Force

ADDED GAMEPLAY

If you shot at Menendez, you assume control of
Section on the VTOL. If you shot at your comrade,
then you move on to the next Objective.

————————————————— TACTICS

Scan the area for RPGs on the rooftops and the street
below. Blow up the vehicles to eliminate any nearby men.

CHALLENGE

ELIMINATE ENEMY PERSONNEL (X5) AS VTOL GUNNER

While on the mounted machine gun, take out at least
five of Menendez's men.

OBJECTIVE
D Pursue and Capture Menendez

"KRAKEN, I NEED TO ASSUME OPCON OF THE DRONE FLEET IN SUPPORT OF CAPTURE OF MENENDEZ."

Now you are teamed up with
Salazar and gain control
of the American MQ-27
Dragonfires. Follow him
through the alley until you
get to an open area. Kill the
guy in the left window and
enter that room.

MQ-27 DRAGONFIRE CONTROLS

When the quad drone icon appears in the bottom-right corner of the HUD, press Up on the D-pad to pair it with your data glove. As you move around, a blue circle signifies where you can aim the drone's attack. Press Fire once you're lined up with your intended target.

————————TACTICS

In the first building on the left, search behind the ammo crates to find the second Intel.

Take down the man who descends the stairs and continue to the rooftop. Direct the quad drones to take out Menendez's men as you make your way to the east. Eliminate the MG if it hasn't already been disposed of, and take cover at the exit.

Keep the MQ-27 Dragonfires busy with the enemies on the building ahead as you move outside, taking down the enemies to the left. Move through the right house, clearing it out as you go.

CHALLENGE

> ## DIRECT QUAD DRONES TO ELIMINATE ENEMY PERSONNEL (X25)

Kill 25 enemies in total by directing the quad drones to attack.

Take cover at the upstairs window and continue to exploit the quad drones' firepower, using Menendez's men as targets. Help out the drones with your own target practice, as his men will attempt to eliminate the drones.

"ENEMY HAS QUAD DRONES INBOUND. WE ARE RE-TASKING YOUR QUAD DRONES TO ENGAGE."

Keep using the MQ-27 Dragonfires as support as you follow Salazar down the path. Once you reach the next building, the drones are rerouted elsewhere. Fortunately, a containment team is dropped in to help your advance.

Turn right toward the structure and run up the steps. Look to the left to find an ammo crate. Refill your weapons before proceeding.

INTEL ③

Climb the ladder found next to the ammo crate to reach the roof. The final Intel sits next to a fuel tank.

Eliminate any bad guys that you can spot from the roof before regrouping with Salazar ahead. You now have enemy quad drones to contend with, though they may be kept busy with your own drones.

E ▶ OBJECTIVE
Capture Menendez

Enter the building ahead and move to the balcony on the right. Eliminate the RPGs on top of the structure on the other side of the valley. Then take the stairs down to ground level and fight your way across the bridge.

Push up the left path, taking cover whenever possible. Several of Menendez's men are ahead, so keep your weapon loaded and rest if damage gets too high. Jump aboard the VTOL, where Menendez conveniently waits for his capture.

> ACHIEVEMENT/TROPHY
> **DEEP COVER**
>
> Capture Menendez to complete Achilles' Veil and get this Achievement/Trophy.

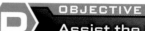

OBJECTIVE
D | Assist the SEALs Using a Sniper Rifle

Head down the steps and exit the bridge. Grab the XPR-50 that leans against the wall, if you do not already have one. Fire at the enemies on the far side of the deck, looking for any RPGs first. Once you have taken enough out, the objective is updated and you need to proceed to the security room.

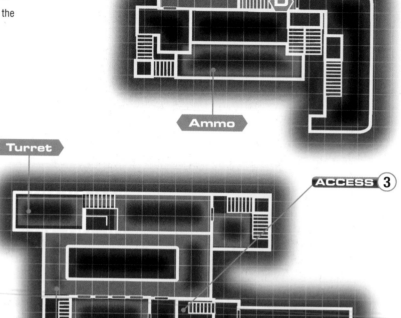

Ammo

Turret

ACCESS ③

Turrets

CHALLENGE
> PROVIDE SNIPER OVERWATCH FOR SEAL TEAM ADVANCE ACROSS FLIGHT DECK

By stopping and helping the team eliminate the assault on the flight deck, this challenge is completed.

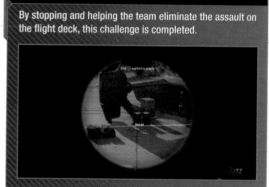

Enter the next door and descend the stairs to find more enemies. Kill them before running down another set of steps. In the hallway, a turret and more enemies make your journey a little tougher.

Once eased, weave through the rooms on the right, using anything as cover. After the next stairs, take cover at the doorway and clear out the office ahead.

"OUR ONLY CHANCE IS TO REBOOT THE ENTIRE SYSTEM."

ACCESS ③

Another Access panel hangs on the far wall to the office. Quickly cut it open to take control of another turret.

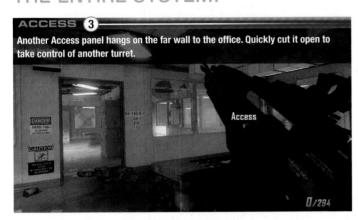

Your first target with the turret should be the other turret in the same room. Then eliminate the rest of the enemy presence. Let go of the turret and follow the walkway through the engine room. Be careful, as enemies wait around every corner—at least you have a turret on your side now.

OBJECTIVE
E Check the CCTV Feed

Head downstairs and run to the northeast corner. Climb another set of steps, reload your weapons, and enter the door to find the security room. Approach the soldier on the computer to find Menendez's location in the server room.

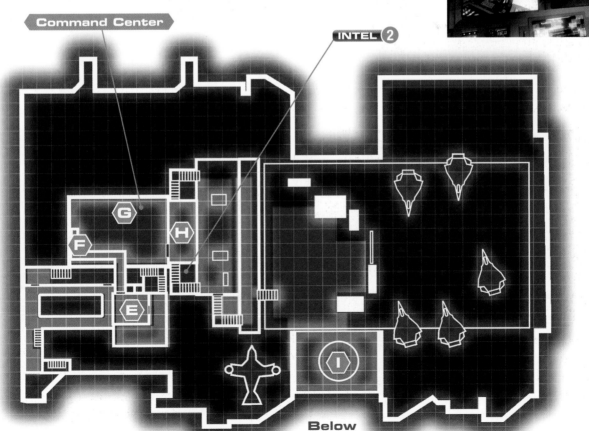

Command Center

INTEL ②

Below Deck

OBJECTIVE
Subdue Admiral Briggs

"I LOST COMMS TO ADMIRAL BRIGGS—HE MAY BE IN DANGER."

As Menendez, approach Admiral Briggs to take him hostage and move him into the next room. Here you are faced with another decision: kill or wound Admiral Briggs. At this point, Menendez uploads a virus that spreads to command center and on to the American drones.

INTEL ②

Leave the server room and, after a couple turns, take the steps on the right. This Intel sits on the desk.

BRANCHING STORYLINES

Your decision to wound or kill Briggs and who is still alive have story consequences.

——————————————————— TACTICS

> GOOD KARMA   ACHIEVEMENT/TROPHY

Crack the Celerium worm. To get this award, Karma must survive through this mission. Farid must have killed Harper, so that he can take the bullet here. Plus, you must get Ship Shape—if the ship goes down, so does Karma.

> SHIP SHAPE   ACHIEVEMENT/TROPHY

Reinforcements are on the way. To get this award, you must first complete all of the Strike Force missions so that China is on your side. Then, you must wound Admiral Briggs by not shooting him in the head.

G
OBJECTIVE
Reach the Server Room

After resuming as Section, duck into the opening created by your troops and follow the path all the way to a vent cover. This gets you directly to the server room—but a moment too late. Approach the central computer to find out the destruction that Menendez has created.

H
OBJECTIVE
Get to Hangar Bay

Menendez has escaped the ship in a fighter, so your next destination is the hangar bay. Exit out the other side of the server room and descend into a room that has been decimated. Proceed into the hangar bay, where Salazar has been captured.

I
OBJECTIVE
Find Menendez

Refill your weapons at the ammo crate as you exit the hangar bay to the right. Look up and behind you to find more of Menendez's men landing on the flight deck.

Take them down as you ride up to the main deck.

"OUR DEFENSE NETWORK HAS BEEN COMPROMISED. ALL HANDS PREP FOR EVAC. ABANDON SHIP."

< 104 105 >

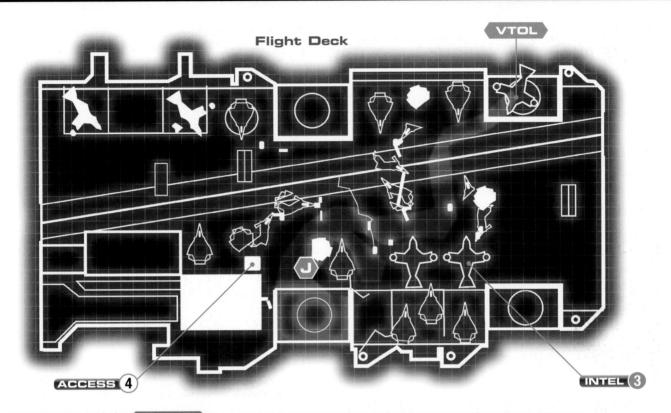

Flight Deck

VTOL

J

ACCESS 4

INTEL 3

> ELIMINATE AIRBORNE ENEMIES (X8) BEFORE THEY LAND

Menendez's men parachute onto the flight deck. Knock eight of them out of the air to score a challenge. This should be your first action as you ride the elevator up.

J OBJECTIVE

Get to the VTOL for EVAC

Take cover behind the aircraft and debris, while siccing the CLAW on the enemy troops. Fight through the enemy assault as you head for the VTOL to the northeast.

INTEL 3

Head east past one open VTOL and approach the second. The final Intel sits just inside.

ACCESS 4

Move to the control room on the left and use Access to force your way inside. This allows you to direct a CLAW to attack specific locations.

> GET TO EXTRACTION IN UNDER 90 SECONDS

As soon as you reach the flight deck, quickly get control of the CLAW and sprint to the VTOL located to the northeast.

> SINKING STAR

Interrogate Menendez. Complete Odysseus on any difficulty.

> DIRECT CLAW TO ELIMINATE ENEMY PERSONNEL (X5)

Press Up and place the aiming reticle on the incoming enemies to instruct the CLAW to attack.

O_CORDIS DIE

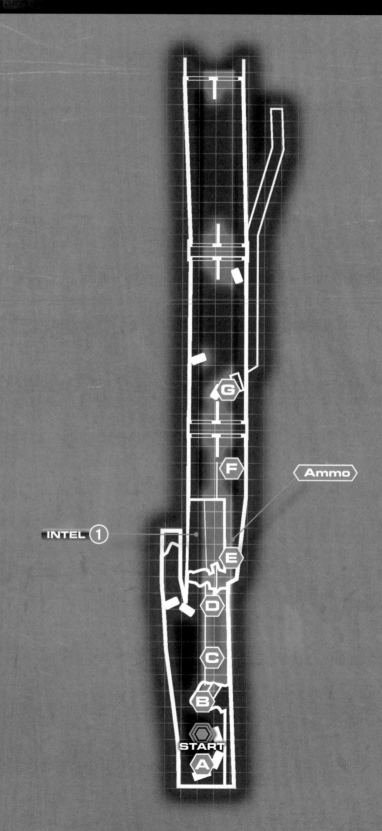

OPERATIVE:
David "Section" Mason, JSOC Counter Terrorist Force

ID#: 86900711

HEIGHT: 6'1"

WEIGHT: 200 lbs.

○ **SUPPORT:**

Mike Harper (if available)

○ **SUPPORT:**

Samuels

○ **SUPPORT:**

Jones

MISSION DETAILS

Marine One is shot down over Los Angeles, and David Mason must escort President Bosworth to safety as US drones under Menendez's control destroy the city.

PRIMARY OBJECTIVE

Protect POTUS

LEVEL OBJECTIVES

A Get POTUS to the "Prom Night" bunker.

B Use the SAM Turret to shoot down the drones.

C Regroup with protection detail.

D Protect POTUS.

E Save all three MRAPS.

F Get to the MRAP vehicles.

G Head for the "Prom Night" bunker.

H Regroup with POTUS.

I Destroy the CLAWs (x2).

J Save G20 leader.

K Get to the FA-38.

L Follow Anderson's ambulance.

M Destroy the drones.

NTEL ———— ③

RECOMMENDED LOADOUT

PRIMARY

> Type 25 with Reflex, Fore Grip, Fast Mag

SECONDARY

> Storm PSR

GRENADES & EQUIPMENT

> Concussion
> EMP Grenade
> XM31 Grenade

PERKS

> Access Kit
> FMJ
> Extended Clip

CHALLENGES

> 100% impact ratio with SAM engagement on highway.

> Perform headshot (x10) sniper kills from the upper freeway.

> Direct quad drones to eliminate enemy personnel (x8).

> Rescue trapped SSA in damaged vehicle.

> Destroy enemy drone (x30) using SAM on roof.

> Protect G20 Cougar at the intersection.

> Destroy drones (x3) with one shot.

> Protect all G20 vehicles.

> Collect Intel (x3).

> 100% survivability rating.

WEAPON/ATTACHMENT UNLOCKS

COMPLETE CHALLENGES	UNLOCK...
2	THROWBACK PERK
5	AMMO PICKUP PERK

"SEAL COMMANDER WHO CAPTURED MENENDEZ REQUESTED TO HEAD UP YOUR SECURITY DETAIL."

Los Angeles is under attack by the United States' own drones, which are currently under Menendez's control. Marine One is one of the casualties as it attempts to carry President Bosworth to safety. Now David Mason must get her to the safe zone, the "Prom Night" bunker.

A   OBJECTIVE
Get POTUS to the "Prom Night" Bunker

After the vehicle crashes, you emerge from the wreckage along with the President. Sleeper cells around L.A. have been activated. Combine that with our own drones attacking, and this will be a tough fight to get her to safety.

HARPER IS MISSING

If Harper is unavailable, he is missing from this mission.

TACTICS

OBJECTIVE
Use the SAM Turret to Shoot Down the Drones

Sprint ahead to the precariously sitting truck and man the Stinger mounted on top. Once enough drones have been taken out, Mason abandons the gun as it falls off the road.

SAM CONTROLS

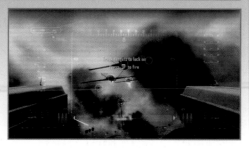

Use the Left Analog Stick to turn around in the seat—360 degrees. The Right Analog Stick aims. As you track the drones, the gun locks onto them. The more drones locked on, the more missiles fired—up to six. Press the Fire button when you are ready to take them down. On the bottom of the screen is radar that shows where your targets are in relation to your view. Spin around until icons appear on the radar and then line them up with your reticle.

———TACTICS

CHALLENGE
> 100% IMPACT RATIO WITH SAM ENGAGEMENT ON HIGHWAY

Make sure every missile you fire hits a target. Do this by waiting for the weapon to lock onto the drones.

OBJECTIVE
Regroup with Protection Detail

Sprint down the street where the others are waiting. Here you are given the choice to Sniper or Rappel.

CHOOSE SNIPER

CHOOSE RAPPEL

OBJECTIVE
Protect POTUS

Select Sniper, pull out the Storm PSR, and take out the enemy in the parking lot to the right. Zoom in on the targets on the street below and start taking them out. If you selected Rappel, this Sniper section must be played from the street below.

STORM PSR

The Storm PSR is an extremely powerful sniper rifle. As you aim through the scope, targets are highlighted for easy recognition. Pressing the Fire button fires one bullet at your target, but this gun is capable of much more. If you hold the Fire button down, the five blue boxes on the right fill up. These represent the power of the shot and how much ammo is used—up to five bullets.

If you are shooting at someone through a barrier, a grid pattern shows up on the surfaces. It appears in red if the shot will not penetrate, and it appears in green if it will. Wait for the grid pattern to turn green before releasing your shot to take advantage of this gun's extreme material penetration.

———TACTICS

OBJECTIVE E
Save All Three MRAPs

"TARGET THE SNIPERS."

Watch for the two trucks, one on each side of the highway, to pull up. Charge up a shot and hit each one to destroy them. Continue to scan the street and pick off anyone who appears until you hear the order to target the men on the overpass.

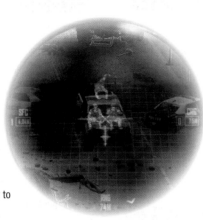

CHALLENGE
PERFORM HEADSHOT (X10) SNIPER KILLS FROM THE UPPER FREEWAY

You must choose Sniper to get this challenge, as it needs to be performed from the upper freeway. Aim for headshots, but you need to be quick.

Look straight across for the cross street and charge up a shot. Use it on the truck that drives up to destroy it. Scan to the right for more incoming enemies. Once you get the all clear, Mason rappels to the street below.

INTEL ①

When you reach the lower street, run past the destroyed bus and search the ground before the MGs to find the first Intel.

OBJECTIVE F
Get to the MRAP Vehicles

As you make your way down the right side of the road, take out another MG that appears in the distance. Continue in that direction until you meet up with the others.

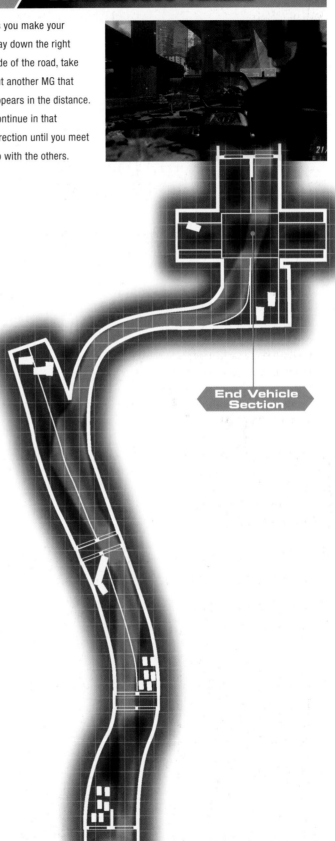

End Vehicle Section

G — OBJECTIVE
Head for the "Prom Night" Bunker

Climb into the cab of the truck and take off. Plow through the enemies, veering into the left lane and back when blocked. Continue to follow the street until you are struck by a semi.

TRUCK CONTROLS

Press Right Trigger/R2 to accelerate the truck and Left Trigger/L2 to brake or reverse. Steer with the Left Stick.

H — OBJECTIVE
Regroup with POTUS

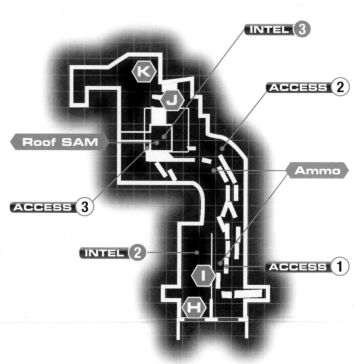

"WE'LL FIND A WAY THROUGH THE STREETS. WE'LL REGROUP EN ROUTE!"

After the truck crashes, grab the RPG that lies on the ground and take out the CLAW to the right.

OBJECTIVE
Destroy the CLAWs (x3)

There are three CLAWs in total on this street that must be taken down in order to reach POTUS.

HARPER HELPS OUT

If Harper is still alive, he takes out the first CLAW, leaving only two for you to destroy.

——————————————————— TACTICS

ACCESS ①
Once the first CLAW is eliminated, enter the truck that sits on its side. Use Access to cut open the gate and get drones of your own.

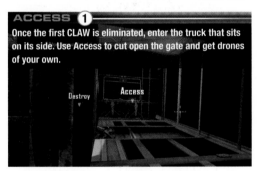

A second CLAW shows up on the other side of the blown-out bus. Get a good view of it and destroy it with a few rockets. Refill your weapons at the ammo crate if needed. Take advantage of the drone help and fight your way into the hotel on the left.

› DIRECT QUAD DRONES TO ELIMINATE ENEMY PERSONNEL (X8)

Whenever the MQ-27 Dragonfires are available to use, target more enemies for them.

INTEL ②
Enter the hotel lobby on the left and grab an Intel that rests on the main desk.

Move to the other side of the lobby and look for the incoming reinforcements. Use the Storm PSR and the drones to eliminate them. Exit out the nearby door and look left to find the final CLAW. Send the drones its way and launch a rocket to finish it off.

Eliminate the group of enemies who appear at the Plaza Downtown ahead. Move up to their old position and take cover. Use the Storm PSR's penetration ability to take out enemies who hide around the plaza.

"OUR IAV IS ON FIRE! YOU'VE GOT TO GET US OUT, PLEASE!"

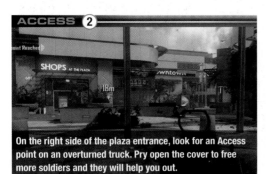

ACCESS 2

On the right side of the plaza entrance, look for an Access point on an overturned truck. Pry open the cover to free more soldiers and they will help you out.

CHALLENGE

RESCUE TRAPPED SSA IN DAMAGED VEHICLE

By "accessing" the overturned armored vehicle, a challenge is complete.

Enter the mall on the left and fight to the escalator. Ascend to the second floor, being sure to dodge the flower pot thrown your way.

ACCESS 3

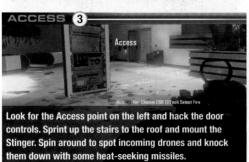

Look for the Access point on the left and hack the door controls. Sprint up the stairs to the roof and mount the Stinger. Spin around to spot incoming drones and knock them down with some heat-seeking missiles.

CHALLENGE

DESTROY ENEMY DRONE (X30) USING SAM ON ROOF

Eliminate as many drones with the SAM as you can. Track the groups until several are locked-on and let the missiles fire. Quickly spin around until you find another group and repeat. It takes 30 drones total from this one SAM to get this challenge.

Use the open skylight to rain fire down on the enemy combatants. Move down the openings to the left until you have eliminated everyone you can. Drop down onto one of the advertisements to limit damage taken or just return down the stairs.

INTEL 3

Look for the big kiosk on the right called LA Best T-Shirt. An Intel sits on the bottom shelf.

Continue to fight your way through the mall until you reach the next checkpoint to the west.

18m

OBJECTIVE
J Save G20 Leader

"DAMMIT, SECTION! THE FRENCH VEHICLE IS TAKING HEAVY FIRE FROM ALL SIDES!"

You hear from Anderson that the French President is under heavy fire and she can't hold them off for too much longer. You need to immediately head that way in order to save the leader. Before reaching the next street, look for an RPG or two on the far roof and take them out. Continue to take out the enemy combatants who hide between the cars, including two who are on truck-mounted guns, until the objective is complete.

> **PROTECT G20 COUGAR AT THE INTERSECTION**

Saving the G20 leader as explained here, earns a challenge.

K OBJECTIVE
Get to the FA-38

When Mason comes to, run over to Anderson's FA-38 and take over for her in the cockpit.

FA-38 CONTROLS

Use the Left Analog Stick to move and strafe and the Right Stick to aim the weapons. Right Trigger/R2 fires the cannon and Left Trigger/L2 fires missiles. The Sprint button uses your afterburners, which is very useful in catching up with the drones. Eventually, the Sky Buster will come online as indicated in the lower-right corner of the HUD. Press Left Bumper/L1 to fire multiple missiles.

——————————————— TACTICS

L OBJECTIVE
Follow Anderson's Ambulance

"I'VE SECURED AN FA-38 TO PROVIDE AIR SUPPORT."

Look for the three G20 vehicles (outlined in white) below. Stay close to them and protect them from any approaching dangers. After following them around a few turns, enemy trucks and drones approach from all sides. Keep the cannon firing and hit enemies with heat-seeking missiles.

Semis block the road ahead, so follow the convoy to the right. Lock onto the two gunships at the next intersection.

> **PROTECT ALL G20 VEHICLES** CHALLENGE

If all of the G20 vehicles survive, then this challenge is yours.

OBJECTIVE
Destroy the Drones

A group of drones zip past, along with a couple ally fighters. Hit the afterburners and lock onto the enemy aircraft. Once they are eliminated, another group flies through the skyline to the east.

Pull back to clear the buildings or carefully navigate between them as you shoot down the rest of the drones. After a while, Mason ejects from the cockpit and lands hard on the street below.

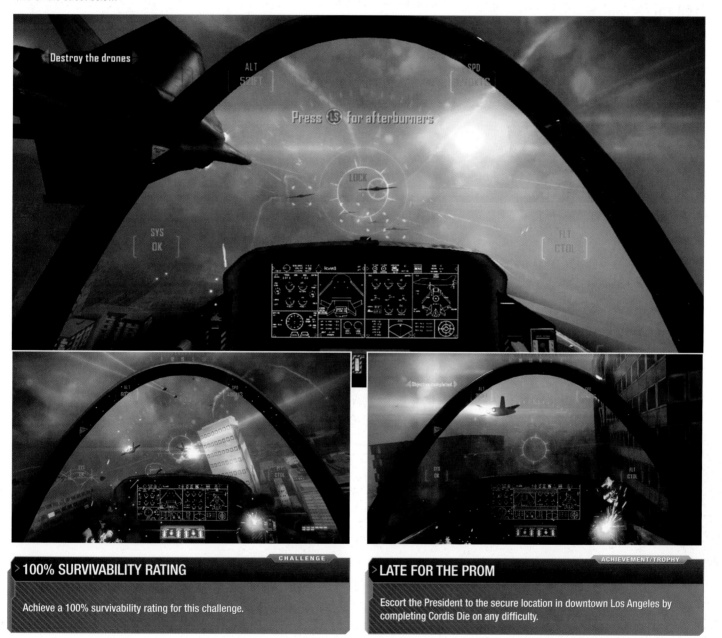

CHALLENGE

> 100% SURVIVABILITY RATING

Achieve a 100% survivability rating for this challenge.

ACHIEVEMENT/TROPHY

> LATE FOR THE PROM

Escort the President to the secure location in downtown Los Angeles by completing Cordis Die on any difficulty.

11_JUDGMENT DAY

OPERATIVE:
David "Section"
Mason, JSOC Counter
Terrorist Force

ID#: 86900711
HEIGHT: 6'1"
WEIGHT: 200 lbs.

○— **SUPPORT:**
Mike Harper
(if available)

MISSION DETAILS
JSOC launch a massive
assault against the Haitian
facility broadcasting the
signal controlling the US
drone fleet.

PRIMARY OBJECTIVE
Find Raul Menendez

LEVEL OBJECTIVES

Ⓐ Shut down the transmission.

Ⓑ Avoid the aircraft debris and
enemy missiles.

Ⓒ Gain entry to the military facility.

Ⓓ Advance to the control room.

Ⓔ Shut down the drone control.

Ⓕ Find Menendez.

INTEL —————— ③

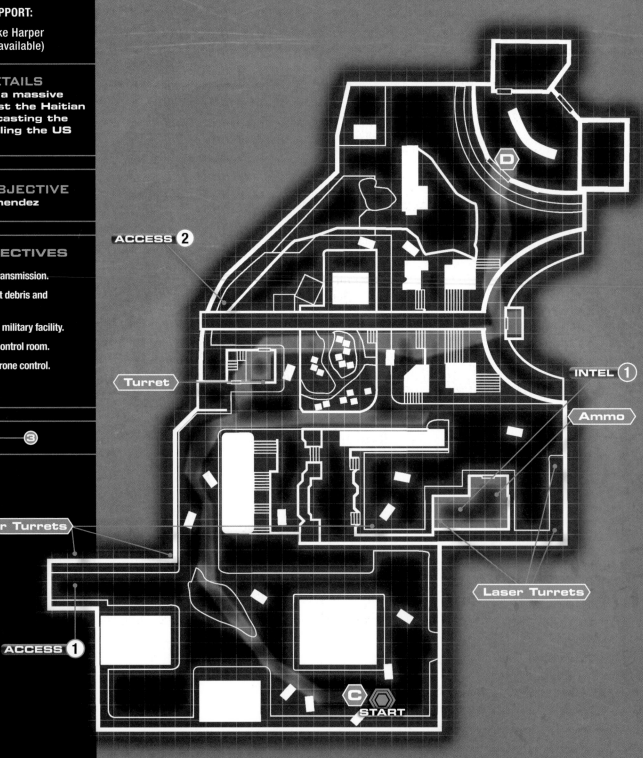

RECOMMENDED LOADOUT

PRIMARY
> SCAR-H with Target Finder, Grenade Launcher, Fast Mag

SECONDARY
> XPR-50 with Variable Zoom, Dual Band, Ballistics CPU

GRENADES & EQUIPMENT
> Concussion
> EMP Grenade
> XM31 Grenade

PERKS
> Access Kit
> FMJ
> Hold Breath

CHALLENGES

> Avoid ALL anti-air missiles.
> Destroy ALL laser turrets.
> Destroy enemy quad drones (x3) while disabled.
> Perform sniper kills (x10) from more than 40m distance.
> Melee camouflaged enemy personnel (x3).
> Direct quad drones to eliminate enemy CLAW.
> Eliminate enemy personnel (x5) with one strike of the kinetic projectile weapon.
> Protect ASD resource to the objective location.
> Collect Intel (x3).
> 100% survivability rating.

WEAPON/ATTACHMENT UNLOCKS

COMPLETE CHALLENGES	UNLOCK...
2	FAST MAG PERK
5	DEATH MACHINE WEAPON

"MADAME PRESIDENT, MAY GOD HELP US."

The drones are still under Menendez's control, but the signal has been tracked to the west coast of Haiti. JSOC is presently in route to shut it down.

OBJECTIVE
Shut Down the Transmission

Along with a few other American soldiers, Section is set to jump out of an airplane. As the aircraft loses control, you are forced to abandon a little early.

"I VOTE KILL. TAKING HIM ALIVE DIDN'T WORK OUT LAST TIME."

OBJECTIVE
Avoid the Aircraft Debris and Enemy Missiles

Steer yourself to avoid the debris and enemy missile explosions as you descend to the ground. There are only so many hits you can take from the explosions before you are taken out, so be careful. Steer well clear of the missiles, as they have a big blast radius.

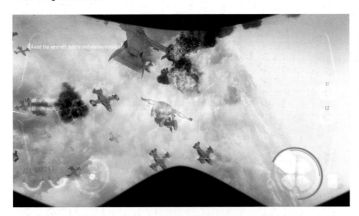

> AVOID ALL ANTI-AIR MISSILES
CHALLENGE

Do not take any damage from the missiles to complete the first challenge. Steer to the extreme left or right to miss the explosions. Keep an eye ahead to the next incoming missile and anticipate where it is going.

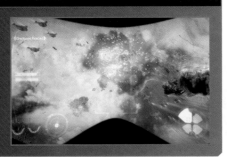

OBJECTIVE
Gain Entry to the Military Facility

Once you are on the ground, sprint to the north to reach the action.

ACCESS ①

Sprint past the building to find an Access crate. Use it to gain control of some quad drones.

> DIRECT QUAD DRONES TO ELIMINATE ENEMY CLAW
CHALLENGE

Immediately sic the drones that you just found on the CLAW to the east.

> DESTROY ALL LASER TURRETS
CHALLENGE

Pull out your sniper rifle and knock out the AA laser mounts on the roofs. There are five along the buildings to the right and another a little further back.

< 118 119 >

Take cover behind some debris and start taking out any enemy soldiers you can see. A friendly CLAW heads up the ramp to the east. Use it as cover as you blast away your foes.

PERFORM SNIPER KILLS (X10) FROM MORE THAN 40M DISTANCE

CHALLENGE

Pull out your sniper rifle and take out the distant enemy snipers and RPGs. A few are on the walkway above. Look for the rocket trails and trace them back to find them. Scan the ground for distant targets to help reach the required 10.

Continue up the road until you reach building 26. Take cover at the doorway and clear out the room. Toss an EMP grenade to disable the turret, step inside, and finish it off.

ACCESS ②

Exit out the back of building 26 and approach the Access point at the downed aircraft. This gives you control of a Kinetic Strike Weapon.

USING THE KINETIC STRIKE WEAPON

Press Right to bring up a red aiming reticle and place it on the intended target. Press Fire to take out anything at that location. This is good for taking out the anti-air gun vehicles that litter the map.

TACTICS

> ELIMINATE ENEMY PERSONNEL (X5) WITH ONE STRIKE OF THE KINETIC PROJECTILE WEAPON

There are a few opportunities to eliminate five enemies with one strike before you reach the military facility. Here are two good ones.

Step into the cargo area just south of building 26 and aim the Kinetic Projectile Weapon at the far wall. Clear out of the area and let the weapon wipe out the camouflaged combatants. Be careful, as your guys may enter before the weapon hits and friendly fire ends the mission.

Another opportunity is just to the west of there. Before going up the steps to building 27, a truck jumps off the upper level. Aim the Kinetic Strike Weapon at the wall behind it. Take cover and watch it obliterate the guys above and below.

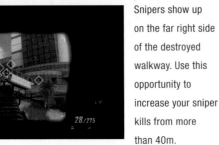

Snipers show up on the far right side of the destroyed walkway. Use this opportunity to increase your sniper kills from more than 40m.

Head south up the steps to building 27. Carefully fight your way through to an ammo crate in the garage area.

Run up to the second floor of building 27 to find an Intel sitting on a desk.

Take cover at an eastern window and send a Kinetic shot at the enemies who take cover at the top of the steps ahead. Move east and step into the small room on the right to reload your weapons if needed. Pause before descending the next steps and use the Kinetic Strike Weapon to take out the two CLAWs who patrol the area. Once the coast is clear, move up to the military facility entrance.

D OBJECTIVE
Advance to the Control Room

INTEL 2

ACCESS 3

E

F

Ammo

START

INTEL 3

ACCESS 3

END

"EVERYONE ON ME! PUSH INTO THE BUILDING."

Since you are entering a building, the Kinetic Strike Weapon is no longer available. Pick off as many combatants inside the building that you can from this position. Be careful, as friendlies assault the second floor.

Kinetic Strike Weapon - Offline
18m

Push into the building, down the stairs, and through a couple rooms. At the walkway that overlooks the lower floor, fire on the lower level.

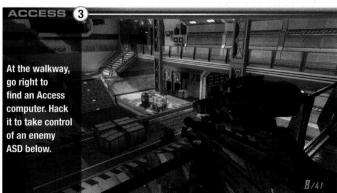

ACCESS 3

At the walkway, go right to find an Access computer. Hack it to take control of an enemy ASD below.

Head downstairs, take cover, and finish off the enemy
ASDs and combatants who occupy the next area.
Fight your way through the hallway until you reach the
broadcast room. Hunker down at the doorway and pick off
the soldiers and quad drones that enter from the right side.

INTEL ②

After clearing out
the broadcast
room, move up to
the third tier of
computers and
search the desks
to the left for the
second Intel.

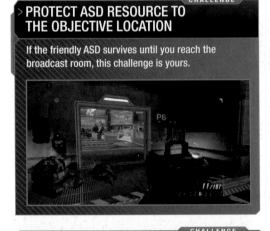

CHALLENGE
> ## PROTECT ASD RESOURCE TO THE OBJECTIVE LOCATION

If the friendly ASD survives until you reach the
broadcast room, this challenge is yours.

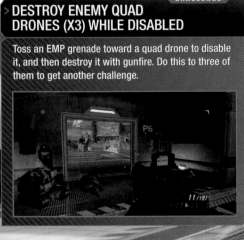

CHALLENGE
> ## DESTROY ENEMY QUAD DRONES (X3) WHILE DISABLED

Toss an EMP grenade toward a quad drone to disable
it, and then destroy it with gunfire. Do this to three of
them to get another challenge.

E OBJECTIVE
Shut Down the Drone Control

"I'M LOCKED OUT. CAN YOU HACK INTO THE SYSTEM?"

Run through one of the upper doors and up the steps to reach the control room. Eliminate the guys
inside and then step up to the computer.

OBJECTIVE
F Find Menendez

"ALL CHECKPOINTS, DETAIN ANYONE ATTEMPTING TO LEAVE AO—EVEN THOSE IN UNIFORM!"

Enter the open door and take cover as you kill Menendez's men who are converging on your location. When the ceiling caves in ahead, run up the left steps and move to the second opening. Take out those inside and take cover at the next doorway.

Pick off the combatants who litter the hallway and opposite room. Move south until you reach another set of stairs. From above, fire down on the men on the lower level. Descend the steps and finish off any remaining foes. Enter the Celerium core room to the south.

INTEL ③

Run around the outer edge and descend the stairs to the lower level. On the north side of the room, look for the final Intel that shines brightly in the darkness.

Climb to the upper floor and fight your way south through the hallway. Approach the partially open gate and Section slides underneath. After grabbing the pistol, the scene goes into slow motion. Take out the two soldiers on the right as you pass them to complete the final mission. You can now decide how to handle Menendez.

CHALLENGE
MELEE CAMOUFLAGED ENEMY PERSONNEL (X3)

Keep an eye out for enemies with the Optical camo suits. Melee attack three of them to get this challenge. The area before the Celerium core room is the best location to get it.

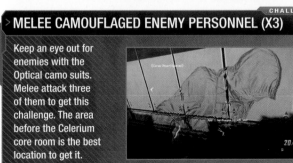

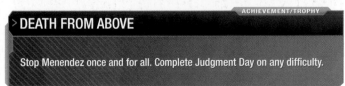

ACHIEVEMENT/TROPHY
DEATH FROM ABOVE

Stop Menendez once and for all. Complete Judgment Day on any difficulty.

REPLAY MISSION

[FOB SPECTRE]
2025

MISSION DETAILS
DEFEND Forward Operating Base "Spectre",
and prevent SDC troops from detonating an
ElectroMagnetic Pulse bomb inside the
facility.

Select   Back   Corner Record   TOGGLE DEV LEVELS   DEV SP STORY

Up to five Strike Force missions open up at different times during
the campaign. Campaign gameplay affects how many Strike Force
missions become available. Completing them is optional and you have
a limited number of attempts to do so. They can be replayed outside
of the story at any time by selecting Replay Mission.

In Strike Force, you play as multiple squads of soldiers and drones on one side of a battle. You can directly control a unit in first-person or control the units in an overhead, Tactical mode. In either mode, you can issue commands, such as attack a specific enemy or go to a location. If the unit you are controlling dies, the game doesn't end. You gain control of another unit and continue playing.

When you begin your first Strike Force mission, a tutorial is playable. You can pause the game and skip the tutorial or you can play through it to learn how to control your troops.

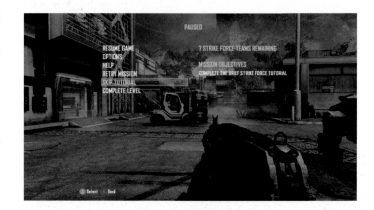

Selecting Squads in Strike Force

The Active Unit panel at the bottom of the screen shows what squad types are available. Use the D-pad to select and switch between the squads. Tapping a direction on the D-pad will select a squad, so that you can command them. Holding down a direction on the D-pad will switch you to that squad, so that you can control one of them.

Each Squad icon shows you what type of squad is available and how many members are in the squad. When selected, the Squad icon glows orange.

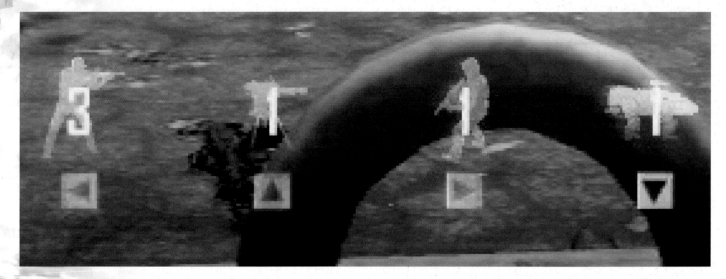

Setting Waypoints for Squads

To send a squad to a specific location, first tap the corresponding direction on the D-pad to select the squad type. Then, point the cursor at a desired location in the world and press LB to place the waypoint.

> Tap Left Bumper/L2 to create a waypoint. The selected squad will automatically proceed to that waypoint.

> Holding Left Bumper/L2 sends all squads to the created waypoint.

Targeting objectives and enemies are both done in the same way. Position the cursor over an objective or enemy and tap Left Bumper/L2 to send the selected squad to the objective or engage the enemy. Hold Left Bumper/L2 to have everyone go to the objective or engage the enemy.

< 126   127 >

Tactical View

The Tactical View gives a strategic view of the battlefield where you can see your squad, enemy troops, and objectives. Commanding squads from the Tactical View is identical to commanding squads on the ground. Press the Back/Select button to access the Tactical View.

To exit the Tactical View and switch back to a squad on the ground, hold the D-pad directional or position the cursor over a squad member and press the Back/Select button.

Availability of Missions

When the first Strike Force mission, FOB Spectre, becomes available, you get three Strike Force teams or three attempts at the mission. Each campaign mission you complete gives you another team. If you attempt a Strike Force mission and fail, you lose a team.

Each Strike Force mission becomes available at a certain time during the campaign. You then only have a certain amount of time to complete it. Once the campaign level listed in the left column of the table is complete, the Strike Force missions listed as available can be played if not already completed.

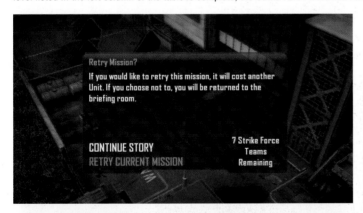

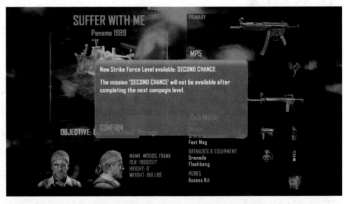

CAMPAIGN	FOB SPECTRE	SHIPWRECK	IED	SECOND CHANCE*	DISPATCH**
PYRRHIC VICTORY					
CELERIUM					
OLD WOUNDS	AVAILABLE				
TIME AND FATE	AVAILABLE	AVAILABLE			
FALLEN ANGEL	AVAILABLE	AVAILABLE	AVAILABLE		
KARMA	AVAILABLE	AVAILABLE	AVAILABLE	AVAILABLE	
SUFFER WITH ME				AVAILABLE	
ACHILLES' VEIL					AVAILABLE
ODYSSEUS					
CORDIS DIE					
JUDGMENT DAY					

*Second Chance is available if Karma was captured by DeFalco and still alive. Otherwise, this mission is not playable during the story.
**Dispatch is available if you have prevented SDC from occupying three countries by completing FOB Spectre, Shipwreck, and IED.

B SPECTRE

HIMACHAL PRADESH, NORTHERN INDIA_ 2025

SION DETAILS

end Forward Operating Base "Spectre,"
prevent SDC troops from detonating an
troMagnetic Pulse bomb inside the facility.

FOB SPECTRE
India 2025

PRIMARY OBJECTIVES:
DEFEND THE FACILITY FROM SDC ATTACKS

STRIKE FORCE TEAMS:
7

UNITS AVAILABLE:

SEALS   SENTRY   CLAW

Start Level   Back   Career Record

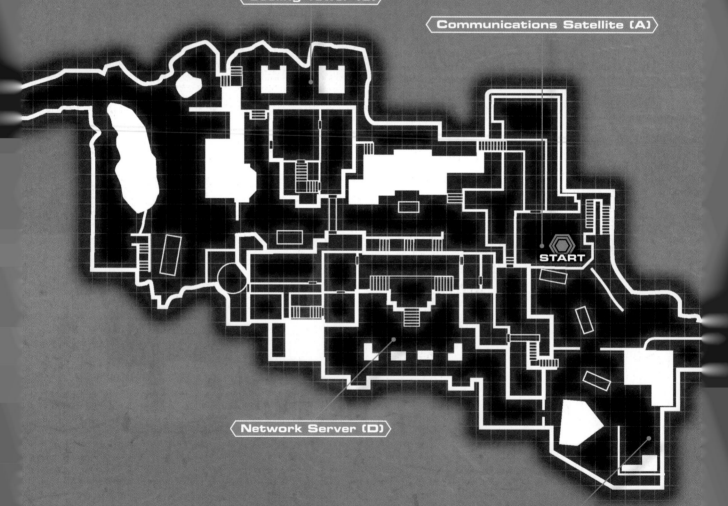

Cooling Tower (C)

Communications Satellite (A)

START

Network Server (D)

Power Transformer (B)

LEVEL OBJECTIVES

> Defend A—Protect the Communications Satellite.

> Defend B—Protect the Power Transformer.

> Defend C—Protect the Cooling Tower.

> Defend D—If SDC lowers the factory's defense field, defend the Network Server from enemy hacking modules.

UNITS AVAILABLE
SEALs, Sentry Turrets, CLAW

CHALLENGES

> Melee enemy personnel (x10).

> Eliminate enemy personnel (x20) using sentry turret.

> Eliminate enemy personnel as CLAW (x10).

> Complete mission with enemy never lowering defense field.

> Eliminate enemy ASD (x3) using only sentry turrets.

> Eliminate enemy personnel (x20) with headshots.

> Destroy enemy quad drones (x12).

> Prevent enemy from planting more than one hacking module.

> Allow no more than one sentry turret to be destroyed.

> Complete the mission in Tactical View only.

"IF RUSSIA CAVES IN AND JOINS SDC, THEY'D BE THE LARGEST MILITARY FORCE ON THE PLANET."

Chairman Tian Zhao, the leader of China's military and the SDC coalition's armed forces, nearly has Russia in SDC, which would make it the largest military in the world. Menendez is counting on this so the superpowers can take each other out.

SDC's current target is a drone factory in Northern India at the forward operating base "Spectre." This is an important post for securing India's border. An attack nearly wiped out their defenses and they cannot withstand another.

That is where JSOC comes in. They must drop in and fight off any subsequent attacks.

Defend the Communications Satellite, Power Transformer, and Cooling Tower

"ONCE ALL ELEMENTS ARE ON THE GROUND, MOVE TO ESTABLISH A DEFENSIVE PERIMETER."

Your first objective is to defend points A, B, and C from the attacking SDC troops. If any two of these points fall, the factory will be vulnerable and the enemy then attempts to hack into the mainframe.

HEALTH BAR OF DEFENSE POINTS

Defend icons appear at the three points with a letter signifying which one it represents. A white health bar encircles the icon. This shows how much damage that point has taken. It will flash red when its health is dangerously low. Once depleted, that point is gone and any enemies will proceed to their next target.

TACTICS

Enemy troops are one minute out when you gain control of your units. This is your opportunity to set up your troops for an ideal defense. You begin the mission with two squads of four soldiers, two sentry turrets, and a CLAW. Once enemy troops arrive, you have to defend the facility for 11 minutes.

Since the SDC must take out two of your points to lower the defense shield, one point can be mostly ignored. The Power Transformer and Communications Satellite are close together making them the ideal positions to concentrate on.

One SEALs team immediately heads for the Cooling Tower. This will slow down any assaults from the northwest. You can let them do their own thing for the most part, but occasionally check in on them to make sure they are targeting who they should be.

The CLAW starts near the Power Transformer. Move it to the area between there and the Communications Satellite platform. This is a good spot for taking out two drop zones and anyone coming through the tunnel.

The second team of SEALs sticks to the satellite platform. Be careful, as SDC troops can fire from all four sides. They will reach the platform by the stairs to the north and east.

One sentry turret sits next to the Power Transformer. You can pull it out a little to the west to get a better angle on anyone entering from the north, but you want to make sure it has a shot at the nearby door.

 The other turret sits on the satellite platform. Move it back a little so it has a good view of the balcony to the south, the road to the west, and the doorway to the north. Man this gun with one of the soldiers for a good view of most of the attacking SDC troops.

You will want to mix up which units you control if you want to max out the number of challenges you earn, but the central turret and the CLAW are the two most effective units.

ELIMINATE PERSONNEL CHALLENGES

CHALLENGE

Most of the challenges for this mission are self-explanatory—eliminate X enemy personnel in one way or another. Try for headshots and melee attacks whenever possible and split your time up between the three types of units to secure these six challenges.

Helicopters drop the enemy units at several spots on the map. These units include soldiers, ASDs, CLAWs, and quad drones. If you can get a jump on them as they are dropping, you can whittle their health down before they can attack.

RADIO CHATTER

Pay attention to what your units are saying. They will warn you when new enemies appear and what location is under attack.

The quad drones are difficult to take out quickly as they are extremely quick, so snap your gun's reticle to its position to keep up with it. The enemy CLAW requires a constant barrage of gunfire and grenades. Some of your soldiers carry EMP grenades. Use some against the drones to stun them and make the kill easier.

The easiest way to complete this mission is to take a soldier and man the turret near the satellite or jump into the CLAW. From these two locations you can reach most anyone who can attack points A and B.

ALLOW NO MORE THAN ONE SENTRY TURRET TO BE DESTROYED

This challenge requires that one of the sentry turrets survives the mission. Keep an eye on both turrets. If one gets mobbed, take the CLAW over to help or send over some troops.

If the SDC gets inside the factory, chances are you've already lost both turrets. But if not, you need to keep two of the three turrets safe for the challenge to be completed.

Watch the radar to see where the next enemies are being dropped off and move into position so you can target them. If they drop in the northwest, switch to the turret so you can eliminate any who come down the road. Otherwise, stick to the CLAW. Do not forget about its grenades, as these make quick work of most of the foes.

Look out for enemy drop-offs outside the east fence. Take them out as they climb over the barrier. Keep your troops fighting off any SDC units who get near the Transformer and Satellite. When the timer hits zero, you must defeat any remaining enemies to complete the mission.

COMPLETE MISSION WITH ENEMY NEVER LOWERING DEFENSE FIELD

If you successfully fight off the SDC attack without losing more than one of the defend points, then this challenge is earned.

OBJECTIVE

Defend the Network Server from Enemy Hacking Modules

If the SDC manage to take out two of the three points, the factory becomes vulnerable. Redirect all units to the factory interior and protect its mainframe computer.

You have another turret inside, but it will not be much help without plenty of support. Switch to one of the soldiers and take cover in a small room outside the mainframe room. Keep one eye on the radar, so you can react to anyone who comes up behind you, and the other eye on the computer area. It is possible to take the CLAW inside, but it is more difficult to move around.

When a soldier gets inside and near the computer, he attempts to plant a hacking module. When you see this happening, quickly take him out. Otherwise, a Destroy D icon appears on the device with a progress bar encircling it. This bar counts down the time until a successful hack. Once the white bar is completely gone, the mission is over. Destroy the device before the hack is complete.

> ## PREVENT ENEMY FROM PLANTING MORE THAN ONE HACKING MODULE

CHALLENGE

If the enemy does get inside the factory, then you need to make sure they do not get more than one of the hacking modules placed. If you've already destroyed one of the devices near the mainframe, keep an eye out for soldiers kneeling in the area. Take them out before another is set. Once you see the Destroy D icon again, it is too late.

If no hacking modules exist when the timer hits zero, eliminate any remaining enemies to complete the mission.

> ## COMPLETE THE MISSION IN TACTICAL VIEW ONLY

CHALLENGE

To complete FOB Spectre with Tactical View only, you will need to make sure your troops are doing what you want from them. Again, you only need to worry about points A and B to be successful, so don't worry as much about the Cooling Tower. Whenever you see enemies being dropped off, highlight the nearest turret or CLAW and target them. Try to keep the CLAW around the central area between points A and B.

> ## DEFENDER

ACHIEVEMENT/TROPHY

Successfully defend FOB Spectre from incursion.

HIPWRECK

SION DETAILS

troy the **SDC** freighter and its cargo of Don-Feng
ersonic cruise missiles.

F.E.L. (A)

START

Defense System (B)

F.E.L. (C)

Kraken Target
Location

< 134   135 >

LEVEL OBJECTIVES

> Destroy primary defense system single DFH cruise missiles.
> Use HPM explosives to scramble the guidance system.
> Disable secondary defense system FEL beams (free electron lasers).
> Hack and disable FEL.
> Call in the Kraken.

UNITS AVAILABLE
SEALs, ASDs, CLAW

CHALLENGES

> Destroy CLAWs (x2) using only soldiers.
> Use only three network intruders to complete the mission.
> Complete mission with more than 2:00 minutes remaining.
> Eliminate enemy personnel (x10) with headshots.
> Melee enemy personnel (x15).
> Destroy enemy ASD (x3) as a CLAW.
> Eliminate enemy personnel (x15) with explosives.
> Eliminate enemy personnel (x15) while they are stunned.
> Run over enemy personnel (x20) with ASD.
> Complete the mission in Tactical View only.

"ONE STRIKE CAN TAKE OUT ANY OF OUR AIRCRAFT CARRIERS."

A freighter is delivering hypersonic cruise missiles, which the SDC plan to launch against Iran, to the Port of Singapore. This plan must be thwarted or the SDC just grows stronger.

There are five steps to destroy the freighter along with these missiles: take out the single cruise missile, use explosives to scramble its guidance system, disable the two electron lasers, hack the lasers, and then call in the Kraken. It is up to JSOC to accomplish this.

"ALL EAGLES ON DECK. CUT ROPES."

Three points, A, B, and C, must be captured and then defended. Point B is the Defense System that gets scrambled. Points A and C are the two FEL beams that need to be disabled.

Both tasks are accomplished by placing a network intruder next to the equipment. It takes some time for it to work, so you need to stick around and defend it from enemy attacks. If the hacking module is destroyed, another must be replaced.

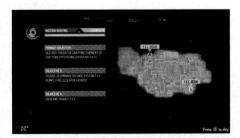

> ## USE ONLY THREE NETWORK INTRUDERS TO COMPLETE THE MISSION

Place a network intruder at each of the three locations. If they are each protected from incoming attacks, without needing replaced, a challenge is complete.

It doesn't matter in which order you capture the points. Once all three are captured and defended, you can call in the Kraken and it will destroy the freighter.

Once the team's feet are on the ground, a mission timer starts counting down from 10 minutes. Once this hits zero, the mission is failed.

As you progress through this mission, reinforcements are dropped in as follows: first an ASD, then a team of SEALs and ASD, and finally a CLAW. Watch out, as the enemy will gain quad drones, ASDs, and a CLAW during this time.

Use HPM Explosives to Scramble the Guidance System of the Defense System Cruise Missile

The cruise missile—look for the Capture B icon—is found in the central hub of Keppel terminal. This location is wide open making you an easy target from all sides, especially from above if the quad drones have arrived.

These flying pests can be avoided in this area by going after point B first. Storage boxes and the small barrier around the missile can be used as cover as you eliminate the enemies who protect it.

Disable Secondary Defense System FEL Beams (Free Electron Lasers) with Hacking Modules

Points A and B are the free electron lasers. Target A to the northwest has the best protection. Enter through the narrow doorway from the south, clear out the enemies around the laser, and then move in to defeat more enemies who take cover to the east.

< 136   137 >

Bring all of your troops in to defend the network intruder as it hacks into the laser. With protection from the walls to the north and west, this is the easiest point to capture.

For point B to the southeast, you are a little more in the open, especially with the quad drones flying around. Fight your way in from the west and clear the area out. If you have the CLAW available, take control of it to make this task a bit easier and more fun.

Protecting this position can be difficult with the drones flying all around and ground troops entering from two points to the north. Spread your guys out and command the CLAW if available.

CHALLENGES
> CHALLENGES

Most of the challenges are eliminating X personnel with different methods or units. Use up the SEAL members' grenades, melee attack when possible, and mix up who you control to max out your challenges.

OBJECTIVE
Call in the Kraken

Once all three points are completely hacked, press the button as indicated on screen to let the Kraken know it is time to take out the freighter.

CHALLENGE
> COMPLETE THE MISSION IN TACTICAL VIEW ONLY

Send everyone to each point, waiting for them to fully capture the point before moving them to the next.

ACHIEVEMENT/TROPHY
> SINGAPORE SLING

Successfully neutralize the SDC freighter at Keppel Terminal.

SSION DETAILS

ort a convoy of Afghan and Russian dignitaries to extraction site and destroy any landmines king its path.

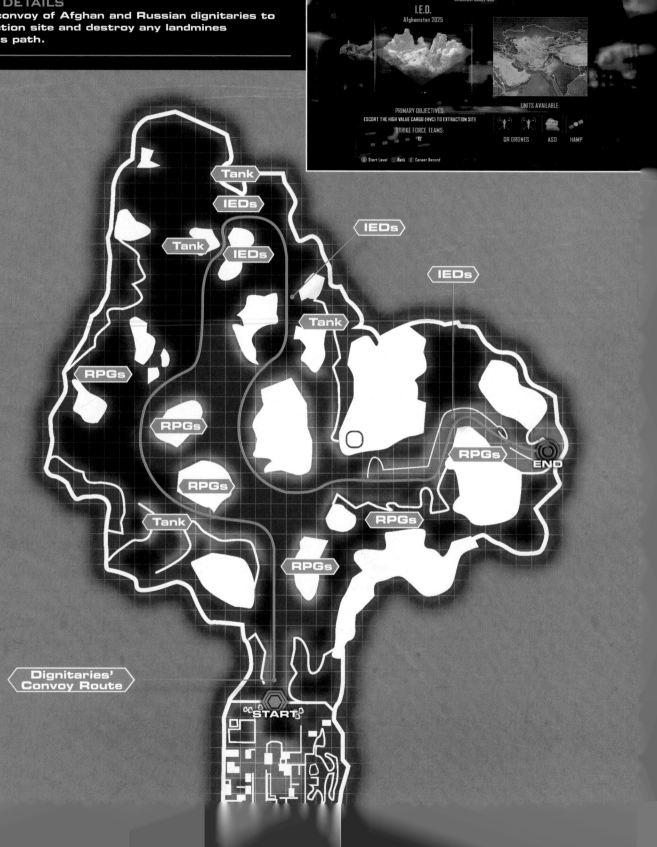

MISSION BRIEFING

I.E.D.
Afghanistan 2025

PRIMARY OBJECTIVES:
ESCORT THE HIGH VALUE CARGO (HVC) TO EXTRACTION SITE
STRIKE FORCE TEAMS:
12

UNITS AVAILABLE:
QR DRONES   ASD   HAMP

Start Level   Back   Career Record

Tank
IEDs
IEDs
Tank
IEDs
IEDs
Tank
RPGs
RPGs
RPGs
RPGs
RPGs
Tank
RPGs
RPGs
END

Dignitaries'
Convoy Route

START

"CENTRAL INTELLIGENCE AGENCY INTERCEPTED AN ASSASSINATION ORDER, DIRECTED BY RAUL MENENDEZ HIMSELF."

The Russian foreign minister is set to sign a peace treaty with the Afghan president, but an assassination order from Menendez has been intercepted by the CIA. Therefore, the location has been changed.

LEVEL OBJECTIVES

> Utilize Quadrotors, ASDs, and HAMP to protect the Afghani Dignitaries.

> Escort the convoy to the rendezvous point.

> Seek and destroy any IEDs planted in the path of the oncoming convoy.

> Use the ASDs or HAMP on enemy heavy armor threats.

UNITS AVAILABLE
Quad Drones, ASDs, HAMP

CHALLENGES

> Eliminate enemy personnel (x3) while they are planting IEDs.

> Eliminate enemy personnel (x10) on horseback.

> Convoy never stopped by presence of an IED.

> Destroy tanks (x3) with Kinetic Strike weapon.

> Destroy helicopter with Kinetic Strike weapon.

> Eliminate enemy personnel (x20) as a quad drone.

> Run over enemy personnel (x10) as ASD.

> Use only ASDs to destroy tanks.

> Keep all vehicles in convoy safe.

> Complete the mission in Tactical View only.

JSOC is sent in to protect the convoy—four vehicles of Afghan and Russian dignitaries. They follow a winding route to the extraction point, but tanks, helicopters, RPGs, soldiers on horseback, and IEDs litter the route.

"NO BOOTS ON THE GROUND THIS TIME. JUST DRONES AND THE EYE IN THE SKY."

OBJECTIVE
Utilize Quadrotors, ASDs, and HAMP to Protect the Afghani Dignitaries

There are no SEALs on the ground for this mission, but you do get two squads of QR drones and a group of ASDs. The Kraken patrols the skies, ready with a High Altitude Munitions Platform (HAMP).

Scan just ahead of the convoy for RPGs on the mountains and tanks in the valleys. Direct the quad drones to attack the soldiers and have the ASDs and HAMP eliminate the heavy armor.

Men on horseback attack about mid-way through the mission; send quad drones their way to fend them off. Keep an eye on your units' locations, as they occasionally need to be corralled in if they stray too far from the action.

As the convoy moves closer to its destination, more enemies of various types join in on the assault. All units should have a target at all times. The convoy is long at four armored vehicles, so be sure to scan the entire area around them.

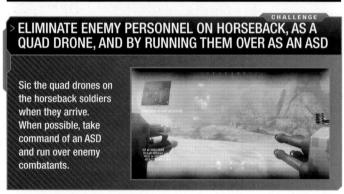

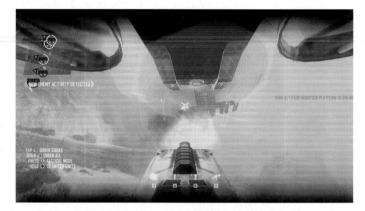

It is ideal to get all four vehicles to the extraction point, but the mission is a success with only one making it. Don't think this means you can let up, because the action gets quite intense around the final destination.

CHALLENGE

> ## ELIMINATE ENEMY PERSONNEL ON HORSEBACK, AS A QUAD DRONE, AND BY RUNNING THEM OVER AS AN ASD

Sic the quad drones on the horseback soldiers when they arrive. When possible, take command of an ASD and run over enemy combatants.

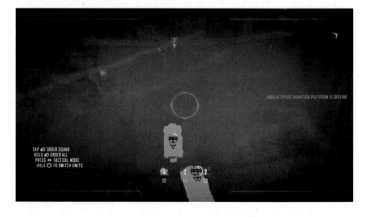

OBJECTIVE

Escort the Convoy to the Rendezvous Point

The health of the vehicles—A, B, C, and D—can be seen as white bars around the defend icons. When the white is completely drained, that vehicle is destroyed. Watch the radar and send units at any nearby enemies.

< 140 141 >

RADIO CHATTER

Pay attention to what is being said on the radio. You are warned when new enemies appear and who is under attack.

———————————— TACTICS

OBJECTIVE
Seek and Destroy Any IEDS Planted in the Path of the Convoy

Enemy soldiers plant IEDs across the path at various points along the way. You will hear a warning when they are being planted. Immediately send a squad of drones to take them out before they can be set. Otherwise, they will also need to destroy the IEDs.

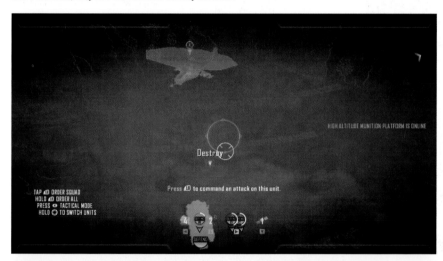

> ELIMINATE ENEMY PERSONNEL (X3) WHILE THEY ARE PLANTING IED
CHALLENGE

Have the quad drones take out the soldiers who plant the IEDs as soon as you notice them. If three personnel can be taken out before the IEDs are set three times during this mission, this challenge is done.

> CONVOY NEVER STOPPED BY PRESENCE OF AN IED
CHALLENGE

The convoy will come to a complete stop if any IEDs are present just ahead of them. Be sure to keep the road clear or you will be spending more time defending the dignitaries.

OBJECTIVE
Use the ASDs or HAMP on Enemy Heavy Armor Threats

The ASDs and HAMP are most effective against the stronger enemies. At the northern point of the route, two tanks present a danger to the convoy. Send the ASDs at the first one and direct the HAMP to hit the second.

> USE ONLY ASDs TO DESTROY TANKS
CHALLENGE

Use the HAMP on the helicopters and soldiers, as you concentrate the ASDs' attacks on the tanks. They will take a bit longer than the HAMP, but they will get the job done. Take control of an ASD to make sure the job is getting done properly.

DESTROY TANKS (X3) WITH KINETIC STRIKE WEAPON

Whenever the HAMP is online, have it attack the next tank in line. You need to take out three of the four tanks in this manner, so be prepared once the Kraken is ready.

DESTROY HELICOPTER WITH KINETIC STRIKE WEAPON

Helicopters will join in the assault late in the route. Target one with the HAMP when it is available to take it out with one shot.

As you make your way through the narrow pass with the bridges, it can get hectic. RPGs line both sides, helicopters attack from above, and IEDs are planted on the ground. Be sure everyone has an assignment and take control of one of the quad drones. Use it to destroy the bridges and eliminate the RPG soldiers. As each helicopter enters, have the HAMP take care of it or, if it is recharging, sic quad drones on them.

As you reach the extraction point, a group of RPG soldiers gets in the way. Send all units at them. A final surge comes from enemy horseback combatants, but a couple CLAWs are there to finish them off.

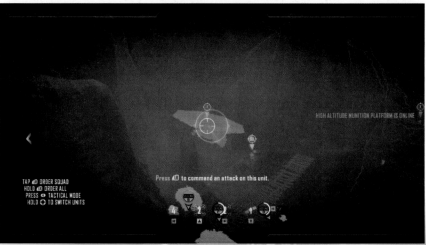

< 142   143 >

NEW ENEMY ACTIVITY DETECTED

TAP ⬤ ORDER SQUAD
HOLD ⬤ ORDER ALL
PRESS ⬤ TACTICAL MODE
HOLD ⬤ TO SWITCH UNITS

> KEEP ALL VEHICLES IN CONVOY SAFE

Keep some units around the convoy at all times to protect them. Watch the radar for approaching enemies and send your drones their way. Get all four vehicles to the extraction point in one piece. A message will pop up below the mini-map showing how many of the transports are still intact, whenever one is lost.

> COMPLETE THE MISSION IN TACTICAL VIEW ONLY

This may be the best Strike Force mission to use Tactical View. Sometimes your drones can get a mind of their own and wander out of the action. Keep them focused on the biggest threats to the convoy and destroy the heavy armor with the HAMP.

> DESERT STORM

Successfully escort the dignitaries to safety.

SECOND CHANCE

SOCOTRA ISLAND, YEMEN_ **JUNE 14TH, 2025**

MISSION DETAILS

Locate and Rescue the HVI (High Value Individual)
for extraction.

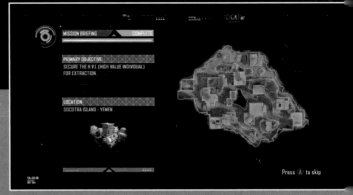

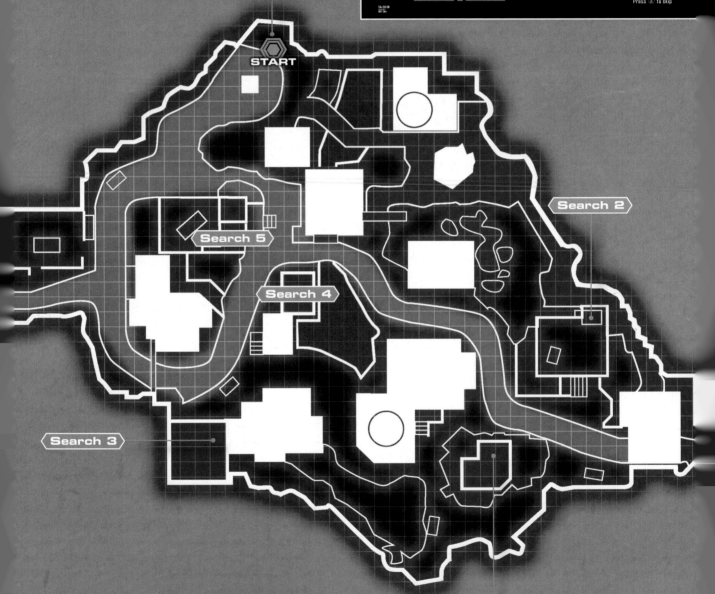

Extraction

START

Search 2

Search 5

Search 4

Search 3

Search 1

"HIGH VALUE INDIVIDUAL EXTRACTION IS A GO. REMEMBER, WE NEED THEM ALIVE."

LEVEL OBJECTIVES

> Use Tactical view to review potential holding points for the HVI.

> Search and clear each point until the HVI is located.

> Secure the HVI and lead them to the extraction point immediately.

> Support VTOL will extract the HVI and squad.

UNITS AVAILABLE
SEALs, VTOL

CHALLENGES

> Eliminate enemy personnel (x10) as an HVI.

> Eliminate enemy personnel (x10) as VTOL turret gunner.

> Melee enemy personnel (x10).

> Eliminate enemy personnel (x15) with headshots.

> Destroy enemy quad drones (x4).

> Eliminate enemy personnel (x15) with explosives.

> Eliminate enemy personnel (x5) by exploding vehicles.

> Extract the HVI in less than 60 seconds.

> Find the HVI in less than 90 seconds.

> Complete the mission in Tactical View only.

If Defalco escaped the Colossus Resort with Karma and she is still alive, the Second Chance Strike Force mission becomes available. This is your chance to correct your mistake of losing Defalco in the Cayman Islands. If you saved Karma from Defalco, or wait too long, this mission is unavailable in the campaign.

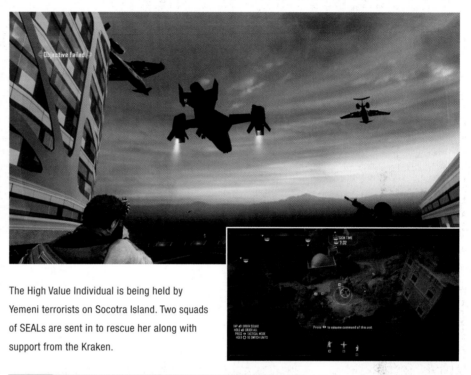

The High Value Individual is being held by Yemeni terrorists on Socotra Island. Two squads of SEALs are sent in to rescue her along with support from the Kraken.

OBJECTIVE
Use Tactical View to Review Potential Holding Points for the HVI

Surveillance has narrowed the possible locations to five buildings around the island. Two are located on the west side of the island and the other three are directly north of the start and extraction.

As soon as you have control, use Tactical mode to send your troops to the furthest points to the northwest. For speed, you can split them up between the two. For an easier time, send them all to the same building.

OBJECTIVE
Search and Clear Each Point Until the HVI is Located

Take control of one of the soldiers and clear out the search point. Each time one is cleared out, the Search icon disappears and text appears below the mini-map that states another point has been searched successfully.

> ELIMINATE ENEMY PERSONNEL AS VTOL TURRET GUNNER AND WITH MELEE ATTACKS, HEADSHOTS, EXPLOSIVES, AND EXPLODING VEHICLES. DESTROY ENEMY QUAD DRONES

CHALLENGE

These challenges are all about taking down the enemy personnel and quad drones in different manners. Explode cars enemies hide behind and vary your attacks to get them all.

Next, send your troops to the northeast building to search for the HVI. Once three locations have been searched, Karma can be found in one of the last two spots. It is always the case that she is in one of the last two locations searched.

< 146 147 >

OBJECTIVE
Secure the HVI and Lead Them to the Extraction Point Immediately

Once you secure Karma, she becomes one of your available units and the Kraken heads to the extraction point to the south. Take control of her and fight your way that direction. Once you eliminate one of the terrorists, pick up the better weapon.

FIND THE HVI IN LESS THAN 90 SECONDS
CHALLENGE

To reach Karma in less than 90 seconds, you have to split your troops up. Send the two squads to different locations. Once a squad has cleared a location, move them to the next building. Best case scenario, she will be in the fourth spot searched.

ELIMINATE ENEMY PERSONNEL (X10) AS AN HVI
CHALLENGE

Once you rescue the HVI, switch to her and use her newly acquired M1911 pistol to take down a terrorist outside. Pick up his gun and use it to take out nine more as you move to the extraction point.

OBJECTIVE
Support VTOL Will Extract the HVI and Squad

Once the HVI reaches the VTOL, the mission is complete and Karma is available to help the JSOC.

EXTRACT THE HVI IN LESS THAN 60 SECONDS
CHALLENGE

Search the three outside locations first—narrowing the possible location of the HVI to the two buildings closest to the extraction site. Once rescued, quickly move to the south as Karma.

COMPLETE THE MISSION IN TACTICAL VIEW ONLY
CHALLENGE

Unless you are attempting to also get the speed challenges, send all of your troops to each search point. Wait for word that the location is clear and send them to the next. Keep the Kraken around the guys for support. Once the HVI has been rescued, highlight her and send her directly to the extraction point. Keep the support and SEALs around her location.

BLIND DATE
ACHIEVEMENT/TROPHY

Successfully rescue HVI.

SPATCH

PESHAWAR, PAKISTAN_ **JUNE 17TH, 2025**

SION DETAILS

assinate SDC Chairman Tian Zhao.

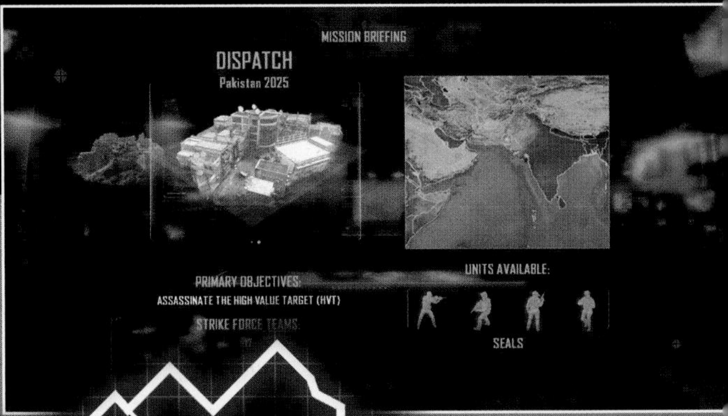
MISSION BRIEFING
DISPATCH
Pakistan 2025
PRIMARY OBJECTIVES:
ASSASSINATE THE HIGH VALUE TARGET (HVT)
STRIKE FORCE TEAMS
UNITS AVAILABLE:
SEALS

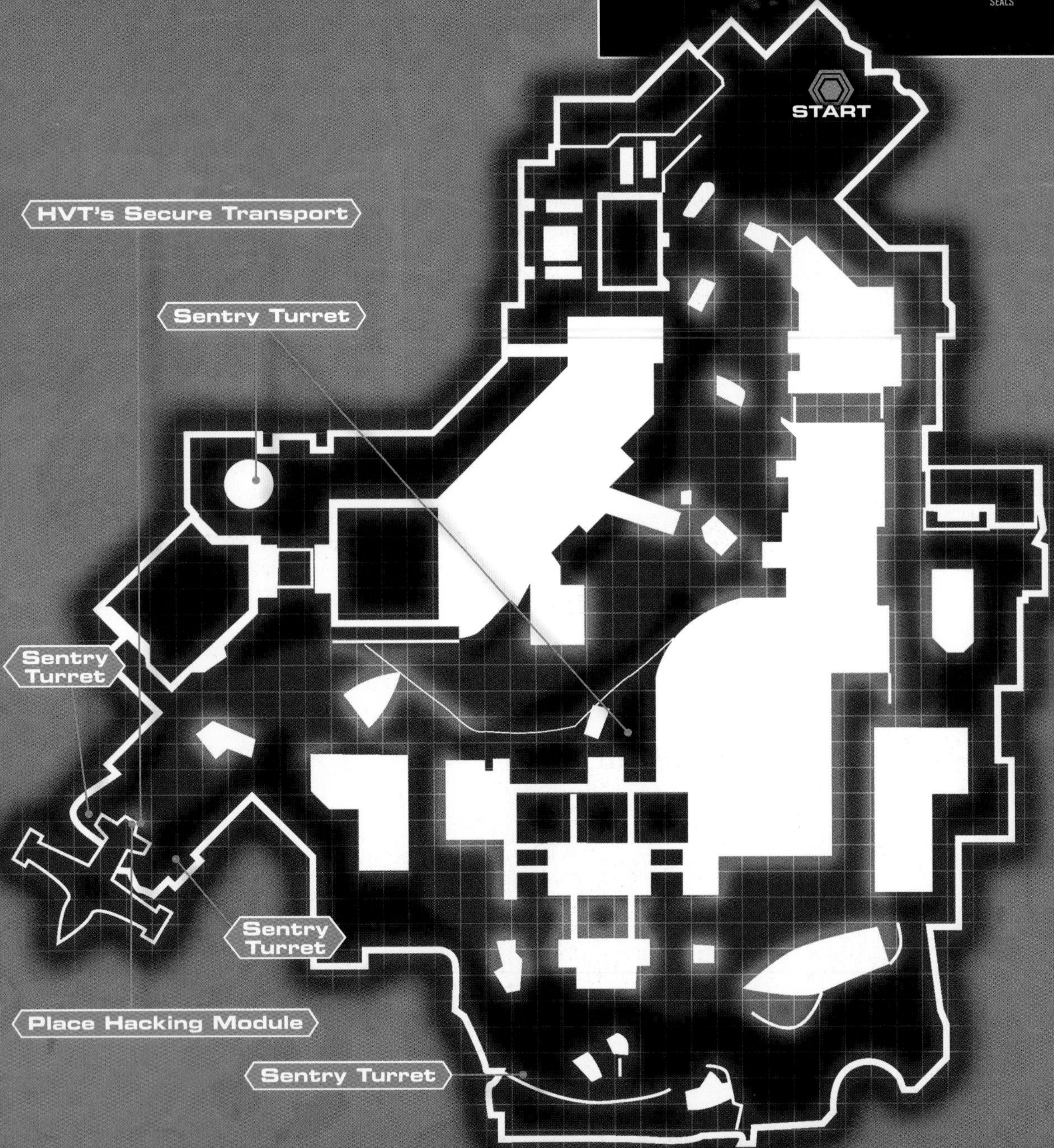
START
HVT's Secure Transport
Sentry Turret
Sentry Turret
Sentry Turret
Place Hacking Module
Sentry Turret

In order to play the final Strike Force mission in Pakistan, you must have prevented SDC from occupying three countries by completing FOB Spectre, Shipwreck, and IED.

LEVEL OBJECTIVES

> Utilize Tactical view and squad command to penetrate General Zhao's protection team.

> Locate General Zhao's downed VTOL and hack through its defense systems.

> Protect the hacking module as it disables the VTOL's security.

> Eliminate General Zhao.

UNITS AVAILABLE
SEALs

CHALLENGES

> Melee enemy personnel (x10).

> Destroy enemy ASDs (x6) while disabled.

> Complete mission with more than 3:00 minutes remaining.

> Eliminate enemy personnel (x20) with headshots.

> Eliminate enemy personnel (x15) with explosives.

> Destroy sentry turrets (x3) while disabled.

> Destroy multiple ASDs (x2) with one explosion.

> Use only one hacking module to complete mission.

> Eliminate enemy personnel (x10) while they are stunned.

> Complete the mission in Tactical View only.

JSOC troops are in Peshawar, Pakistan as Tian Zhao flies over in a fleet of VTOLs. The aircraft are brought down by JSOC rocket launchers and Zhao's VTOL goes down at the end of the street. Your mission here is to fight your way through his protection team, hack into the VTOL, and assassinate SDC Chairman Tian Zhao.

"REINFORCEMENTS DEPLOYED. EAGLE'S ON GROUND."

OBJECTIVE
Utilize Tactical View and Squad Command to Penetrate General Zhao's Protection Team

You start in the far north with four teams of SEALs—each with their own weaponry. Some have the M8A1 assault rifle, and others carry the Mk 48 light machine gun. They all carry the SMAW launcher as their secondary. Half of them carry EMP grenades and the rest have frags.

Once the teams are on the ground, the mission timer starts to count down from eight minutes. There are three routes to the downed VTOL: the alley to the right, up the street in the middle, and the long way around the south side.

The southern route gives you the best coverage from gunfire, but the north alley will get you there the fastest. Going straight up the middle leaves you the most vulnerable, but it gives the best view of the final area.

Each route has a sentry turret guarding the path, so be careful as you fight your way toward the goal. Make your first priority to get rid of this obstacle. Use a SMAW or Mk 48 to destroy it quickly. Using an EMP grenade on a turret or ASD disables it, making it an easier target.

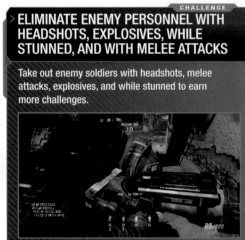

CHALLENGE

> ELIMINATE ENEMY PERSONNEL WITH HEADSHOTS, EXPLOSIVES, WHILE STUNNED, AND WITH MELEE ATTACKS

Take out enemy soldiers with headshots, melee attacks, explosives, and while stunned to earn more challenges.

CHALLENGE

> DESTROY ENEMY ASDs (X6) AND SENTRY TURRETS (X3) WHILE DISABLED

Toss an EMP grenade at ASDs or sentry turrets to disable them and finish them off with your other weapons. Taking out six ASDs and three turrets this way earns these two challenges.

CHALLENGE

> DESTROY MULTIPLE ASDs (X2) WITH ONE EXPLOSION

Look for two ASDs in close proximity to each other. Toss a frag grenade in between them when they are at their closest. A few guard the VTOL—giving a great opportunity to complete this challenge. In fact, it may be possible to get four with one explosion.

OBJECTIVE

Locate General Zhao's Downed VTOL and Hack through Its Defense Systems

Just before reaching the overturned car, take cover inside the restaurant on the right and place some soldiers on the other side of the street. Destroy the ASDs and two sentry turrets that guard Zhao's aircraft.

OBJECTIVE

Protect the Hacking Module as It Disables the VTOL's Security

Run outside and clean up any remaining enemies and plant the network intruder next to the VTOL. Place everyone you have available behind the car and hunker down.

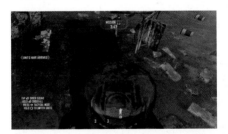 

> USE ONLY ONE HACKING MODULE TO COMPLETE MISSION

Protect your first hacking module without the need to replace it.

OBJECTIVE

Eliminate General Zhao

Protect the device until the VTOL is opened and Zhao is taken care of.

CHALLENGE

> COMPLETE MISSION WITH MORE THAN 3:00 MINUTES REMAINING

Send all of your units down the right alley and quickly dispose of the sentry turret. Move to the left window in the restaurant and take out the ASDs and left turret with your rocket launcher. Move down the steps, destroy the other turret, and then immediately place the network intruder. Have everyone join you behind the overturned car and protect the device.

CHALLENGE

> COMPLETE THE MISSION IN TACTICAL VIEW ONLY

Handle this mission in Tactical View in the same way; just make sure your troops are headed in the right direction.

ACHIEVEMENT/TROPHY

> ART OF WAR

Successfully assassinate SDC Chairman Tian Zhao.

BRANCHING STORYLINES

Certain actions and choices made during the campaign have an effect on the story of *Call of Duty: Black Ops II*. The following table breaks it down by level and lists the results of these actions and choices.

MISSION	EVENT	RESULT	CONSEQUENCE
Old Wounds	Kravchenko Interrogation	Succeed	Reminded of it in Panama (Suffer With Me) (Achievement/Trophy: Dirty Business [during Suffer with Me, as long as CIA File is found in Time and Fate])
Old Wounds	Kravchenko Interrogation	Shoot Kravchenko before full interrogation	Nothing
Time and Fate	CIA File	Found	Reminded of it in Panama (Suffer With Me) (Achievement/Trophy: Dirty Business [during Suffer with Me, as long as you resist shooting Kravchenko in Old Wounds])
Time and Fate	CIA File	Not Found	Nothing
Fallen Angel	At end of mission on SOC-T, Avoid Fire	Not Avoided	Harper injured, face is burned for rest of game
Fallen Angel	At end of mission on SOC-T, Avoid Fire	Avoided	Harper unharmed, face is normal (Achievement/Trophy: Hey Good Looking)
Karma	Defalco Escape	Chloe Captured / Defalco Alive	Second Chance Strike Force mission available Defalco appears in Achilles' Veil and is present in standoff during Odysseus
Karma	Defalco Escape	Chloe Rescued / Defalco Dies	Second Chance Strike Force mission unavailable Defalco is replaced in Achilles' Veil and is not there in Odysseus
Suffer With Me	Kill or wound "Menendez"	Mason Killed	Nothing
Suffer With Me	Kill or wound "Menendez"	Mason Wounded	Meets David during ending (Achievement/Trophy: Family Reunion)
Achilles' Veil	Shoot Harper or Menendez	Harper Dies	VTOL gameplay is skipped Harper no longer appears in rest of game Salazar lives in Odysseus
Achilles' Veil	Shoot Harper or Menendez	Shoot at Menendez / Farid Dies	VTOL gameplay is played Harper appears in Odysseus and kills Salazar Farid does not appear in Odysseus, therefore Chloe dies Harper appears in rest of game, often alongside player (Achievement/Trophy: Ultimate Sacrifice)
Odysseus	Command Center Standoff	Defalco and Farid Alive / Chloe Rescued	Defalco attacks Chloe, Farid kills Defalco, Salazar kills Farid Chloe lives Defalco absent in Judgment Day (Achievement/Trophy: Good Karma [as long as Ship Shape is earned])
Odysseus	Command Center Standoff	Defalco and Farid Alive / Chloe Captured	Farid kills Defalco, Defalco returns fire and kills Farid Defalco absent in Judgment Day (Achievement/Trophy: Showdown)
Odysseus	Command Center Standoff	Defalco Alive / Chloe Rescued / Farid Dead	Defalco kills Chloe Chloe is no longer around Defalco appears in Judgment Day
Odysseus	Command Center Standoff	Chloe Rescued / Defalco and Farid Dead	Salazar kills Chloe Chloe is no longer around
Odysseus	Command Center Standoff	Chloe Captured / Defalco and Farid Dead	Salazar kills the two US service men

MISSION	EVENT	RESULT	CONSEQUENCE
Odysseus	Command Center Standoff	Chloe Captured / Defalco Alive / Farid Dead	Defalco slits Chloe's neck
Odysseus	Kill or Wound Admiral Briggs	Briggs Killed	USS Obama is destroyed
Odysseus	Kill or Wound Admiral Briggs	Briggs Wounded	USS Obama survives CLAWs join player in Judgment Day (Achievement/Trophy: Ship Shape [as long as Strike Force is complete and China is an ally])
Cordis Die	Harper is Alive or Dead	Harper is Alive	Harper appears in scenes including in truck Harper kills the first CLAW after driving sequence Harper assists in street fight
Cordis Die	Harper is Alive or Dead	Harper is Dead	Harper is replaced in many scenes and does not assist player
Strike Force	FOB Spectre	Completed/Incomplete	India does not join SDC / India joins SDC (Achievement/Trophy: Defender)
Strike Force	Shipwreck	Completed/Incomplete	Iran does not join SDC / Iran joins SDC (Achievement/Trophy: Singapore Sling)
Strike Force	IED	Completed/Incomplete	Afghanistan does not join SDC / Afghanistan joins SDC (Achievement/Trophy: Desert Storm)
Strike Force	Second Chance (only available if Chloe was captured in Karma mission)	Completed/Incomplete	Chloe in Command Center in Odysseus / Chloe not there (Achievement/Trophy: Blind Date)
Strike Force	Dispatch	Completed/Incomplete	China becomes ally (Achievement/Trophy: Art of War) / China not an ally
Judgment Day	Allied with China or Not	Friendly with China	Chinese troops appear in Judgment Day
Judgment Day	Allied with China or Not	Not Allied with China	No help from Chinese troops
Judgment Day	Capture or Kill Menendez	Capture Menendez	Menendez goes to prison
Judgment Day	Capture or Kill Menendez	Kill Menendez	Menendez is dragged off

For the best ending, the following must happen:

> Avoid fire at end of Fallen Angel.
> Defalco escapes with Chloe in Karma.
> Rescue Chloe in Second Chance.
> Shoot Harper in Achilles' Veil.
> Wound Alex Mason in Suffer With Me.

> Wound Admiral Briggs in Odysseus.
> Capture Menendez at end of Judgment Day.
> Complete Dispatch.

This way, China becomes an ally because you complete the Strike Force missions. Farid and Defalco take out each other in Odysseus. Because of this, Chloe survives and cracks the Celerium worm. Alex Mason is reunited with his son, David, and the USS Barack Obama survives.

To get all of the Achievements/Trophies, you will have to play through Achilles' Veil again and shoot at Menendez. That earns you the Ultimate Sacrifice award.

If *Call of Duty: Black Ops II* could be summed up in any single sentence, it would be: "*Play it your way.*" With unprecedented levels of customization for your classes (and even your weapons!), you can choose to face the battlefield the way *you* prefer.

Dig in to this multiplayer material to learn about all of the weapons, Attachments, Equipment, streaks, maps, and modes that make up the *Call of Duty: Black Ops II* multiplayer experience.

MOVEMENT

Movement is simple and fundamental to your success in multiplayer. Remember, in *Call of Duty*, movement is life. You should always be strafing while hipfiring or even ADSing if you are fighting at short to medium range. At greater distances, you may need to remain still for a moment to take a shot. But once you do, get moving again. Stationary targets are easy targets.

Move quickly and decisively toward key overwatch points, objectives, and hotspots. Use terrain to your advantage. Move behind hard cover, conceal your advance from enemy eyes, and flank the enemy team.

BASE MOVEMENT SPEEDS

Your speed in multiplayer is determined by the *item you are carrying*. This means the weapon, secondary weapon, Scorestreak, or even *turret* that you are lugging around sets your base movement speed.

MOVEMENT SPEEDS

SPEED CLASS	ITEMS
FASTER	Combat Knife only (no weapon equipped in primary/secondary slot), Sentry Gun/Guardian while carried
NORMAL	Shotguns, SMGs, Snipers, Pistols, Ballistic Knife, Crossbow, Hunter Killer, Care Package, and AGR Grenades
SLIGHTLY SLOWER	ARs
SLOWER	LMGs, Launchers, Riot Shield, War Machine, Death Machine

The Perk *Lightweight* and the Attachment *Stock* affect your movement speed as well. Lightweight gives you about a 7% bump to your movement speed. The Adjustable Stock lets you move at full (walking) speed while in ADS. The difference between the "normal" and "slower" class speeds is only about 10% (with ARs in the middle at 5% slower). So Lightweight can bump you up quite a bit. The Combat Knife is a special case, allowing you to sprint about 50% further than a "normal" speed item.

> ### IMPORTANT!
>
> Your movement speed is set by the *item in your hands*. This means that you can switch to a secondary combat knife or pistol and sprint farther than if you are carrying around an LMG or AR.
>
> Naturally, this carries the risk of running into an enemy with the wrong weapon in your hands. Keep this in mind when you are starting a fresh round in any objective mode and you need to reach a key area.

SPRINTING

Sprinting allows you to move around more quickly, but at the cost of lowering your weapon and making louder movement sounds. This is very dangerous in enemy territory. Sprinting around a blind corner can lead to a quick death for new *Black Ops II* players.

After sprinting, you automatically recover your breath for another sprint as long as you are walking around normally. This allows you to reach full sprint distance again after several seconds of walking. The Extreme Conditioning Perk doubles the distance you can sprint. Dexterity brings your weapon up more quickly after sprinting.

Use sprints to move quickly in areas without cover, to reach objectives, or to evade enemies. Be very cautious about sprinting in known enemy territory.

MANTLING AND CLIMBING

You can mantle or climb over many objects in the world, including short walls, rocks, windows, and other bits of terrain. Mantling gives you increased battlefield maneuverability. It is even possible to use mantling to "grab" an item after a jump. Naturally, you can also climb ladders.

Note that both mantling and climbing lowers your weapon. This makes either action very dangerous with hostiles nearby. Dexterity doubles the speed at which you can mantle or climb objects, reducing your vulnerability.

CROUCHED AND PRONE

You can crouch or go prone to lower your silhouette and move more quietly. Crouching in particular is extremely important for making use of short cover. Crouching to duck behind cover while reloading is a key skill in any mid-range firefight. Crouching and standing from a crouch are both much faster than going prone.

Going prone lowers your silhouette completely. This allows you to take cover behind very low cover. Take note that going prone also restricts your movement, only allows a slow crawl for moving, and presents your head toward the enemy. Crouching or (especially) going prone increases weapon stability. Given the opportunity, lining up a burst of suppressive fire while prone can easily down multiple enemies if they come into your line of sight unaware of your position.

You can sprint out of a crouch or prone position. Doing so is faster than standing up first.

JUMPING

Jumping is typically used to mantle onto objects or get some height before climbing a ladder. Several maps also have areas where you can jump over short gaps. You can make only one full-strength jump without resting for a short time. If you try to jump again immediately, you can only make a short hop. The Lightweight Perk prevents all falling damage. This can be useful on some levels, especially if you prefer a high vantage point.

Jumpshots and Dropshots

There are two types of combat movement you can take advantage of by using prone and jump. The first is the dropshot. This is simply going prone while continuing to fire at your target.

The dropshot has the advantage of instantly removing your upper body from your enemies' view, causing them to miss a crucial bullet or two before they compensate and aim down. The downside is that it immobilizes you, making you more vulnerable to an accidental headshot from anyone in front of you. You're also easy prey while prone if a second hostile is nearby.

The second is the jumpshot. Simply sprint, jump, and fire while in the air. This is typically most useful when rounding a corner. If you sprint at a corner and jump, aiming where you suspect your target to be, you can open fire while in midair. You have only a split second to start shooting, but this can surprise opponents who are expecting you to simply walk or sprint around the corner. Your accuracy while doing this is poor. Plus you take another hipfire penalty as you land and recover from the jump.

Combat Dive

If you are sprinting, holding the Crouch button causes you to perform a combat dive to prone. This propels you forward, similar to a jump, while at the same time laying out your body and landing prone. The combat dive allows you to instantly reach a prone position from a sprint, and round a corner or even jump out of a window. You can't fire while in the dive. As soon as you recover from the landing while prone, you can open fire from your new position.

MOVEMENT SOUNDS

Any time you are moving, you are making noise. Normal walking makes moderate noise, which differs depending on the surface you are walking over. Sprinting makes your movement sounds louder. Jumping, mantling, and climbing all make noise as well. Reloading and throwing grenades also make noise.

The Dead Silence Perk eliminates your movement noises. The Awareness Perk allows you to hear enemy movement at twice the normal distance (or at the normal distance if they have Dead Silence).

VISIBILITY

Moving makes you highly visible. What feels like a "small adjustment" to you, while standing framed in a window or behind cover, can instantly give away your position. If you happen to get killed while moving slightly behind cover, watch the killcam. It should be instantly obvious how and why you were spotted.

Staying stationary for long periods is a good way to eat a grenade or get shot through a wall. With that being said, you also need to know when stillness is necessary.

COMBAT

Movement is the foundation that supports you while fighting. Combat is where you put your skills to the test.

AIM DOWN SIGHTS (ADS)

ADS is simply the act of bringing up your sights with your weapon. You should be in ADS during any medium-range or longer engagement. It's often a good idea to begin hipfiring and then pull up ADS as you engage, even at shorter distances. Entering ADS lowers your movement speed. Be aware that holding ADS while a fast-moving SMG or shotgun user strafes you with hipfire may not be the best idea.

Weapons ADS at different speeds, and some Attachments can affect ADS time slightly.

> SMGs, shotguns, and pistols have fast ADS times.

> ARs have normal ADS times.

> LMGs and sniper rifles have slow ADS times. The Ballista has a *slightly* faster ADS than other snipers.

> The Quickdraw Perk cuts ADS times in half, or by a quarter for LMGs.

> The Adjustable Stock Attachment allows for full speed movement while in ADS.

> Dexterity brings up your weapon more quickly after sprinting, allowing you to ADS more quickly.

> Toughness reduces flinching while you are in ADS.

HIPFIRE

Hipfiring is simply shooting without ADS. Hipfiring is inaccurate, and typically only worth using at short ranges with weapons that have better hipfire spreads. The Laser Sight Attachment significantly reduces hipfire spreads.

> Pistols, shotguns, and SMGs have the best hipfire spreads.

> ARs have average hipfire.

> LMGs and snipers have poor hipfire accuracy.

ACCURACY

Knowing what affects your accuracy in combat is critical for survival.

> Standing still, crouching, going prone, using a Foregrip or Laser Sight Attachment, or holding your breath with a sniper rifle scope improve accuracy.

> Moving, firing, jumping, and taking damage all reduce accuracy.

> The Rapid Fire Attachment significantly reduces accuracy, and a few scopes have a slight recoil recovery penalty.

With a full-auto weapon, make use of ADS at medium range, a Laser Sight when hipfiring at close-medium, or hipfire at close range. At longer distances, use ADS and short bursts of two to three bullets to land hits.

Sway

When in ADS, all weapons have some amount of *sway*. This is the gentle motion of the gun moving while you try to hold it steady. Sway is minimal when using Iron Sights on most weapons. It is more visible when you use a zooming or sniper sight. The ACOG Sight, Target Finder, and Ballistics CPU all reduce your weapon's sway.

Sway doesn't have any impact on the recoil of your weapon. It can affect your accuracy with your first few shots when you're trying to line up a shot on a distant target. A few optical attachments affect sway.

RELOADING

Reloading is a dangerous action in combat. Always try to duck behind cover while reloading if you know or suspect enemies are nearby. There are actually two stages to reloading any weapon:

> The time it takes for the ammo to enter the magazine.

> The time it takes to reload from a partially empty magazine (faster), or a fully spent magazine (slower).

The first stage (ammo entering the magazine) can be *reload cancelled*. If you sprint or switch weapons, the remaining animation is cancelled. Whenever possible, you should cancel your reload animation as soon as the magazine enters the weapon—even a split-second sprint or double-weapon switch instantly reloads the weapon. Just don't try this while in direct combat.

Keep in mind that reloading on an empty magazine is slower than a partial reload for most weapons. You have an additional animation of pulling the charging handle or racking the slide. The Fast Mag Attachment reduces reload times.

MELEE

By pressing the Melee button, you take a swing with your offhand knife, main-hand combat knife, or pistol tactical knife. In all cases, if you are at point-blank range with an enemy, you instantly kill him or her.

In *Call of Duty: Black Ops II*, you only ever lunge at someone if you are moving toward them. You cannot lunge toward them while standing still, moving sideways, or moving backward. The lunge range is actually only slightly reduced from *Black Ops*. However, this new mechanic makes it much more difficult to knife in many of the situations where it used to excel. You should go for a melee kill *only* if you are attacking a stationary enemy from behind, or if you literally run into someone rounding a corner or going through a doorway. Otherwise, whiffing with a knife can easily get you killed by anyone who has the reaction of simply pulling the trigger.

The Assault Shield can also perform a melee shield bash, but it takes two hits to down a target, unlike the knife. Melee kills do have the advantage of being silent.

WEAPON SWITCHING

Switching weapons takes time, but it is faster than reloading for certain types of weapons. As a result, switching weapons when your magazine runs dry in combat can save your life if you switch and begin firing immediately instead of attempting to reload. Weapons switch at speeds corresponding to how cumbersome they are.

> Pistols switch the most quickly, followed by SMGs, Shotguns, ARs, LMGs, and sniper rifles.

Because of pistols fast swapping, they are ideal backup weapons for when you run dry in CQC. At greater distances, you're better off simply ducking behind cover and reloading.

The Fast Hands Perk doubles weapon switch speeds. This is very useful for Burst/Semi-auto ARs, LMGs, and sniper rifles that need a backup weapon for CQC. Even SMGs can be a useful backup weapon with the Fast Hands Perk.

EXPLOSIVE OBJECTS

Vehicles of all sorts and explosive barrels can be detonated to cause a fatal explosion to anyone nearby. Use your own explosive weapons to detonate vehicles on a map to take down any hostiles nearby.

Be careful around burning vehicles. Once on fire, they automatically burn down until they detonate. Keep your distance or finish the explosion with a few rounds.

EQUIPMENT AND SCORESTREAKS

Equipment and Scorestreaks are both critical tools for supporting your battlefield role. When covering or assaulting an objective, or guarding your back in Deathmatch, you can use both Equipment and Scorestreaks to tip the odds in your favor.

Choose Equipment and streaks that best fit your expected role. If you know you're going to be sprinting across the map and assaulting a fixed position, grenades and EMPs can come in handy. If you're defending an objective, C4 and Shock Charges may fit the bill. For dismantling enemy defenses, use the Engineer Perk, EMP grenades, and the Black Hat PDA. When you plan to make extensive use of Equipment, bring the Scavenger Perk.

GAME MECHANICS

DAMAGE RULES

All players in multiplayer matches have 100 health each. All weapons deal a flat amount of damage. For most weapons (and weapons other than sniper rifles), this decreases at a distance. Some Attachments can affect how quickly this damage falloff occurs, notably the Suppressor, Rapid Fire, and Long Barrel.

Most guns can kill in two to five shots. Shotguns fire multiple "pellets" per shot, and can potentially kill in one shot. Sniper rifles can kill in one shot to certain areas of the body. Burst-Fire weapons shoot three to four rounds per burst, so they too can kill in one "shot" if all the bullets in the burst hit their mark.

Explosives typically deal a flat amount of damage at the epicenter of the blast, decreasing in a linear manner to the outer edge of the explosion. Most are lethal near the explosion, and heavily damaging even at the outer edge.

A handful of attacks are instant kills, regardless of the situation—notably melee attacks, but a few Scorestreaks as well. Headshots grant a damage boost for most weapons, but only for the KSG among the shotguns. Sniper rifles get a damage boost for hitting higher on the body. Headshots are lethal. Shots to the chest or waist may or may not be lethal depending on the particular sniper rifle.

Damage Falloff

For pistols, SMGs, ARs, and LMGs, hitting targets at longer ranges causes reduced damage. Each different weapon starts with a certain damage per bullet, typically enough damage to kill in three shots at short range. Then the damage falls to a minimum amount at the maximum range for that weapon, usually one or two shots more to kill.

Shotguns and sniper rifles are special cases. Shotguns deal *no* damage past their maximum range whatsoever. Sniper rifles deal a flat damage amount at any distance. Sniper rifles also have multipliers from the waist up, depending on the particular rifle, which can result in a one-shot kill at very long range.

Several Attachments affect damage falloff. The Suppressor and Rapid Fire Attachments increase falloff. The Long Barrel reduces it. This means that a weapon equipped with a Suppressor may take an extra shot to kill at a shorter distance than normal. But remember, no Attachment affects maximum or minimum damage.

At short range, a weapon with a Suppressor is just as lethal as one without. Even with a Long Barrel, your weapon will still drop to its minimum damage at long range. It simply maintains its damage for a greater distance than usual. Again, shotguns and sniper rifles are special. Changing the range on a shotgun *does* impact how far you can shoot with it. A Suppressor-equipped shotgun has a shorter distance before its bullets simply vanish. One with a Long Barrel can inflict damage at a greater distance.

Sniper rifles on the other hand, actually *do* suffer reduced damage from a Suppressor. Typically, the way it works is that a Suppressor-equipped sniper rifle has to hit higher up on the body to score a killshot, or it takes two shots if you hit low on the body. This makes semi-automatic rifles easier to use with a Suppressor than bolt-action rifles.

Time to Kill

Time to kill is simply a measurement of how quickly a given weapon *can* kill another in ideal circumstances. In theory, the simplest way to look at this is how many shots in how much time, or damage multiplied by rate of fire.

In practice, however, this can be a very misleading way to look at the weapons. Outside of extremely short-range combat (as in, so short you could be knifing your target), not every shot lands on target. On top of that, headshots act as another variable. Scoring a headshot typically takes one shot off the number needed to down a target (or is instantly lethal with sniper rifles).

If you're trying to evaluate what weapons are good at a given range, one-shot kills and high fire rates *are* useful for CQC. Just don't fall into the trap of assuming that a good time to kill makes any given weapon the best in every situation; it does not.

> Sniper rifles and shotguns can kill in one shot. But sniper rifles have terrible hipfire spread, making them a poor choice for CQC.
> Assault Rifles and SMGs with burst fire can sometimes kill in one burst at close range. They often take more than one burst at a distance.
> The Rapid Fire Attachment reduces time to kill at close range, particularly for SMGs (at the cost of reduced range and accuracy).
> Dual-wielded pistols can have surprisingly low time to kill, but again, only at close range.
> Among automatic weapons, the order usually goes: rapid-fire SMG, auto Pistol/SMG, AR or rapid-fire LMG, LMG at close range.
> At longer distances, sniper rifles and burst-fire ARs (or occasionally SMGs) are typically more dangerous, with semi-automatic ARs and LMGs also faring well.

Remember: No player has perfect accuracy, so the general effectiveness of weapons is defined as much by recoil and range as it is by damage and rate of fire.

PENETRATION

All weapons in *Call of Duty: Black Ops II* can penetrate surfaces and strike players on the other side. In order from best to worst penetration:

> **Sniper rifles and light machine guns**
> **Assault rifles**
> **SMGs**
> **Pistols**

The FMJ Attachment maximizes penetration values. It does *not* directly increase damage, only the ability for a bullet to penetrate a wall. When you penetrate a wall, the bullet loses damage as it goes through the surface. You can expect to need quite a few more bullets on target to down a player through any hard cover.

Bullets lose more damage the sharper the angle of penetration is. Ideally, you want to fire at a target behind hard cover or a wall directly perpendicular to the wall. This isn't always possible, just be aware that you'll need to pump more lead into the target if you're firing at a sharp angle.

LMGs are particularly well suited for taking out targets behind cover. They have both great penetration and the large magazines to sustain fire through cover (ARs with FMJ are passable as well).

PICK 10

A massive overhaul to Create a Class, the Pick 10 system allows you to literally pick 10 items. You can pick from the full selection of weapons, Attachments, Perks, and Equipment, with very few restrictions (and even a few picks that break *those* rules).

You can run a build with six Perks, one gun with no Attachments, and nothing else! You can even run a build that doesn't have a primary weapon. Those are extreme examples. In general, most common builds tend to *resemble* builds from previous *Call of Duty* titles, but they aren't identical. Here are the specifics:

> You have 10 picks to create your build.

> *Any* item takes up a pick, including an Attachment.

> You can choose up to two weapons, with two Attachments on the first, one on the second. Up to three Perks. And up to two Tactical and Lethal choices.

> You can take up to three *Wildcard* selections. Wildcards allow you to break the normal rules in a few ways, including an extra Attachment, an extra Perk, or extra Tactical or Lethal Equipment.

> You can take *less* than the full 10 picks, but never more, and Wildcards do take a pick.

WILDCARDS

There are eight Wildcards available for use. Of the eight, you can have a maximum of three active at a time. Three affect Perks, three affect weapons, and two affect Equipment. The Wildcards are:

> PERK 1-2-3 GREED: Enables the selection of an additional Perk in any one of the three Perk categories.

> OVERKILL: Allows a second primary weapon to be chosen as your secondary weapon.

> PRIMARY GUNFIGHTER: Allows a third Attachment to be equipped on your primary weapon.

> SECONDARY GUNFIGHTER: Allows a second Attachment to be equipped on your secondary weapon.

> TACTICIAN: Replaces your Lethal slots with a second bank of Tactical slots.

> DANGER CLOSE: Allows you to take a second Lethal equipment of the same type.

Note that for Tactician, you cannot choose the same item for both unlocked banks. That is, you could have two Flashbangs and two Concussion grenades with Tactician, but not four Flashbangs! The same rule applies to Overkill. You must choose a different type of primary weapon.

Remember: Taking a Wildcard *does* take a pick, so taking Perk 2 Greed to grab Scavenger means giving up a point for Perk 2 Greed and a point for Scavenger.

PICK 10 CATEGORIES

The default Pick 10 layout is as follows:

> One primary weapon slot with two Attachment slots

> One secondary weapon slot with one Attachment slot

> Three slots for Perks in three categories (Perk 1/2/3)

> Two slots for Tactical equipment

> One slot for Lethal equipment

> Three slots for Wildcards

Taking a pick in *any* of those areas consumes one of your available points.

HOW TO BUILD A CLASS

While the freedom can initially be a bit overwhelming, it's important to understand that a bog standard "normal" build still takes up (surprise!) 10 picks exactly. That's one primary weapon (1) with two Attachments (3), a secondary weapon with an Attachment (5), three Perks (8), and one Lethal and Tactical selection (10).

Say you wanted an extra Perk. You can take a Wildcard called Perk Greed that lets you take one extra Perk in any of the normal Perk 1-2-3 slots. Because both the Perk and the Wildcard take a pick, you need to drop two items.

You could drop both your Lethal and Tactical Equipment. Or drop your secondary weapon entirely. Or drop one Attachment and one Tactical. Or drop an Attachment and a Perk. It doesn't matter where you pull the picks from, only that you free up two slots.

We have prepared example classes later in the guide that showcase a variety of builds for various roles in different objective modes. You'll find that most builds we consider strong don't deviate heavily from a "standard" build. They simply use the added flexibility to enhance a chosen role.

USING PICK 10 FOR *YOU*

The Pick 10 system has two major strengths. First, it allows you to build the class that *you* enjoy playing. And second, it allows you to heavily specialize your classes for very specific roles. The first point is just plain fun. If you really enjoy ultra-customized weapons, you can use the Primary Gunfighter Wildcard and bling out your main weapon. Want to run a ton of Perks? Go for it!

The second point allows you to build some extreme classes. Enjoy explosives? Take an assault rifle with a Grenade Launcher Attachment (two explosives), a secondary RPG (four explosives), and two Frag grenades (six explosives). Now cap that entire pile off with the Scavenger Perk and you are a one-man walking arsenal that can refill on the battlefield.

We recommend using your first prestige to experiment heavily with the Pick 10 system, before you settle down into a mix of classes specialized for more specific battlefield roles. It can definitely feel a bit strange choosing between a Reflex Sight or Extreme Conditioning, or wondering if a Shock Charge is somehow equal to the Ghost Perk. But remember, nothing forces you to create "unbalanced" classes.

You can create very functional and effective all-around classes mixed in with builds that emphasize weapons, Perks, or Equipment as you see fit.

SCORESTREAKS

The classic Killstreak system in *Call of Duty* has been revamped for *Call of Duty: Black Ops II*. Killstreaks are now *Scorestreaks*. The basics are still the same. Racking up consecutive kills without dying builds your score, which earns you Scorestreaks.

The key difference is that now performing almost *any* action that is beneficial to your team builds your score toward your Scorestreaks. Also, playing the objective in objective game modes rewards far more points than simply hunting alone for kills. This provides a direct positive feedback loop for good teamplay. Put up UAVs, guard the objective, defeat attackers, and you will score far more than someone running six Perks behind enemy lines who never touches the objective—even if they outkill you!

SCORESTREAK RULES

Dying resets your Scorestreak progress completely. However, you still earn Scorestreak points generated by active streaks even after death. This means that an active UAV or Guardian earns you points the entire time it is active.

Scorestreak points earned in a controlled streak (the RC-XD, Sentry Gun, AGR, Hellfire Missile, Dragonfire, Lodestar, or VTOL Warship) are lost if you are killed while in control. You still earn the points toward your overall *match* score, but they won't help your Scorestreak progress once you've been knifed in the back. Hide carefully before taking control!

Streak rewards *can* be looped. If you earn your highest streak, you reset to your first reward. Streak rewards *cannot* be stacked. Use your early rewards before you earn them again or lose them!

Care Package streaks, and the Death Machine and War Machine occupy a special fourth slot that is not overwritten by your normal three streak slots. The Death Machine and War Machine persist through death until their ammo is expended.

You can switch between any earned Scorestreak rewards and activate them in any order at any time, unless you are under the effects of an EMP.

MULTIPLAYER ARSENAL DATA

We have prepared a new visual presentation for the raw data that makes up the weapons in *Call of Duty: Black Ops II*. Check out these notes so you can get the most out of this valuable information.

WEAPON RANGES AND DAMAGE

First of all, we have correlated information on weapon range (and other items) to the maps in this guide. The maps are gridded with a scale that you can use to check the distances involved in combat at any point on any level. This also ties into the damage charts we have prepared for all of the weapons. You can use these charts in combination with the maps to gain an insight into the right weapon for the job in any given area.

A few notes before you dig into this data:

> Your personal weapon preference is the most important point of all. Use the information on these pages to inform your choices amongst *your* favorite weapons. In other words, don't rely solely on specs and numbers when you choose a weapon—they don't tell the whole story. Your personal play style and subjective feel are also important.

> Remember that the broad overviews of the weapon classes are the most important variables for choosing the right weapon for the job. Use SMGs and shotguns in close quarters combat, LMGs and sniper rifles at long range, and custom ARs at close-medium to medium-long, and you'll do just fine.

> Look at the *totality* of a weapon, not simply its damage or rate of fire. How accurate is it? How fast does it reload? Does it have low recoil or high? Can you compensate for that recoil? Are the iron sights to your liking? How deep is the magazine? How fast do you move while carrying it? How accurate is the hipfire? How fast do you ADS? How quickly does it switch? Does it have favorable penetration statistics?

> You can ask and answer a dozen questions about any weapon in the game, and that's part of the fun. Use this information to help guide your exploration of *all of*

DAMAGE CHARTS

We provide a set of damage charts for each weapon class. They show you the *number of shots to kill* a target at a given distance. You can use these ranges in combination with the maps to determine just how effective your chosen weapon will be in any engagement area. Generally, weapons in *Black Ops II* require anywhere from one to six shots to kill. One-shot kills are reserved for pointblank shotgun blasts and accurate sniper killshots.

Two-shot kills are possible on only a handful of weapons: a few pistols at very close range, near misses with shotguns, and the semi-automatic assault rifles. Three to four shots is the "average" for most of the guns. Five-shot kills typically show up only at long range on a few weapons. SMGs and pistols all bottom out at six shots to kill.

Sniper rifles present a special case. We do not include a damage-over-range chart for them. The reason for this is the way sniper rifles deal damage. Rather than having a damage amount that drops off over distance, they instead inflict a flat amount of damage per bullet. The more accurate your shot to a lethal part of the target is, the more damage you inflict—aim high!

To read a damage chart, simply look at the color key. It is graded from high damage (fewer shots to kill) at short range to lower damage (more shots to kill) at long range.

With the exception of shotguns, every other gun in the game does *not* have a maximum distance. The "end" of the range on these charts simply shows you the distance at which the weapons stop losing damage. In other words, if you have an assault rifle that drops to a maximum of four shots to kill, that is the most shots the weapon will need to do the job no matter how far away the target is (assuming, of course, that your shots are on target). Keep this in mind when you examine the maps and choose your weapons.

> ## Headshot!

For almost all guns, a headshot reduces the number of shots to kill by one. If you have a steady hand, aiming high in CQC situations or even medium-range firefights can give you an edge in combat. A few weapons have no headshot multiplier or other unusual traits; these are noted in the weapons' individual notes.

> ## Multishot!

Remember that burst-fire weapons shoot multiple bullets per shot! If a three-round burst weapon is inside its three-shot kill distance, it can kill with a single trigger pull if the shots are on target. Anywhere outside short range, it's common for at least one shot to go astray, so you often need more than one burst to get the number of hits needed for a kill.

Shotguns are unusual in that they *do* have a maximum range past which they don't inflict any damage at all. Don't use shotguns outside CQC engagements! They make up for their range deficiency with the ability to score one-shot kills at close range, often even when fired on the move from the hip.

Remember that no player has perfect accuracy, *and* the weapons have built-in recoil. The combination of your aiming skill, the weapon's recoil pattern, and its rate of fire all combine to make landing those precious few shots to kill a lot more difficult than it might seem at first glance.

It's easy to look at the more damaging weapons at short range and then look at the Rate of Fire chart and think, "Aha, strong weapon!" Which is true…at close range. But at close range, just about every weapon can be lethal. Plus, you're exposed to a host of other risks, from explosive equipment, melee attacks, lucky shots from burst-fire weapons or snipers, and short-range specialist weapons that are built to be deadly in CQC.

A high rate of fire weapon is more difficult to land shots with at a distance, especially if that weapon also has intense recoil. Again, for emphasis, the weapons that *feel* right for you *are* right for you—use the info here to refine your selection between favorites!

Several Attachments affect shot-to-kill ranges: the Long Barrel, Suppressor, and Rapid Fire Attachments all have an impact on your damage profile.

USING THE DAMAGE CHARTS

Look up your preferred weapon, check its ranges for different shots to kill, and then flip to the maps section and examine the gridded maps. You can use the map grids in conjunction with the Objective map, the Hotspot markings, and even the Routes maps to determine the distances involved in all sorts of engagements.

> Map Grid Quick Reference

Each gridded map also has a small scale beside it that shows four "cheat" ranges: shotguns, SMGs, ARs, and LMGs. These are simply a quick reference to give you a general idea of where those weapons operate near their maximum damage potential.

You can use these shorthand distances to quickly get a rough idea of which weapon is suitable for an area on any map. However, be sure to use the more specific information in this chapter to accurately examine a particular weapon on a given map.

RECOIL PLOTS

A very special new addition to our guide is the inclusion of weapon recoil plots. These scatter charts are built by simulating thousands of rounds of fire, incorporating all the complex recoil forces that act on the weapon every time you squeeze the trigger.

The *red* dots indicate where the first ten rounds of your shots are likely to hit. The *blue* dots indicate where your shots are likely to scatter if you keep the trigger pressed while you continue emptying the magazine. One obvious and important takeaway here is the oft-repeated and always true mantra: short, controlled bursts. If you want to hit anything at a distance, aim down the sights and use burst fire—don't spray and pray.

Use the recoil plots to get a *rough idea* of the recoil for a given weapon. A host of variables can influence your actual battlefield accuracy, including: the distance to your target; whether it is above or below you, or behind cover; where you are standing; if you are moving; what sort of scope you have equipped; and a host of other factors. Nevertheless, all other things being equal, these recoil plots should help you identify roughly how intense the recoil is on any given weapon *and* what *direction* its recoil favors.

Weapons that bounce left and right (or around) center can be difficult to control, because they may bounce off target. This is especially true if you are aiming for a headshot or are shooting at a distance. On the upside, they can also bounce *onto* a target if you are slightly off center. Weapons that recoil mostly vertically—or vertically with a slight angle—are more *predictable* in their recoil pattern. This lets you compensate automatically when you aim. These "climbing" weapons can also go from an upper chest shot to a headshot if you let the recoil go unchecked.

Some weapons have very intense recoil that is strong both vertically and bounces around the center. These weapons are extremely difficult to aim on full auto. They require skilled trigger control to get the most of them at longer ranges. They sometimes compensate for this harsh recoil with greater damage, higher rates of fire, better hipfire spreads, or other benefits.

Finally, some weapons are blessed with relatively low recoil even on full auto. As with high-recoil weapons and their balancing factors, these weapons sometimes pay for their comparative stability in other areas: raw damage, rate of fire, magazine size, etc.

> Several Attachments affect recoil, either positively or negatively. See the Attachments section for more information. However, in brief: the Fore Grip, various optical sights, the Suppressor, Rapid Fire, and using burst fire with the Select Fire Attachment all have an impact on your accuracy.

> These Attachments don't change the basic recoil *pattern*. Rather, they slightly reduce or exaggerate the effects of recoil, requiring more or less trigger discipline to hit your target.

> Remember that crouching or going prone also aids your accuracy. Several other factors can affect accuracy in combat, from getting hit with the Toughness Perk equipped to recovering from a jump. Check the Gameplay chapter for more information on general accuracy modifiers.

RATE OF FIRE CHARTS

The Rate of Fire tables in this chapter simply illustrate the rounds per minute (RPM) of any given weapon. We show both the base rate and the rate with the Rapid Fire Attachment for the weapon classes that can use it. This is important for a few reasons.

> A weapon with a high rate of fire reaches its maximum recoil very quickly. That is, if you hold the trigger, you'll send bullets off target very quickly.

> A weapon with a low rate of fire is often more controllable, even if its overall recoil pattern is harsh. This is especially true when you fire in short bursts.

> A weapon with a high rate of fire can kill more quickly at close range. However, it requires more careful trigger control to use effectively at a distance.

> The Rapid Fire Attachment has additional range and hipfire penalties. This emphasizes its intended purpose to boost short-range lethality at the cost of long-range precision.

RELOAD CHARTS

Reload speed is very important, as it often means the difference between life and death if a second enemy comes for you. Hint: a second enemy always comes for you.

The Reload charts on the following pages consist of stacked bars that show the time it takes to reload in three chunks. These chunks correspond to three different reloading situations. There is an extra bar for weapons that can use the Fast Mag Attachment, which significantly speeds reload times.

> Magazine Refill is the first part of the bar (in green). This is the time it takes for the magazine to refill with ammo. If you sprint or change weapons, you can cancel the remainder of the animation and the gun stays reloaded, thus giving you the fastest time.

> Reload Time is the second, middle portion of the bar (in yellow). This is your reload speed if you reload with any ammunition in the magazine.

> Finally, reloading with a completely empty magazine is the last portion of the bar (in red). This is the longest time. It takes longer than a reload with a partial magazine because you have to pull a charging handle or rack the slide to put a round in the chamber.

> Remember that some weapons reload via individual shells: shotguns and the Executioner. Or with no magazine at all: a speed loader for a Fast Mag Executioner, or an ammo belt for the Mk48 and LSAT LMGs. These lack a "magazine empty" reload time for obvious reasons.

AMMO LOADOUT

The ammo tables in this chapter simply show you the magazine size with or without the Extended Clip Attachment. Most weapons within a class tend to have similar magazine sizes. However, there are a few outliers. Weapons with smaller or larger magazines can be more or less dangerous when engaging multiple enemies on one mag. Weapons that already have a large magazine can get away with firing on full auto for longer, and can more easily engage multiple enemies.

Conversely, weapons with a smaller magazine need more careful trigger control. They may need the Extended Clip Attachment to operate at combat parity with "standard-magazine" weapons when you engage multiple foes.

IRON SIGHTS

Finally, the following pages include images of the iron sights for each weapon. This is simply a convenience we have included so you can glance over the various iron sights for all of the weapons in one place.

GAME ON!

Dig in, see what we have prepared, and play with the new range tools and the rangefinder map grids. Use these to help narrow down your favorite weapons and evaluate different maps in different game modes.

PRIMARY WEAPONS

ASSAULT RIFLES

PROS	
Strong all-around weapon	
Multiple fire types	
Good penetration	
CONS	
Weaker than specialist weapons in their range bands	
COMBAT ROLE	All-purpose weapon
PREFERRED ENGAGEMENT	Close-medium to medium-long with mixed cover

If you're unsure of what weapon to take, use an assault rifle.

Assault rifles are the workhorse weapon of the *Call of Duty* series. They are flexible, powerful, and effective in almost any situation.

With the right Attachments, assault rifles can function as room sweepers or long-range suppression weapons.

If any weapon is the standard weapon of *Call of Duty*, it's an automatic assault rifle with a Reflex sight.

ASSAULT RIFLE TYPES

Assault Rifles come in three varieties:

> Fully Automatic
> Burst-Fire (M8A1 and SIG556)
> Semi-Automatic (FAL OSW and SMR)

Fully automatic rifles are the easiest to use all-around weapons. They are comfortable at medium range, and usable at close range on full-auto, or at longer ranges when burst fired.

Burst-fire weapons are inherently easier to use at medium to long range, where their improved accuracy helps with hitting distant targets. Burst-fire weapons *can* instantly kill targets in CQC, but the delay between shots makes them a poor match for weapons fired on full auto.

Semi-automatic rifles have the best overall damage profiles of any of the ARs, but they require a fast trigger finger and a steady hand to deal their damage. They are the weakest of the three types in CQC.

> ASSAULT RIFLE TYPES

Assault rifles are the most flexible weapon group. They have access to semi-auto, fully auto, and burst-fire modes.

Fully-automatic rifles can be considered the most standard weapon type in the game. They are flexible, effective at almost any range, and easy to use.

Burst-fire rifles trade continuous rate of fire for increased accuracy and lethality at long range, firing in three- or four-round bursts with each pull of the trigger.

Semi-automatic rifles are the most accurate and have the highest individual damage per bullet of any weapon outside sniper rifles. However, they only fire a single bullet per pull of the trigger.

Note that the Select Fire Attachment muddies the waters a bit in terms of categorizing assault rifles. Any assault rifle can swap between fully automatic and either burst or semi-auto (depending on the original mode of the weapon).

The important point to take away here is recognizing where each fire type is most effective. Fully automatic fire is more useful at shorter distances, while burst or semi-auto is stronger at a distance.

WEAPON NOTES

> The M8A1 fires four-round bursts, with little delay between bursts.
> The AN-94 fires the first two rounds of any burst of shots at a higher rate of fire, making short bursts very accurate.
> The SCAR-H, SMR, and FAL OSW have better penetration than the other ARs.

ASSAULT RIFLE PROFILES

NAME	MAG SIZE	EXTENDED MAG
AN-94	30	40
FAL-OSW	25	34
M27	30	40
M8A1	32	42
MTAR	30	40
SCAR-H	30	40
SMR	20	26
SWAT-556	30	39
TYPE-25	30	40

ASSAULT RIFLE DAMAGE: SHOTS TO KILL OVER DISTANCE

This chart illustrates the number of shots needed to kill a target from a given distance.

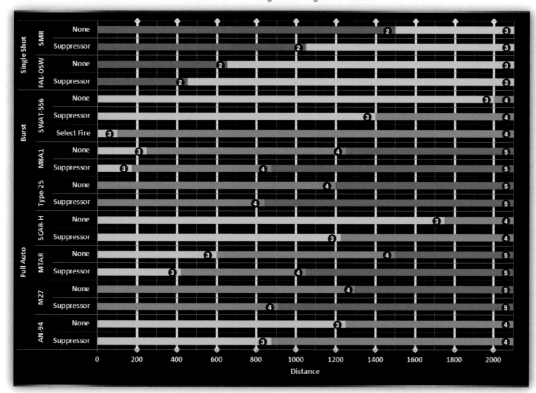

ASSAULT RIFLE RATE OF FIRE: ROUNDS PER MINUTE

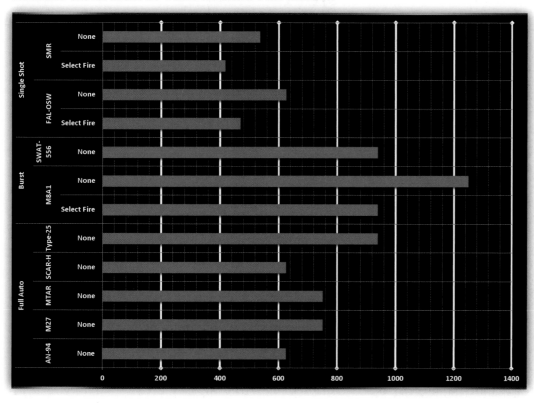

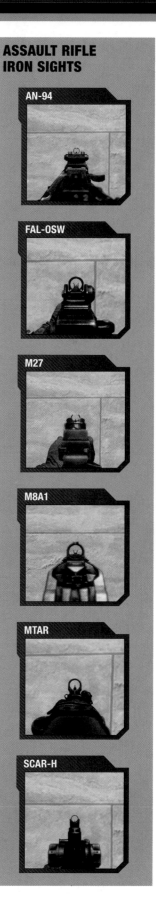

ASSAULT RIFLE IRON SIGHTS (CONTD.)

SMR

SWAT-556

TYPE-25

ASSAULT RIFLE RELOAD: TIME IN SECONDS

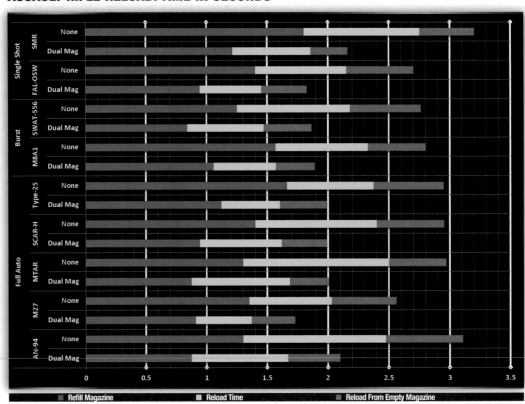

Legend: Refill Magazine | Reload Time | Reload From Empty Magazine

ASSAULT RIFLE RECOIL PLOTS

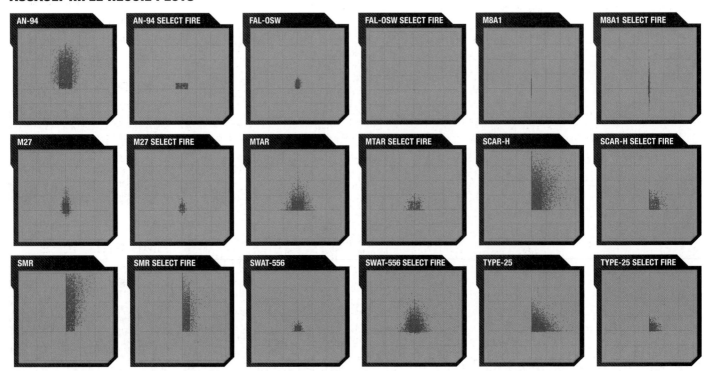

| AN-94 | AN-94 SELECT FIRE | FAL-OSW | FAL-OSW SELECT FIRE | M8A1 | M8A1 SELECT FIRE |

| M27 | M27 SELECT FIRE | MTAR | MTAR SELECT FIRE | SCAR-H | SCAR-H SELECT FIRE |

| SMR | SMR SELECT FIRE | SWAT-556 | SWAT-556 SELECT FIRE | TYPE-25 | TYPE-25 SELECT FIRE |

SUBMACHINE GUNS

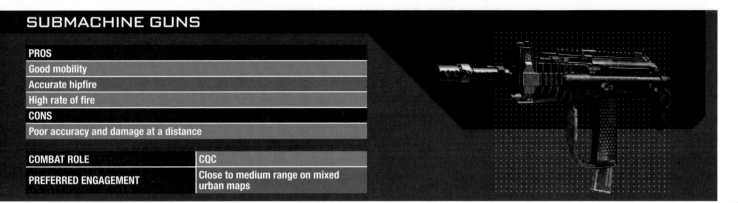

PROS
Good mobility
Accurate hipfire
High rate of fire

CONS
Poor accuracy and damage at a distance

COMBAT ROLE	CQC
PREFERRED ENGAGEMENT	Close to medium range on mixed urban maps

SMGs are fast-moving CQC beasts. They are built for short-range firefights and high mobility.

SMGs have good base movement speed, fast ADS times, good hipfire spreads, and high rates of fire. This makes them ideal for engaging and eliminating targets at short range while on the move.

SMGs trade off long-range damage potential for these benefits, and have significantly more damage falloff than ARs or LMGs. You can definitely still take down targets at medium range with ADS and careful trigger control, but longer-range engagements become dicey due to the number of shots you need to land on the target.

SMGs work best on maps that have more short-range encounters than medium- to long-range ones. They are also very useful in objective modes that demand high mobility.

As with shotguns, SMGs benefit from stealthy setups utilizing Ghost, Suppressor, Dead Silence, etc. You need an edge to force an engagement at your preferred distance, rather than being stuck out in the open engaging ARs at long range.

SMGs are extremely flexible weapons. You can take Attachments like Quickdraw, sights, or a grip to skew them towards medium-range viability, or take a Laser Sight or Rapid Fire to emphasize hipfire or close-range bullet spraying.

SMG TYPES

With the exception of the Chicom CQB (a 3-round burst SMG), the other SMGs differ in more subtle ways.

The other SMGs have differing rates of fire, recoil patterns, damage falloff, and magazine sizes.

Experiment with the SMGs to find which you prefer. They each trade off close-range lethality with more efficiency at close-medium to medium-range combat. It is likely you will find that you prefer several different SMGs for different map and mode combinations.

WEAPON NOTES

> All SMGs have average penetration, only slightly worse than ARs.

> The Skorpion has no headshot multiplier, but the highest rate of fire.

SMG DAMAGE: SHOTS TO KILL OVER DISTANCE

This chart illustrates the number of shots needed to kill a target from a given distance.

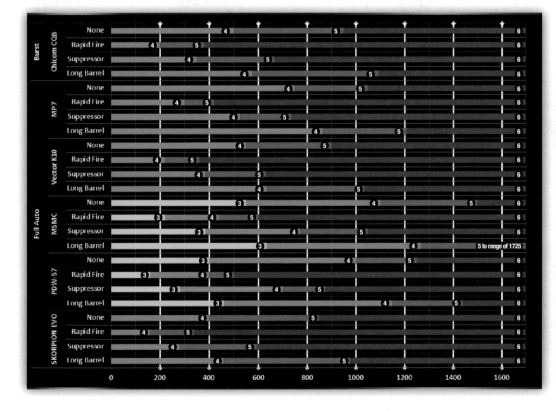

SMG PROFILES

NAME	MAG SIZE	EXTENDED MAG
Chicom CQB	36	48
MP7	40	54
MSMC	30	40
PDW-57	50	65
SKORPION EVO	32	42
Vector K10	36	48

SMG IRON SIGHTS

CHICOM CQB

MP7

MSMC

PDW-57

SKORPION EVO

VECTOR K10

SMG RATE OF FIRE: ROUNDS PER MINUTE

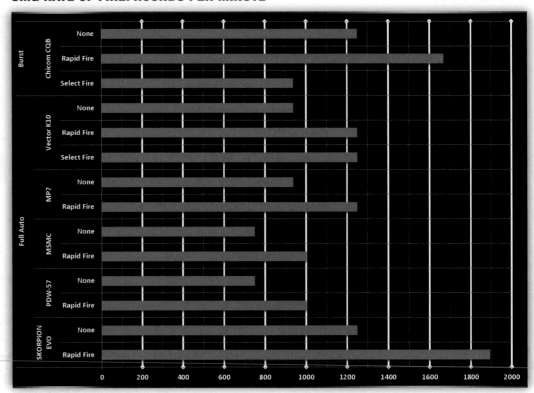

SMG RELOAD: TIME IN SECONDS

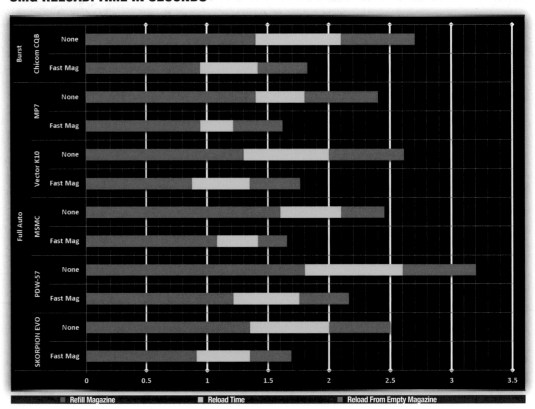

■ Refill Magazine   ■ Reload Time   ■ Reload From Empty Magazine

SMG RECOIL PLOTS

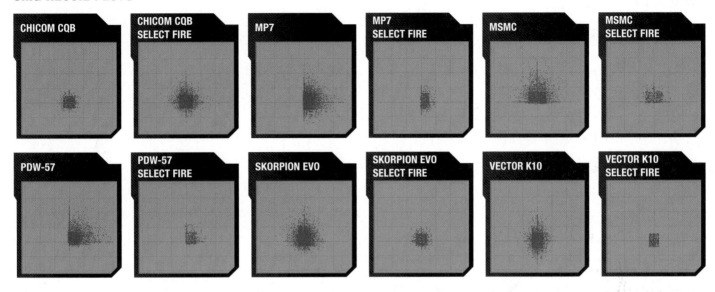

SHOTGUNS

PROS	
One shot kills at close range	
Good mobility	
Accurate hipfire	
CONS	
No ranged capability	
Lengthy reload times	

COMBAT ROLE	Room clearing, extreme CQC
PREFERRED ENGAGEMENT	Short range, small to medium maps with high urban density

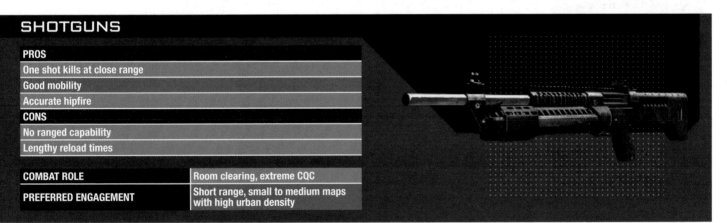

Shotguns are powerful CQC weapons, capable of downing targets in a single shot from the hip while staying highly mobile.

Shotguns have some overlap with SMGs in a CQC role, but they trade off distance for close-range power. Unlike other weapons, shotguns cannot damage targets outside their maximum range.

Note that the Suppressor and Long Barrel Attachments have special meaning for shotguns. They either reduce or increase the range at which you can actually *hit* targets. This is unlike most other weapons, where they simply change damage falloff distances.

The Laser Sight is also important for shotguns, as it allows for a tighter pellet spread for each shot when hipfired. Although you should note that the KSG only fires a single slug, so it is still better to ADS with it.

Another viable setup is using Quickdraw and ADS almost every shot (if you can ensure a more accurate delivery of buckshot to the face). Adjustable Stock and a Millimeter Scanner also work well, giving you quick ADS movement and automatic target sweeps while in ADS.

Much of the challenge of using a shotgun is simply getting into close range to begin with. They do work if you can get there, so consider stealthy Perk setups and aggressive flanking play to get into range.

Alternatively, a shotgun makes a nasty backup weapon for room clearing or defending at short range.

SHOTGUN TYPES

There are two pump-action shotguns, the R-870 and the KSG, a semi-automatic (the Saiga 12), and a fully-auto, the M1216.

The R-870 is an all-around shotgun. It has a solid rate of fire, good damage, and good accuracy.

The KSG is a slug shotgun, firing a single high-damage round. It demands high accuracy in exchange for much greater range than the other shotguns.

The Saiga is a semi-auto shotgun. It is better for engaging multiple targets, but drains ammunition rapidly to score kills. Bring Extended or Fast Mags!

Finally, the M1216 is fully-auto. It has a very unusual 16-shell magazine that fires four shells before you must rotate it to load the next four. This "gap" in firing can be lethal if your shots aren't on target.

WEAPON NOTES

> The KSG is the only shotgun with (poor) penetration. The other three shotguns do not penetrate.

> Shotguns do not deal bonus headshot damage, with the exception of the KSG which has a high headshot multiplier.

> The R-870 and KSG reload two shells at a time with Fast Mags.

SHOTGUN PROFILES

NAME	MAG SIZE	EXTENDED MAG
KSG	14	19
M1216	16	22
R 870 MCS	8	11
Saiga 12	10	13

SHOTGUN IRON SIGHTS

KSG

M1216

R870 MCS

SAIGA 12

SHOTGUN DAMAGE: SHOTS TO KILL OVER DISTANCE

This chart illustrates the number of shots needed to kill a target from a given distance.

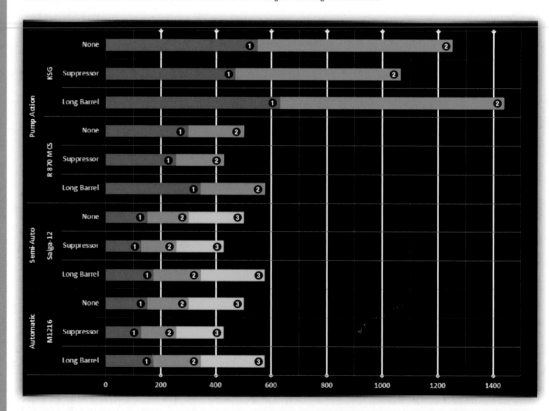

> IMPORTANT: SHOTGUN DAMAGE

Excepting the KSG, shotguns fire a burst of pellets in a cone.

Because of this fact, these ranges show the distances at which you can score a one- or two-shot kill—not a *guarantee* that you will do so every time.

Using ADS or a Laser Sight can tighten the spread. However, when you are in a mobile CQC fight, your aim needs to be dead on and you need a bit of luck to score reliable one-shot kills.

< 174   175 >

SHOTGUN RATE OF FIRE: ROUNDS PER MINUTE

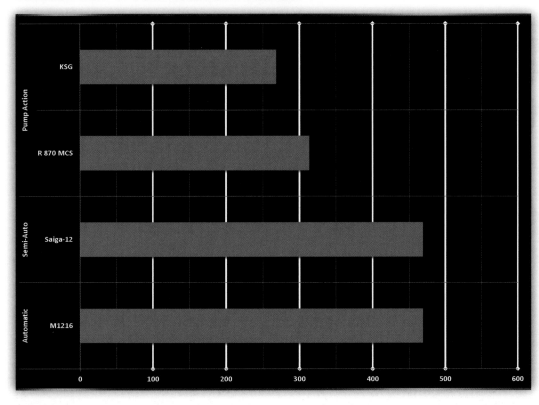

SHOTGUN RELOAD: TIME IN SECONDS

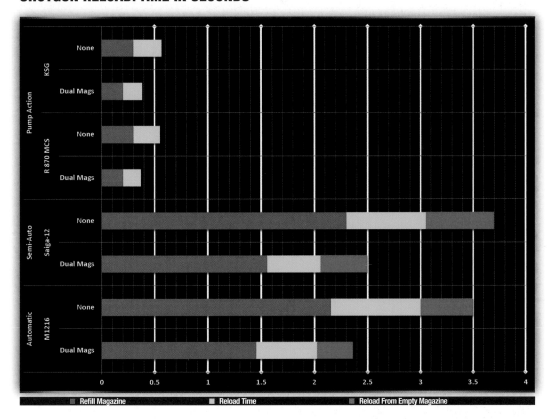

■ Refill Magazine   ■ Reload Time   ■ Reload From Empty Magazine

> SHELL LOADS

Remember that the reload times for the R-870 and KSG are *per shell*.

SHOTGUN RECOIL PLOTS

KSG

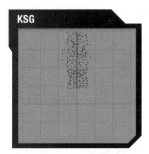

M1216

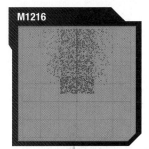

R870 MCS

SAIGA 12

LIGHT MACHINE GUNS

PROS
High damage, good penetration
Large magazines
Stable while prone

CONS
Poor mobility, ADS time, and hipfire spread
Loud and highly visible when fired full-auto

COMBAT ROLE	Long-range combat, medium-range suppression
PREFERRED ENGAGEMENT	Medium to long range with a good overwatch position

LMGs are powerhouse ranged weapons, with high damage, good range, and good penetration. In exchange, however, they are cumbersome, slow to move and bring to bear, with poor hipfire and slow reloads.

As SMGs are to close-range highly-mobile combat, so are LMGs to slower defensive play. They are ideal for locking down an objective area or chokepoint with their deep magazines.

While an AR needs to reload after downing a target or two, an entrenched gunner with an LMG can easily mow down the entire enemy team (if they're foolish enough to charge into an open area in line of sight).

Despite the magazine sizes of LMGs, trigger discipline is still important. Much like ARs, short controlled bursts are much more effective at taking down targets at a distance.

Remember to abuse your deep magazine sizes by shooting targets through hard cover. With their strong penetration, LMGs have the ammo and the penetration to take out targets through cover at any distance.

Quickdraw, the Fore Grip, and an optical Attachment are all good choices for an LMG. They help minimize the slow ADS penalty and let you easily identify and eliminate targets at long range, where you should be fighting.

Remember that when using an LMG, if you are close enough that an AR would work just as well, you're *probably* too close. Take advantage of your superior range and whenever possible engage targets at long range.

This nullifies shotgun users and considerably weakens SMGs. Only some AR builds are well suited to fight you on even terms, leaving you up against other LMGs or sniper rifles as serious threats.

LMGs are the only other type of weapon besides SMGs that can take Rapid Fire. But be aware that taking it can make long range combat more difficult, in exchange for raising your lethality in close-medium combat, where LMGs are typically weaker than CQC specialists.

With the slowest movement speed of the basic weapon classes, remember to switch to a secondary pistol or combat knife to move more quickly.

WEAPON NOTES

> The HAMR has a very unique firing pattern. Its rate of fire *slows* as you continue to shoot, stabilizing over time. This allows for rapid-fire bursts, or more stable suppressing fire if you hold the trigger. Just be aware of the ammo consumption involved.

> The QBB and HAMR reload via a drum magazine, rather than the ammo belts of the LSAT and MK48, allowing them to reload more quickly.

> The QBB and HAMR do not have a headshot multiplier.

> LMGs are quite good at taking down Scorestreaks from a distance due to their damage and magazine sizes.

LIGHT MACHINE GUN PROFILES

NAME	MAG SIZE	EXTENDED MAG
HAMR	75	100
LSAT	100	135
MK48	100	135
QBB LMG	75	100

LMG DAMAGE: SHOTS TO KILL OVER DISTANCE

This chart illustrates the number of shots needed to kill a target from a given distance.

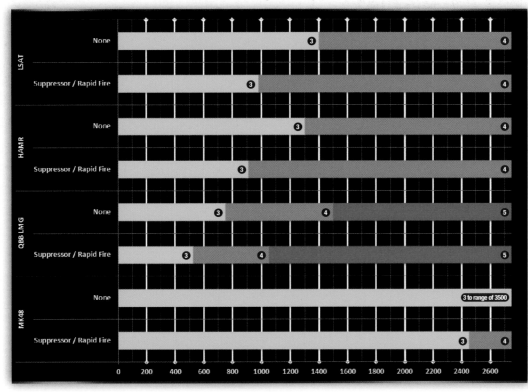

LMG RATE OF FIRE: ROUNDS PER MINUTE

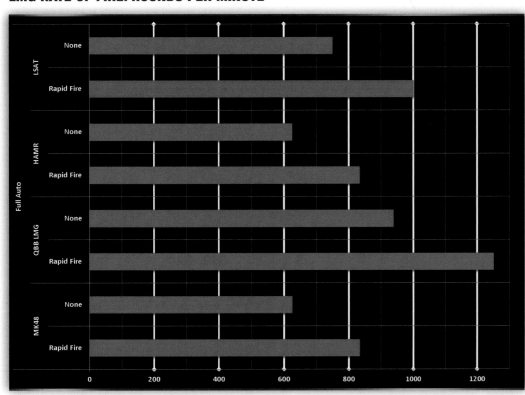

LMG IRON SIGHTS

HAMR

LSAT

MK48

QBB LMG

LMG RECOIL PLOTS

HAMR

HAMR BURST FIRE

LSAT

MK48

QBB LMG

LMG RELOAD: TIME IN SECONDS

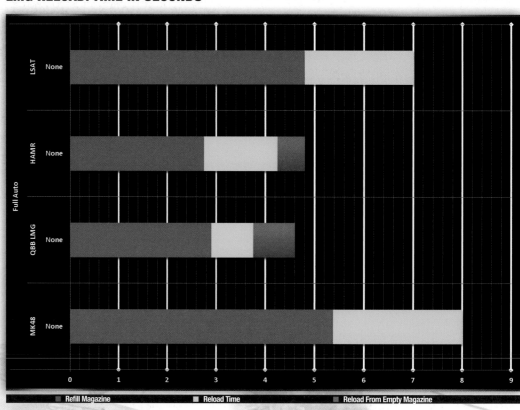

Full Auto

LSAT	None									
HAMR	None									
QBB LMG	None									
MK48	None									

0 1 2 3 4 5 6 7 8 9

■ Refill Magazine   ■ Reload Time   ■ Reload From Empty Magazine

< 178   179 >

SNIPER RIFLES

PROS	
One-shot kills	
High damage at any range	

CONS	
Poor at close range	
Demand high accuracy from operator	

COMBAT ROLE	Long-range assassination, objective overwatch
PREFERRED ENGAGEMENT	Medium-long to long range with clear sightlines

Sniper rifles are supreme long-range weapons, capable of scoring kills in a single shot at any distance. They are ideal for covering long lines of fire and can take down many enemies at distances that are impossible to retaliate from.

Sniper rifles have very poor hipfire spread and lack the high rate of fire to compete effectively at close range. Although you *can* get lucky with a hipfire shot and take down an enemy in one shot.

In *Call of Duty: Black Ops II*, sniper rifles have good mobility. Take advantage of their speed to reposition yourself constantly. Because of killcams, it's easy for a target to pinpoint your location and track you down if you stay immobile for too long.

Sniper rifles come with a sniper scope by default, which requires steadying your breath. You can equip an ACOG Sight (or Iron Sights on the Ballista) if you want to try mobile sniping at shorter distances. Note that snipers do still sway while using an ACOG Sight, which can cause missed shots at range.

The Ballistics CPU is a special sniper-only Attachment that reduces sway while equipped. This can make the initial acquisition of your target a bit faster, particularly at very long distances.

Be careful about getting myopic while sniping. If you spend too much time zoomed in with your scope, it's easy to lose awareness of the situation around you, which can get you stabbed in the back.

Sniper rifles benefit from a reliable secondary weapon. A pistol, SMG, or shotgun can be very helpful when you need to defend yourself at close range. Dual Pistols, the B23R, or the Kap 40 all work quite well as close-range defense. Because pistols switch more quickly than other weapon types, they're ideal if you aren't using Fast Hands.

If you *are* camping in one area, Claymores, Bouncing Betties, and Shock Charges can all be used to cover your back.

HOLD YOUR BREATH...

When you sight in with a sniper scope, you have to hold your breath by pressing the Sprint button.

Doing so steadies your aim as you hold your breath, quickly reducing the sway of the rifle so you can take a pinpoint accurate shot.

If you fire before your sight is fully steady, the bullet may deviate from your intended target, causing a miss, particularly at long range.

WEAPON NOTES

> Sniper rifles deal static damage at all ranges.

> Sniper rifles receive a damage multiplier when they hit higher up on the body.

> Suppressors reduce sniper rifle damage directly.

> The Ballista has slightly faster ADS than other sniper rifles.

> The Ballista can "mount" Iron Sights, allowing for midrange ADS shots.

SNIPER RIFLE TYPES

The Ballista and DSR-50 are bolt-action rifles, with relatively low rates of fire. The SVU-AS and XPR-50 are semi-automatic. The SVU-AS in particular has a high rate of fire in exchange for its weaker damage profile.

SNIPER RIFLE PROFILES

NAME	MAG SIZE	EXTENDED MAG
Ballista	7	10
DSR-50	5	7
SVU-AS	10	16
XPR-50	8	11

SNIPER RIFLE	KILLSHOT FROM
Ballista	Chest up
DSR-50	Waist up
SVU-AS	Headshot only
XPR-50	Chest up

SR CROSSHAIRS

BALLISTA   DSR-50

SVU-AS   XPR-50

SR RECOIL PLOTS

BALLISTA

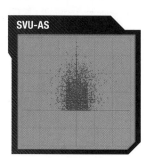

DSR-50

SVU-AS

XPR-50

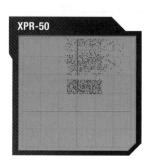

SNIPER RIFLE RATE OF FIRE: ROUNDS PER MINUTE

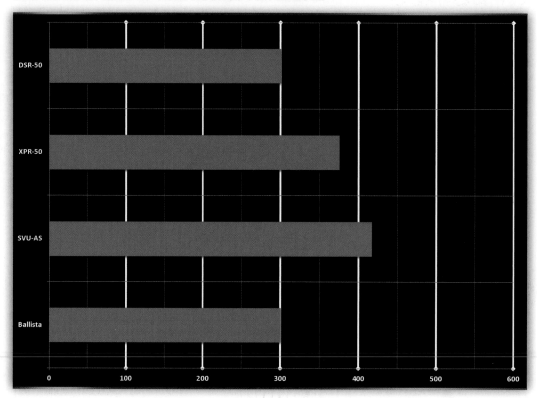

SNIPER RIFLE RELOAD: TIME IN SECONDS

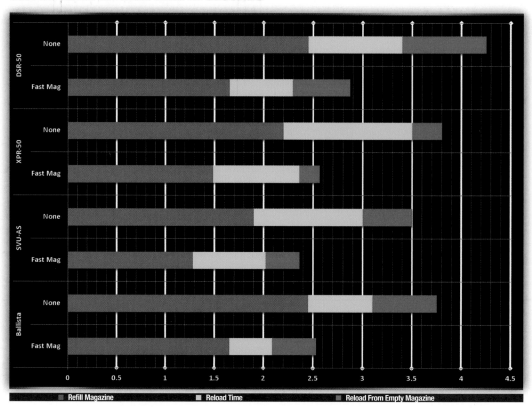

■ Refill Magazine   ■ Reload Time   ■ Reload From Empty Magazine

SPECIALS

Specials are special Equipment that can be taken as a primary "weapon."

ASSAULT SHIELD

The Assault Shield is a protective shield that can be carried in front of you or on your back to block shots. It can also be deployed on the battlefield as a mobile piece of cover. When carried as a "weapon," you can only attack with shield bashes, which require two hits to kill. However, the primary use of the Assault Shield is not directly attacking; it is blocking incoming fire.

While you are moving, only your feet are exposed. You can minimize even this weakness by crouching as you move forward, keeping the Assault Shield aimed at any hostiles in front of you.

Remember that due to internet latency, if you are at very close range with an enemy strafing around you firing, aiming the shield perfectly to block all incoming attacks is very difficult. It is much easier to block incoming fire straight on from a distance, or if you are tucked in a corner with the shield guarding your front.

You can deploy the Assault Shield as a piece of waist-high cover. You can't shoot through it, but you can shoot over it. Crouching down gives you complete frontal cover. This is particularly useful at long range in any situation where you have *no* other available cover.

The Assault Shield also pairs well with the Flak Jacket and Tactical Mask Perks when you must secure an objective at all costs.

Because the Assault Shield takes up your primary slot, you must either take a pistol secondary, use the Overkill Wildcard to bring another primary weapon, or scavenge a weapon on the battlefield.

COMBAT KNIFE

You do not "choose" a Combat Knife. Instead you are given one in place of a primary or secondary slot if you leave it blank. The Combat Knife functions as a "normal" knife in most respects. It is a one-hit silent kill at close range, and swings at a regular speed.

However, the Combat Knife has one very useful special benefit. You can run almost 1.5x as far with a Combat Knife as you can with the fastest main-hand gear: SMGs, shotguns, and pistols. Combined with Extreme Conditioning, this allows you to run farther than any other player that isn't holding a Combat Knife.

The downside to that speed boost is the fact that you're running around the map with a knife in your hand instead of your gun. Sprinting into an armed enemy typically ends poorly.

Fast Hands can help, but otherwise, use the speed to travel long distances only when you are relatively certain your path is clear (or you have friendlies ahead of you). Be sure to swap back to a ranged weapon before you reach areas of likely enemy contact!

SECONDARY WEAPONS

Secondary weapons increase your flexibility, giving you backup explosive firepower, or a quick swapping secondary pistol.

LAUNCHERS

PROS	
Effective against air support	
Can clear large groups or rooms	
CONS	
Limited ammunition	
Low rate of fire	
COMBAT ROLE	Anti-air, area clearing

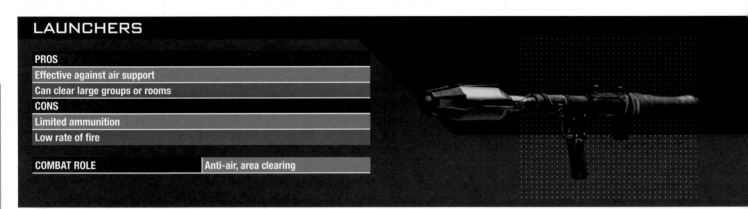

Launchers are explosive weapons useful for taking down enemy air support or ground-based Scorestreaks and Equipment. The SMAW and RPG can also be direct fired on the ground to flush out campers or blast groups of enemies near an objective. The FHJ-18 is an anti-air lock-on missile launcher *only*, while the SMAW can lock onto Scorestreaks or fire unguided.

The RPG is completely unguided. It is *possible* to hit aerial streaks with it, but difficult. The Crossbow is a unique weapon. It fires explosive-tipped bolts that stick and instantly kill any enemy with a direct hit. Although they can also inflict damage (or kill, with the Tri-Bolt Attachment) if you land a shot near your target.

The Crossbow has a three-round arrow "clip," allowing you to take three shots in quick succession before reloading.

The Crossbow makes a good backup weapon for a short-ranged primary (typically a shotgun or SMG) if you don't want to take a pistol and would rather have some longer range ability. A Crossbow with a precision sight attached can take down enemies at a surprisingly long range (if your aim is true).

BALLISTIC KNIFE

The Ballistic Knife is a "secondary weapon" version of the Combat Axe. This knife gives you an instantly lethal, stealthy projectile that you can fire and pick up from the ground (or your target's face) by simply stepping over it.

You only get a few shots with the Ballistic Knife. However, you can pick the knives back up (or get more with Scavenger), allowing you to rack up quite a few kills with limited ammo.

The Ballistic Knife does have a slight arc to its trajectory, so learning to use the Ballistic Knife (alongside the Combat Axe) is a bit of an art.

The Ballistic Knife also allows you to make very quick melee stabs while wielded. Although, as with other melee attacks, there is next to no lunge, and you need to be nearly point blank to down a hostile with a melee strike.

PISTOLS

PROS	
Quick weapon switch times	
Accurate	
Good damage at close range	
CONS	
Poor damage at range	
Shallow magazines	
COMBAT ROLE	Fast switching backup weapons

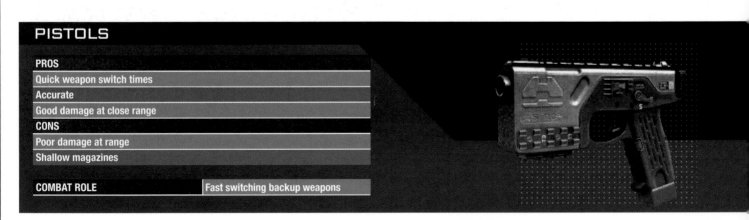

Pistols are fast-switching accurate backup weapons. They are ideal for finishing off a damaged opponent when your primary weapon runs dry.

Pistols don't make for great primary weapons due to their severe damage falloff and relatively shallow magazines. Up close, they work quite well, and can even outperform some primary weapons in CQC.

Pistols are the only weapon in the game that can be dual wielded, trading off any ranged ability for increased lethality in CQC. If you only care about protecting yourself in CQC, the Dual Wield Attachment is quite useful.

Because pistols switch more quickly than any other weapon type, training yourself to fast swap to your pistol exactly as you run out of ammo on your primary weapon is an important skill to master. If you switch and start firing immediately, you will almost always come out on top against an opponent who runs dry and chooses to reload instead.

PISTOL TYPES

The Tac-45 and Five-Seven are semi-automatic pistols. Of the two, the Tac-45 can reliably kill in two shots at a greater range, while the Five-Seven is remarkably accurate at a distance and has a larger magazine.

The B23R is a three-round burst pistol, while the KAP-40 is fully automatic. Both are very effective at close range.

Finally, the Executioner is a very unusual weapon; it is a shotgun in pistol form! The Executioner is *very*, very short range, but at that range, it can potentially kill in one shot.

PISTOL DAMAGE: SHOTS TO KILL OVER DISTANCE

This chart illustrates the number of shots needed to kill a target from a given distance.

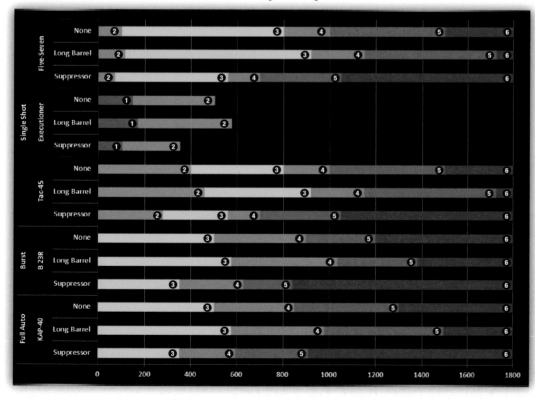

WEAPON NOTES

> The Executioner deals no headshot damage.
> All pistols have poor penetration.

PISTOL IRON SIGHTS

B23R

EXECUTIONER

FIVE-SEVEN

TAC-45

KAP-40

PISTOL RECOIL PLOTS

B23R

EXECUTIONER
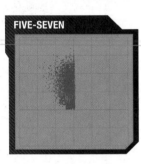

FIVE-SEVEN

FNP-45

KAP-40
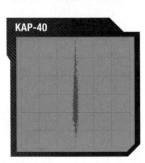

PISTOL RATE OF FIRE: ROUNDS PER MINUTE

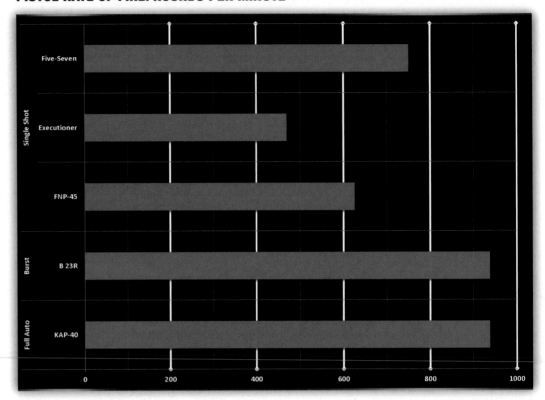

PISTOL RELOAD: TIME IN SECONDS

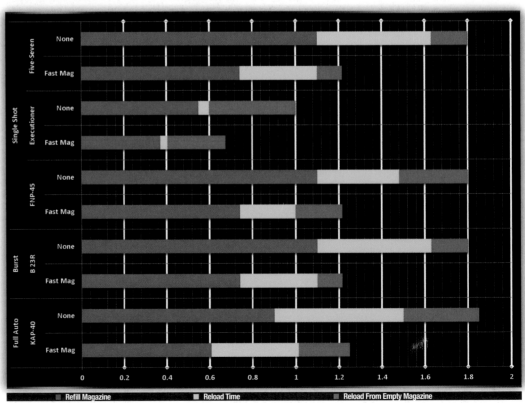

Refill Magazine   Reload Time   Reload From Empty Magazine

< 184   185 >

ATTACHMENTS

Attachments modify your weapons. Among the many types of modifications, you can give your weapons sophisticated optical scopes, underslung grenade launchers, fire rate adjustments, and ergonomic grips.

Customizing your weapons to fit your preferred playstyle is one of the best parts of *Call of Duty*. This section is loaded with information to help you make the best choices.

Because custom weapons are so personal, we strongly recommend you spend time with *every* Attachment on *every* class of weapon. This is also good for earning experience from completing challenges. You can earn rewards while you learn!

> **Mutually Exclusive Attachments**
>
> Attachment rules are pretty straightforward; you can't jam two optics onto a gun!
> - No more than one optic
> - One magazine modifier: Fast Mag or Extended Clip
> - One weapon modification: Select Fire, Grenade Launcher, Hybrid Optic
> - One barrel modification: Suppressor, Long Barrel

ATTACHMENTS BY WEAPON CLASS

ASSAULT RIFLE

- Reflex Sight
- Quickdraw Handle
- Suppressor
- EOTech Sight
- ACOG Sight
- Fore Grip
- Select Fire
- Adjustable Stock
- Laser Sight
- FMJ
- Fast Mag
- Target Finder
- Extended Clip
- Hybrid Optic
- Grenade Launcher
- Millimeter Scanner

SMG

- Reflex Sight
- Quickdraw Handle
- Suppressor
- EOTech Sight
- Fore Grip
- Select Fire
- Adjustable Stock
- Laser Sight
- FMJ
- Fast Mag
- Target Finder
- Extended Clip
- Long Barrel
- Rapid Fire
- Millimeter Scanner

SHOTGUN

- Reflex Sight
- Quickdraw Handle
- Suppressor
- Adjustable Stock
- Laser Sight
- Fast Mag
- Extended Clip
- Long Barrel
- Millimeter Scanner

CROSSBOW

- Reflex Sight
- ACOG Sight
- Dual Band
- Tri-Bolt
- Variable Zoom

LMG

- Reflex Sight
- Quickdraw Handle
- Suppressor
- EOTech Sight
- Fore Grip
- ACOG Sight
- Variable Zoom
- Adjustable Stock
- Laser Sight
- FMJ
- Target Finder
- Extended Clip
- Hybrid Optic
- Rapid Fire
- Dual Band

SNIPER RIFLE

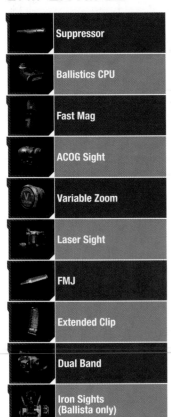

- Suppressor
- Ballistics CPU
- Fast Mag
- ACOG Sight
- Variable Zoom
- Laser Sight
- FMJ
- Extended Clip
- Dual Band
- Iron Sights (Ballista only)

PISTOLS

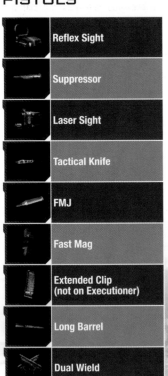

- Reflex Sight
- Suppressor
- Laser Sight
- Tactical Knife
- FMJ
- Fast Mag
- Extended Clip (not on Executioner)
- Long Barrel
- Dual Wield

ATTACHMENT DESCRIPTIONS

REFLEX SIGHT

Basic red dot optic; clean, clear view

The Reflex Sight is a simple, clean optic Attachment that gives a clear view of your target with a simple red dot as a crosshair. The Reflex Sight has very clear visibility, with a small frame that does not obscure your view. For guns that you are not comfortable with Iron Sights, the Reflex Sight Attachment is a great choice.

It is also slightly easier to use than even good Iron Sights at medium to long range. While the Reflex Sight is not a zooming optic scope, the clear visibility and tiny dot can allow you to land shots on targets with careful trigger discipline. The Reflex Sight in *Call of Duty: Black Ops II* is one of the cleanest in *Call of Duty* history. If there is a standard *Call of Duty* weapon, an assault rifle with a Reflex Sight is it.

> ### Custom Crosshairs
>
> The Reflex and EOTech Sights allow you to customize the reticle. After you attach the scope, tap the Switch Weapon button on the Attachment to pick a custom crosshair.
>
> While the simple red dot is one of the best all-around sights, there are other options that have clearer views at slightly shorter or longer distances.

EOTECH SIGHT

Basic holographic optic with slightly greater zoom than the Reflex Sight

The EOTech Sight is very similar to the Reflex Sight, with a holographic crosshair suspended in a slightly larger housing. The only gameplay difference between the two is a very slight zoom factor increase with the EOTech Sight over the Reflex Sight. Also, the Holographic frame is slightly more obscuring.

With the slightly higher zoom, an EOTech Sight is also slightly better for semi-auto or burst fire ARs or SMGs, or LMGs at medium to medium-long range. Otherwise, the choice of a basic optic comes down entirely to personal preference. Experiment with each and see what you prefer!

ACOG SIGHT
Basic zoom optic; high zoom, reduced sway

The ACOG Sight (Advanced Combat Optical Gunsight) is the last of the basic scopes. It acts as the long-range option of the three basic types, providing a greater zoom factor than either the Reflex or EOTech Sights. The ACOG Sight works well on ARs and LMGs when you want to focus on medium- to long-range combat, or in reverse on sniper rifles, when you *don't* want to focus solely on long-range combat.

The ACOG Sight has reduced sway when you are in ADS. You have both the benefit of greater zoom and slightly more stable target acquisition. However, it has only a negligible effect on weapon recoil. It simply makes lining up the shot a bit easier. The ACOG Sight does not have an ADS speed penalty. Other than the slight loss of situational awareness and peripheral vision when zoomed, the ACOG Sight is a viable scope for mid-range combat.

The ACOG Sight works best with semi-auto or burst ARs, or LMGs, which have the long-range punch needed to down targets at greater distances. Sniper rifles benefit from it as well, but be aware that SRs *do* take a slight recoil penalty from using an ACOG Sight. This barely affects you, even when rapidly firing shots with the semi-automatic rifles. You're unlikely to see a difference with the bolt-action variety. An ACOG Sight equipped SR is slightly less stable than a fully-scoped sniper scope with your breath held. But it is faster if you're simply scoping and firing immediately.

Remember that when you're using an ACOG Sight, you need to keep your engagement distances at a range band farther out than normal to really maximize the potential of the ACOG Sight. If you're fighting at the same distances you normally do with a Reflex or EOTech Sight, you're not taking full advantage of the scope. If anything, anyone using those scopes or Iron Sights has a slight edge over you. Check your positioning and try to step back one line of cover when using an ACOG Sight!

LASER SIGHT
Reduces hipfire spread

The Laser Sight is a powerful Attachment that modifies the hipfire spread of your weapon. When equipped, the Laser Sight reduces hipfire spread—this is similar to the effect from Steady Aim in previous *Call of Duty* titles.

A Laser Sight equipped SMG is a serious threat at close to close-medium range. An SMG user can reliably down targets that would be more easily killed with ADS on an SMG or AR without a Laser Sight. The only slight downside to using the full-range advantage granted by the Laser Sight is the extra ammo you can burn to score kills at a greater distance.

Laser Sights also have a dramatic impact on the performance of shotguns. Unless you are using ADS with your shotguns (which takes time, losing some of their speed advantage in CQC), hipfiring is the way to go. Because three of the four shotguns fire a spread of pellets, the Laser Sight can help you to more reliably land one-shot kills at close range. However, this also requires that you *aim* more accurately. The tighter spread means less chance of glancing hits on highly evasive targets. Experiment with the Laser Sight on the shotguns. You may find you prefer using Quickdraw Handle and ADS with some, and regular or Laser Sight hipfire with others.

Laser Sights on ARs give them roughly the hipfire profile of a regular SMG, which can make the full-auto ARs quite effective in CQC. LMGs do benefit from a Laser Sight, but they're still not amazing CQC weapons (although a Laser Sight, Rapid Fire LMG with Lightweight equipped isn't bad!). Pistols benefit significantly from the Laser Sight. Although, if you're going to be regularly hipfiring your pistol, you should seriously consider taking the Dual Wield Attachment. Whether you prefer to keep the option of ADS targeting is a personal choice!

The Laser Sight doesn't have exactly the same percentage reduction in hipfire spread on every weapon class: SMGs get the least reduction from it (though it still makes them exceedingly lethal); ARs, LMGs, and pistols get an average amount. If you regularly take no-scope shots instead of weapon switching, consider taking a Laser Sight!

TARGET FINDER
Advanced zoom optic; paints targets with a red diamond

The Target Finder is the first of the "advanced" optics. Advanced optics means sights with more sophisticated electronics or zooming capabilities than the "basic" optics (the Reflex Sight, EOTech, and ACOG Sight).

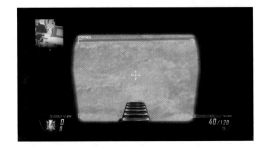

When you enter ADS, the Target Finder paints all hostile targets in view with a red diamond. This makes picking out targets at a distance *extremely* easy. Only foes with Cold Blooded can avoid the target acquisition in your scope, and you can still spot them normally. The Target Finder is ideal for covering a static area at medium to long range. It makes picking targets out of busy cover extremely easy.

A good long-range AR or LMG with a Target Finder can be a real terror when covering an objective area.

The Target Finder is a very obscuring optic, essentially taking up your entire view like a sniper scope while in ADS. This makes the Target Finder a slightly worse choice than a basic optic or Iron Sights if you are concerned about situational awareness when fighting with a mobile build. The target highlighting makes the Target Finder better for camping out and covering a static objective area.

If you are a new player, the Target Finder can also help you with locating players hiding behind hard cover on any map. But be careful about relying too much on the Target Finder; it can hamper training your ability to spot threats without the targeting assistance. Use it to learn common camping spots. Then remember to keep an eye on those areas when you round corners or sweep an area in ADS.

HYBRID OPTIC
Dual scope; combines Reflex and ACOG Sight functionality

The Hybrid Optic is exactly what the name implies: a combination optical sight that has both a Reflex Sight-style red dot and an ACOG Sight-style zooming sight. Switch between the scopes by pressing Sprint while in ADS. The transition between scopes is nearly instantaneous, so the Hybrid is very flexible and easy to use at medium to medium-long range.

The Hybrid doesn't have the same sway reduction as the ACOG Sight. In exchange, it gives you the benefits of both a medium- and a longer-range optic for the price of one Attachment slot; not a bad deal.

> Scope Switching

Because the transition between scope modes is nearly instant, it's easy to cycle view modes based on the distance of your target. However, because fractions of a second matter when you're facing an alert opponent with a gun aimed in your direction, it's best to have the appropriate scope already selected.

Note that you cannot switch scopes until you are fully in ADS. This can be awkward if you were in ACOG Sight mode and you ADS against a close-medium range opponent. Try to switch to the scope that most suits the area you are patrolling before you drop ADS after downing a target.

MILLIMETER SCANNER

Range: 1000
Wall penetrating millimeter wave scanning optic

The Millimeter Scanner (MMS) resembles the Reflex Sight as a general optical Attachment, but it also has the powerful ability to quite literally see through walls. While in ADS, periodic scanning waves project from the scope into the world, giving you a glimpse at hostile targets through any nearby surfaces.

The further a target is, the more unclear the scan is. A target with Cold Blooded is all but impossible to spot unless they are completely stationary when they are hit by a scanner sweep. The MMS is a powerful tool for room clearing in urban areas, and is equally effective when defending an area. It allows you to detect incoming threats before they come into view.

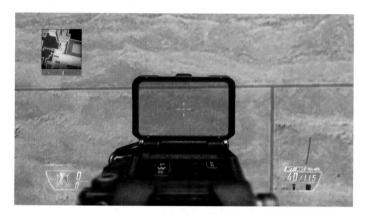

The MMS pairs especially well with the Adjustable Stock Attachment and a shotgun or SMG. You can then move at full speed while still sweeping for hostile targets. You can also use it with Smoke grenades and Scavenger. Smoke an area, use the MMS to down targets through the smoke, then restock from the packs they drop, and do it again.

The MMS actually has a touch *less* zoom than the Reflex Sight, so it is a poor choice for long distance combat. However, it does have a remarkably clear frame, giving easy target acquisition at short ranges. It's easy to get myopia with the MMS equipped. Don't fall into the bad habit of looking for targets behind walls, instead of targets out in the open that can shoot you! Use the MMS to *augment* your situational awareness; don't let it distract you.

FAST MAG

Dual taped magazines for most weapons, faster reload for others

On most assault rifles and SMGs, Fast Mag provides an equal speed increase on reloads and when exchanging the mag for a fresh one. While the reload animations look different, they take the same amount of time. On weapons that have the Fast Mag Attachment but don't actually use taped twin magazines, Fast Mags simply speeds up the reload time. For weapons like the Executioner, this is a speed-loader, while the R-870 and KSG shotguns reload two shells at a time; on other weapons the animation is quicker.

Fast Mags are extremely important for any build expecting to engage in a lot of mid- and close-range combat, where a slow reload can get you killed. For builds where you expect to engage at long range, or where you are completely stealthy, fast reloads are less critical.

FORE GRIP

Very slightly reduces recoil

The Fore Grip is a simple Attachment that reduces recoil while in ADS. This can be very useful for stabilizing long-range fire, and increases your overall accuracy slightly. The Fore Grip tends to be most useful on weapons that have significant recoil. Already stable weapons don't receive much benefit. The HAMR LMG receives a larger recoil reduction than other weapons.

SUPPRESSOR

Eliminates red dot on radar when firing

The Suppressor is a powerful stealth Attachment that eliminates your red dot on the minimap when you fire your weapon. It also reduces muzzle flash and dampens the sound of your weapon firing, providing additional stealth benefits.

The Suppressor is essential for stealthy CQC builds running Ghost and an SMG or AR. It allows you to operate in enemy territory more effectively. The tradeoff for the stealth power of the Suppressor is slight loss of effective range. The Suppressor increases damage falloff, meaning you will need an extra shot or two to down your target at a shorter distance than usual. Because the Suppressor has no effect on your shots to kill at close range, it is especially well suited to SMGs and CQC combat in general. You can certainly take down targets at a distance, just be aware you may need a few extra bullets.

The Suppressor has slightly less of an impact on damage falloff for shotguns, due to their already short range. Be aware that losing range on a shotgun means losing *actual* range. Unlike other weapons, once shotguns reach their maximum distance, the pellets no longer deal any damage. A Suppressor reduces the range at which you can hit your target period.

Sniper rifles also have a significant penalty to damage when using a Suppressor that is different from the way other weapons are handled. SRs typically kill in one shot when you score a hit on a certain part of the body.

The Suppressor bumps that target area "up." This means that where a waist shot would be fatal without a Suppressor, you need to score a neck or head shot to kill with a Suppressor. This usually makes the Suppressor a poor choice for the bolt-action rifles. However, it is usable on the semi-automatics, where you can fire two quick shots and down a target reliably.

The SVU-AS sniper rifle also suffers a slightly greater recoil recovery penalty than other suppressed weapons. Although, this is still easily manageable given its semi-automatic fire type.

The Suppressor has a very slight penalty to recoil recovery, though the penalty is small. Also, because the Suppressor dampens muzzle flash, it can actually improve *perceived* recoil while aiming—that is, you have a clearer view of your target while firing.

ADJUSTABLE STOCK

Full speed ADS movement

The Adjustable Stock Attachment allows you to move at your full movement speed while in ADS. Normally, entering ADS slows your movement, but the Stock lets you continue to strafe at high speed while firing precision shots. The Adjustable Stock is very effective at close-medium to medium range, where your increased mobility can help evade incoming fire. This is especially true with the Lightweight and Toughness Perks equipped.

However, be aware that moving at a faster speed while in ADS can impact your aim. This is true if you are used to moving at a certain speed while in ADS with a given weapon class, particularly for targets at long range.

QUICKDRAW HANDLE

Halves ADS time

The Quickdraw Handle Attachment has a simple and powerful effect. It allows you to enter ADS more quickly. For LMGs, it shaves about a quarter of the time off, while all other weapon types lose about half the normal ADS time. This is a very powerful Attachment for mid-range combat where you expect to ADS often. It can save your life at shorter ranges when up against weapons that have accurate hipfire.

Quickdraw Handle is also surprisingly strong on shotguns. All of them benefit from the increased accuracy while in ADS. However, using ADS regularly in CQC is usually a bad idea—Quickdraw Handle can mitigate that weakness.

GRENADE LAUNCHER

Provides an under-barrel grenade launcher with two grenades

The Grenade Launcher Attachment gives you an under-barrel launcher with two grenades that you can use to flush out campers, bombard objective areas, or nail targets behind cover. The grenade fired from the launcher must reach a minimum distance before they are armed. Don't waste your time trying to "hipfire" a grenade at a nearby target.

At a distance, aiming for the ground near your target is the best way to score a kill. For targets at longer ranges, you need to practice with the flight arc of the grenade to hit targets inside windows or doorways. If you manage to hit someone directly with the grenade while it is in flight, it is an instant kill (even at close range). However, this isn't a common occurrence.

Note that the Fast Mag Attachment has *no* effect on the reload speed. The Grenade Launcher does not reload quickly. Be careful about using it if you suspect enemies are nearby.

SELECT FIRE

Allows fire select between burst/semi and fully auto

Select Fire is a new Attachment to the *Call of Duty* series. It allows you to switch an SMG or AR between semi-auto or burst-fire and fully-automatic fire modes. In the case of SMGs, this gives them an unusual degree of medium-range flexibility, though it does *not* improve their damage profiles. Hitting targets at medium range gets a bit easier, but you still need to land more shots than ARs on average. For ARs, semi-auto and burst-fire variants get more close-range punch, while fully-auto types can use burst-fire mode for better mid- to long-range accuracy. When using Select Fire on what is normally an automatic weapon, the burst mode has a greater recenter speed per shot. This actually reduces recoil in a way that you can't get when burst-firing on full auto.

Select Fire is a useful Attachment, but keep a couple things in mind. First, you must *use* Select Fire for it to have a significant impact on your performance. This sounds obvious, but if you take Select Fire and don't switch fire modes as you shift around the battlefield, you're wasting an Attachment choice. Second, for some weapons, Select Fire takes up an Attachment slot to do something that you can arguably do yourself—control your fire-rate with automatic weapons to burst at a distance. In the case of the semi-auto and burst-fire SMG and ARs, however, it does give you a fully auto option that can be quite helpful for CQC engagements.

Experiment with the Select Fire Attachment. In some ways it *doubles* the number of SMGs and ARs in the game. It changes up the accuracy profile and combat behavior of the weapons significantly. While equipped, Select Fire conveniently remembers the last fire mode it was set to if you die, so you don't have to constantly switch. Changing fire modes is also quick. Shifting as you move in and out of CQC to medium-range engagement areas is fairly safe.

FMJ

Maximizes penetration, boosts bullet damage against Scorestreaks

FMJ is a simple and useful Attachment. It maximizes the penetration value of your weapon, letting you penetrate surfaces more easily. It also greatly increases bullet damage against Scorestreaks. This includes *all* aerial streaks such as the UAV or VTOL Warship, as well as ground-based streaks like the AGR and Guardian turret.

LMGs are noticeably powerful against streaks with this Attachment. They already inflict good damage at range, and the FMJ multiplier lets them down streaks easily with their deep magazines. However, even SMGs and ARs benefit. SMGs in particular get a big boost in their penetration, which is normally quite weak.

Experiment with the FMJ Attachment and the Engineer Perk. It lets you "see through walls," giving you a very powerful battlefield advantage. You can spot and eliminate enemies, Equipment, and Scorestreaks safely and easily.

EXTENDED CLIP
Boosts magazine capacity by roughly 30%

The Extended Clip Attachment simply boosts your magazine size. These deeper magazines can be very useful with the high fire rate SMGs, or for ARs to keep enough ammo for downing multiple targets. Note that the Extended Clip increases reload time by 10%.

It's very important to get used to using the deeper magazines by forcing yourself to *not* reload after downing a single target. You frequently have enough ammunition after taking out one enemy that you can easily down a second (and sometimes a third). Avoiding that reload can save your life if another enemy investigates the death of a teammate. Because of this ability, the Extended Clip has a very similar function to that of the Fast Mags Attachment. It strengthens you in CQC to close-medium range, by cutting down on the danger of reloading with enemies nearby.

The Extended Clip is also helpful for any weapon with the Rapid Fire Attachment. You burn through ammo at a ferocious rate when using it. Most snipers and shotguns don't need this Attachment, though the Saiga-12 and M1216 do gain some benefit from it.

LONG BARREL
Extends damage falloff range slightly

The Long Barrel is a specialized Attachment that *improves* damage falloff, extending the range at which you can take down a target in fewer bullets.

For SMGs, this effect is minor, but it can be helpful on builds using a Laser Sight to hipfire targets at a distance. The Long Barrel has a similarly small impact on pistol performance. Remember that the Executioner is a "shotgun" in pistol form, so it benefits in the same manner as other shotguns with increased range. In the case of shotguns, this Attachment is important. It actually extends the range at which you can hit targets *period*. It is a valuable Attachment once unlocked.

RAPID FIRE
Increases rate of fire but weakens accuracy and range

Rapid Fire is an unusual Attachment that greatly strengthens a weapon in CQC at the cost of long-range performance. Equipping Rapid Fire boosts your rate of fire, worsens hipfire spread, and worsens your weapons ability to recover from recoil while in ADS. In essence, you are trading increased rate of fire for close-range time to kill, at the cost of long-range accuracy and some damage falloff.

This makes SMGs into absolute powerhouses in CQC, but weakens their ability to fight effectively at medium range. If you plan on using an SMG to hipfire at close-medium range, you may want to keep the Laser Sight and skip Rapid Fire.

You lose the very precise hipfire benefits of the Laser Sight while using Rapid Fire.

Of course, if you want absolutely supreme hipfire at close range only, Laser Sight and Rapid Fire do work well! In the case of LMGs, this can simply make them more lethal due to their high damage *if* you can handle the increased recoil. Experiment with each LMG, as well as using a Fore Grip to moderate the recoil.

The Skorpion EVO, which already has an extremely high rate of fire, gains slightly less rate of fire than other weapons, and suffers a bit more damage falloff and hipfire spread. That said, it also makes the Skorpion even more lethal than it already is in CQC (just be sure to bring Fast Mags or Extended Clip!).

DUAL BAND
Advanced Optic; moderate zoom, provides thermal and night vision

The Dual Band is an advanced optical scope that provides *both* thermal and night vision in one sight. This gives you a clear view of targets in almost any situation. The Dual Band is especially useful for spotting targets in low light areas, heavy cover, or through smoke.

Because the Dual Band is a full screen sniper style scope, it is somewhat obscuring. You can easily lose situational awareness if you spend too long staring down the scope and not enough time checking your surroundings.

The Dual Band gives a slight penalty to recoil recovery while in ADS. The penalty is a bit large for LMGs—a tradeoff for the ease of target acquisition. Cold Blooded targets are completely grey while looking through the Dual Band, which makes them a bit harder to spot.

Because the Dual Band can pierce smoke, Smoke grenades combined with Scavenger can let you obscure an objective or key chokepoint and easily cover any targets that enter the area.

VARIABLE ZOOM
Simple sniper-style scope; also usable on LMGs

The Variable Zoom scope is simply a modified "basic" Sniper scope that allows you to adjust the level of zoom while sighted in. This makes the Variable Zoom perfect for a mobile sniper that engages targets at a variety of distances. It can also be used on LMGs if you plan on engaging at primarily long ranges. Note that LMGs take a slight penalty to recoil recovery while using the Variable Zoom scope. Exercise trigger discipline while firing at great distances.

BALLISTICS CPU
Reduces sway significantly

The Ballistics CPU has a simple and useful effect. It reduces visible sway while in ADS with a sniper rifle. Note that this doesn't change how you stabilize a sniper rifle by holding your breath. It just makes getting your crosshair centered in on a target or area a bit easier.

IRON SIGHTS
Special Attachment for Ballista; allows for medium-range unscoped sniping

The Iron Sights "attachment" is a special case for the Ballista sniper rifle only. It allows you to use the Ballista with Iron Sights instead of a sniper scope. This means you can take quicker ADS shots than would be possible with a sniper scope, but at the cost of having no long-range zoom.

Note that Ballista retains its normal sniper damage profile with this Attachment. You need to score upper body shots to reliably down targets. Accuracy is still critical for success if you're going to get into heads-up firefights with ARs and LMGs or SMGs while on the move.

DUAL WIELD
Special Attachment for pistols; allows twin pistol usage

Dual wield allows you to put a pistol in both hands for double the firepower! Of course, this comes at the cost of any ability to fight at a distance. You can no longer ADS, and your hipfire spread is significant. With that in mind, Dual Wield gives you superb close-range firepower. A pair of dual wielded Kap-40s, B23Rs, or Tac-45s makes a very strong fast-swapping backup weapon for an AR, LMG, or sniper rifle.

TACTICAL KNIFE
Special Attachment for pistols; wields an offhand knife with pistol

The Tactical Knife Attachment allows you to use your combat knife at the same time as your pistol, giving you a much speedier stabbing animation and recovery time. You don't suffer any penalties to the use of your pistol while using the Tactical Knife. It gives you a stealthy edge in very tight CQC encounters. The Tactical Knife does slightly increase your lunge range, as long as you are moving toward the enemy when you melee.

TRI-BOLT
Fires all three crossbow bolts simultaneously

The Tri-Bolt is a special Attachment for the crossbow that fires all three of the loaded explosive bolts simultaneously. This depletes your ammo more quickly, but ensures that near-misses are fatal when the bolts explode. Because it does not provide any benefit for direct hits, you need to decide if the increased ammo consumption is offset by the ability to kill with indirect shots (or bring Scavenger!).

EQUIPMENT

Equipment gives you more options in combat, featuring tools to help you either clear a room or defend one. Because of the Pick 10 system, it is now possible to run builds that have no Lethal or Tactical Equipment. You now have to weigh the value of a single grenade against that of a Perk or a weapon.

Remember that the Scavenger Perk allows you to resupply all Equipment. This makes any build that plans to utilize Equipment heavily much more viable and effective.

The Fast Hands Perk is also extremely useful for any build planning to use Equipment regularly. It allows for double-speed Equipment usage, which can save your life. It also makes Equipment usage in combat effective instead of risky.

> Blast Radius

The "Kill" and "Hitmarker" ranges on the Lethal explosives are directly usable on the maps in this guide. Use the range grid on any map and you can get a rough idea of how large of an area the blast from an explosive covers.

LETHAL SLOT

GRENADE
Range: Kill 200, Hitmarker 240
Basic thrown grenade

The Frag grenade is a timed hand grenade that can be "cooked" by holding the Grenade button before tossing it. The grenade has a 3.5-second fuse. Each second that you hold it, your crosshair pulses, allowing for easy timing of your throw. You can use the timer pulses to airburst the grenade, precisely taking down targets just inside windows or over key objectives.

Grenades roll or bounce after landing, which can make precise targeting a bit tricky if you don't airburst them. However, they do have the best blast radius of the basic explosives, so landing anywhere near your target is good enough!

Frag grenades are typically better at slightly longer ranges than Semtex. This is simply because you need time to cook a grenade to properly airburst it (something you cannot safely do in CQC situations). Even Fast Hands doesn't help with the timer!

> Toss It Back

You can throw Frag grenades back if they land very close to you. But make the decision quickly! If that grenade was cooked at all, it's going to blow up in your hands. The Fast Hands Perk resets the grenade timer if you pick one up, guaranteeing you can always throw a live grenade back safely.

SEMTEX
Range: Kill 130, Hitmarker 230
Sticky grenade with a short fuse

Semtex is a special type of grenade that sticks wherever it lands—to walls, floors, ceilings, and even other players! Semtex has a shorter effective explosion radius for a kill than the other explosive Lethal Equipment. It makes up for this with ease of delivery.

Semtex can be thrown and instantly sticks and detonates quickly thereafter. Also, while its fatal blast radius is short, it still inflicts serious damage to about the same distance as the other explosives. When deciding between Semtex and Frags, Semtex is generally a better choice if your explosive delivery is time sensitive. For instance, if you're playing a highly-mobile class or you need an explosive to threaten an objective quickly.

< 194 195 >

C4
Range: Kill 220, Hitmarker 280
Remotely detonated high-power explosive

The most powerful of the Lethal explosives, C4 is a remotely detonated explosive that can stick to any surface (but *not* to other players like Semtex). C4 is ideal for covering objectives or key chokepoints. It's especially useful if you are in a situation where you can monitor the route the C4 is guarding while also covering another approach with your gun.

You can detonate C4 very quickly by double-tapping the Reload button. This works even while it's in midair as you throw it! This allows you to use C4 as an instant "grenade" of sorts. But be aware that its throwing distance is worse than the other thrown explosives.

Because C4 has a large effective blast radius, consider sticking it to ceilings inside small rooms or hallways. Players tend to notice C4 packs sitting out in the open, *especially* on objectives. That said, you can abuse C4's remote detonation in objective modes (especially Domination) by listening for sounds from the objective or via announcer updates. Hear a flag changing hands? Trip your C4 and score a kill!

> Which Explosive?

Grenades and Semtex are the most "basic" of the explosive Lethal Equipment. Use grenades if you're planning on fighting mostly at medium range, and Semtex if CQC is expected.

Grenades are more lethal if you learn to airburst them effectively. Semtex is easier to use, but it can't be thrown around corners or bounce around in rooms like a Frag grenade.

C4 is a bit of a mix. It's not as fast as Semtex, or as slow as a grenade, but it lacks the throwing distance and is more visible than either (though it does *not* throw up a nearby explosive HUD warning like grenades do).

You can use C4 to cover an area or objective, similar to the way that Claymores or Betties can. But it lacks a proximity trigger, making it somewhat weaker unless you can monitor it yourself.

The type of explosive you take should mesh well with your intended role on the battlefield. Consider if you're going to be playing offense or defense, CQC or long range, and if you plan to take Scavenger or Fast Hands to make heavy use of your Lethal Equipment.

BOUNCING BETTY
Range: Kill 210, Hitmarker 220
Motion-sensitive 360-degree proximity mine

The Bouncing Betty is a proximity mine that triggers when any hostile walks within range. Triggering the Betty causes it to jump into the air and explode, showering the area immediately around it with lethal chest-high shrapnel. You can duck or go prone to avoid half or all of the explosion. If you are standing, odds aren't in your favor for surviving. The Bouncing Betty is easier to use than the Claymore, but skilled players can also avoid it more easily.

CLAYMORE
Range: Kill 195, Hitmarker 230
Motion-sensitive proximity mine with a frontal blast arc

Claymores launch a frontal explosion that is almost always lethal to any unfortunate hostile that trips them.

However, scoring kills with Claymores requires that you place them carefully. Poorly placed Claymores *can* simply be outrun by a sprinting player. To score kills with your Claymores, place them just around corners or inside doorways facing *away* from the doorway or corner. You want your targets to walk past the Claymore and trip it so the explosion hits them as they move away from it.

If you place a Claymore right in a doorway facing forward, not only can enemies easily see and shoot it from a distance, they can also potentially sprint at it from the side and slip through the entrance before the explosion can hit them.

> Which Type of Mine?

Claymores are a bit more effective at guarding areas with lots of sharp corners and narrow pathways. Betties, on the other hand, are better in open terrain where you can't be completely certain which direction an enemy will approach.

Both are most effective if you spend a bit of time examining the terrain on the map, *especially* in objective modes. In all modes, Claymores and Betties are useful for protecting objective areas or guarding your back if you're camping an area.

Remember, there are a lot of Perks and Equipment that can bypass mines. But even having your mine detonate without a kill can alert you to an enemy nearby, which can easily save your life.

COMBAT AXE
Stealthy, instantly lethal throwing weapon

The Combat Axe gives you a throwing weapon that is instantly lethal if it makes contact with a target. The Combat Axe can be picked back up to be reused. The Combat Axe flies very quickly, with a slight arc to its flight path. It bounces off of hard surfaces, making bank shots possible. Unlike the other Lethal Equipment options, the Combat Axe doesn't give you much indirect fire ability, nor can it guard your back. However, it does give you a quick weapon that can kill in one shot, almost silently.

Remember that you can throw a Combat Axe at any time, even while climbing a ladder or reloading. You can also use Equipment while mantling, which can allow you to throw a Combat Axe when traversing through a window or up a cliff. This can save your life in some situations if a target comes into view at close range.

> **Enhanced Visibility**

In previous *Call of Duty* titles, tracking down your thrown weapons was tricky. This time around, the Combat Axe and Ballistic Knife have a bright highlight and flash while on the ground. This makes locating and recovering them much easier. Even better, you no longer have to hold Reload to pick them up—simply walking nearby is good enough!

TACTICAL SLOT

SMOKE GRENADE

Creates an obscuring cloud of smoke for instant cover

Smoke grenades are invaluable for creating cover. They detonate as soon as they hit the ground, and instantly fill the area with smoke. This instant effect really enhances their utility. Smoke grenades are useful over objectives, in open areas where enemies have a clear line of sight to you (or your team), or when crossing an open area. Use Smoke grenades to generate cover to secure an objective or to cross a dangerous area. Remember that the MMS and (particularly) Dual Band Attachments can both see through smoke. You can only carry one Smoke grenade. Although they can be replenished with Scavenger.

CONCUSSION

Stuns and staggers targets

Concussion grenades stagger enemies that are even grazed by the blast, stopping their sprint, slowing their movement, causing their aim to sway wildly, and making them turn extremely slowly. This makes Concussion grenades very lethal when used on a highly-mobile CQC build. You can tag enemies with Concussion grenades and finish them with ease while they are nearly immobilized.

Unlike Flashbangs, which can blind targets to varying degrees, Concussion grenades *always* have an impact on your target if you get a hitmarker. Concussion grenades can also be used to temporarily disable Equipment. Bouncing Betties, Claymores, Shock Charges, and C4 can all be shut down briefly if you hit them with a Concussion.

Concussion grenades do not detonate until they hit the ground, so they cannot be airbursted. However, you can throw them a good distance.

FLASHBANG

Blinds and disorients hostiles

Flashbang grenades blind your enemies. Flashbangs completely blind enemies if they are looking at the grenade when it detonates, and partially if they are looking away. A perfect hit from a Flashbang can *completely* disable multiple enemies for several seconds. The tricky part about using Flashbangs is that you never know *how* blind your targets are.

You do get a hitmarker when the Flashbang goes off and it affects someone, but there is no indication if the blinding effect was total or partial. As a result, be careful about using Flashbangs to attempt a room clearing. A target behind cover may be barely affected by the blinding flare. Also, if they are pointing towards the door you threw the grenade in, you can expect a hail of bullets to meet you when you run in, blind or not.

Flashbangs can be airburst. They have a short timer and detonate once it expires, whether in the air or on the ground. This makes Flashbangs useful for throwing at or airbursting over objective areas. Timed right, you can guarantee that several enemies will be at least partially impaired, because any defenders camping around an objective are very likely to be looking *at* that objective.

SHOCK CHARGE

Electric shock temporarily paralyzes hostiles

The Shock Charge is a new support tool, a *Tactical* proximity mine. When thrown, the Shock Charge sticks to any surface (if it contacts a player it simply detonates instantly). Once in place, the Shock Charge trips if a hostile moves anywhere near it.

Any enemy hit by the Shock Charge is temporarily paralyzed. The blast from the Shock Charge is *very* disorienting and powerful—more debilitating than a Concussion and about as bad as eating a Flashbang right in the face. The duration on the paralysis is very short. However, it all but guarantees a free kill if you, or a teammate, are watching an area with Shock Charges guarding any avenues of approach. Shock Charges can guard your back as an early warning tool. When you hear the charge go off and get the hitmarker, you can swing around to intercept the hostile coming from your flank or rear.

< 196   197 >

EMP GRENADE

Disables and destroys hostile Equipment

The EMP grenade is a powerful tool for shutting down enemy Equipment and ground-based Scorestreaks. All regular Equipment is instantly destroyed by the EMP, as well as the Sentry and Guardian turrets. Even the AGR can be destroyed in two EMP hits, and a single hit shuts it down for several seconds. EMP grenades do have a slight impact on players. The grenades can disable their radar, shut down any advanced optics they are using, and disable their ability to call in Scorestreaks. EMP grenades are very useful in combination with Engineer and Scavenger. This combination allows you to single-handedly dismantle the enemy team's defenses around an objective or area.

SENSOR GRENADE

Provides localized positional information on hostiles

The Sensor grenade is a new type of grenade that creates a temporary scanning field. This field gives you precise locational and directional information on any enemy tagged by the grenade. The radar info provided by the Sensor grenade is identical to that of an Orbital VSAT, but the area covered is much smaller.

When a Sensor grenade hits the ground, it projects sensor beams to *any hostile within line of sight*. This means that it *can* be blocked by terrain, so don't trust the Sensor grenade to catch absolutely every enemy in an area with heavy cover. The Sensor grenade is particularly good at catching targets in open, high-traffic areas. Lobbing a few grenades ahead of your team as you move towards an expected conflict zone can give you an edge, especially if you report enemy positions to your flanking or long-range teammates.

The Sensor pulses four times after landing, and then explodes. This gives you a brief overview of any enemies in the area. The final explosion paints enemy targets on the mini map for an additional five seconds. If it detonates in a small room, you can keep several hostiles painted for a breach or wall penetration shots. Be wary of advancing if you are tagged by the blast! This is good to know if you're the one using it, or if an enemy Sensor grenade explodes near you. The explosion doesn't inflict any meaningful damage, but it can stop someone from sprinting if they happen to get tagged by it.

BLACK HAT

Hack and disable hostile Equipment or Scorestreaks

An unusual new tool, the Black Hat PDA is a hacking device that can be used to disable hostile Equipment or damage enemy Scorestreaks. When used against Scorestreaks, the Black Hat counts as a "missile hit." If you use it on an aerial Scorestreak that has flares, it uses up one of the flares just as though you had fired a locking missile at it. Against ground-based Equipment or Scorestreaks, a single hack is sufficient to disable the device. You can also use the Black Hat to recover friendly and enemy Care Packages. On an enemy Care Package, you steal the contents and booby trap it. This works through walls out to a distance of 750. Beyond that, it needs line of sight.

The Black Hat gives you extra flexibility. You can take it instead of a launcher to help deal with enemy streaks or Equipment. But be aware that using the Black Hat takes time. You have to hold the Black Hat on target while you hack, just as though you were locking on with a missile. And because it does take time, you risk exposing yourself to danger while you are defenseless. On the upshot, the Black Hat is a lot less visible and has a decent range (unlike standing out in the open trying to target a UAV with a launcher). So in some situations (particularly when paired with Engineer), you can disable enemy defenses safely.

TACTICAL INSERTION

Allows you to place your own spawn location

The Tactical Insertion drops a piece of Equipment on the ground that fixes your next respawn point. This is near vital Equipment when on offense in certain objective modes, and less critical in other game modes. Use Tactical Insertions to cut down travel time to an objective point by tucking your insert away behind cover about halfway to the objective on "your" side of the map. Any explosion can destroy a Tactical Insertion. A hostile can destroy it, or even worse, camp it and wait to kill you as soon as you respawn.

TROPHY SYSTEM

Intercepts and destroys any hostile projectiles

The Trophy System provides perfect projectile defense. It destroys *any* type of incoming projectile, including grenades, launcher shots, Scorestreak rockets, and even throwing axes! Each Trophy System can only destroy two incoming projectiles. You can carry a maximum of two, but this is typically enough to protect you against incoming explosives when securing an objective. With Scavenger, you can use Trophy Systems liberally, dropping them near any point of conflict as you see fit.

WILDCARDS

Wildcards allow you to "break the rules" of the Pick 10 system slightly. Each Wildcard does take up a pick, so you need to decide if the added cost is made up for by the benefit offered by the Wildcard. You can take up to three Wildcards.

PRIMARY GUNFIGHTER

Allows a third Attachment on your primary weapon

Primary Gunfighter lets you take a *third* Attachment on your primary weapon. Want a Suppressed, Extended Clip, Laser Sight SMG? Rapid Fire, Fore Grip, Hybrid LMG? Go for it! Primary Gunfighter works well with Scavenger. If you're going to heavily customize your weapon, you want to be able to use it indefinitely.

SECONDARY GUNFIGHTER

Allows a second Attachment on your secondary weapon

Less crucial than Primary Gunfighter, Secondary Gunfighter lets you put a second Attachment on your secondary weapon. Because secondaries tend to be backup weapons anyway, it's rarely a good idea to burn two picks on an extra Attachment for a pistol.

OVERKILL

Allows a second primary weapon

Overkill lets you take a second primary class weapon in your secondary weapon slot. This is most useful for mixing range bands. That is, taking a medium- to long-range weapon along with a CQC powerhouse. An AR, LMG, or sniper rifle paired with a Shotgun or SMG is the typical Overkill setup.

Note that like certain Attachments, Overkill is only worth it if you *use it*. You have to make a point of switching weapons *before* you get into a firefight, so that you have the right weapon in hand. If you don't, you're not fully exploiting Overkill's potential, and it's not worth consuming the pick!

< 198 199 >

PERK 1-2-3 GREED

Allows a second Perk to be taken in any of the three Perk slots

Perk Greed is very powerful. It allows you to take up to six Perks total. However, it is expensive in terms of picks, as you are paying two points for each second Perk in a category. Perk Greed is one of the most useful Wildcards for customizing builds for specific purposes. Whether building a short-range stealth class or a medium-range brawler, Perk Greed allows you to double up on crucial Perks in each Perk category.

DANGER CLOSE

Allows you to take a second Lethal equipment of the same type

Danger Close allows you to take a second Lethal item, giving you the option of taking two explosives (or axes) into battle. When you take Danger Close, you can only double up on the *same* Lethal item you have selected. So, two Frags or two Claymores is okay, but you can't take two different items. Consider bringing Fast Hands and Scavenger if you want to take full advantage of an explosive loadout.

TACTICIAN

Replaces your Lethal slot with a second Tactical slot

Tactician lets you exchange your Lethal slots for a second bank of Tactical Equipment. You can take two Shock Charges and two EMP grenades, but not four Flashbangs. And like Danger Close, bringing Scavenger is advisable if you intend to get the most mileage out of your extra Tactical Equipment. This is very useful for defensive or support builds with Scavenger.

PERKS

Perks are special abilities that grant you advantages on the battlefield. Some Perks are very situational and only useful in certain objective modes, or if your opponents are using certain types of loadouts. Others are much more general and simply enhance your performance at all times.

Choosing how to customize your build with the possibility of equipping six Perks can be daunting, so here are a few words of advice.

> **Use our custom classes as templates.** Each of the custom classes in the Modes section of this guide is built for a specific battlefield role. You can look at the Perks we chose for each class to get a feel for what Perks are useful in what roles.

> *Experiment!* Many Perks come down to personal preference and playstyle. Spend time using them all, especially on your first Prestige while you are learning the game.

> Situational Perks: Flak Jacket, Blind Eye, Hard Wired, and Tactical Mask.

> General-use Perks: Hardline and Scavenger.

> Stealthy Perks: Ghost, Cold Blooded, and Dead Silence.

> Perks that impact your performance in combat: Lightweight, Toughness, Fast Hands, and Dexterity.

> Perks that affect your mobility: Lightweight, Dexterity, and Extreme Conditioning.

> Perks that grant you an information edge: Engineer and Awareness.

Because Perks grant abilities that no Attachment, gun, or piece of Equipment can, they are often central to any build. Choosing your Perks should be one of the first things you do when putting together a new class.

TIER 1

LIGHTWEIGHT

Increases movement speed by 7%
Eliminates falling damage

Lightweight gives a slight boost to your movement speed. Note the difference between the fastest movement classes (pistol, SMG, shotgun, and sniper rifle) and the slowest (LMG and launchers) is 10%, with ARs right in the middle at 5% slower.

While the speed boost is slight, it is very meaningful on SMG or shotgun builds, particularly when combined with Extreme Conditioning. The extra speed can get you into position to seize an objective or flank the enemy team at the start of the round.

Consider keeping a class around with a speedy build specifically for this purpose. This is especially noticeable for flag running in CTF, and reaching the bomb plant site in Demolition or Search & Destroy, but it can also be meaningful to get into a key overwatch or flanking position.

Lightweight's effects in actual combat are subtle. It can give an advantage to hipfiring builds with SMGs or shotguns, or ARs using the Adjustable Stock for full speed ADS movement. However, the benefits are slight in a heads-up firefight.

The positional benefits are more difficult to quantify. Getting into position and sweeping half the enemy team is certainly a good way to start a round, but Lightweight is always a solid Perk in objective modes where speed makes a difference. Lightweight also eliminates falling damage, making some jumps safer to perform, and making it (marginally) safer to drop out of windows or from high ledges.

GHOST

Conceals you from UAVs while moving
Also conceals you while planting or defusing, or controlling Scorestreaks

Ghost is an extremely powerful stealth Perk because so many players rely heavily on UAV sweeps for positional information on enemy movement.

Ghost pairs especially well with a Suppressor for a stealthy build. Without Suppressor, firing your weapon gives away your position, which is especially dangerous if you are fighting away from your team.

Because you are concealed from UAVs while moving, Ghost favors aggressive, mobile, and stealthy builds. Taking an SMG or AR with a Suppressor and constantly flanking the enemy team can make you a serious threat. Stay alert to the position of your teammates relative to the position of the enemy if a hostile UAV goes up. You can expect the enemy to move toward the blips it can see, often moving right past you if you are staying concealed.

Staying mobile hides you from UAVs, you cannot simply stand in place and wiggle to remain concealed. Watch your mini map arrow to learn how much movement you need to stay invisible. It fades out while Ghost is actively concealing you from enemy UAV cover. Ghost does remain effective if you are planting or defusing a bomb, or using a controlled Scorestreak.

If you value stealth, but other blue Perks are important to your build, consider running a CUAV—it's not a complete replacement, but it serves a similar role. Ghost does not conceal you from an enemy VSAT, but a CUAV can conceal you.

FLAK JACKET
Heavily reduces explosive damage

Flak Jacket has a very simple and very powerful effect—it reduces *all* incoming explosive damage. With Flak Jacket active, no single basic explosive, from grenade launchers to Semtex can kill you unless they score a dead-on direct hit. You can run clean over a Claymore or Bouncing Betty without fear, and you may even survive some air support strikes.

Flak Jacket is a generalist "nice to have" Perk, but it is near vital for any build that is serious about tackling objectives. Objective hotspots tend to be constantly bombarded with explosive weapons, so using Flak Jacket to secure such positions is very important.

> **Objective Hero**
>
> Keep a build around with Flak Jacket, Tactical Mask, two Trophy Systems, and Scavenger for the ultimate in objective defense.

BLIND EYE
Automated air support cannot target you

Blind Eye grants total immunity to the targeting of unmanned aerial Scorestreaks, including the Hunter Killer, Stealth Chopper, Escort Drone, Warthog, and Swarm. However, you *can* still be killed by such streaks if a teammate *without* Blind Eye happens to be standing near you when enemy air support opens fire. Mind your positioning!

Blind Eye's protection against Hunter Killers is actually one of the stronger aspects of a Perk that is otherwise somewhat weak in comparison to Cold Blooded. Cold Blooded provides targeting protection against all player-controlled Scorestreaks (and protection against ADS targeting with advanced scopes on top of that).

Protection against the Stealth Chopper and above is important and useful. But because all of the streaks past the Hunter Killer are on the high end of the

Scorestreaks in cost, they are comparatively more rare—meaning Blind Eye isn't always pulling its weight, making it a situational Perk.

However, if you need to take down a stealth chopper, drone, or Warthog that is threatening your team, a build that has Blind Eye, an FHJ-18, and one or two Black Hats with Scavenger can be effective. Otherwise, consider Blind Eye to primarily be protection against the streak-breaking and rage-inducing random Hunter Killer from the sky.

HARDLINE
Earn Scorestreaks roughly 20% faster

Hardline is a very useful utility Perk that speeds up your acquisition of Scorestreaks. Hardline's power is unusual in that it is directly related to *your* personal skill as a player. If you can consistently rack up mid-level Scorestreaks, Hardline can give you the boost needed to hit high-cost Scorestreaks more consistently. However, Hardline is still extremely helpful with low-end streaks. If you run one common support build consisting of UAV and Counter-UAV, and one of Guardian, Lightning Strike, Hellstorm, or Sentry, Hardline can allow you to secure your UAV and CUAV more consistently and potentially loop your entire Scorestreak repeatedly during a match.

Hardline is a worthwhile choice on many builds. The only knock against it is consuming a pick and the slot for another blue Perk that can be more useful for a specialized build. However, if you don't have need for the other blue Perks (or you're willing to burn a Wildcard on Perk 1 Greed), Hardline is a worthy choice for many builds.

In general, taking Hardline on builds that you intend to play in a defensive or supporting manner is more effective than on builds you expect to use in a very aggressive or objective-oriented manner. This is simply due to the risk involved; such builds tend to die more often, breaking their Scorestreak. One last thing to consider is that Hardline acts as a multiplier on the cost of your Scorestreaks; it does *not* increase the actual match score you earn at the end of a game. Hardline speeds up Scorestreak acquisition, not leveling!

TIER 2

COLD BLOODED
Conceals you from Dual Band, Target Finder, Sensor grenade, MMS, and player-controlled Scorestreaks
Removes your red name when targeted

Cold Blooded is another powerful stealth Perk. It gives you protection from all Scorestreak target highlighting, all advanced optic scopes, *and* completely removes your red name when an enemy aims in your direction. The removal of the red name sounds minor but is remarkably powerful. It pairs extremely well with Ghost and a Suppressor to create a stealthy, lethal class.

Cold Blooded is also very useful for medium- to long-range builds that expect to spend a lot of time engaging in ADS battles. The extra time it takes for someone to notice you can give you the edge you need to down your prey. Note that Cold Blooded isn't great for "hiding" from enemies that are aware you're already guarding an area. It's more useful for stealth when you are playing offensively and rapidly shifting your position. Cold Blooded is *more* powerful when you're near enemy players, as they may mistake you for a friendly for a split second too long. The protection from advanced optics is a nice added Perk, but not a defining reason to use Cold Blooded. Enemies may or may not be using those sights, but they'll definitely be targeting you! Cold Blooded also provides some protection against the *controlled* Scorestreaks by hiding the highlighting reticle. This can often save your life against aerial Scorestreaks, and may give you enough time to get into cover against the Sentry Gun, AGR, etc.

HARD WIRED

Immune to the effects of EMP grenades, EMP Systems, and the Counter-UAV

Hard Wired grants immunity to CUAV and EMP disruption, including EMP grenades. Hard Wired is a very specialized Perk. It can be extremely useful for catching complacent enemies off guard. However, the protection against EMPs is less useful in most matches, and even the CUAV immunity is only useful if the enemy team is making use of CUAVs heavily.

If you do run into a situation where the enemy is outright spamming EMP grenades and CUAVs, Hard Wired can protect you. Otherwise, several other green Perks are much more versatile and powerful in a wider range of builds. Like Flak Jacket, Blind Eye, and Tactical Mask, Hard Wired is a situational Perk.

SCAVENGER

Refill ammunition and equipment from packs dropped by enemies killed with non-explosives

Scavenger refills ammunition, including Lethal and Tactical Equipment. Scavenger packs are only dropped by enemies who are killed with bullets, *not* explosives.

Because Scavenger grants you nearly infinite ammunition, it is extremely powerful when making heavy use of Lethal and Tactical Equipment, as well as launchers or the Grenade Launcher Attachment. Scavenger is also very useful when using heavily modified weapons—the extra ammo allows you to maximize your use of your customized weapons. If you love your Gunfighter blinged-out weapons, Scavenger is a must.

Scavenger is a near automatic pick if you plan on using equipment heavily. Being able to constantly resupply your Tactical and Lethal grenades massively increases their battlefield impact. Note that Scavenger is somewhat less valuable if you're planning on deliberately getting yourself into dangerous situations around objectives. You need to stay alive to maximize Scavenger's power!

TOUGHNESS

Heavily reduces flinch when shot

Toughness heavily reduces flinch when you are hit by bullets. This can give you a decisive edge in a heads-up firefight with another player. Toughness is at its best on AR and LMG builds where you plan to engage at medium range or further using ADS. It can also be very helpful for customized SMGs built for close-medium to medium-range ADS combat. Toughness is still helpful on pistols, shotguns, and sniper rifles. Although it's somewhat less consistent than it is on the other weapon classes.

Toughness is a very simple, very effective Perk. It is aimed toward a specific playstyle, rather than a specific situation or enemy behavior. You're *always* going to be taking bullet fire, so Toughness is active and useful during any match in any mode.

FAST HANDS

Doubles weapon swap speed and Equipment usage

Resets fuse when throwing back Frag grenades

Fast Hands doubles your weapon switch times and cuts the use time on *all* types of Lethal and Tactical Equipment. This makes Fast Hands extremely useful when carrying a weapon that switches slowly in your secondary slot (anything other than a pistol!). Fast Hands can also save your life if you are engaged in a close-range battle and need to quickly switch to your secondary if your weapon runs dry (or is simply ill-suited to CQC, in the case of LMGs or sniper rifles).

The Equipment speed boost is also extremely handy. This opens up grenade usage in CQC—something that is normally a very bad idea. It pairs extremely well with any build utilizing Scavenger alongside Tactical and Lethal Equipment. Fast Hands is also very useful with the Overkill Wildcard. Though because of the cost in picks, you may simply wish to use Fast Hands with a second weapon acquired on the battlefield. That said, pairing Fast Hands with an Overkill build using a sniper/AR/LMG mainhand and a shotgun/SMG offhand gives you the best of medium-to-long and close-range combat all in one class.

Curiously, Fast Hands can be handy for battlefield mobility. Because switching to a lightweight weapon allows you to sprint further, Fast Hands reduces some of the risk of weapon switching before and after sprinting. This effect is minor overall, but it can and will save your life now and again.

Finally, Fast Hands resets the timer on Frag grenades if you pick them up to toss them back. This is a very minor benefit, as it requires a specific grenade in a specific situation, but hey, it's a free perk for your Perk!

TIER 3

DEAD SILENCE

Eliminates movement sounds

Dead silence all but eliminates your normal movement sounds, and severely reduces your sprinting sounds. It is extremely useful in Search & Destroy, and any stealthy build where you expect to spend a great deal of time in enemy territory or near hostiles. Dead Silence does *not* help with other sounds that you make while jumping, planting, using Equipment, defusing a bomb, or firing your weapons.

One strange quirk worth mentioning: Dead Silence is more useful if your opponents have decent audio setups and are alert to movement sounds—something you cannot control or guarantee. This makes evaluating how effective Dead Silence is for you in any given situation difficult!

A bog standard stealthy build is a Suppressor-equipped weapon with Ghost, Cold Blooded, and Dead Silence. You can often get away with removing Dead Silence or Cold Blooded, but if you're playing in organized League play (or in S&D!), we do recommend using Dead Silence, as you often run into more alert players in those matches.

< 202 203 >

ENGINEER

Highlights enemy Equipment and ground Scorestreaks through walls

Delays triggered explosives

Reroll and booby trap Care Packages

Engineer is a powerful Perk that highlights *all* placed Equipment and ground-based Scorestreaks in bright red, and makes them visible through walls! On top of that already powerful effect, Engineer also allows you to reroll friendly Care Packages, booby trap enemy Care Packages, or defuse a friendly package.

Engineer is extremely useful when assaulting a defended objective, as it allows you to spot all Shock Charges, Claymores, Betties, C4, Sentry Guns, Guardians, and so on well before they are a threat. You can also provide information on the location of any dangerous equipment or streaks to your entire team, magnifying the impact of Engineer on a match. Engineer can also be handy to locate campers—players often place Claymores, Betties, or Shock Charges near their camp grounds. If you spot a Claymore at the top of a staircase leading to a room, tossing a grenade into the room is usually a safe bet.

A single player running Engineer can reroll an entire team's Care Packages and spot hostile equipment for the whole team if they communicate well! And if all that isn't enough, Engineer also delays the detonation of Bouncing Betties, Claymores, or Shock Charges if you *do* trip them.

TACTICAL MASK

Reduces effect of Flashbangs, Concussion grenades, and Shock Charges

Tactical Mask is a powerful defensive Perk that renders you nearly immune to the effects of Concussion, Flash, and Shock Charge grenades. This is very useful when attacking or defending a static objective area where you expect to be bombarded with grenades. Although its overall power depends entirely on the loadout of the opposing team—if they don't use those Tacticals, Tactical Mask is a wasted pick.

Pairing Tactical Mask with Flak Jacket works well, as it guarantees that no matter *what* type of grenade is thrown in your direction (or explosive that you stumble across), you are likely to walk away unscathed.

EXTREME CONDITIONING

Sprint for twice as long

Extreme Conditioning has a simple and useful effect: It doubles the distance you can sprint. This is both powerful and dangerous. It is vital and useful in any mode where you need to cover a great deal of ground, or on larger maps simply to reach critical locations. However, it also encourages constant sprinting, which is a very bad habit to get into. Sprinting around a corner with someone waiting for you is near the top of lethal tactical mistakes you can make.

Use Extreme Conditioning to reach objective areas or the "front lines," so to speak, but try to avoid blindly sprinting into enemy territory. If you're out in front of your entire team, odds are there's an enemy lying in wait nearby.

> **Sprinting Distance**
>
> Remember that your movement speed and distance you can sprint are both controlled by what weapon or item you are holding in your hands. If you're trying to cover a lot of ground quickly, pulling out a lightweight weapon before you start sprinting is the way to do it.
>
> Just don't do this if you're in hostile territory. Encountering an enemy while you're sprinting with the wrong weapon in hand gives away kills!

AWARENESS

Doubles range at which you can hear players moving

Hear players with Dead Silence at normal range

Awareness is the inverse of Dead Silence. Instead of dampening your movement sounds, it amplifies the audio of enemy players' footsteps, doubling the distance at which you can hear walking or sprinting. Awareness *nullifies* Dead Silence, putting the range you can hear anyone running that Perk back to normal distance.

This does create an unusual problem, however. The range at which you can hear players with or without Dead Silence is different, which can make pinpointing locations very tricky without a lot of practice. Similarly, switching between builds that do or do not run Awareness can also cause you problems as you get used to detecting players at a certain distance and then that distance changes when you swap out Awareness.

Also like Dead Silence, Awareness is more useful if *you* have a good audio setup. With headphones and in-game music turned off, you can more easily hear incoming threats. But if you're playing on quiet speakers in a noisy room, Awareness won't do much for you!

We recommend either running Awareness on a *lot* of your builds, with your audio settings tuned for it, or avoiding its use most of the time. It's important that you become accustomed to the battlefield audio and detection of other players on every map in a consistent manner. Awareness is a Perk that rewards you for dedication to using it!

DEXTERITY

Regain use of weapon more quickly after sprinting

Mantle and climb at double speed

Dexterity doubles the speed you climb or mantle over objects, and reduces the delay before your weapon comes up after sprinting or mantling an object. This makes Dexterity a very useful all-around mobility Perk, and improves your chances of survival if you are sprinting often—very useful for mobile SMG or shotgun builds. It can also help for mid-range AR builds that make use of the Quickdraw Attachment to bring up your sights as quickly as possible.

Dexterity pairs well with builds using Lightweight and Extreme Conditioning that expect to sprint a lot. It also pairs well with builds utilizing Fast Hands and the Quickdraw Attachment for the absolute fastest possible response times from sprinting, switching weapons, or going into ADS.

Because you can only equip three Scorestreaks at a time, choosing them carefully is important.

The Scorestreak system encourages "rolling" from Scorestreak to Scorestreak, by taking a few easy-to-earn lower Scorestreaks that generate more points, and using those points to slingshot yourself into a medium- or high-end Scorestreak. Naturally, the lower Scorestreaks (everything from the RC-XD up to about the Lightning Strike) are fairly easy to acquire in a match if you play smart. For less experienced players, picking the three low-cost Scorestreaks is a good way to maximize your potential rewards.

The midline Scorestreaks, from Death Machine up to Orbital VSAT, take a bit more effort. You need to play conservatively, not take any suicidal risks, and ideally, rack up bonus points near an objective.

The high-end Scorestreaks, from Escort Drone all the way up to Swarm, require dedication. Skilled play, heavy objective play with a bit of luck, the Hardline Perk, teammate support, a good build, and rolling Scorestreaks all help you reach these powerful Scorestreaks.

> Scorestreak Slingshots

Among the lower Scorestreaks, the UAV, Counter-UAV, and Guardian can all generate a lot of assist points to roll into midline Scorestreaks.

Once you hit the middle, the Sentry Gun, AGR, Stealth Chopper, and VSAT can all generate a lot of assist points. The Dragonfire *can* do so as well, but it is very fragile, so using it to boost yourself to the higher Scorestreaks is risky.

Automated Scorestreaks are preferable to controlled Scorestreaks for slingshotting yourself to higher Scorestreaks more quickly. Automated Scorestreaks allow you to continue to fight and earn points, while controlled Scorestreaks can earn you points more safely if you choose your hiding spot with care!

Choose the right Scorestreak for the job:

> Team support: UAV, Counter-UAV, Guardian, Sentry Gun, AGR, Stealth Chopper, Orbital VSAT, EMP Systems.

> Clearing an area: RC-XD, Hunter Killer, Hellstorm Missile, Lightning Strike, Warthog, Lodestar, VTOL Warship, K9, Swarm.

> Suppressing the enemy team: Dragonfire, Stealth Chopper, Warthog, Lodestar, VTOL Warship, K9, Swarm.

> Defending an area: Guardian, Sentry Gun, Death/War Machine, AGR, Stealth Chopper, Escort Drone, VTOL Warship, Swarm.

> Eliminating enemy Scorestreaks: RC-XD, Hunter Killer, Counter-UAV, War Machine, Hellstorm Missile, Lightning Strike, Dragonfire, EMP Systems, Lodestar, VTOL Warship.

Also remember that you don't have to take all three Scorestreaks; run UAV-CUAV and loop them all game long!

Keep in mind that the power of some lower Scorestreaks is magnified when your entire team uses them. UAVs and CUAVs can keep your team perfectly informed while denying the enemy intel. A mass of Hunter Killers can take down any air support. A maze of Guardians is extremely difficult to break through, and so on.

Dealing with Scorestreaks

The Ghost, Cold Blooded, Blind Eye, Flak Jacket, Hard Wired, and Engineer Perks, and the SMAW, FHJ-18, Black Hat, and EMP grenades, all can help to avoid or eliminate enemy Scorestreaks.

For heavy duty Scorestreak elimination, we recommend keeping a build with an FMJ-equipped LMG, Blind Eye, Cold Blooded, Engineer, an FHJ-18, a Black Hat, and two EMP grenades. This allows you to take out *any* type of enemy Scorestreak (or Equipment!) with ease.

If your entire team runs Ghost, Blind Eye, and Cold Blooded, your team can completely ignore enemy UAVs and Hunter Killers, along with any air support.

RC-XD

Ground, Directly Controlled

The RC-XD is a remote-controlled car strapped with a C4 charge. You can detonate the car at any time, killing any enemies in the vicinity.

The RC-XD has the ability to perform a speed boost. The speed boost facilitates better ramp-jumping and helps you propel the car into an enemy-packed area.

The RC-XD does have a limited timer, so you can't simply roam the map (or camp) endlessly. However, you can use it to cross a lot of terrain, or protect an objective area (or route to an objective).

Because the RC-XD requires your personal control, the longer you are driving it, the longer your team is missing your body on the frontlines, which can be vital in many objective modes. Use the RC-XD when you are in a safe position and can afford the time out of the fight to use the explosion to maximum effect.

You can destroy the RC-XD with *any* gunfire or a nearby explosion. However, it's usually fast enough to sneak in and detonate, as long as you don't drive it out in the open on a main pathway.

Note that Flak Jacket does not protect from a direct hit by the RC-XD explosion, though it can save you if you are only hit by the periphery of the blast.

UAV

Missiles to destroy: 1
Aerial, Unmanned

The UAV is an unmanned aerial drone that performs periodic reconnaissance sweeps of the map, revealing all enemy locations to your team.

If you aren't near the front lines or have some hard cover to duck behind, do a quick check of your main map when a UAV comes online. It gives you an overview of the position of all enemy forces on the map.

Despite being one of the cheapest Scorestreaks in the game, the UAV is *absolutely vital* and should be a key Scorestreak in many of your builds in almost any game mode. If the assault rifle is the workhorse of the guns, the UAV is the all-around champion of the Scorestreaks.

If the UAV's powerful utility weren't enough to convince you, you also earn Scorestreak assist points every time a teammate downs an enemy while you have a UAV active! Remember that UAVs do not detect moving enemies using the Ghost Perk, and enemy Counter-UAVs or (more rarely) EMPs can shut down your radar completely.

HUNTER KILLER

Aerial, Unmanned

The Hunter Killer is an advanced automated seeking drone, packed with explosives. When released, the Hunter Killer immediately flies towards the nearest hostile enemy target and detonates, killing the target and anyone unfortunate enough to be standing nearby.

If the Hunter Killer cannot find a target immediately (and you didn't throw it inside an enclosed area), it then takes flight and begins orbiting the battlefield. While orbiting, it constantly scans for a target in the open. When the Hunter Killer locates one, it swiftly dives and explodes.

The Hunter Killer is also effective as an anti-air "missile" of sorts. It will automatically seek out other aerial Scorestreaks and ram them, dealing one missile's worth of damage (or triggering a flare).

The Hunter Killer can also be used to destroy the Sentry Gun, Guardian, or AGR. Note that it prioritizes nearby enemy players over ground-based Scorestreaks, and air-based Scorestreaks over ground targets (if you throw it into the air that is).

Because the Hunter Killer is automated, it is not always going to strike the exact target that you might want, but it is a quick way to take down hostile UAVs or CUAVs. It can occasionally be very useful for quickly and safely destroying a well-placed enemy Sentry or Guardian on an objective.

Because Hunter Killers do not require any lock-on time like the SMAW or FHJ-18, or hacking time like the Black Hat PDA, you can use them as a very effective tool for instantly downing enemy air power (*if* they are used by the team).

The basic idea here is to have everyone on the team take a Hunter Killer, and save them solely for downing enemy air support.

This is particularly effective against Scorestreaks like the Warthog, which can be devilishly difficult to destroy with normal anti-air equipment. Hunter Killers, however, are comparatively simple to use against it.

There are other ways to nullify enemy Scorestreaks when playing as a team (mass Blind Eye/Cold Blooded/Hard Wired/Ghost), but Hunter Killers take up a Scorestreak slot instead of a Perk slot—something to consider!

CARE PACKAGE

Missiles to destroy: 1
Aerial, Airdropped

The Care Package Scorestreak reward calls in a support helicopter that drops a package containing a random Scorestreak reward.

Keep in mind that the chopper does drop the package directly where you place the drop zone marker, so be careful not to place it on the roof of a building! Also be aware that the package *can* crush you (or anyone else) who happens to be nearby when it lands. Furthermore, you can use Engineer or the Black Hat PDA to steal and booby trap enemy packages.

The Care Package can be riskier than more focused options because it takes time for the package to drop, requires a safe open drop zone, and you never know what you're going to get from it.

That said, Care Package *is* a good choice if you simply want to gamble on occasionally picking up a high-end reward (they do drop rarely). There's also one other decent reason to use Care Package: the Engineer Perk.

If you're running Engineer, you can reroll Care Package contents. This greatly improves the odds of getting at least a midline Scorestreak. It's also extra useful if multiple players on your team are running Care Package.

It is possible to destroy the Care Package chopper, causing it to drop the package early, but this is rarely worth the effort. The chopper is fast and difficult to hit, and you are usually better off using the drop placement to identify the location of an enemy.

COUNTER-UAV

Missiles to destroy: 1
Aerial, Unmanned

While active, the Counter-UAV scrambles enemy radar, shutting down not just other UAV scans, but also the enemy minimap entirely. This is functionally similar to granting your entire team Suppressors and Ghost. The enemy team can no longer pinpoint friendly locations via gunfire, and that's ignoring the loss of tactical information because they can no longer locate friendly players at a glance.

The CUAV is a very powerful support Scorestreak. It can be difficult to gauge its impact because it is not as immediately satisfying as a Scorestreak that can kill enemy players. But keeping the enemy blanketed with CUAV coverage for an entire match can be a decisive advantage for your team.

The CUAV is also the only way to counter an enemy VSAT, short of calling in an EMP blast. Just like the UAV, while the CUAV is in the air, you earn bonus support Scorestreak points every time a teammate kills an enemy. The Hard Wired Perk protects you completely from the effects of a Counter-UAV.

> ## Information Warfare

UAVs and CUAVs are cheap, but they are two of the most
important Scorestreaks in the game.

UAVs give your team a powerful edge in the tactical
game, and CUAVs deny the enemy team any sort of
tactical information.

Whenever you're unsure what Scorestreaks to use, UAV
and CUAV are a safe bet.

Both UAVs and CUAVs enter the battlefield airspace and
hover overhead, circling the battlefield for a short time
before they depart.

While in the air, they can be shot down and destroyed
easily with any lock-on missile attack, or any AR or LMG
with the FMJ Attachment.

Denying the enemy their UAV and CUAV coverage is
a strong play, as long as you don't expose yourself to
danger to destroy them.

GUARDIAN

Range: 750
Ground, Placed, Movable

The Guardian places a microwave
dish that can stagger, stun,
disorient, and eventually kill any
hostile target that comes into
range of the microwave beam.

The Guardian does not affect you
or friendly players, making it an ideal
Scorestreak for covering objectives and
narrow passages on any map.

When an enemy steps into the beam, they are stunned and
slowed, and constantly take damage. This also blurs their
vision, and makes effective combat next to impossible.
The Guardian beam is essentially an impenetrable barrier
if placed well.

The Guardian *can* kill if a target stands in the beam for too
long, so attempting to run through a hostile Guardian beam
to attack it is a bad idea.

The key to utilizing the Guardian well is placing it in such a
way that it completely blocks any attempt at destroying it
from the front, while you cover its flanks and rear. A Guardian
facing down a narrow path that has a 90 degree turn at the
end is next to impossible to eliminate from the front.

The Guardian beam has very significant width and height to its effect. It works just fine when placed
up on a ledge, and can cover a surprising amount of area if placed out in the open. The Guardian earns
Scorestreak points every time it damages or kills any player with the microwave beam.

Destroying a Guardian is best done by shooting it while out of range. Even an SMG or AR without FMJ
can destroy a Guardian fairly quickly and safely while out of range. This is distinct from a Sentry, because
the Guardian has a lot less effective range, making it easier to destroy from the front. Otherwise, you can
destroy the Guardian with an EMP or use a launcher or explosives to eliminate it quickly.

> ## Mobile Turrets

The Sentry Gun and the Guardian can be picked up and moved (at full movement speed even!), but if
you die while carrying them, they are lost.

Try to reposition them when you know the area is secure, or you have teammates in front of you.

Note that you do not lose either turret if you fail to place them immediately after activating
the Scorestreak.

> ## Turret Limits

You can have at most four turrets, in any combination of Sentry or Guardian on the map at any time.

> ## Sturdy Turrets

The Guardian and Sentry last for a *long* time if not destroyed, and you *cannot* destroy them simply by
knifing them from behind. Break out the EMP grenades, shoot them with FMJ, or use explosives to
eliminate them quickly. Neither Cold Blooded nor Blind Eye protects you from either turret!

HELLSTORM MISSILE

Aerial, Directly Controlled

The Hellstorm Missile is a remotely launched guided MIRV precision missile.

You can control the Hellstorm directly while in flight and give it a speed boost, or split it into multiple missiles that strike a wide area. Using boost grants the Hellstorm a large burst of speed towards your target, but at the cost of some fine control. If you're trying to get the missile on target against an enemy or group of enemies in the open, line it up swiftly and use boost. If you're trying to strike an enemy that is just inside cover (in some cases even inside a door or window), don't use boost. It is possible to steer the missile directly into an opening and kill the target within with the large blast radius!

However, the Hellstorm has another trick up its sleeve. While it is in the air over targets, it constantly acquires and locks onto multiple enemies within range. If you press the Deploy Button, the Hellstorm deploys a massive barrage of submunitions, saturating the area with miniature guided rockets that seek out any locked target. The area that the cluster bomb will hit is represented in the missile's HUD with a circle shape. Targets that will be hit by the cluster bomb are also highlighted with square box corners. This gives the Hellstorm devastating area denial against targets in the open. It can easily eliminate half (or more!) of a team if they are out in the open, even if they are spread out over a decent distance.

The Hellstorm is a very powerful weapon in objective modes. It can easily clear an objective of any targets, or at the very least, force them all indoors as soon as they hear the incoming Hellstorm warning. Even if they immediately take cover, you can still often guide the Hellstorm into a building if you don't split it!

To defend yourself against the Hellstorm, seek cover immediately when you hear it inbound, or deploy a Trophy System. Cold Blooded can hide you from the automatic target spotting, and Flak Jacket *might* protect you from a submunition strike if you are moving fast, but don't rely on it!

LIGHTNING STRIKE

Aerial, Directed

The Lightning Strike calls in a lethal triple bombing run on three target areas of your choosing.

The Lightning strike is a deadly Scorestreak for two reasons. First, it hits almost instantly after you pick the locations, giving very little time for hostiles to react to the warning of an incoming barrage. And second, the blast radius from the strike is *huge*.

Lightning Strike is amazing for clearing outdoor objective areas, or clearing a path *towards* an objective.

Note that the strikes are staggered. But because they occur so swiftly, it is rarely worthwhile to place them all on the same target, unless you are dealing with a situation so time-sensitive you can't even afford to move the targeting crosshair!

Lightning Strike contains a very nice bonus. When you call in a Lightning Strike, you are given a "free" UAV sweep of the map when you bring up the targeting control to choose the three locations for the strike.

DEATH MACHINE

Special, Equipped Weapon

The Death Machine Scorestreak grants you control of your own personal minigun. A 200 round, fully automatic minigun with impressive accuracy and a lethal rate of fire.

The Death Machine lives up to its name. It can easily mow down an entire enemy team if they are in the open and in your line of sight.

You cannot ADS with the Death Machine. Holding the ADS button causes the Death Machine to spin up and slightly tightens the targeting reticle. This means there is no delay when you pull the trigger, and slightly more accurate fire.

The Death Machine is an unusual Scorestreak in that it replaces your carried weapon, and it does not grant you any special durability. You're still just as vulnerable to enemy fire, even if you *feel* invincible with this weapon in your hands.

The best use for the Death Machine is typically covering an area, as it slows your movement speed to LMG speeds. Move into position, *then* bring out the big gun.

The Death Machine occupies its own inventory slot and can be equipped or de-equipped at will. Until you run out of ammunition, the Death Machine sticks around, even if you die!

SENTRY GUN

Ground, Placed, Movable

The Sentry Gun is an automated turret that tracks and quickly eliminates any hostile targets within its line of sight. With an impressive range and a good arc of fire, you can use the Sentry Gun to lock down an area of the map.

Much like the Guardian turret, the Sentry Gun is an area denial tool. But with a greater range and much faster lethality, it is significantly more deadly.

Everything that applies to the Guardian in terms of placement also applies to the Sentry Gun. Use it to lock down avenues of approach to objectives while you cover other directions.

Unlike the Guardian, the Sentry Gun has no effective range limit, which makes it a more lethal defensive tool for locking down an area. And remember, you can always take both!

The Sentry also has one other trick up its sleeve. You can take direct control of the Sentry Gun by holding the Reload button while it is active.

This allows you to prioritize targets and call enemies behind hard cover, as the Sentry Gun view has automatic target marking. Only Cold Blooded can stop this effect, and neither Cold Blooded nor Blind Eye protects from the Sentry when it is in automatic mode.

WAR MACHINE

Special, Equipped Weapon

The War Machine Scorestreak equips you with a six-round semi-automatic grenade launcher, giving you the ability to saturate an area with high explosives.

Like the Death Machine, the War Machine occupies its own inventory slot, and remains through deaths as long as you have ammo remaining.

Unlike the Death Machine, the War Machine *does* require reloading. Reloading the War Machine is quite slow. Make sure you are safe and behind cover before attempting to reload. Instead of reloading manually, simply switch back to a regular weapon and then re-equip the War Machine; doing so fully reloads the War Machine.

The War Machine is harder to use effectively compared to the Death Machine because you have comparatively less ammunition. Thus, it is much easier to run dry quickly. In addition, the War Machine is slightly more expensive to acquire, but the amount of rapid damage that it can deliver justifies the added difficulty of acquiring it.

Just like the regular Grenade Launcher Attachment, the War Machine grenades have a minimum distance they must travel before arming. Be sure to use the War Machine from at least medium range. Resist the urge to spam an area with grenades; you can inflict a lot more damage by selectively pulling out the War Machine and lobbing a grenade or two at a key objective area or a room that you know (or suspect) someone is camping within.

The War Machine is also a good counter to other ground-based Scorestreaks or placed Equipment. You can simply lob as many grenades as necessary at the "problem" until it goes away.

Note that the War Machine is heavily affected by the Flak Jacket Perk. It takes around three direct or near direct hits to down a target equipped with it.

DRAGONFIRE

Missiles to destroy: 1
Aerial, Directly Controlled

The Dragonfire is a remote-controlled quadrotor armed with a machine gun.

Small and nimble, the Dragonfire can hover over difficult terrain and pick off targets with ease. While it is not especially sturdy (having the equivalent of roughly two players' worth of health), it can make use of altitude, speed, and cover to avoid incoming fire.

The Dragonfire is most effective when used with your team. Hovering over or near your teammates keeps enemies on the ground distracted, giving you easy targets, and keeping their guns trained on the ground-based threats.

With infinite ammunition and automated target highlighting, acquiring and eliminating targets in the open is quite easy. Don't expose yourself to excessive risk while piloting the Dragonfire. It lasts a full minute, and you can inflict serious casualties on the enemy team if you pilot it carefully.

Cold Blooded screens you from the Dragonfire's target highlighting. But because the Dragonfire is typically close to the ground and has clear vision from a height, this does *not* mean that Cold Blooded is perfect protection. An operator can still spot you moving and take you out.

You can exit the Dragonfire early by holding the Reload button if you are in an objective mode and an urgent situation calls for your presence. You can't hold or interact with objectives while in the Dragonfire!

AGR

Ground, Airdropped, Unmanned, Directly Controlled

The Autonomous Ground Robot is an automated *or* remote-controlled armored combat robot that enters the battlefield via airdrop.

You can choose the dropzone for the AGR the same way you call in a Care Package, by tossing a smoke grenade to mark the DZ. Like the Care Package, be careful not to throw it in an area where the AGR cannot land! When the AGR lands, it immediately breaks out of its container and enters automatic mode. While automated, it patrols the map, engaging any hostile targets in range.

In addition to automatic mode, you can also directly take control of the AGR by holding the Reload button. This gives you direct control of movement, machine guns, and rockets!

Even better, you can switch between automatic and directly controlled whenever you wish. Because the AGR lasts a long time on the battlefield, it is very possible to move the AGR from one hotspot to another as the match progresses.

In automatic mode, the AGR will seek enemy players, but has a short targeting delay before firing. It lacks the instincts of a player, and the altitude of a Stealth Chopper, but it does function very effectively as a guardian for a small area.

This makes the AGR the perfect tool for denying a key area of the map, typically around an objective. Drop the AGR directly onto the objective you want to lock down, or drop it nearby and pilot it in manually. Then leave it on automatic mode.

If you suspect the AGR is at risk of being overrun, you can take control of it manually to down hostile enemy targets.

Cold Blooded protects you from the target highlighting of the AGR if it is manually controlled, but neither Cold Blooded nor Blind Eye protects you if it is on automatic!

The AGR is remarkably sturdy, taking two EMP grenades, multiple explosive hits, or a lot of gunfire to destroy. Don't get overconfident with it if you're controlling it manually, but don't be hesitant against players trying to hide. You can easily withstand a few shots.

The AGR *can* be destroyed with a single Black Hat hack, but it is extremely difficult to keep the AGR targeted if it is mobile.

STEALTH CHOPPER

Missiles to destroy: 2
Aerial, Unmanned, Directed

The Stealth Chopper Scorestreak calls in a friendly gunship with stealth technology. It is completely hidden from the enemy's minimap.

The Stealth Chopper flies onto the battlefield to the area you select. It then proceeds to open fire on any hostile enemies within its line of sight.

The Stealth Chopper is very aggressive and dangerous. Any nearby enemies out in the open aren't likely to last long.

Make use of the Stealth Chopper to lock down an area of the map. Between its quick kills and the difficulty of locating it immediately, you can often clear an area of the map before your enemies are aware of its position.

Even once the enemy *is* aware of the presence of the chopper, it is reasonably resilient, taking two missiles or quite a few bullets to destroy. Plus, the enemy usually has to risk exposure to take a clean shot.

If an objective you are trying to control is indoors where the chopper would have no line of sight, try to place it over a major hotspot with a lot of open terrain. Doing so turns the entire area into a no man's land for the enemy team until they deal with the chopper.

Blind Eye provides total protection from the Stealth Chopper. It won't target you while you have that Perk active.

ORBITAL VSAT

Unmanned

The Orbital VSAT activates perfect surveillance of the entire enemy team for a limited time. While active, your team has a "super UAV" effect, giving you the exact location and facing of every member of the enemy team.

This is a massively powerful advantage, and tends to turn the match into a lopsided contest while the VSAT is active. It can easily shift the balance of a match in your team's favor.

If you really want to shut down the enemy team, combine a CUAV with the VSAT to deny the enemy radar coverage while your own team has perfect battle intel.

The only way to counter the effects of the VSAT is an active Counter-UAV. Unlike the UAV or CUAV, the VSAT is *not* visible in the sky, nor can you attack it, for obvious reasons.

ESCORT DRONE

Missiles to destroy: 2
Aerial, Unmanned

The Escort Drone calls in a miniature drone helicopter as a personal escort. While active, the drone hovers near you, automatically gunning down any enemies that get in range. The drone provides excellent protection while it is in the air and is extremely dangerous to the other team while active.

Because the drone hovers overhead, it can give away your general location. Naturally, since it protects you, this usually isn't an issue, but it's something to be aware of. Also note that an opponent with Blind Eye can close in safely.

If you wish to use the Escort Drone offensively, you have to close in on the enemy positions so that it moves into range. This also means that using it defensively is easier (and safer), so locking down an objective location with an Escort Drone overhead is quite effective. Only one Escort Drone can be active on the map at a time.

WARTHOG

Missiles to destroy: 3
Aerial, Unmanned

The Warthog Scorestreak calls in an A-10F Warthog to make multiple strafing runs across the battlefield, mowing down enemy opposition with cannon and missile fire.

The Warthog flies quickly across the map, then out to the edges of the battlefield's airspace, before returning for another pass.

Because the Warthog travels so quickly, it is remarkably difficult to destroy with anti-air. This means that often the only safe way to handle a Warthog strike is to stay indoors or use Blind Eye.

Because the Warthog makes a straight pass across the map, it *is* possible to survive in the open if you keep a large piece of hard cover between you and the Warthog. Just be aware that if a teammate is nearby in the open, you might be the unlucky recipient of some splash damage from Warthog missiles.

The Warthog is a devastating Scorestreak. It often allows a free lockdown of any objectives out in the open while it is active, and at the very least, pins enemy players inside buildings or behind hard cover while it is active.

Because players tend to flee indoors while the Warthog is in the air, this is a perfect time to take control of outdoor objectives or to sweep buildings for kills.

EMP SYSTEMS

Unmanned

Deploying the EMP Systems Scorestreak unleashes a massive EMP blast that shuts down the entire enemy team's electronics systems. This disables their radar, destroys *all* of their Scorestreaks, shuts down their equipment, and even disables their powered advanced optic Attachments like the Dual Band or MMS!

Deploying the EMP is the counter-intelligence equivalent of the VSAT. It gives your team a very powerful advantage while active, and only enemies with Hard Wired can continue to function at anything approaching full combat readiness.

When you acquire the EMP, time its usage to destroy a powerful enemy Scorestreak. Or if you are in a round-based objective mode, deploy it at the start of a new round to give your team a crushing advantage right out of the gate.

LODESTAR

Missiles to destroy: 3
Aerial, Directly Controlled

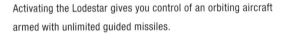

Activating the Lodestar gives you control of an orbiting aircraft armed with unlimited guided missiles.

These missiles are both easy to aim and *extremely* powerful. Landing a missile anywhere near a target in the open is guaranteed to take them down.

You can also guide the missiles with enough precision to land them inside doorways or windows with care. Holding down the ADS button zooms in slightly to aid in guiding the missiles to your target.

Because the Lodestar is on an orbiting flight path around the map, you may have your view of some maps obscured by terrain. When you can't reach targets with missiles, be sure to call out their positions to your teammates. One of the strengths of a controlled aerial Scorestreak with targeting systems is superior battlefield awareness. As with the Warthog, enemies tend to flee indoors once the Lodestar is active. This frees up outdoor objectives to be taken and gives your teammates obvious areas to sweep for hostiles.

You can rack up a *lot* of kills with the Lodestar, so be sure that you pick a safe and hidden location to take control of it. You don't want to waste all those potential Scorestreak points by dying while you are in the Lodestar.

Enemies with Cold Blooded are concealed from the automatic targeting highlights. Because you are so far up in the sky, they can be quite difficult to spot.

The Lodestar is rather vulnerable to anti-air. It flies on a very predictable path at a distance that makes it easy to target with launchers, and it can be hard to spot enemies targeting you. Fortunately (or unfortunately, if you're on the receiving end), with two flares, it still takes a concentrated effort to shoot it down.

VTOL WARSHIP

Missiles to destroy: 3
Aerial, Directly Controlled

The mighty VTOL Warship is an extremely powerful Scorestreak, granting you control of a hovering gunship armed with both rapid-fire machine guns and quad rockets.

In addition, you can force the VTOL Warship to relocate. Once one area of the battlefield is clear of hostiles, you can switch to another position to gain line of sight on your unfortunate prey below.

As with the Warthog and Lodestar, enemies are very likely to flee indoors while you have the VTOL Warship active. Be sure to call out enemy locations if you spot someone running into a building.

The VTOL Warship is somewhat exposed to anti-aircraft missiles. It is relatively easy to target, so it is very important that you exterminate enemies in the open quickly, especially if you notice the telltale silhouette of a player aiming a launcher at you.

The VTOL Warship can completely lock the map down for your team while it is active. Like the Lodestar, you can earn a *lot* of points while using it, so be sure to take control of it from a safe location.

To take down a hostile VTOL Warship, use Cold Blooded to conceal yourself from its sensors and an FHJ-18 AA along with two Black Hats to destroy it in one life. Although, hitting it with all three and staying alive is difficult.

Alternatively, an LMG with the FMJ Attachment can take the VTOL Warship down remarkably quickly. On several maps, the VTOL Warship flies in from off of the map. This gives you a precious few seconds to line up and open fire before it can effectively retaliate.

K9 UNIT

Unmanned

Activating the K9 Unit Scorestreak calls in a vicious pack of combat-trained dogs to assault the entire enemy team. While active, a constant flood of hounds sweep the battlefield, tackling and instantly killing any player they come into contact with.

Unlike the Warthog, Lodestar, VTOL Warship, or Swarm, and the other high-end hard-hitting Scorestreaks, the K9 Unit is special because the dogs can and will attack players absolutely anywhere on the map, including inside buildings. This makes the K9 Unit potentially one of the most lethal Scorestreaks. Because it is autonomous, you can continue to fight while your dogs do work for you.

There is one weakness to the K9 pack, however. Enemies *can* shoot them, and each kill earns 50 points towards a Scorestreak, which is a considerable amount. If a K9 Unit is called in on you, it is possible to find a dead-end to hide out in and simply gun down any that try to reach you. This gives you the potential to rack up a lot of free points.

SWARM

Unmanned

The final lethal Scorestreak, the Drone Swarm calls in a *huge* flight of Hunter Killer Drones that begin orbiting the battlefield, constantly deploying and bombarding every enemy player on the map. While active, the entire map becomes a no man's land for the enemy team. Only players with Blind Eye are spared the bombardment, and even they aren't safe if a player without Blind Eye happens to be standing nearby. Calling in the Drone Swarm gives your team almost total freedom to roam the map and take objectives or hunt the enemy team while they cower inside buildings or under hard cover.

If a Swarm is called in on you, there are a few things you can do to protect yourself and your team. The first is to run the Blind Eye Perk. This completely shields you from the Swarm's targeting systems. The second is to make use of the Trophy System. It won't save you indefinitely, but each Trophy can absorb two drone strikes. This is potentially enough time to secure an objective or cross an open area.

Finally, the EMP System *can* shut down the Drone Swarm. Although it is rare to see both deployed on opposite teams at the same time!

MULTIPLAYER MAPS

Welcome to our tactical maps chapter. We have prepared a carefully crafted set of overlays for each map in *Call of Duty: Black Ops II* to give you an edge in combat.

Please check out our new gridded rangefinder maps! They work hand in hand with our Arsenal to give you a powerful new resource; the ability to measure distances to determine the best tool for the job on any map and in any mode.

MAP TYPES

For every level in multiplayer, we have prepared *three* types of maps:

> A Hotspot map that notes key tactical locations. This map also shows a grid overlay for checking ranges.

> An Objective map that displays all objective modes on one map.

> And finally, four Route maps for four different objective modes, showing key routes through the maps.

THE MAP RANGEFINDER GRIDS

The grid on the Hotspot map gives you a simple overview of the level with few distracting markings, *and* a valuable tactical tool to examine distances.

USING THE RANGEFINDER GRIDS WITH THE ARSENAL

The Arsenal chapter contains detailed charts on many aspects of the weapons in *Call of Duty: Black Ops II*. One of the charts in particular shows you the specific ranges tied to the number of shots required to down an enemy.

You can use these charts to find your *specific* weapon and then examine that weapon's performance on any map in the game. The Hotspot maps' rangefinder grid is the key. Simply check the range distances for your weapon. Find out where your assault rifle drops from three to four shots to kill, for example. Then check the grid scale on the map you're interested in.

With this information, you can quickly and easily determine how long the lines of sight are, and whether an advanced zooming optical Attachment would be beneficial. You can decide if a Suppressor, Rapid Fire, or Long Barrel might help. Perhaps most importantly, you can gauge what weapon classes are likely to work well on that map in general, depending on the mode you are playing.

Use the Objective map to examine where the objectives are located. Use the Hotspot map to check on hotspots. And use the Route map to examine common routes. All of these points tend to see high traffic, and by using that

MAP SCALES

It's very important to note that because the maps are all different sizes in the game *but not on the page*, we have to use a different scale for the grid squares on different maps.

Check the grid scale before you try to check ranges, or it may result in some confusion!

AVERAGE DISTANCES

In addition to the detailed ranges in the Arsenal chapter, each map also has a "cheat sheet" ruler with four average effective ranges for the primary weapon classes: shotguns, SMGs, assault rifles, and LMGs. Sniper rifles do not have an average range, as they are effective at any distance!

These ranges are *rough* estimates. They are useful for quickly examining the distance from an overwatch point to an objective or checking the line of sight range on a key route. When you want to check the specific range of your preferred weapon, hit up the Arsenal and check your weapon. Then flip back to the map and check the ranges.

OBJECTIVE MAP

The Objective map has *all* of the objective locations for each game mode marked on it. Use this map to check objective locations for any game mode you are interested in.

OBJECTIVE MAP ICON KEY

🎖️🎖️	TEAM SPAWNS	🏛️	HEADQUARTERS LOCATION	A B D	DEMOLITION BOMB SITES AND OVERTIME SITE
⬆️⬆️⬆️	CONNECT TO SAME-COLORED ARROWS ON MULTI-LEVEL AREAS	🚩🚩	CTF FLAG STANDS	Ⓐ Ⓑ Ⓒ	DOMINATION CONTROL POINTS
🪜	USABLE LADDER	A B	SEARCH & DESTROY BOMB SITES		
⚠️	HARDPOINT AREAS OF CONTROL	💼	SEARCH & DESTROY BOMB		

HOTSPOT MAP

The Hotspot map marks key tactical locations on every level. Each icon refers to a different engagement type, warning, or pointer for a useful position to hold.

HOTSPOT

These locations are areas that, because of simple geography or level flow, tend to have high traffic. As a result, they are dangerous areas to traverse. You should always be alert for enemy contacts unless you know for certain that your team has the area locked down.

Hotspots are good locations to go hunting for kills. They are bad locations if you are trying to avoid contact while traveling to an objective or to flank the enemy team. Beware of explosives and Scorestreaks when traversing hotspot areas!

CLOSE QUARTERS COMBAT (CQC)

Close quarters combat (CQC) areas tend to force close-range engagements. They are ideal for close-range weaponry because these areas are indoors or because the terrain has lots of cover and sharp corners. Bring your shotguns, SMGs, dual pistols, or fully automatic ARs here. Beware of entering these areas with a long-range assault rifle, LMG, or sniper rifle in hand.

CQC engagements tend to be short and lethal. You can take advantage of CQC areas to force a close-range engagement if your primary weapon is short ranged. They are also particularly good areas to make use of proximity mines and Shock Charges. You can use the Millimeter Scanner Attachment and the Engineer Perk to locate enemies.

OVERWATCH

Overwatch areas are simply locations that have some combination of good hard cover and clear lines of sight. A good overwatch position with a strong-medium to long-range weapon can clean up enemies who move into your line of sight.

Be sure to have your back guarded, either by teammates, Equipment, or Scorestreaks! Overwatch areas vary in importance (and safety!) depending on the game mode you are playing. Make a point of examining them with different weapons and scopes attached so you can check out the sightlines and make use of the cover.

SNIPER PERCH

Sniper locations are overwatch areas that also have very long lines of sight for the map they are on. These locations are ideal for sniper rifles, LMGs, and ARs configured for long-range combat.

JUMP SPOT

These icons denote an area of the map where you can make a useful jump or a useful mantle to cover terrain. Most maps have multiple areas where you can use a bit of agility and speed to cut travel times, flank an enemy position, or stay out of sight by jumping or climbing over gaps, in through windows, or over walls or rocks. If a map has a high number of useful jump or mantle locations, or your favored route has many of them, the Dexterity Perk can speed your movement considerably.

ROUTE MAP

The four Route maps show different routes through the level for four specific objective modes: **Domination**, **Demolition**, **CTF**, and **Search & Destroy**. These modes were chosen because they frequently have both teams running for the objective to and from fixed positions. As a result, the routes players take through the levels are much more predictable than, say, Hardpoint or Headquarters (which randomly changes the objective location), or Deathmatch (where the combat flows all around the map).

Use these routes to get a feel for how you can move through the level. The routes obviously aren't the *only* way to move through the level. They're just common, quick paths that will take you from your spawn to any of the objectives.

ROUTE MAP DIFFERENCES

For Domination and CTF, the route maps are identical. The target areas are placed in the same locations for both teams, so the route paths are the same.

For Demolition and Search & Destroy, however, the offense and defense have slightly different spawn locations relative to the bomb sites. These maps show two different routes, one for each side. Because you swap between offense and defense in both modes, you need to be familiar with the differences.

Generally, the defensive team has a shorter run to both bomb sites, to give them an edge in early preparation. Although this isn't a lot of time on the smaller maps!

SPECIAL RANGES

Finally, we have prepared a few additional useful ranges for you, on top of weapon ranges.

The following charts cover:

> **Running Distance:** How far you can sprint with a specific weapon in your hands, with or without Extreme Conditioning or Lightweight.

> **Hearing Range:** How far you can hear an enemy, with or without Dead Silence or Awareness.

> **Throwing Range:** How far you can toss an explosive!

> **Explosion Range of Effect:** The blast radius of explosives!

Note that for throwing distances "grenade" means any Frag, Semtex, Flashbang, Concussion, Sensor, EMP, Smoke, or Shock Charge. Remember that the Frag and Sensor can roll a bit, possibly giving them a bit of extra distance.

In the case of the running distances, the same speeds noted in the Gameplay intro chapter also apply to those distances. So, a War Machine can run the same distance as an LMG, and holding a Care Package marker grenade lets you move the same distance as an SMG.

> **SMG Speed:** Sniper rifles, shotguns, pistols, Ballistic Knife, Crossbow, Hunter Killer, Care Package, and AGR.

> **LMG Speed:** Launchers, Riot Shield, War Machine, and Death Machine.

Finally, the last special case is the Combat Knife. You can move 50% further with a Combat Knife in hand (no primary or secondary weapon equipped) than an SMG sprint distance. *Carrying* the Sentry or Guardian also lets you move this far.

RUNNING DISTANCE

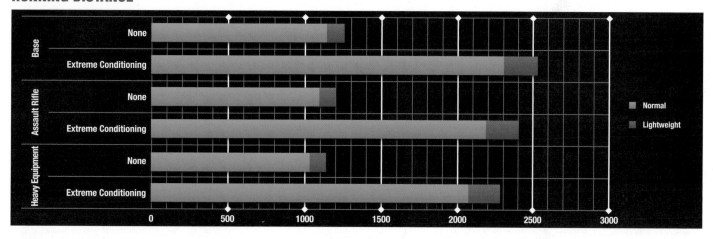

HEARING RANGE

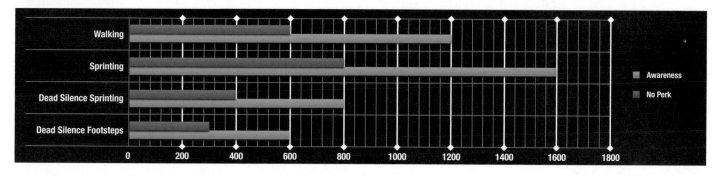

THROWING RANGE

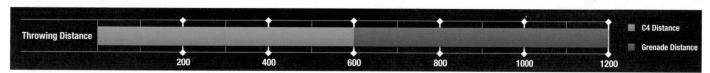

EXPLOSION RANGE OF EFFECT

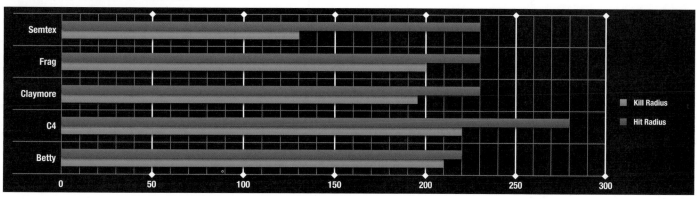

AFTERMATH

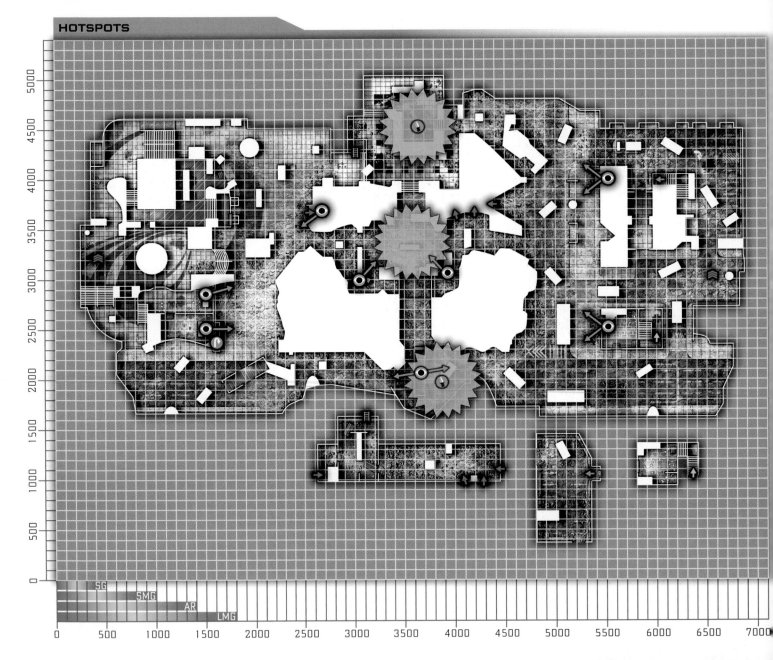

OVERVIEW

Aftermath takes place in the blasted-out ruins of downtown L.A., after it is smashed by a massive Drone attack. Ruined buildings, destroyed vehicles, and craters in the street all make for an unusually devastated urban landscape.

The focus of the map is a large, fallen skyscraper in the middle of the level. It creates a (literally) broken-up mix of terrain in level's central area. On the far east and west, a parking garage and a small shopping center provide 'base' areas with upper levels. They have line of sight over the outer parts of the center ruins.

NOTES

The central hotspot is very hot. Bypass it by traveling north or south, unless you want to get into combat! Be wary of campers in the east and west structures if you're fighting out on the streets. Familiarize yourself with their lines of sight so you can avoid them when necessary.

ACTIVITY HOTSPOT	
CLOSE QUARTERS COMBAT (CQC)	
OVERWATCH VANTAGE POINT	
SNIPER PERCH	
JUMP SPOT	

< 218 219 >

MULTIPLAYER MAPS_AFTERMATH

OBJECTIVE LOCATIONS

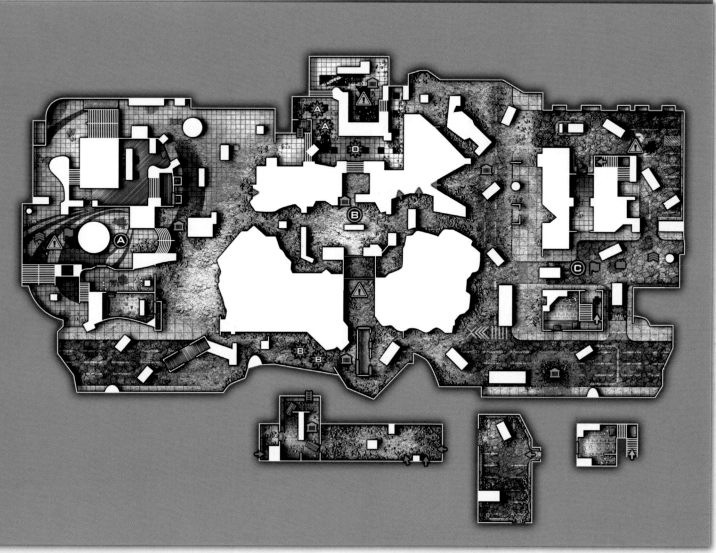

TEAM SPAWNS	HEADQUARTERS LOCATION	DEMOLITION BOMB SITES AND OVERTIME SITE
CONNECT TO SAME-COLORED ARROWS ON MULTI-LEVEL AREAS	CTF FLAG STANDS	DOMINATION CONTROL POINTS
USABLE LADDER	SEARCH & DESTROY BOMB SITES	
HARDPOINT AREAS OF CONTROL	SEARCH & DESTROY BOMB	

CAPTURE THE FLAG

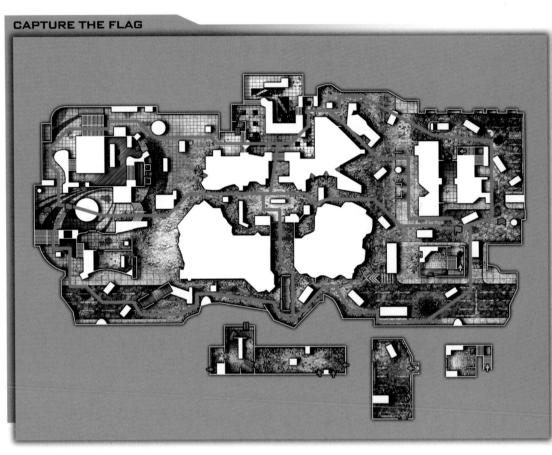

DEMOLITION

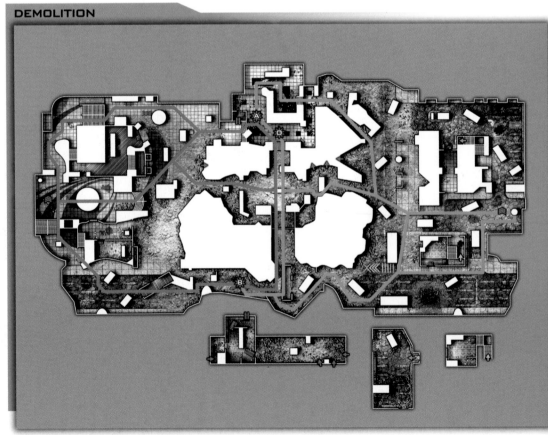

DOMINATION

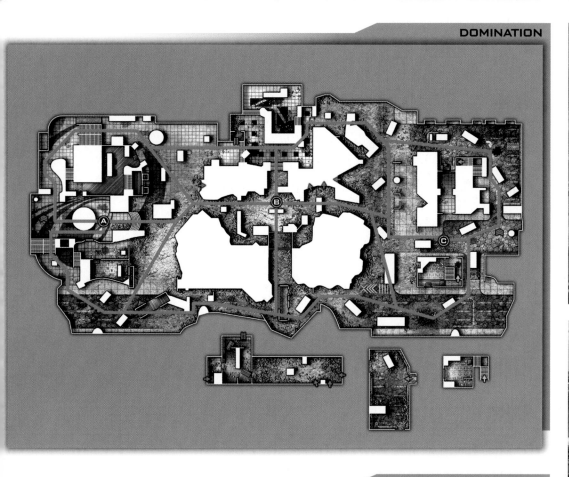

SEARCH & DESTROY

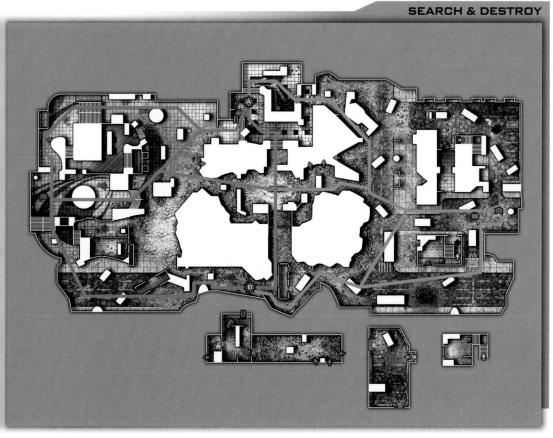

CARGO

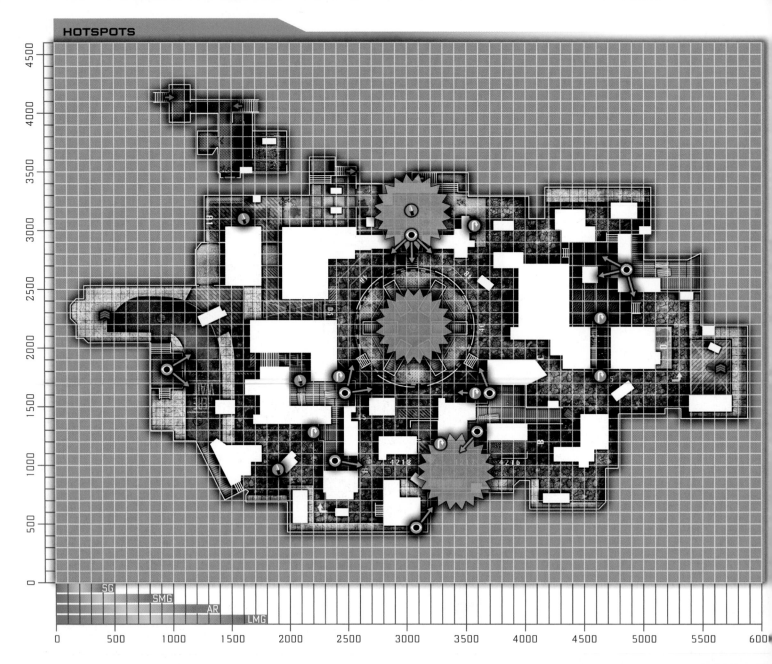

![Activity Hotspot]	**ACTIVITY HOTSPOT**
![CQC]	**CLOSE QUARTERS COMBAT (CQC)**
![Overwatch]	**OVERWATCH VANTAGE POINT**
![Sniper]	**SNIPER PERCH**
![Jump]	**JUMP SPOT**

OVERVIEW

A loading dock in Singapore makes for an unusual battlefield, as automated systems move shipping containers around the center of the map. This dynamically opens and closes line of sight throughout the match. Combat in Cargo flows in and out of the center of the level. Large stacks of shipping containers break up the east, west, and south of the map. A small office building on the north side of the level provides one of the few indoor areas.

NOTES

As cranes move the shipping containers around in the middle of the map, lines of sight between the northern office and east and west overwatch points are constantly shifting. Exploit the newly created cover when you are moving through the center, and expect enemies to do the same.

OBJECTIVE LOCATIONS

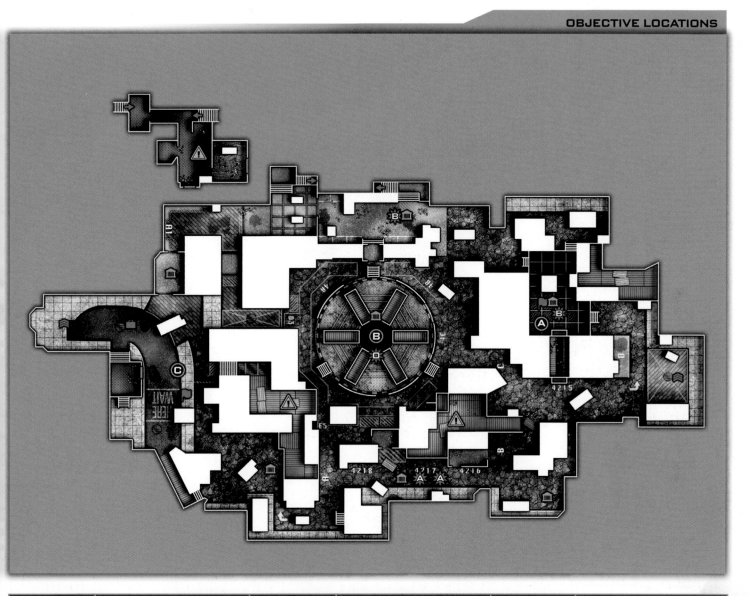

	TEAM SPAWNS		HEADQUARTERS LOCATION	Ⓐ Ⓑ Ⓞ	DEMOLITION BOMB SITES AND OVERTIME SITE
↑ ↑ ↑	CONNECT TO SAME-COLORED ARROWS ON MULTI-LEVEL AREAS	⚑ ⚑	CTF FLAG STANDS	Ⓐ Ⓑ Ⓒ	DOMINATION CONTROL POINTS
	USABLE LADDER	Ⓐ Ⓑ	SEARCH & DESTROY BOMB SITES		
⚠	HARDPOINT AREAS OF CONTROL	💼	SEARCH & DESTROY BOMB		

Bring a CQC weapon or some Equipment to guard your back if you plan on fighting at a distance. Much of the combat around the edges of the level occurs at short ranges.

CARGO

CAPTURE THE FLAG

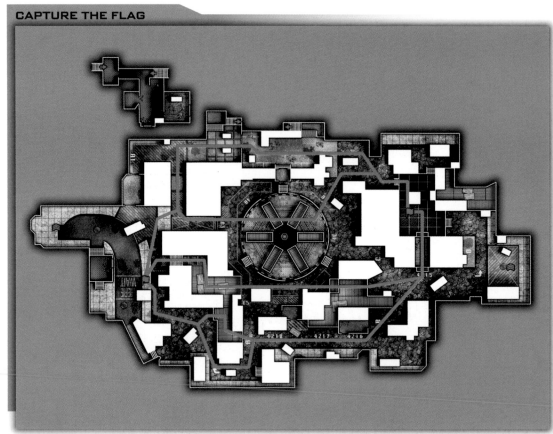

DEMOLITION

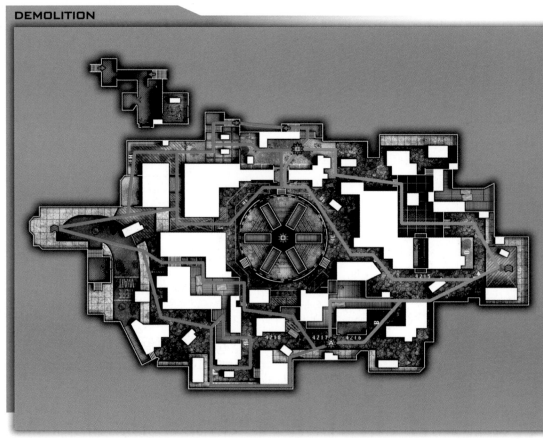

DOMINATION

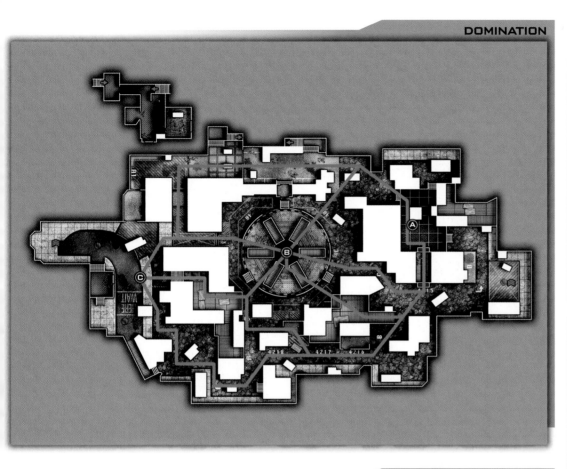

SEARCH & DESTROY

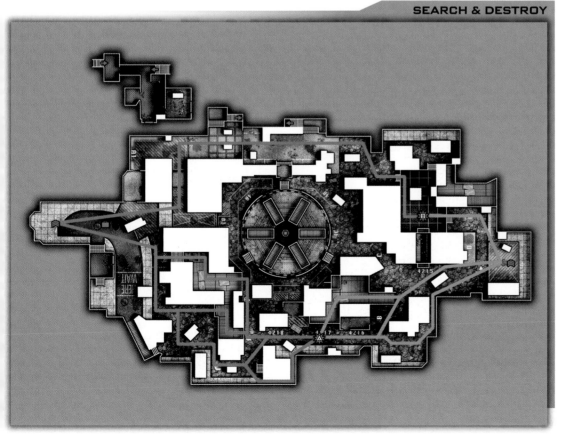

CARRIER

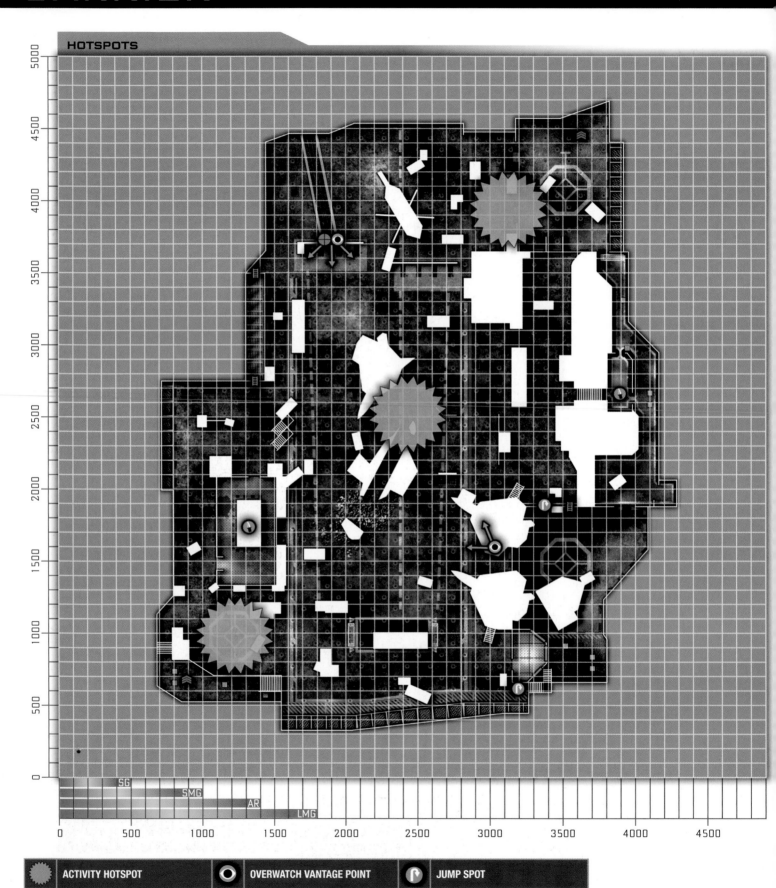

![]	**ACTIVITY HOTSPOT**	![]	**OVERWATCH VANTAGE POINT**	![] **JUMP SPOT**
![]	**CLOSE QUARTERS COMBAT (CQC)**	![]	**SNIPER PERCH**	

OBJECTIVE LOCATIONS

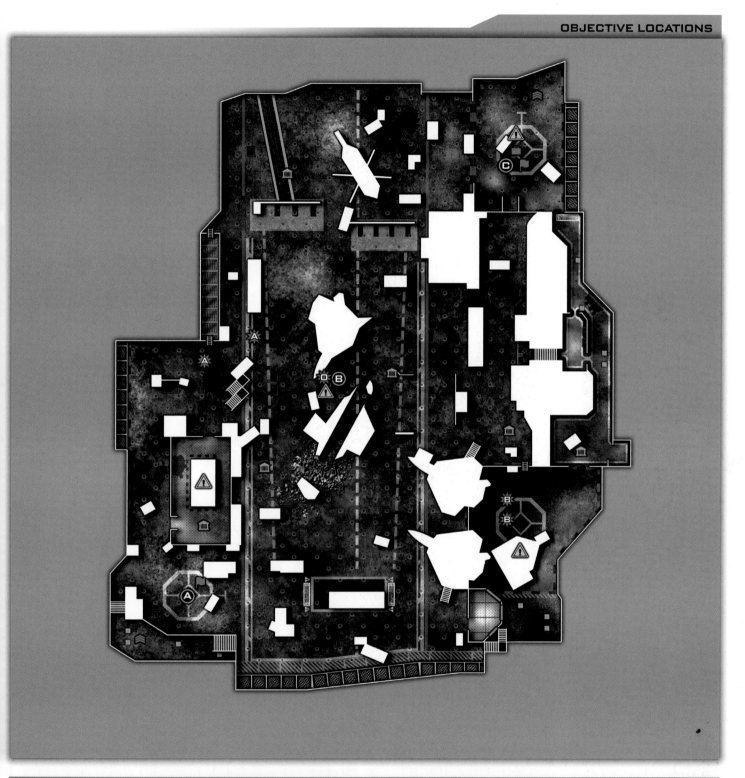

	TEAM SPAWNS		HEADQUARTERS LOCATION				DEMOLITION BOMB SITES AND OVERTIME SITE
	CONNECT TO SAME-COLORED ARROWS ON MULTI-LEVEL AREAS		CTF FLAG STANDS	Ⓐ	Ⓑ	Ⓒ	DOMINATION CONTROL POINTS
	USABLE LADDER		SEARCH & DESTROY BOMB SITES				
	HARDPOINT AREAS OF CONTROL		SEARCH & DESTROY BOMB				

CARRIER

OVERVIEW

The flight deck of a Chinese super-carrier makes an impressive-looking backdrop to the combat on this map. The smoking ruins of advanced fighter jets clutter up the center of the map. Piles of debris and low obstructions severely break up line of sight from point to point. A handful of tiny side routes run along the east, west, and south of the carrier. These allow you to avoid the main deck entirely if you're trying to keep a low profile.

NOTES

Target acquisition is a real issue on this level. The amount of visual noise can make it a little more difficult for you to find targets. Consider bringing an advanced optical scope to locate enemies more quickly.

CAPTURE THE FLAG

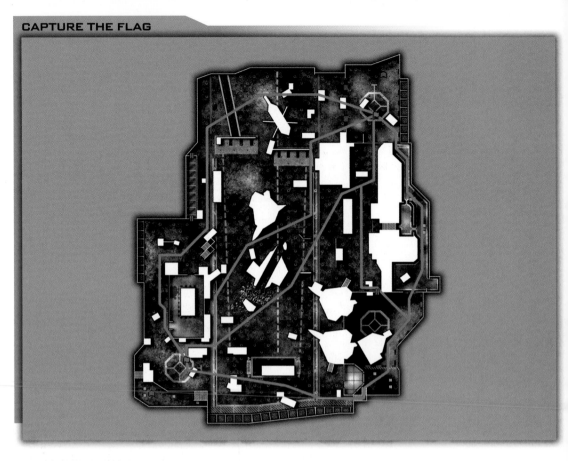

DEMOLITION

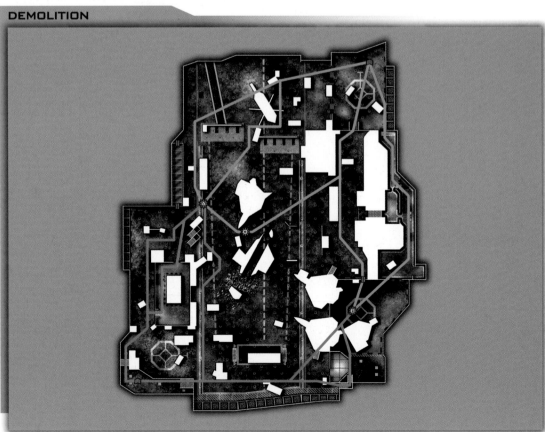

< 228 229 >

MULTIPLAYER MAPS_CARRIER

DOMINATION

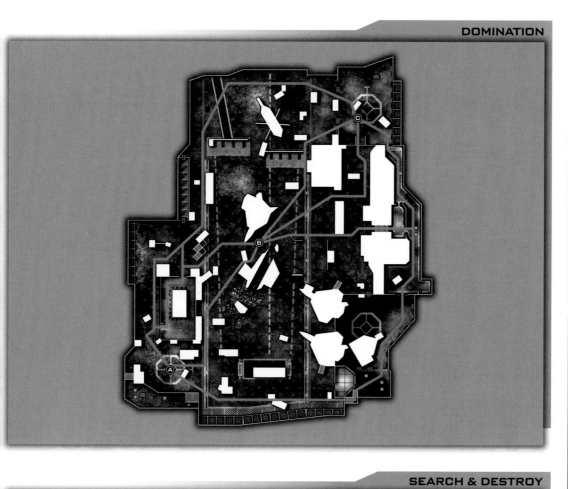

SEARCH & DESTROY

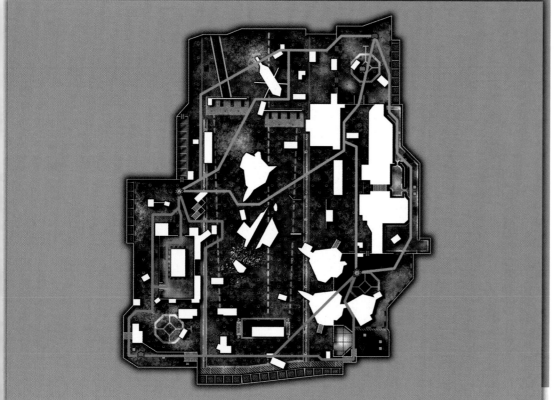

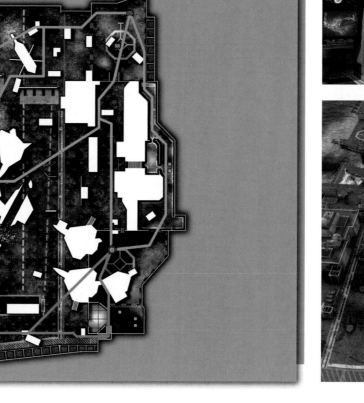

DRONE

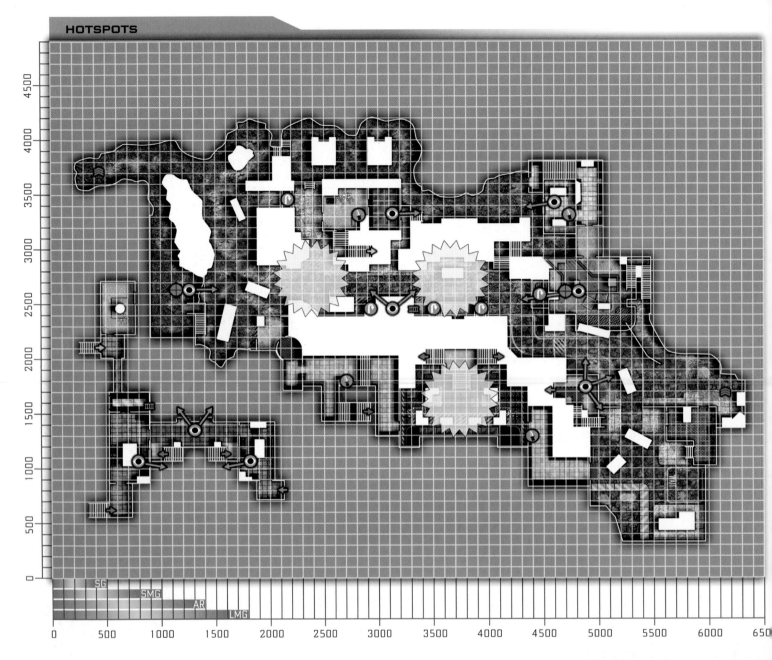

OVERVIEW

Drone features a top-secret and high-tech Drone construction facility located somewhere deep in the Myanmar jungles. This level hosts intense combat over mixed building interiors and a long central street. The Drone facility itself sprawls over the level, with a large multi-level portion on the south center of the map. Several multi-level buildings also occupy the north center.

The central street that divides the structures stretches straight and clear from east to west—be very careful about exposing yourself to this clear sightline.

NOTES

You can choose your engagement type by fighting inside the building or outside in the northwest, southeast, or central street. This map provides a mix of long-range combat in the street and very tight CQC combat inside the buildings.

ACTIVITY HOTSPOT	
CLOSE QUARTERS COMBAT (CQC)	
OVERWATCH VANTAGE POINT	
SNIPER PERCH	
JUMP SPOT	

OBJECTIVE LOCATIONS

TEAM SPAWNS	HEADQUARTERS LOCATION	DEMOLITION BOMB SITES AND OVERTIME SITE
CONNECT TO SAME-COLORED ARROWS ON MULTI-LEVEL AREAS	CTF FLAG STANDS	DOMINATION CONTROL POINTS
USABLE LADDER	SEARCH & DESTROY BOMB SITES	
HARDPOINT AREAS OF CONTROL	SEARCH & DESTROY BOMB	

DRONE

CAPTURE THE FLAG

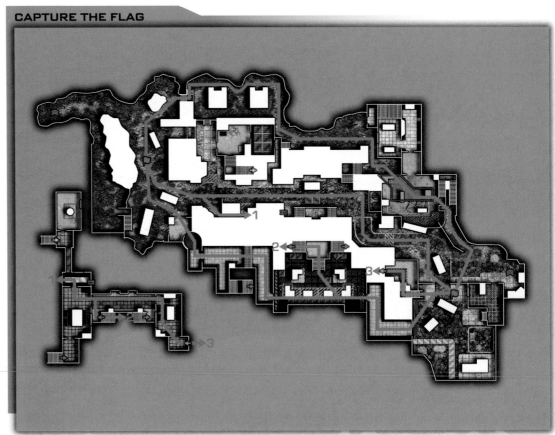

DEMOLITION

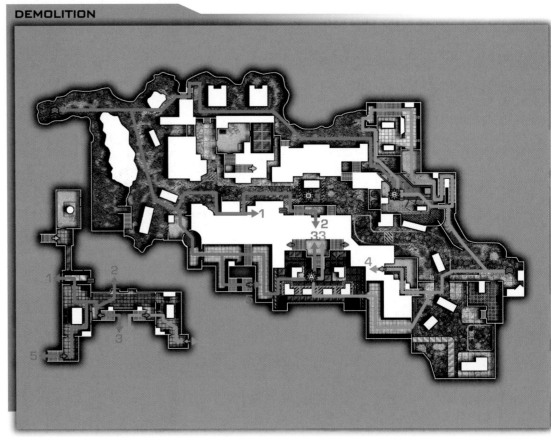

< 232 233 >

DOMINATION

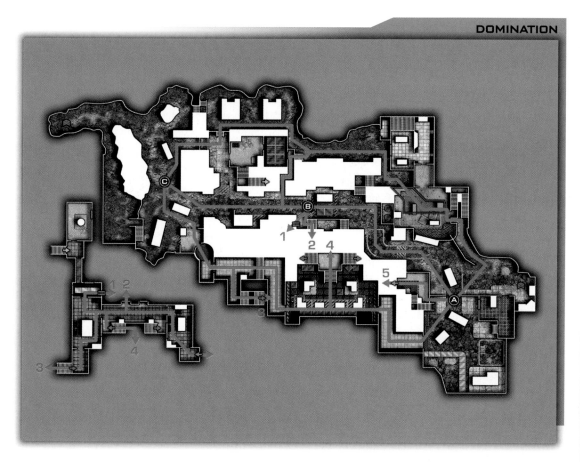

SEARCH & DESTROY

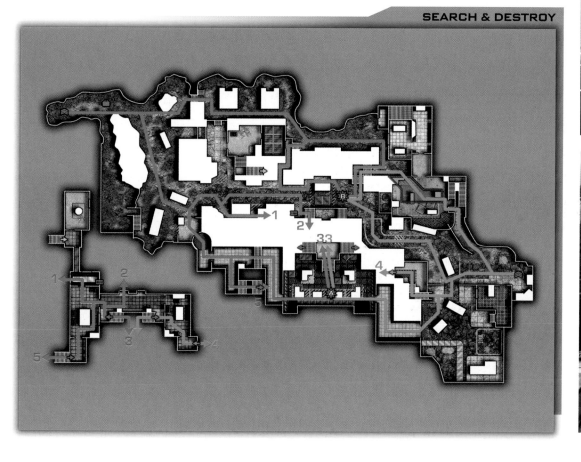

EXPRESS

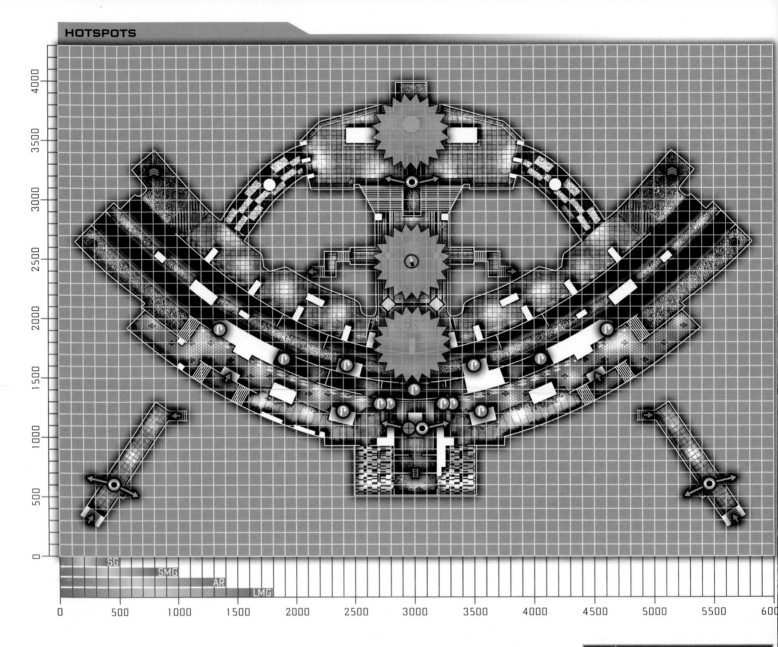

	ACTIVITY HOTSPOT
	CLOSE QUARTERS COMBAT (CQC)
	OVERWATCH VANTAGE POINT
	SNIPER PERCH
	JUMP SPOT

OVERVIEW

This rail terminal for the high-speed California train forces engagements down narrow lanes of fire. Slight curves, obstructions, and a few parked train cars break up lines of sight. Because of the way the routes through this level are very divided, it can take a surprisingly long time to travel from place to place. You are often forced to travel a route that you *know* will have enemies pointing in your direction at the end.

Bring loadouts that help you speed your movement, disrupt enemy positions, or shield your approach. You often have no choice but to face an entrenched enemy at the end of one of the lanes.

NOTES

Periodically an alarm sounds, barriers retract on the train tracks, and a high-speed train whips through the level! Don't be on the tracks when this happens, or you'll end up squished. You can climb in, out, and onto the train cars at the south end of the level. You can also traverse the overhead walkways that cross the tracks.

OBJECTIVE LOCATIONS

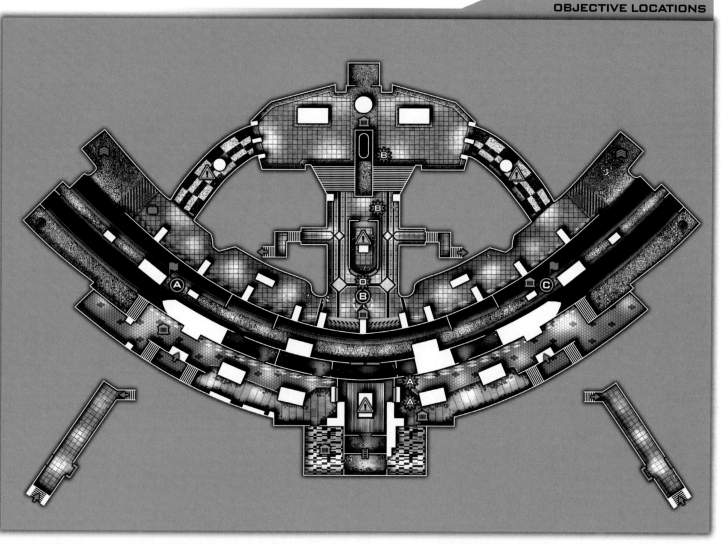

	TEAM SPAWNS		HEADQUARTERS LOCATION		A B O	DEMOLITION BOMB SITES AND OVERTIME SITE
↑ ↑ ↑	CONNECT TO SAME-COLORED ARROWS ON MULTI-LEVEL AREAS	⚑ ⚑	CTF FLAG STANDS		A B C	DOMINATION CONTROL POINTS
▤	USABLE LADDER	A B	SEARCH & DESTROY BOMB SITES			
⚠	HARDPOINT AREAS OF CONTROL	💼	SEARCH & DESTROY BOMB			

EXPRESS

CAPTURE THE FLAG

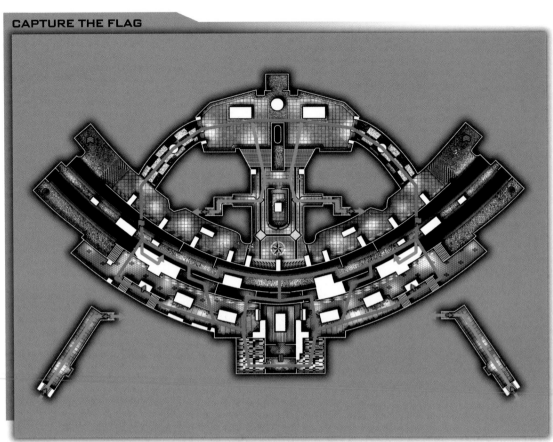

DEMOLITION

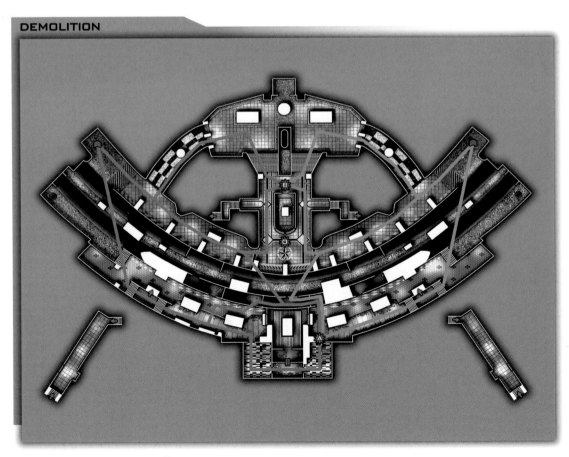

< 236 237 >

DOMINATION

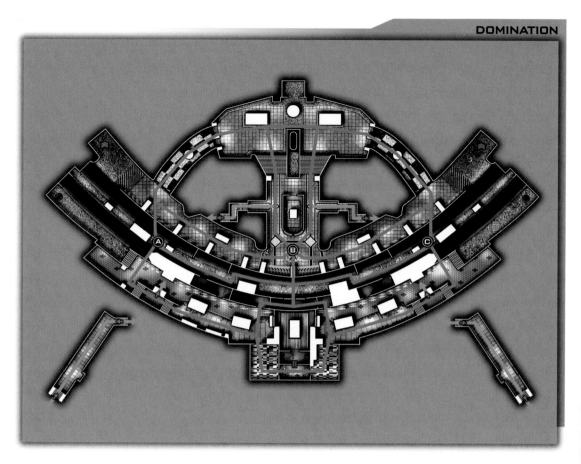

SEARCH & DESTROY

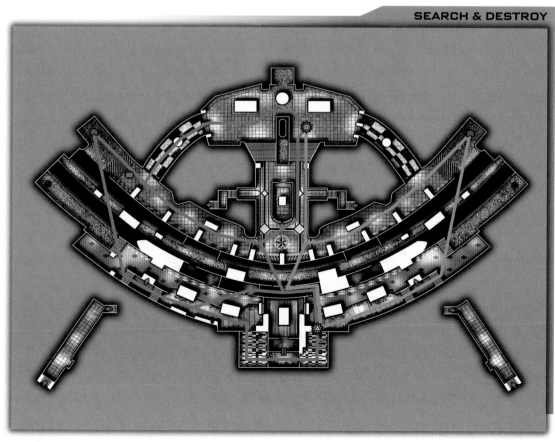

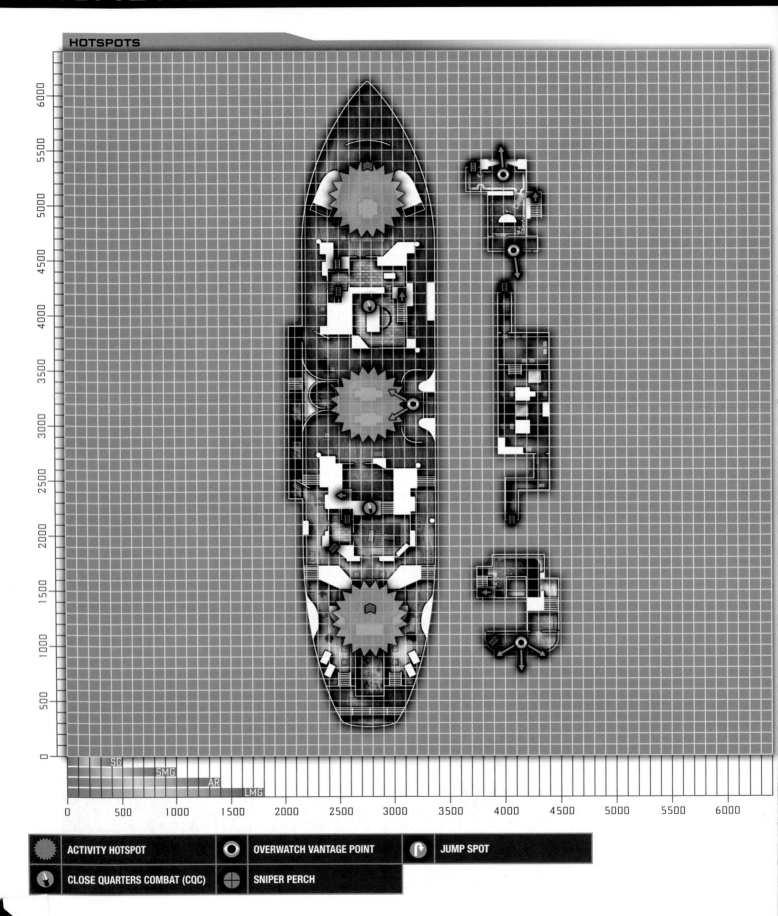

HOTSPOTS

ACTIVITY HOTSPOT	**OVERWATCH VANTAGE POINT**	**JUMP SPOT**
CLOSE QUARTERS COMBAT (CQC)	**SNIPER PERCH**	

< 238 239 >

OBJECTIVE LOCATIONS

	TEAM SPAWNS		HEADQUARTERS LOCATION				DEMOLITION BOMB SITES AND OVERTIME SITE
	CONNECT TO SAME-COLORED ARROWS ON MULTI-LEVEL AREAS		CTF FLAG STANDS	Ⓐ	Ⓑ	Ⓒ	DOMINATION CONTROL POINTS
	USABLE LADDER		SEARCH & DESTROY BOMB SITES				
	HARDPOINT AREAS OF CONTROL		SEARCH & DESTROY BOMB				

HIJACKED

OVERVIEW

A super-luxury yacht creates an intense battle arena. Very narrow paths through the level and an extremely short distance from east to west make this a brutal head-on engagement in most modes. You can use interior areas on the north and south of the yacht to take cover from the madness out on the deck. Below deck is a passage that you can use to traverse the north-south route and avoid the action above.

NOTES

The center of this level is a killing field. Avoid it by going below or using the side path on the west of the deck. Or cover it yourself from a side path or the interior areas. High-powered aerial Scorestreaks are especially devastating on this map. Use the limited canopies on the yacht's north and south tips to take cover if you can't get inside quickly enough.

CAPTURE THE FLAG

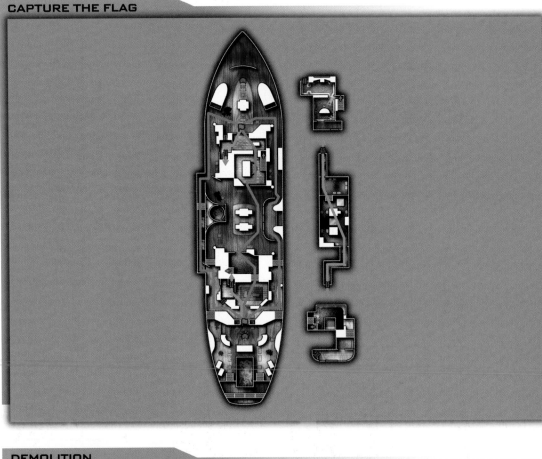

DEMOLITION

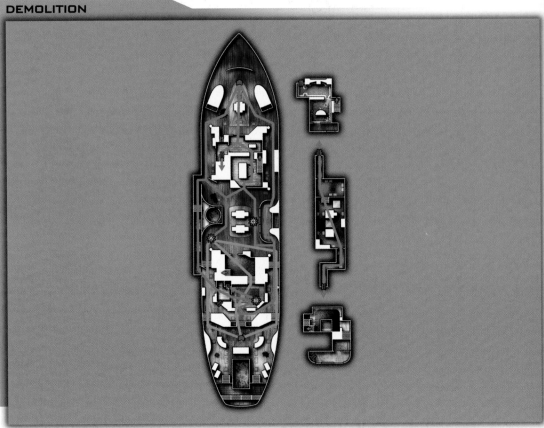

DOMINATION

SEARCH & DESTROY

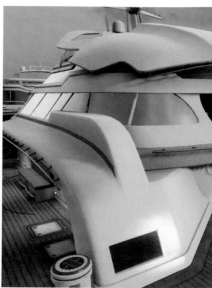

HOTSPOTS

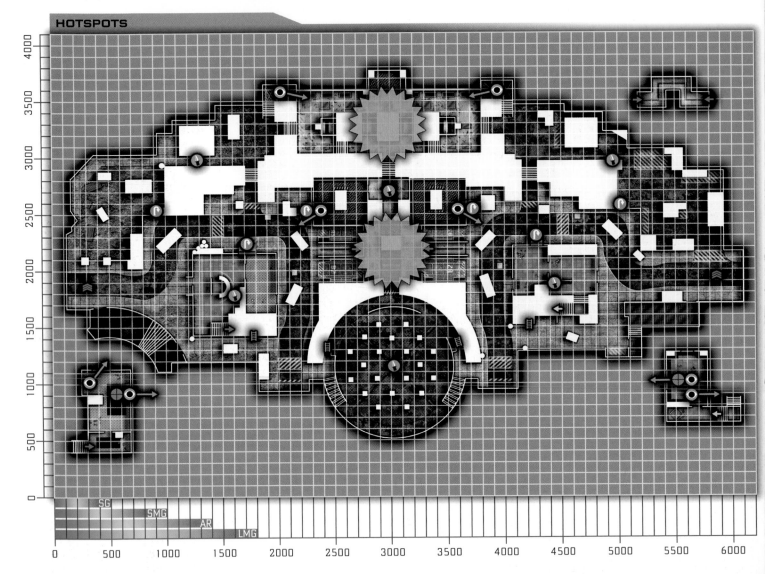

✴	**ACTIVITY HOTSPOT**
◗	**CLOSE QUARTERS COMBAT (CQC)**
◉	**OVERWATCH VANTAGE POINT**
⊕	**SNIPER PERCH**
↺	**JUMP SPOT**

OVERVIEW

A Pakistani nuclear plant is the site of an intense battle over a central dividing line. Despite a relatively simple-looking east-west layout, you can use quite a few routes to pass through the center of the map: north out by the ocean, up over the center, or south inside one of the plants towers. Each route features choices that yield different types of cover.

It's important to use the alternate routes, either climbing inside the rooms beside the center, or going far north or south if the center is heavily locked down. Both sides have buildings that can perfectly cover the middle area (and each other).

The "base" areas on each side are similar, but not symmetrical. Spend some time exploring them to get used to the lines of sight. Familiarize yourself with the available cover for pushing an objective or flanking the enemy team.

NOTES

The raised central platform is an extremely dangerous area. Don't travel over it unless you are forced to because of an objective, or if speed is your sole concern. Expect campers inside the buildings on the east and west of the map. Avoid them or flush them whichever you prefer.

OBJECTIVE LOCATIONS

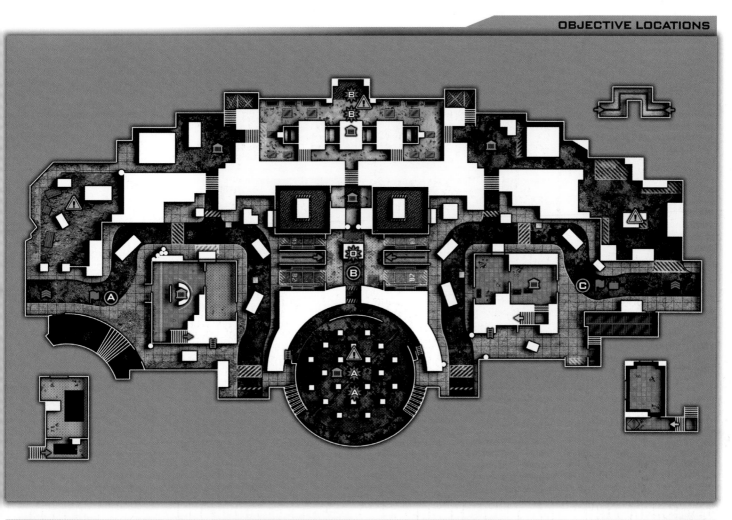

	TEAM SPAWNS		HEADQUARTERS LOCATION		DEMOLITION BOMB SITES AND OVERTIME SITE
	CONNECT TO SAME-COLORED ARROWS ON MULTI-LEVEL AREAS		CTF FLAG STANDS		DOMINATION CONTROL POINTS
	USABLE LADDER		SEARCH & DESTROY BOMB SITES		
	HARDPOINT AREAS OF CONTROL		SEARCH & DESTROY BOMB		

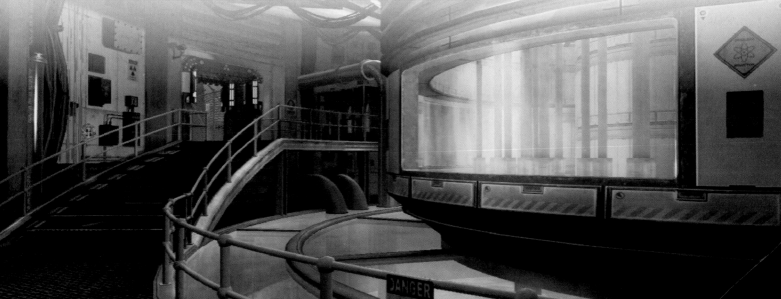

MELTDOWN

CAPTURE THE FLAG

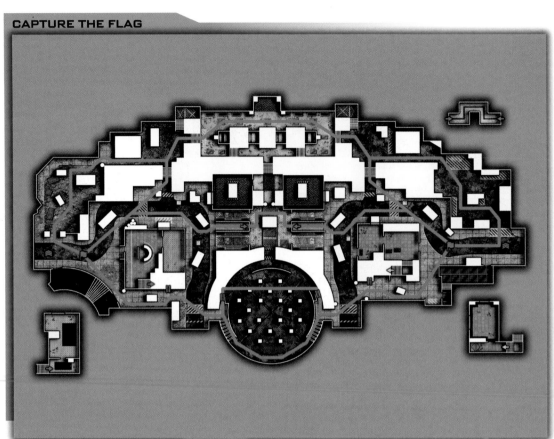

DEMOLITION

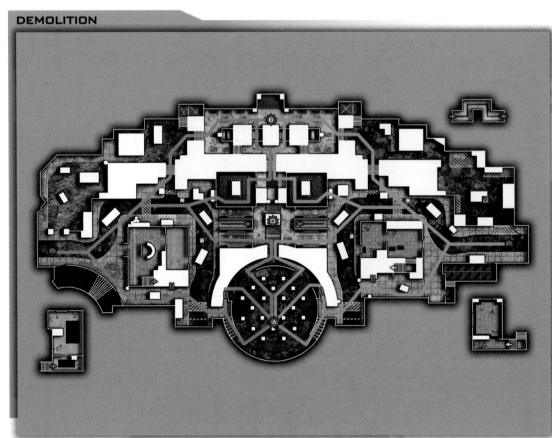

DOMINATION

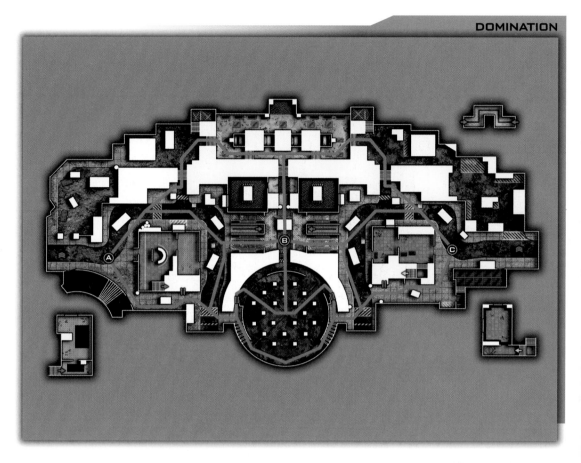

SEARCH & DESTROY

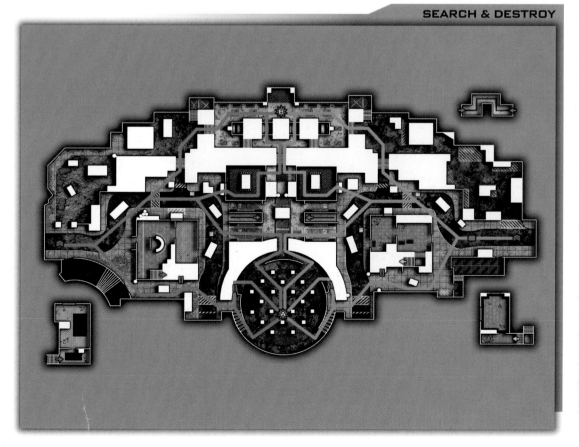

HOTSPOTS

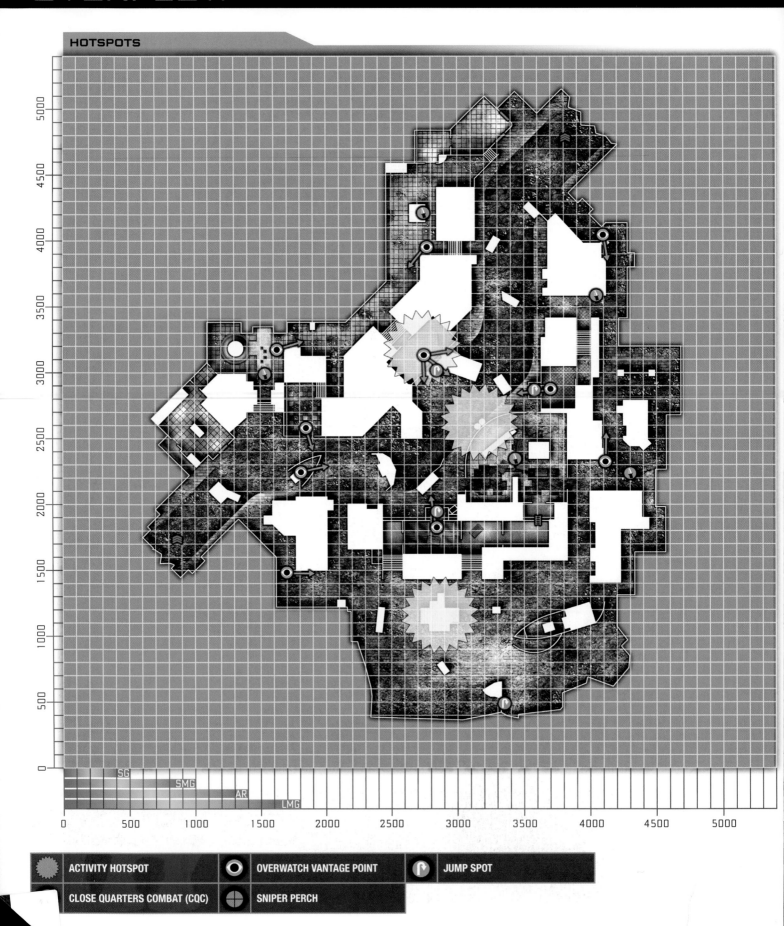

ACTIVITY HOTSPOT	**OVERWATCH VANTAGE POINT**	**JUMP SPOT**
CLOSE QUARTERS COMBAT (CQC)	**SNIPER PERCH**	

OBJECTIVE LOCATIONS

〉〉 〉〉	TEAM SPAWNS	🏛	HEADQUARTERS LOCATION	Ⓐ Ⓑ Ⓞ	DEMOLITION BOMB SITES AND OVERTIME SITE
↑ ↑ ↑	CONNECT TO SAME-COLORED ARROWS ON MULTI-LEVEL AREAS	⚑ ⚑	CTF FLAG STANDS	Ⓐ Ⓑ Ⓒ	DOMINATION CONTROL POINTS
🪜	USABLE LADDER	Ⓐ Ⓑ	SEARCH & DESTROY BOMB SITES		
⚠	HARDPOINT AREAS OF CONTROL	💼	SEARCH & DESTROY BOMB		

OVERFLOW

OVERVIEW

A complex map, Overflow takes place after a massive flood in a Pakistani city. Riverside debris clutters the streets. A mix of long, open sightlines and many interior areas generates interesting tactical engagements. The map is broken up into three areas: a northern walkway takes you behind several buildings that players can enter; a central street has sightlines broken up by debris; and a southeastern area just off the river hosts more interior areas and a muddy, open field behind the buildings.

This level challenges you to adapt to changing engagements in mobile game modes. It forces you to use every area when you compete for static objective areas. Explore the map and learn the many alternate routes that shift between the north, center, and southeastern regions.

NOTES

The central street has a ton of cover, making it safer than most central map areas. However, it is covered by a lot of buildings from the northwest and southeast. Thus, you should still avoid moving through it more than necessary. Expect campers in the various small buildings off the central street. Figure out which direction they are covering and either flank them or avoid them completely. There are plenty of routes that avoid their line of sight.

CAPTURE THE FLAG

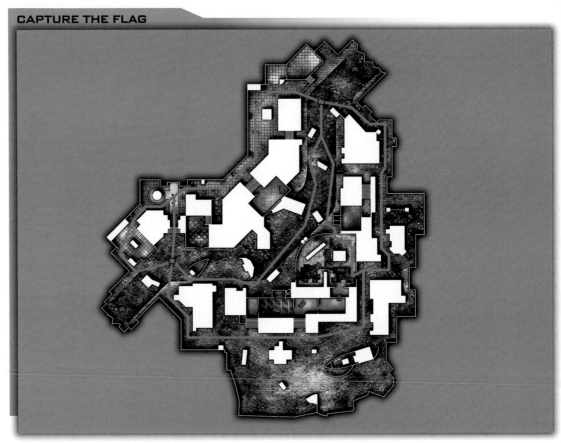

DEMOLITION

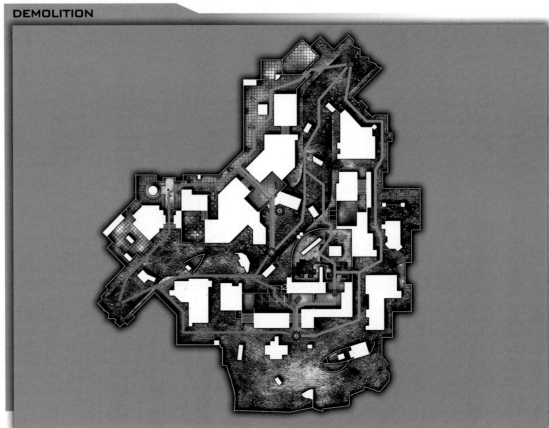

DOMINATION

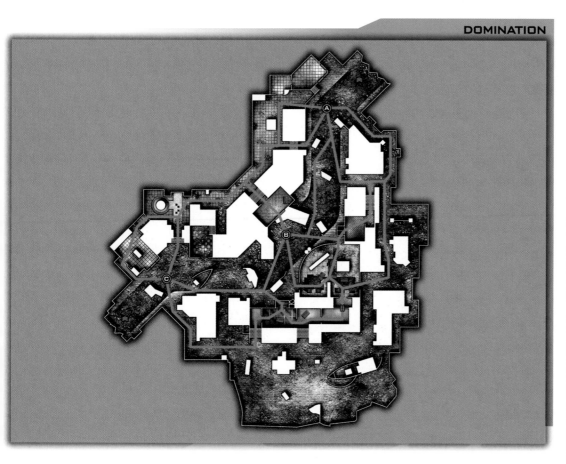

SEARCH & DESTROY

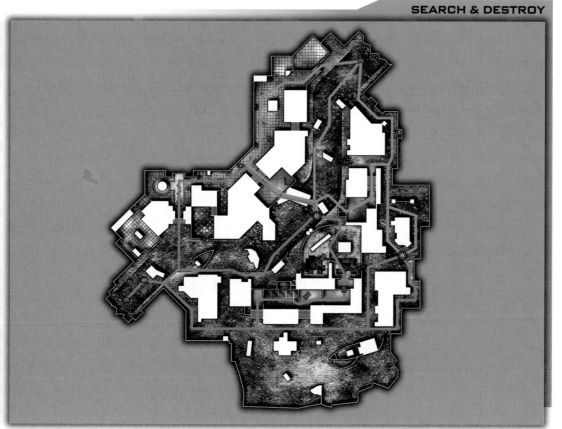

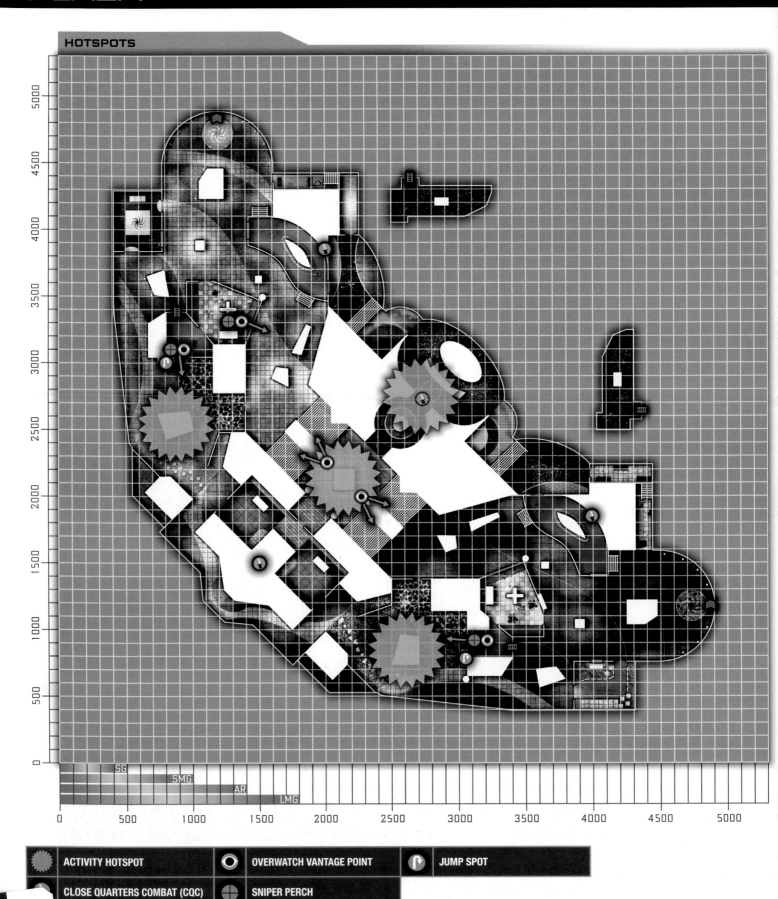

HOTSPOTS

ACTIVITY HOTSPOT

OVERWATCH VANTAGE POINT

JUMP SPOT

CLOSE QUARTERS COMBAT (CQC)

SNIPER PERCH

< 250 251 >

OBJECTIVE LOCATIONS

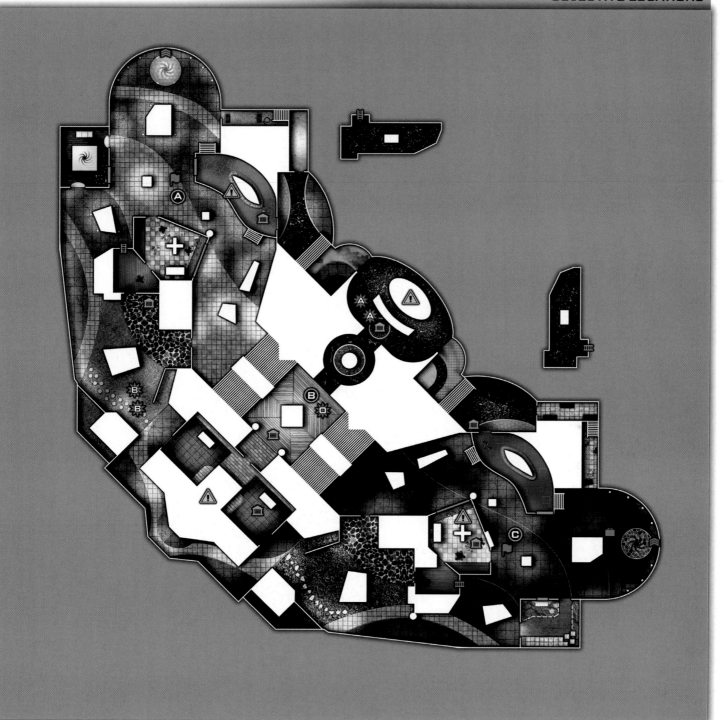

	TEAM SPAWNS		HEADQUARTERS LOCATION		DEMOLITION BOMB SITES AND OVERTIME SITE
	CONNECT TO SAME-COLORED ARROWS ON MULTI-LEVEL AREAS		CTF FLAG STANDS		DOMINATION CONTROL POINTS
	USABLE LADDER		SEARCH & DESTROY BOMB SITES		
	HARDPOINT AREAS OF CONTROL		SEARCH & DESTROY BOMB		

PLAZA

OVERVIEW

A floating tourist paradise on the Indian Ocean, Resort is broken up into two major areas. Storefront buildings take up the northwest and southeast, while a club occupies the center of the map.

There are four discrete routes through the center. Two of them connect to the largest center pathway, a raised platform that is a constant hotspot. Crossing the map's center tends to be the most dangerous if you go directly through, over the stairs in the middle. Also, approach the northwest and southeast areas with caution. There are rooftops on each side and multiple cover areas that can easily shield incoming players.

NOTES

There aren't a lot of long sightlines on this level. Many of the more obvious ones are broken up by obstructions. It's possible to play with CQC setups if you are careful about avoiding the more open areas.

CAPTURE THE FLAG

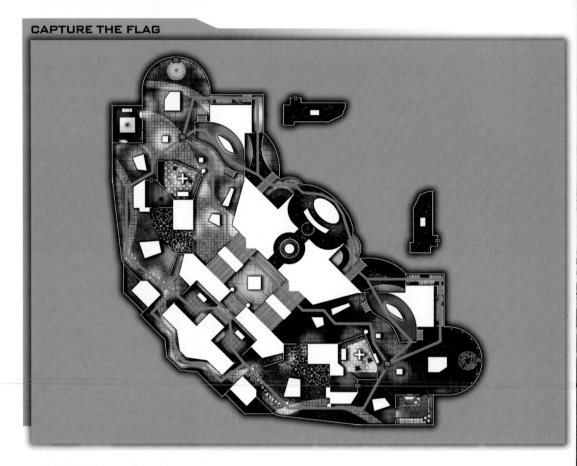

DEMOLITION

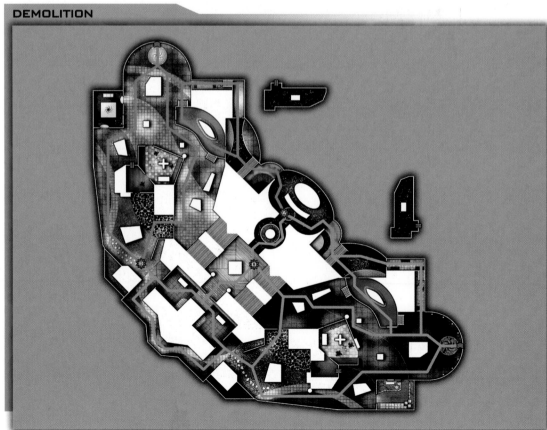

DOMINATION

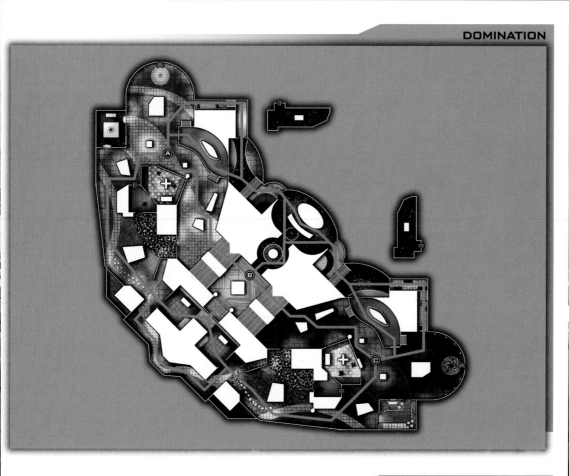

SEARCH & DESTROY

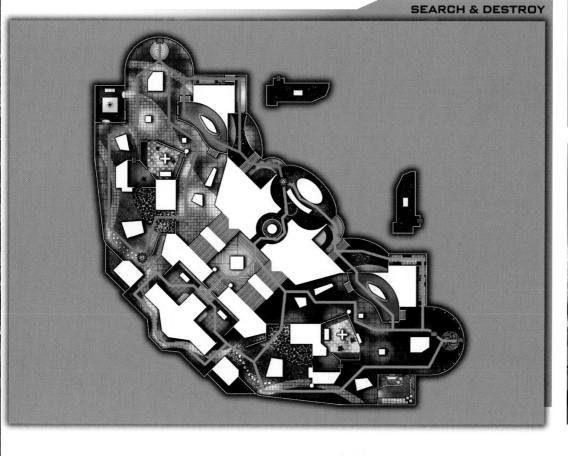

HOTSPOTS

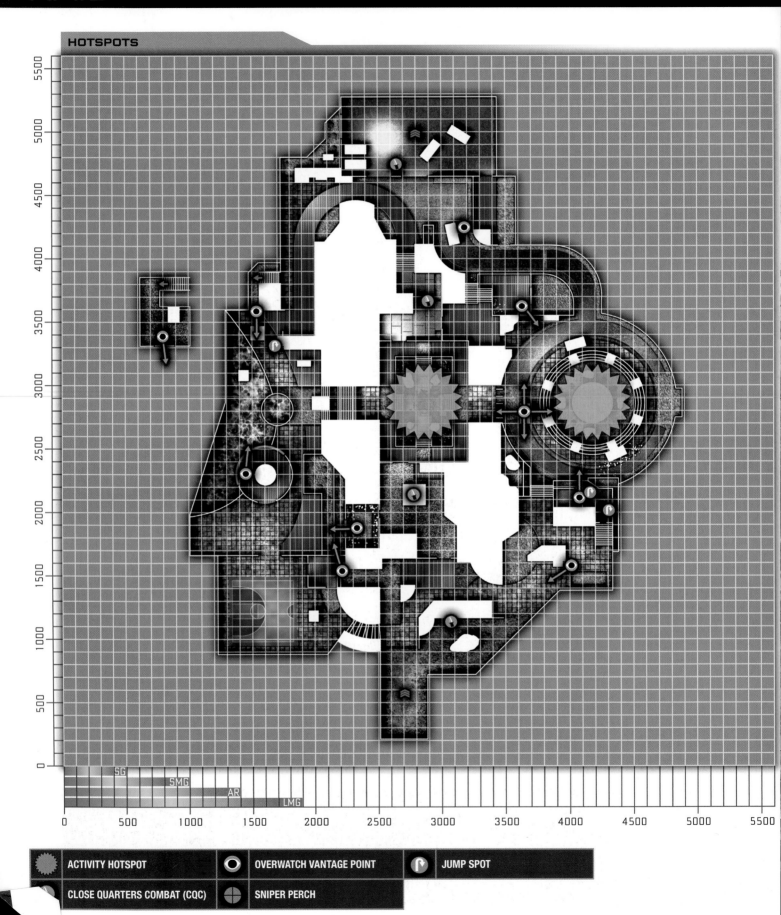

ACTIVITY HOTSPOT		**OVERWATCH VANTAGE POINT**		**JUMP SPOT**	
CLOSE QUARTERS COMBAT (CQC)		**SNIPER PERCH**			

OBJECTIVE LOCATIONS

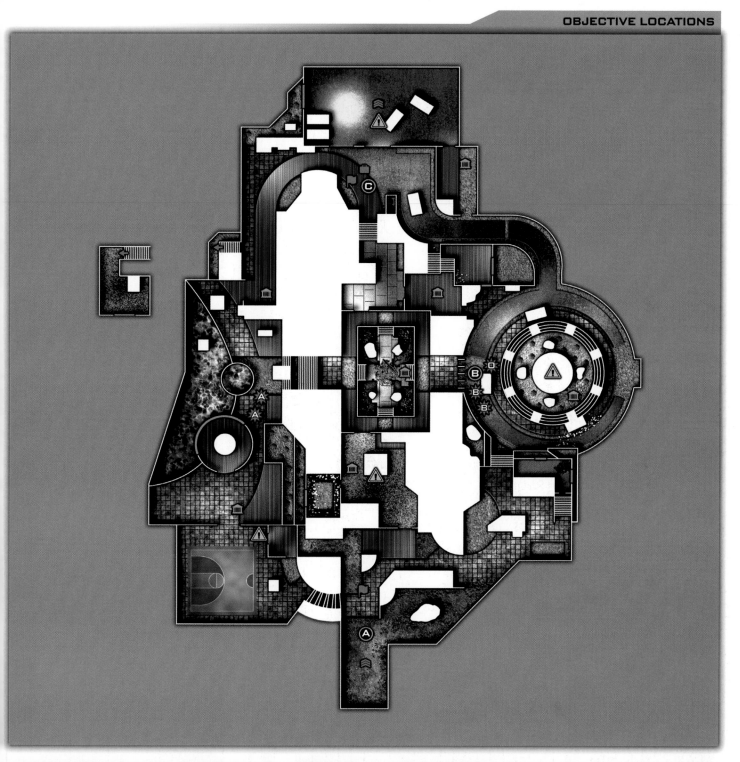

⋙ ⋙	**TEAM SPAWNS**	🏛	**HEADQUARTERS LOCATION**	🅰 🅱 🅾	**DEMOLITION BOMB SITES AND OVERTIME SITE**	
⬆ ⬆ ⬆	**CONNECT TO SAME-COLORED ARROWS ON MULTI-LEVEL AREAS**	🚩 🚩	**CTF FLAG STANDS**	Ⓐ Ⓑ Ⓒ	**DOMINATION CONTROL POINTS**	
🪜	**USABLE LADDER**	🅰 🅱	**SEARCH & DESTROY BOMB SITES**			
⚠	**HARDPOINT AREAS OF CONTROL**	💼	**SEARCH & DESTROY BOMB**			

OVERVIEW

A rich, ultra-modern mansion, Raid is broken up into multiple discrete mini-battlefields. They include the central garden area to the pool, and the small rooms inside the mansion. Stay alert to the entrances into and out of each area. You need to know where your teammates are and where enemies can approach at all times. As long as you know your flanks are secure, you can focus on any threats within or entering the area you're covering or traversing.

Because the areas are divided, if you're being stymied in one part of the level, take an alternate route and come in from an unexpected direction.

NOTES

The center is a proper hotspot, with four entrances that lead to all parts of the level. Travel through it quickly or avoid it entirely. Each part of the map has different types of cover and lines of sight. Explore all of them and familiarize yourself with common camping spots so you know where to look when you enter a new zone.

CAPTURE THE FLAG

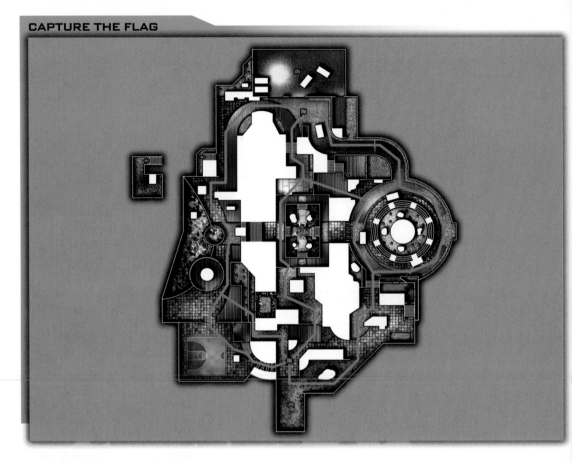

DEMOLITION

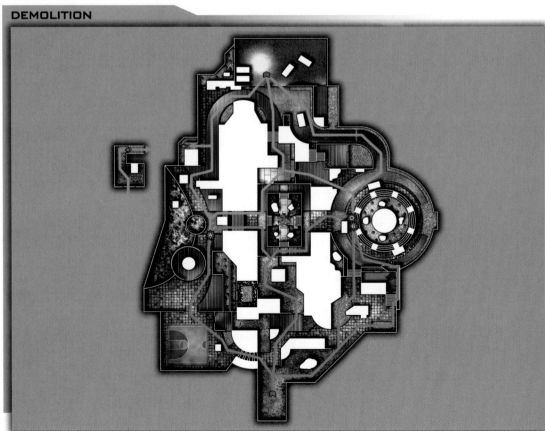

DOMINATION

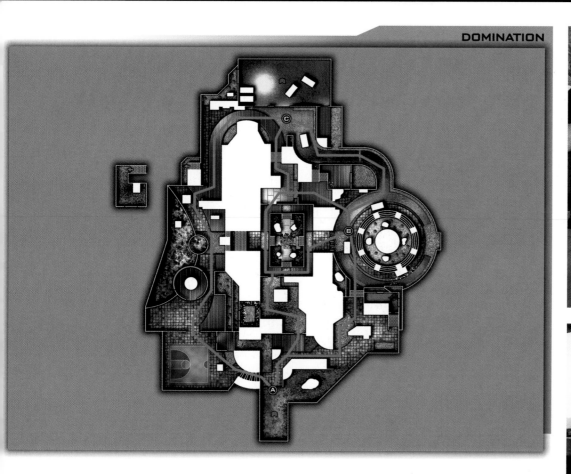

SEARCH & DESTROY

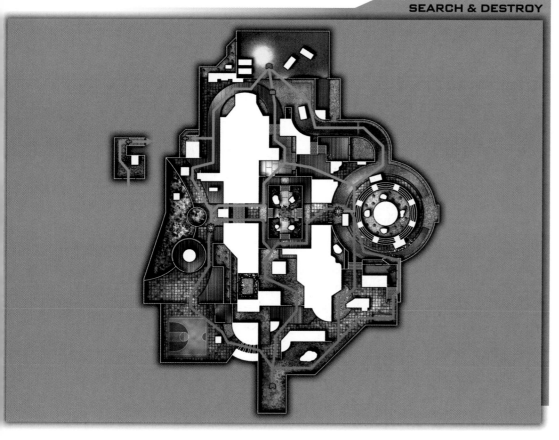

SLUMS

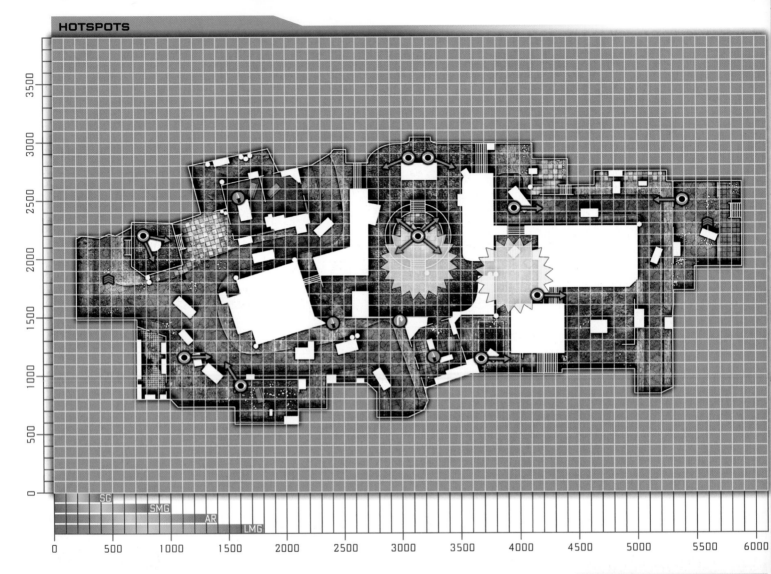

OVERVIEW

The rundown backstreets of Panama City feature intense close-range combat. All paths flow through a central plaza area, which results in brutal conflict in the center of the map. This map is much more asymmetrical than almost any other map in the game. Be aware of the differences between the east and west sides.

In objective modes with static objectives, you may find one side significantly more difficult to fight in. So, be sure to explore both thoroughly and learn their ins and outs. Failing that, bring a Tactical Insertion and break out yourself!

NOTES

Beware of proximity mines and turrets on this level. The narrow lanes and sharp corners are ideal for traps. Bring traps of your own, or use Engineer and Equipment to dismantle those of the enemy.

ACTIVITY HOTSPOT	
CLOSE QUARTERS COMBAT (CQC)	
OVERWATCH VANTAGE POINT	
SNIPER PERCH	
JUMP SPOT	

< 258 259 >

MULTIPLAYER MAPS_SLUMS

OBJECTIVE LOCATIONS

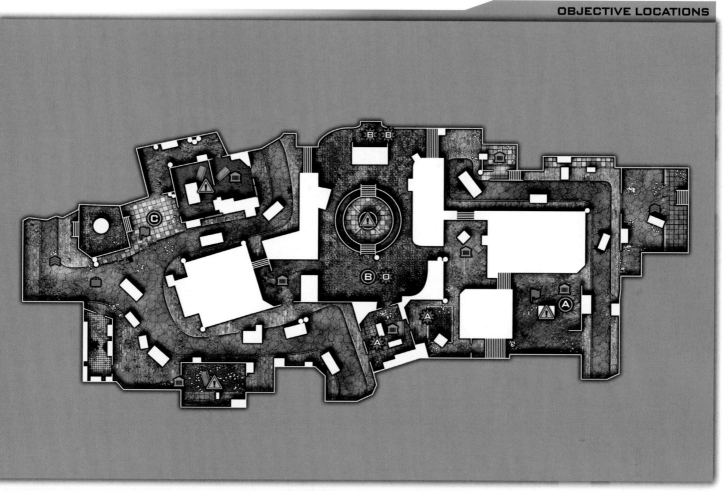

TEAM SPAWNS	HEADQUARTERS LOCATION	DEMOLITION BOMB SITES AND OVERTIME SITE
CONNECT TO SAME-COLORED ARROWS ON MULTI-LEVEL AREAS	CTF FLAG STANDS	DOMINATION CONTROL POINTS
USABLE LADDER	SEARCH & DESTROY BOMB SITES	
HARDPOINT AREAS OF CONTROL	SEARCH & DESTROY BOMB	

SLUMS

CAPTURE THE FLAG

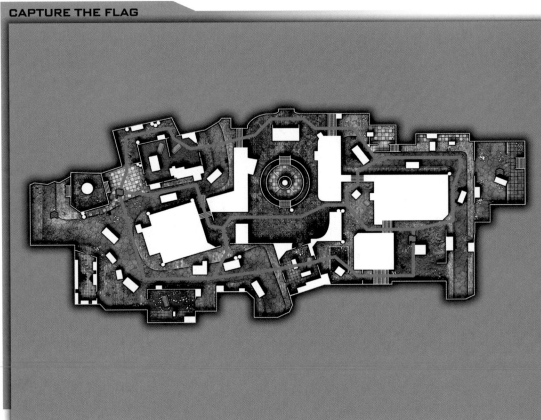

DEMOLITION

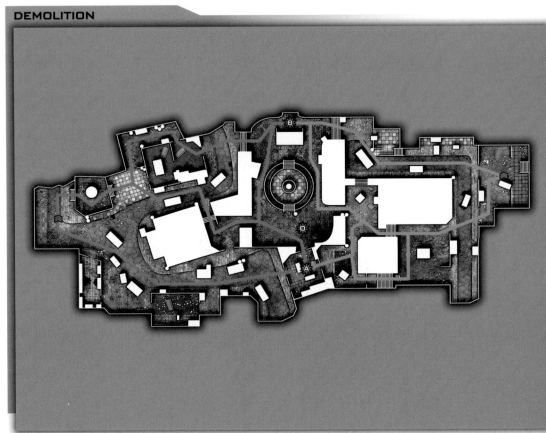

DOMINATION

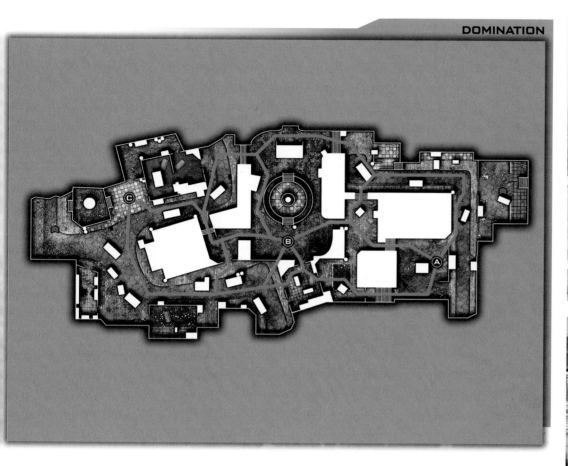

SEARCH & DESTROY

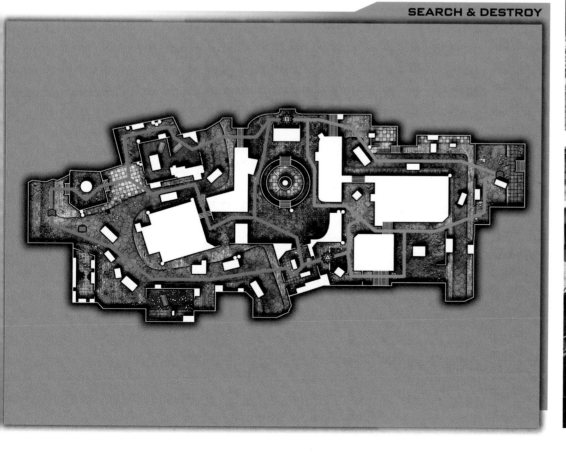

HOTSPOTS

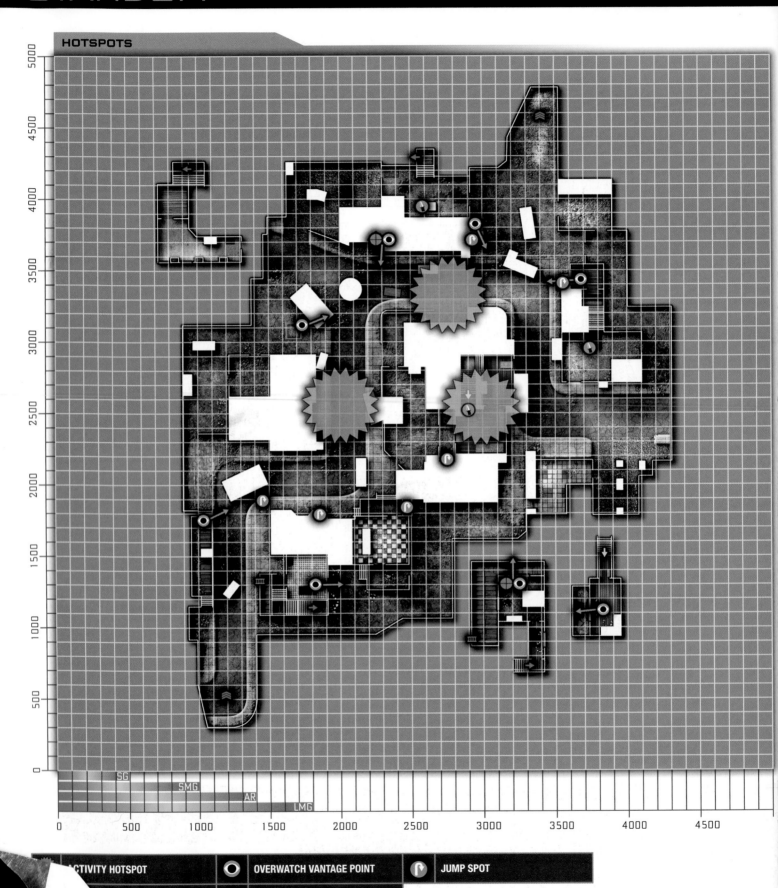

ACTIVITY HOTSPOT

OVERWATCH VANTAGE POINT

JUMP SPOT

QUARTERS COMBAT (CQC)

SNIPER PERCH

OBJECTIVE LOCATIONS

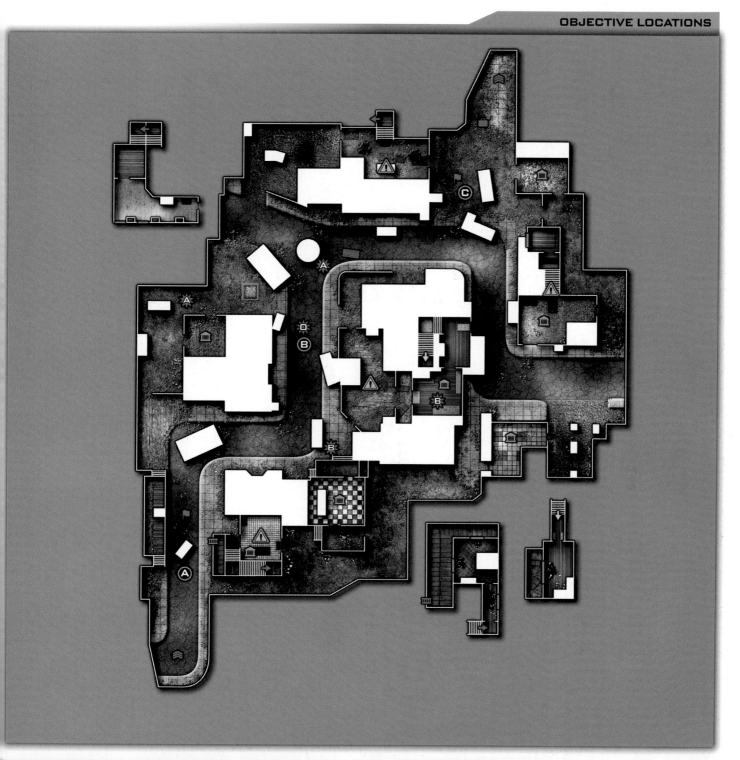

	TEAM SPAWNS		HEADQUARTERS LOCATION		DEMOLITION BOMB SITES AND OVERTIME SITE
	CONNECT TO SAME-COLORED ARROWS ON MULTI-LEVEL AREAS		CTF FLAG STANDS		DOMINATION CONTROL POINTS
	USABLE LADDER		SEARCH & DESTROY BOMB SITES		
	HARDPOINT AREAS OF CONTROL		SEARCH & DESTROY BOMB		

STANDOFF

OVERVIEW

A border town in Kyrgyzstan is the site for conflict on this small, urban map. This level's many buildings and the connections between the different areas encourage a lot of nasty, short-range fights. Meanwhile, the open streets provide ideal killing grounds for long-range specialists.

This level has a lot of sharp ninety-degree corners. It imposes repeated turns no matter what direction you take or what side of the map you begin on. Be aware of corner traps and campers at all times.

NOTES

The streets are extremely dangerous. Try to either be in a building covering the streets, or avoid them by using the back alleys. If you must cross them, move quickly, use what cover exists, and minimize your exposure.

CAPTURE THE FLAG

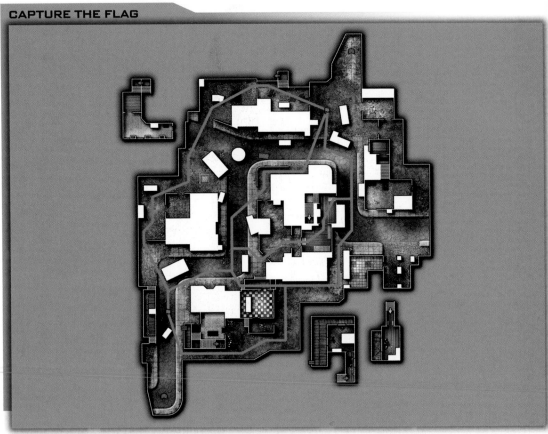

DEMOLITION

DOMINATION

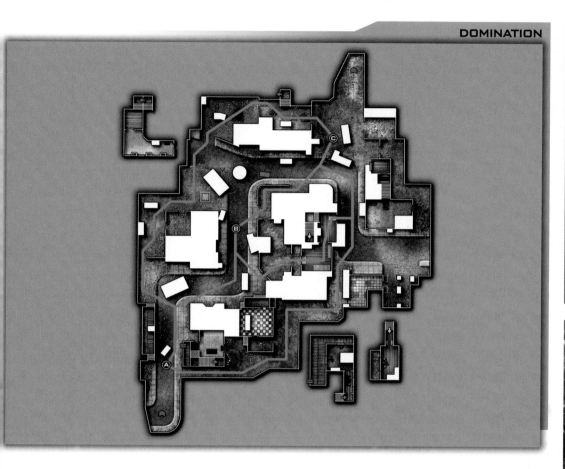

SEARCH & DESTROY

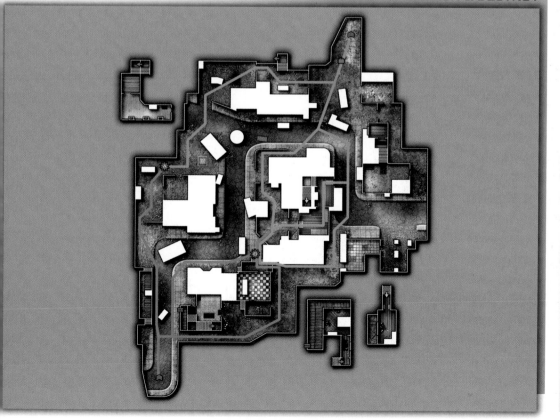

TURBINE

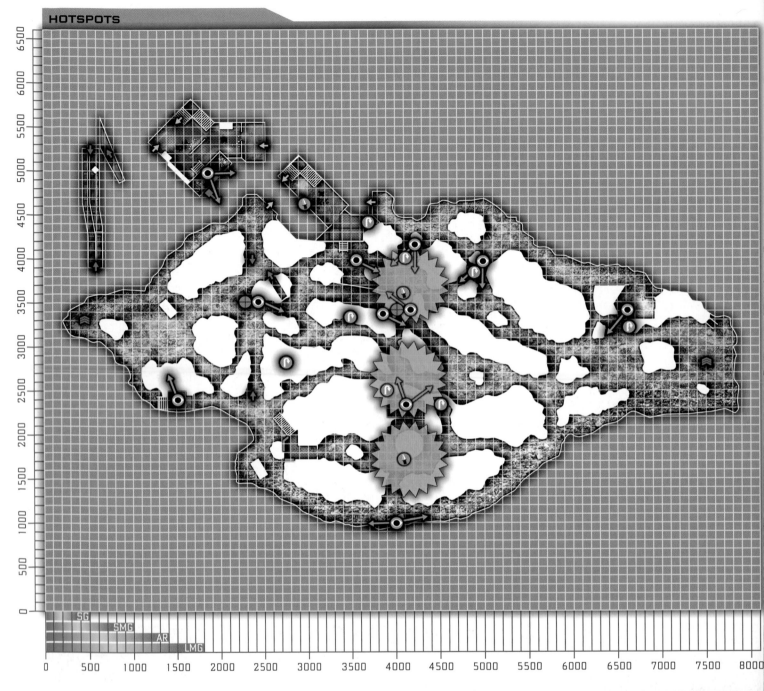

OVERVIEW

A wind farm high in the steppes of Yemen provides challenging, rocky terrain over which to battle. A fallen turbine creates cover and obstructions in the center of the valley. This is one of the largest maps in the game, with a *long* path from east to west. The rocks break up movement paths and sightlines. Travel can be very linear along narrow lanes of engagement. Stay extremely alert when you travel along these lanes. A camper set up at the end can make any path lethal.

This map dips into a valley in the center, with higher altitude on the north and south edges. Use these elevations to shoot down at [ ]s below. However, don't become so focused on the center of the map that you miss threats on the opposite side!

ACTIVITY HOTSPOT	
CLOSE QUARTERS COMBAT (CQC)	
OVERWATCH VANTAGE POINT	
SNIPER PERCH	
JUMP SPOT	

OBJECTIVE LOCATIONS

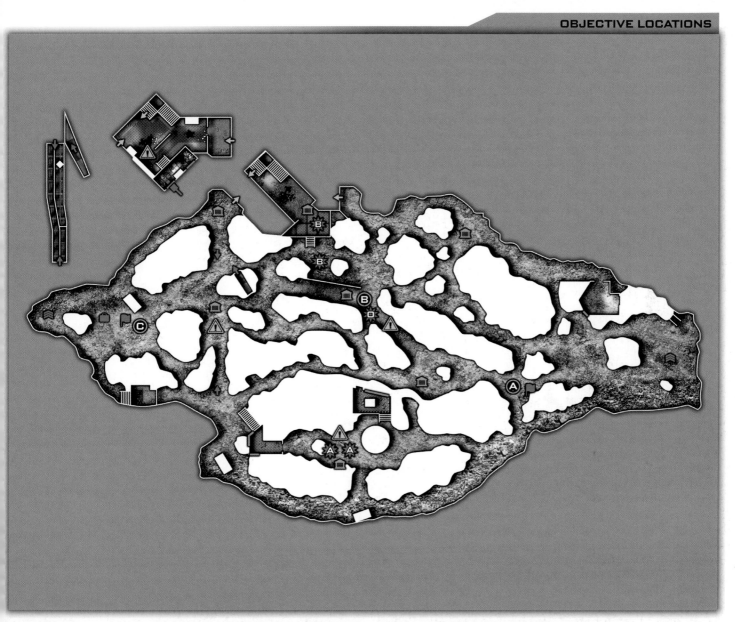

	TEAM SPAWNS		HEADQUARTERS LOCATION		DEMOLITION BOMB SITES AND OVERTIME SITE
	CONNECT TO SAME-COLORED ARROWS ON MULTI-LEVEL AREAS		CTF FLAG STANDS		DOMINATION CONTROL POINTS
	USABLE LADDER		SEARCH & DESTROY BOMB SITES		
	HARDPOINT AREAS OF CONTROL		SEARCH & DESTROY BOMB		

NOTES

Long-range weapons can shine on this map, even with the sightlines frequently broken by rocky outcroppings. Short-range engagements do occur, particularly in objective modes that force movement to specific areas. Still, keep your head down if you're in the open with a short-range weapon.

You can climb on the remains of the titular turbine in the valley's center. Doing so exposes you to fire from all sides of the map, so don't stick your head up there unless you know what you're getting into!

TURBINE

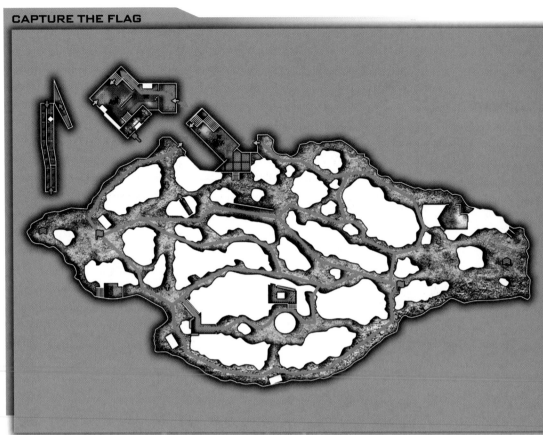

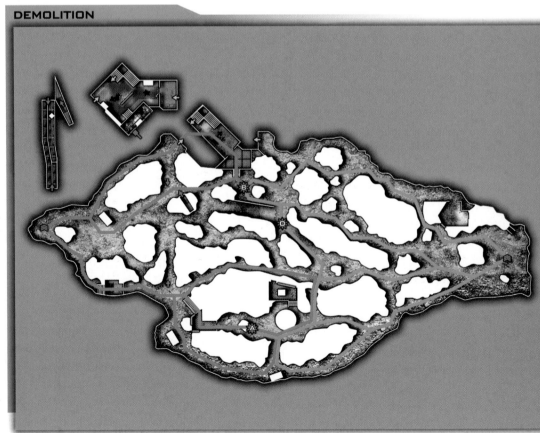

DOMINATION

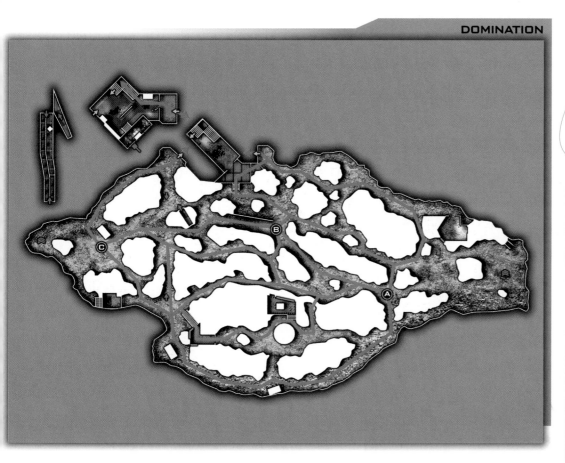

SEARCH & DESTROY

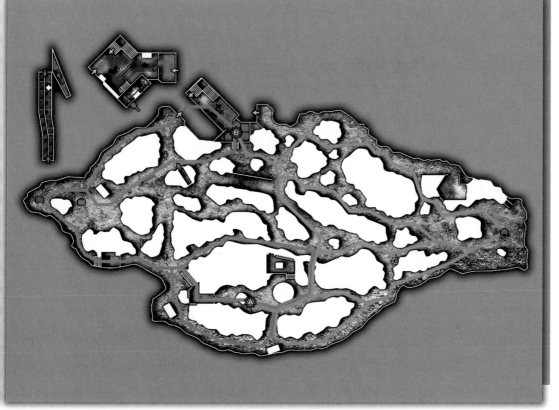

YEMEN

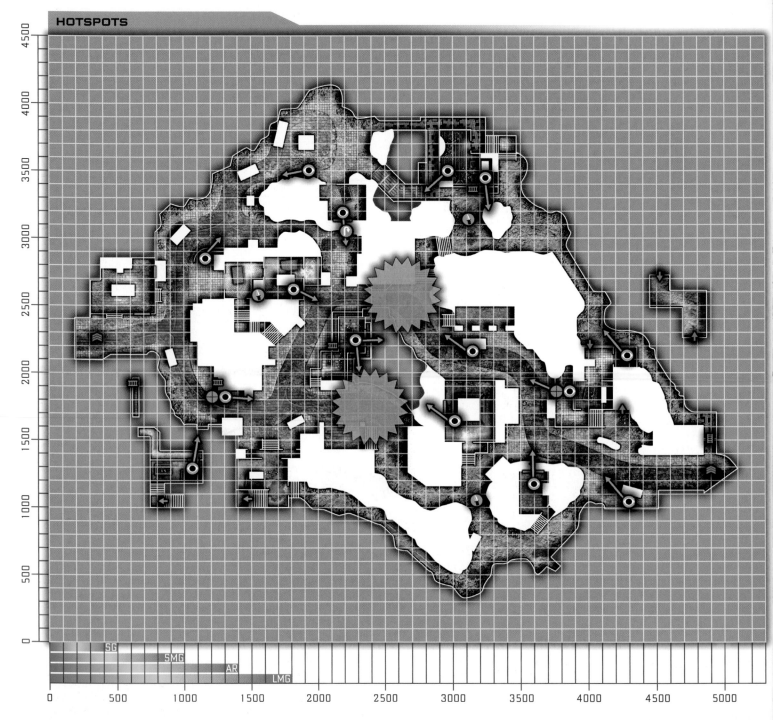

HOTSPOTS

OVERVIEW

... of a small island city in Yemen are the site of an intense urban conflict. The most mazelike and twisting of the urban-
... significant elevation changes. A dip leads down into the center of the map from the higher points
... With buildings on all sides and elevation changes common, situational awareness is absolutely vital
... unicate with your teammates, and bring classes that give you an informational edge.

ACTIVITY HOTSPOT	
CLOSE QUARTERS COMBAT (CQC)	
OVERWATCH VANTAGE POINT	
SNIPER PERCH	
JUMP SPOT	

OBJECTIVE LOCATIONS

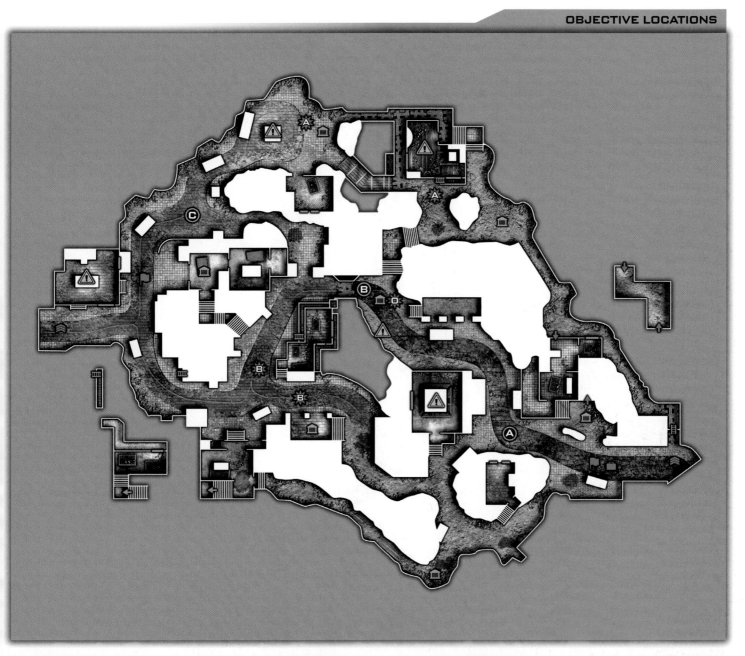

		TEAM SPAWNS		HEADQUARTERS LOCATION	Ⓐ Ⓑ ⓪	DEMOLITION BOMB SITES AND OVERTIME SITE
↑ ↑ ↑		CONNECT TO SAME-COLORED ARROWS ON MULTI-LEVEL AREAS	⚑ ⚑	CTF FLAG STANDS	Ⓐ Ⓑ Ⓒ	DOMINATION CONTROL POINTS
		USABLE LADDER	Ⓐ Ⓑ	SEARCH & DESTROY BOMB SITES		
⚠		HARDPOINT AREAS OF CONTROL	💼	SEARCH & DESTROY BOMB		

NOTES

Don't forget about the very outermost routes around the level. They are definitely slower, but they also tend to see a lot less traffic than the middle of the map. You can off
use them to flank an entrenched team. There are quite a few good sightlines from buildings, so be aware of campers on overwatch. Either flank them or use alternate
to avoid them entirely.

CAPTURE THE FLAG

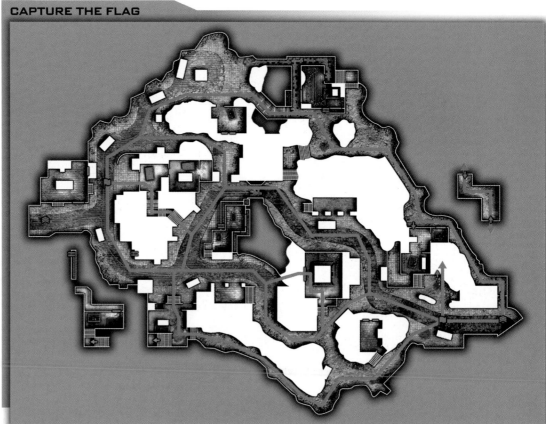

DEMOLITION

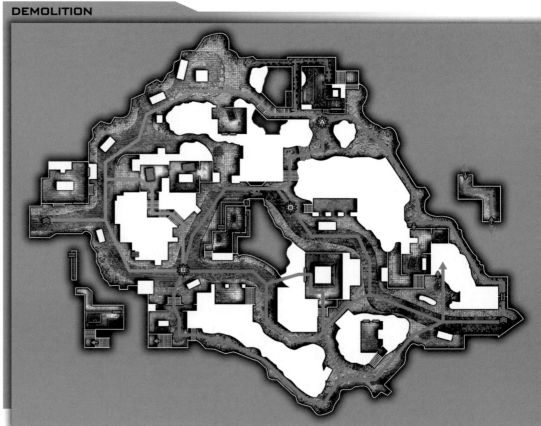

DOMINATION

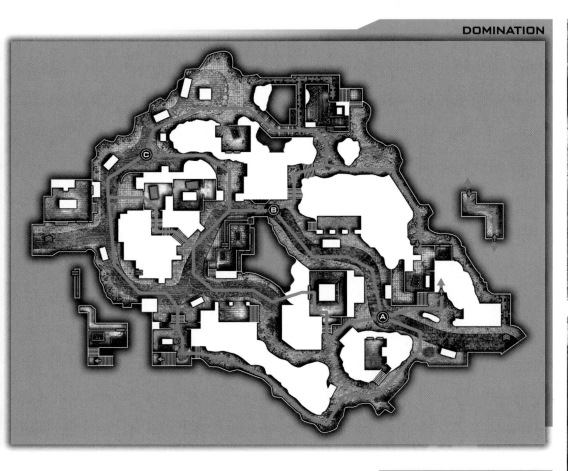

SEARCH & DESTROY

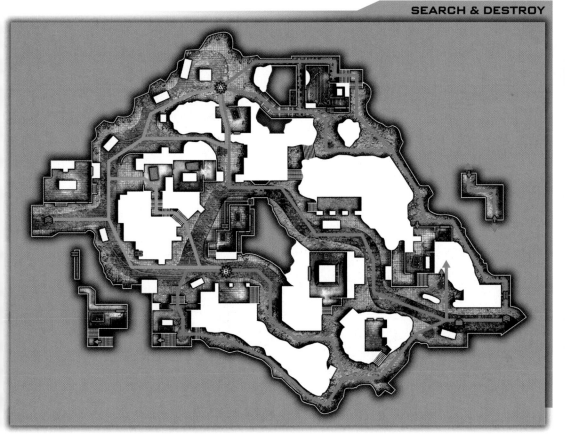

ZOMBIES

Provided by our friends at Treyarch, we present the following overview of *Zombies*, a game unto itself that fans of the series look forward to playing with great anticipation. Enjoy!

Zombies returns to *Call of Duty* for its third installment, following *Call of Duty: World at War* and *Call of Duty: Black Ops*. The game mode has grown wildly popular since its debut in 2008, spawning an additional seven DLC entries and two iOS versions of the game.

Now with *Black Ops II*, *Zombies* is bigger than ever, both literally and figuratively, transporting players to an entire county overrun with the undead. Darker secrets, deeper quests, new weapons, and more zombies than you've ever seen onscreen before; the latest chapter of the *Zombies* epic takes the game to a whole new level. This year's entry offers a variety of game modes to sate every appetite of zombie killer.

We *highly* recommend playing a few rounds of *Zombies* with some friends before digging too deep into this part of the guide. Get a feel for the game. Learn the tendencies of the undead and devise some personal strategies to survive. Try to pick up the trail of some of the game's many, many mysteries.

GREEN RUN
NORTHERN HEMISPHERE

Waiting for other players

Once you get chewed up a few times (and you will), review the material here. We'll set you down a path and help you survive. We may even drop a few hints toward the numerous secrets in the game.

Zombies is not just another game mode. It thrives on the thrill of discovery, the fanning of conspiracy theories, and community cooperation outside of the game. Feel free to search out *Zombies* fan communities. Become a part of the team effort to unravel *Zombies'* secrets. It's this spirit of community off which *Zombies* thrives.

Surviving *Zombies* as long as you can is one thing; being good enough to unravel all of its secrets is another matter entirely. This is *not* a direct walkthrough! So, this chapter avoids story spoilers and focuses strictly on *Zombies* gameplay.

> Strategy Updates

Check out www.bradygames.com for updated *Zombies* content and strategy as it becomes available.

WHAT LURKS INSIDE THE HAZE OF SMOKE & ASH?

...ents of *Black Ops Zombies MOON*, Earth is a shadow of its former self. Zombies ...sh cover much of the landscape, concealing both unknown horrors

...n the remains of a bus depot on the edge of a desolate post-apocalyptic ...e robotic creature sits behind the wheel of a dilapidated bus, waiting to ...nd take them on the ride of their lives.

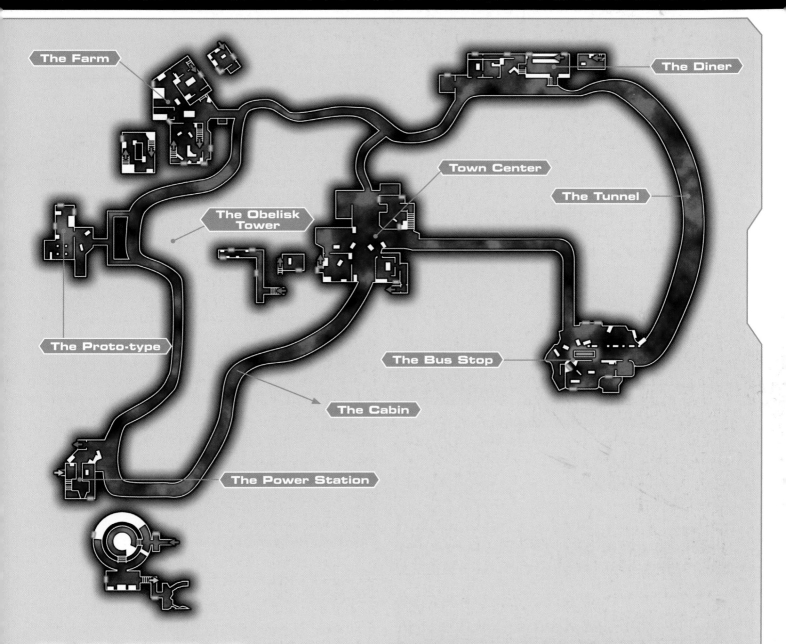

- The Farm
- The Diner
- Town Center
- The Tunnel
- The Obelisk Tower
- The Proto-type
- The Bus Stop
- The Cabin
- The Power Station

THE SETUP

Call of Duty: Black Ops II Zombies takes place in one enormous map the size of a county, which is divided into five major areas. These include:

> The Bus Depot	> The Farm	> The Town
> The Diner	> The Power Station	

Each of the five areas has its own identity rife with secrets to discover, weapons and equipment to acquire, and many, many zombies. The map here is big enough to provide you with some serious options. And, by options, we mean multiple *Zombies* game modes. Here's the breakdown:

BLACK OPS II ZOMBIE MODES

> **TranZit:** Dig into the conspiracies and lore of *Zombies* by exploring the entire county. Be forewarned: it takes serious time, skill, and effort to uncover all of the secrets of TranZit.

> **Survival:** Need a quick fix of *Zombies* mayhem? Survive as long as you can with limited resources in one of three subdivisions of Green Run. How long will you last in the Town, the Farm, or the Bus Depot?

> **Grief:** A spin on the survival game-type, competitive-cooperative. Grief pits two teams against each other in one of Green Run's two custom-fit locations. Compete to survive the longest, and "grief" the opposition to win.

Adjustable Difficulty

Is the game a little too tough in your first couple forays into the fray? You ca[n] now lower the difficulty to hone your zombie-slaying skills.

SURVIVAL AND GRIEF

Survival and *Grief* are, respectively, cooperative and competitive co-op game modes in *Zombies*.

Survival is purely cooperative with up to 4 players.

Grief, on the other hand, involves up to 8 players split into two teams (CDC and CIA) competing in a "last team standing" scenario. The teams are *not* directly pitted against each other. You're not playing *Zombies Deathmatch* here. Rather, the idea is to interfere (or "grief") the opposing team and let the zombies do your dirty work. Only one team can survive. Here's the twist: you can work together for early rounds or the entire game, but ultimately only one team walks out alive. There are opportunities to be cooperative, sure, but there are features where competition plays a heavy role.

It may be a benefit to work together across teams, but eventually you'll have to make a classic moral apocalyptic decision: which team is walking out alive? Both teams cannot, and you're not here to kill the other team. You just have to determine who leaves the arena breathing.

TRANZIT

TranZit is the primary game mode of *Zombies*. Here is the continuation of a legend that began back in *Call of Duty: World at War* and continued through *Black Ops*. TranZit puts you in the shoes of one of four new survivors, each struggling to make their way through the smoldering ruins of the Earth. This is *not* a reboot. Connections to the past are there.

Who are these new survivors? Where did they come from? How will their stories weave into the greater mythos? Listen to them. Follow them. They have mind-boggling insight into the legend of *Zombies*.

TranZit features all of the classic *Zombies* mechanics fans have come to know: rebuilding barricades, killing zombies, earning points, buying weapons, opening passageways, and deep side-quests that illuminate the game's mythology.

But two major additions will help you navigate and survive TranZit's challenges: "Buildables" and the Bus. More on these later.

little support in your fight against the undead? Guess what—you'll have
　　　　　　　t. Need to get around town (relatively) safely? You'll
　　　　　　　Bus lets you travel around to the map's five major
　　　　　　　ian traversing afoot. Be advised—the bus driver is on a
　　　　　　　e you behind.

All Aboard!

The robotic bus driver drives the bus around the map on a continuous circuit, stopping at all five major areas.

The bus itself has boards on the windows, which can be rebuilt like any other barricade in the map. However, zombies can enter the bus via certain locations that *cannot* be barricaded. Zombies *will* attack you while the bus is in motion if you board or ride the vehicle during a wave.

Other than expediting travel around the entire county, the best part about the bus is that it can be upgraded! Search the entire county—and we mean *all of it*—for very specific parts that expand the bus's capabilities and help you defend your transport in later rounds.

Where and what are these pieces? Well, we don't want to make this *too* easy on you. We can tell you that they'll give you a significant edge once you add them to the bus. Hunting down those parts is well worth the time.

Upgrades for the bus are scattered around the entire map. You have to look high and low and in every nook and cranny to find all of the parts.

A little piece of advice: If you happen to have an EMP grenade, we do *not* recommend detonating it in the vicinity of various electrical equipment or devices. A long walk over molten rock, with screeching creatures nipping at your face, is not as much fun as it may seem.

Power!

Zombies veterans already realize how important electricity is, not only to survive, but also to explore and discover. Thus the significance of power in TranZit cannot be overstated. *If you feel so inclined*, find the means of returning power to the county. What can you do with Power?

> **Specific Doors:** Some of the doors in *Zombies* cannot be opened simply by spending points. They require a source of power to see what's hidden behind them. Without power, you cannot access certain locked rooms in each of the five major areas. Trust us—it's worth the effort.

> **Perk-a-Cola Machines:** These perk-dispensing vending machines require electricity to be used. Perk-a-Colas are expensive, but they're a necessity for late-round survival. Note: in the Solo experience, the Quick Revive machine has a slightly different function and is already powered up and ready to use.

> **Equipment:** Even some of the new equipment types require power to function.

This game offers a host of strategic choices, even so far as choosing whether or not you even *want* to activate the power. There just may be instances where *not* turning on the power could be beneficial to your health.

< 276   277 >

Remember the Power Station? Take a good look around the area, and see if you can find a filthy means of getting down into its basement. Once inside, you can *eventually* flip the switch on the *real* power for the *entire* map, *assuming* you've taken the necessary steps to do so. However, don't expect to find that switch hanging out on a wall somewhere, as in previous *Zombies* installments. You have to do some snooping and use a little elbow grease to get the county's power grid back up and running.

Once the power is active, *all* Perk-a-Cola machines are powered up and functional. This lets you stock up on Perks, which is vital for surviving into the later rounds.

You may discover that the main power has not necessarily reached every corner of the county. That means you have to find some workarounds. They're there—again, snooping is key.

While turning on the power has many benefits in TranZit, you may also find that leaving it off can be equally beneficial. Flipping that switch may have an *unintended* electrical side effect…

Buildables!

We've mentioned that you should be on the lookout for various parts to beneficial *accouterments* that will aid your survival. Welcome to the wonderful world of Buildables!

Buildables are very useful items that you, well, *build*. If you can find the right parts in the right part of the county, you'll eventually find a quiet little place where you can perform some craftsmanship. Do your best to survive and find the perfect place to make your masterpiece!

There are some rules when it comes to Buildables. First, you can carry only *one* part to a Buildable at a time. And you can have only one active part of any given Buildable *active* in the world at any given time. If it's destroyed or taken, feel free to go back to where you originally found it and get another. On subsequent play-throughs, those parts may not be in the same place you originally found them.

Second, any player can assemble the parts. Do you have Part A and your teammate has Part B? You can both add them to the assembly. Strategy wise, each player can carry one part and assemble it quickly; or one player can do the item-running while the other players play defense. The best strategy for Buildables is up to you and your teammates.

Once you construct a Buildable, any player can then pick it up and equip it from the location it was constructed. But you can carry only one Buildable at a time. Choose wisely.

Here's a look at the different *types* of Buildables that may be available to you:

> Defensive Buildables
> Offensive Buildables
> Resource Buildables
> Buildables to help you discover new things within the county

If you find a location where you can build something, start scavenging the *immediate* area for objects in the world that look useful. However, some extra-special Buildables will require serious scavenging around the *entire county* to locate. Did you think they were going to make this easy for you?

A Shroud of Smoke & Ash…

A menacing haze of smoke and ash covers the map's five major areas. It is every bit as dangerous as it looks. Should you make the command decision to venture into the murk, be advised that therein reside all sorts of new evils. Your doom may start with an ear-piercing screech. If you hear it, cover your face, keep your knife handy, and be ready to sprint to a clearing—the dense smoke is simply no joke.

Those who have the guts to stray from the path and make their way through it will find a much more dangerous world than exploring the county's five main locations. Zombies *will* continue their onslaught, and there's nothing worse than being surrounded by zombies obscured by the smoke.

Getting lost in the smoke with zombies nipping at your heels is generally fatal. However, the rewards and Easter eggs for braving these no-man's lands are equal to the danger. Nevertheless, be warned: if you're not yet up to snuff, *stay away from the smoke!* If you decide to go in there, we recommend bringing a friend or two.

Traveling as quickly as possible in a coordinated unit is the best way to manage this madness. Communication and teamwork can be crucial. If at all possible, avoid entering unless you've purchased multiple Perk-a-Colas and doubled-up on Mystery Box weaponry. Seriously consider boosting up before venturing the depths of the smoke.

Mystery Boxes

It wouldn't be *Zombies* without the Mystery Box, and this weapon dispensary returns to the franchise in a big way. Featuring a selection of near-future weapons from *Black Ops II*, as well as some tried and true Wonder Weapons from previous installments (Ray Gun anyone?), the Mystery Box is, more than anything else, critical to your survival. The most powerful weapons and special equipment come strictly from this fickle box. You may not always get what you want; but generally, you'll get what you need.

Be careful how many times you dip into that well, however. After you use the Mystery Box a random number of times, a teddy bear appears and a strange, demonic giggle sets the box a-shaking and teleports it to another, unknown location.

The Mystery Box is initially located at the Diner area, the first stop on the bus's circuit after the Bus Depot. But there are many other Mystery Box locations scattered about all five major areas. You'll likely notice a stack of very obvious ammo boxes here and there around the map. These mark the potential locations of a Mystery Box appearance.

Mystery Box weapons can be reloaded only via the Max Ammo power-up drop. This drop comes from killing zombies or via the Pack-a-Punch machine *the first time you put the weapon in*.

Perk-a-Cola Machines

Perk-a-Cola machines are scattered around the map. They dispense Perk-a-Colas, which enhance your abilities just like perks in multiplayer. Perk-a-Colas are highly recommended drinking to reach the later rounds. Saving your points and purchasing these buffing beverages should be a priority for your team. Deposit some points, crack your knuckles, and pop open a bottle of one of these:

> **Quick Revive** In solo play, this Perk-a-Cola allows you to automatically revive yourself. You can do this up to three times before the machine vanishes—permanently. In co-op, Quick Revive triples your revive speed when helping downed allies.

> **Double Tap Root Beer:** This particular Perk-a-Cola dramatically increases your rate of fire, in turn increasing your lethality with all weapons. Warning: when you up the rate of fire, you also up the rate of ammo burn.

> **Speed Cola:** One of the more essential Perk-a-Colas in the game, Speed Cola doubles your reload speed. Pick this up from the Diner the moment you can afford it.

> **Jugger-Nog:** The old standby Perk-a-Cola, Jugger-Nog upgrades your durability, allowing you to take a few extra hits from attacking zombies. It might not seem like much, but in the later rounds you'll need every bit of health you can get. If your entire team is sporting Jugger-Nog, your survivability as a group is boosted considerably. This is a prerequisite for jaunts into the fog.

> **Tombstone:** It wouldn't be a new *Zombies* map without a new Perk-a-Cola. This one is a savior if you happen to spend more time down than up. This is a great perk to have if you go down. You'll have to retrieve *your* tombstone upon respawn at the next round (located where you bled out). Be advised that the tombstone is on a timer and starts counting down the second you respawn. As it ticks down, you will regain less and less of your previous loadout. Good luck. Don't die.

The Zombies

Zombies attack in *all* parts of the town, both out in the haze and in the main areas. They get progressively stronger as you complete each wave. *There is no safe haven*.

To survive, you must earn points and then spend points to acquire better weapons, purchase Perk-a-Colas, and pack some punch to your existing weapons. *Don't die rich!* You can't take it with you. Spend your dough because it'll keep you alive.

Zombies also, on occasion, drop instant-gratification Power-Ups when killed. They provide a temporary bonus to everyone on your team. Power-Ups do not sit on the map indefinitely. If you don't grab it, it will disappear after a while.

Power-Ups

> **Insta-Kill:** Kill a zombie with one shot with any weapon, including your melee knife. This is a very powerful ability. It can save your team in the later rounds. If it drops toward the end of a round and you don't need it, let it sit for a moment and the round reset before you grab it.

> **Nuke:** Pick this up and KABOOM! Every zombie active on the map drops dead in flames the moment you pick up the Nuke. Note that there is a slight delay before zombies fall over dead-dead. Don't get eaten before they drop!

> **Max Ammo:** This Power-Up instantly gives everyone on the team maximum ammo for all of their weapons, both primary and secondary. This is critical, as mentioned, for the special weapons you buy from the Mystery Box.

> **Carpenter:** Pick up this glowing gold hammer, and all of the broken barricades will repair themselves across the entire map. This buys you some time, depending on your location, as zombies have to tear back through the barricades to get at you.

> **Double Points:** Just like the name, this Power-Up doubles your score for every action you perform, be it killing a zombie or repairing a barricade. This is especially helpful to get you to the high-point thresholds that Perk-a-Cola machines and the Pack-a-Punch machine require. With more points also comes more open doors and more visits to the Mystery Box.

When fighting zombies, aiming for headshots whenever possible is advisable. However, some weapons are strong enough that even a body shot will suffice in the early rounds.

As far as general tactics go, keep yourself in a position where you *always, always, always* have an escape route. Never corner yourself into a dead end; you'll find yourself overwhelmed in the blink of an eye.

As the rounds progress, you'll notice that zombies can be dismembered. They lose their arms, their heads, and their legs. Legless zombies can be fatally irritating, but they can also work to your benefit. Give it a try.

> Hellhounds

Demon dogs *do in fact* appear in Survival but not in TranZit, nor in Grief. You have to activate Hellhounds in Custom Games to add some fire and brimstone to your private session.

Roughly every five waves is a special Hellhound round. The nasty beasts swarm you from all sides, appearing out of thin air in a puff of brimstone.

Hellhounds are fast and extremely aggressive. Be sure you are either backed up in a corner with a *lot* of ammo or have plenty of room to maneuver.

A TOUR OF THE TOWN

In TranZit, the bus links all five areas. You can explore the whole of the county and all its surroundings.

THE BUS STOP

TranZit *always* begins inside the terminal in the Bus Depot area.

> Learn to Build

Scattered around the city are locations that can be used to craft...*useful* items. Parts are scattered around, just begging to be acquired and built into something life-saving.

Clear the Room

Shhhhh...

Upon start of Round 1, a handful of inert zombies stand in place around the room, seemingly asleep or utterly zoned-out. If you attack them, they absolutely will wake up and attack anyone inside the depot, as more zombies start ripping at the barricades.

Dispatch them all. In the first couple of rounds, your knife can down them ~~quickly~~ (instantly in the first round). This is a good way to rack up some points ~~before~~ when things get significantly more hairy after the ~~first~~ ... rst wave of zombies to earn enough to open the ... y. You see, *Zombies* is all about personal strategy. But ... ly.

> Barricade Boost

You earn cash for every board you repair on a barricade. However, there is a limit to how much you can earn in any round.

Regardless of how deep into the game you are, rebuilding barricades is easy money. It's up to you and your team to decide how important it is to rebuild barricades in relation to fending off the zombie hordes.

Find *Your* Power!

The first concern of every real world zombie-fearing survivor is getting (or keeping) the lights on. The same holds true for *Zombies*—lightning banishes darkness, as they say, and it's imperative that you eventually find and activate the power in any *Zombies* map if you want to experience all it has to offer.

Speaking of power, as soon as you load in to your first game of TranZit, you'll notice something in the corner that will help you hone the craftsmanship skills we talked about earlier. Trust us, this is not a non sequitur.

Now you need to find what looks like junk, scrap, and throwaway items. You may be just clever enough to build something useful and applicable to this section. We won't tell you what, and we certainly won't tell you where—what's the fun in that? Just know that everything you need for your first attempt at fashioning is *well* within reach.

< 280 281 >

Once *fashioned*, any player in the game can pick up the finished product. Now go have some fun with it. Its usefulness isn't all that far from where you're standing right now.

> Heavy Load

Each survivor can only carry *one* finished "Buildable" and *one* unfinished part. If you pick up a different Buildable or part, you effectively swap it out.

Keep in mind that if you bleed out and respawn at the start of a new round (assuming your teammates survived without you), any unfinished part you were carrying is dropped where you went down. Be sure to tell your teammates where the item is—they'll need it to survive!

Ride the Bus

Once you're outside, you may hear the bus horn beeping. If you hear it while you're inside a location, get outside quickly or you may miss the bus. Hop on the bus for a free ride to the Diner.

> Enjoy the Ride

Zombies can attack while you're riding in the bus, so be prepared to repel boarders.

Barricaded windows are all around the bus. Pay attention to your 3 and your 9, but don't neglect your 12 and your 6. Thankfully, you can rebuild these barricades for some much needed protection…and points.

> Wait For Me!

The bus driver gives a few warning honks before departing. If you miss the bus when it departs, good luck!

Be aware of your distance to the bus at all times. If you plan on departing, you'd better be in range. Otherwise, be prepared to hole up for an extended stay until the bus returns.

THE DINER

Hungry for flesh? You know *they* are! The remains of a Diner and a Garage, along with a lone power-locked storage shed, make up the second area on the bus's tour.

Visit the Diner

The Diner is no longer serving breakfast, but for 750 points you can gain access. At the Diner, you can find a Perk-a-Cola and a wall-buy weapon.

Stop by the Garage

750 points gains you access to the Garage, where you find the first location of the Mystery Box! When starting the game, the Mystery Box is always here in the Garage.

Also, you may have noticed on your way here the giant blue column of light in the sky…

> *Vonderbar* Vunder Veapons

Paying 950 points to open the Mystery Box gives you a random weapon. You might get a pistol. You might get two to dual-wield. You might even get a Ray Gun. You never know! But we do know that the game's very best weaponry is located inside this box.

The Mystery Box is essential to survival in *Zombies*. It is the only way to gain access to a variety of weapons beyond those available as wall-buys in fixed locations around the map.

There are some downsides to the Mystery Box. The first is the random nature of your reward. Sure, you might luck out with an LMG, but your teammate may wind up getting a …or worse.

The other downside is that, after a certain number of uses, the Mystery Box "rewards" you with a teddy bear and then vanishes. Mystery Box locations are scattered around the county in each of the five areas, and never in the vast swaths of smoky haze. Once a box is exhausted at one location, it teleports to another area at random.

Thankfully, you don't lose those 950 points should the Mystery Box up and disappear on you. *You will be refunded your deposit.*

Finally, the only way to refill the ammunition for a Mystery Box weapon is through the Max Ammo Power-Up or the *first* use of the Pack-a-Punch

The Zombie Shield

We've been pretty elusive about the whats and there wheres of the Buildables to this point. If you've made it this far, you deserve a little something, and naming a Buildable is just what you need.

An extremely useful Buildable, the Zombie Shield is the *Zombies* version of the Campaign and Multiplayer Assault Shield. It blocks frontal attacks and can be planted to provide a bit of a roadblock for zombies. Most importantly, it can be used to bash the unliving daylights out of the undead. However, the Zombie Shield is useful for only a limited number of bashes, so bash wisely.

This is a very useful Buildable, but you have to balance Zombie Shield users with carriers of other Buildables. This is all part and parcel with team strategy, and it's up to you to decide what works best for your zombie-slaying unit.

THE FARM

A relaxing countryside farmhouse is the third stop on the bus's circuit. Okay, there are horrific swarms of zombies roaming the land, so maybe it's not all that relaxing. The Farm consists of a two-story barn, a smaller two-story house, and a single shed with a powered door.

The Barn

A two-story barn contains yet another Perk-a-Cola. Also, there is a very useful zombie-clearing wall-weapon tucked behind a stack of crates. Two staircases provide access to the second floor. But if you keep your eyes peeled, you'll find another means of escape beyond the stairs.

You can run around inside the barn a bit while evading zombies, but be careful. It's easy to get trapped if your escape routes are blocked by a swarm of zombies.

The Farmhouse

While the farmhouse is also two stories tall, it is much smaller and potentially easier for zombies to overwhelm you within the narrow rooms and passageways.

The Farmhouse also contains a potential location for the Mystery Box on the second floor—note the stack of boxes sitting out on the balcony. You can drop down from this balcony to reach the ground outside. This is useful if you have zombies in hot pursuit.

Random story for you: an old vet' used to live 'round these here parts, retired to the farm after his tour, before things went to hell. The farmer would work the fields, all day, every day, gnawing on his chaw, happy as a clam. His daughter, always looking out for him, got onto him about his tobacco habit and eventually convinced him to give it up. But the farmer found a pretty *cool* hiding place where he could always sneak a dip.

< 282 283 >

THE POWER STATION

The fourth stop on the bus's tour of terror is the Power Station, where a dormant Reactor is the key to reactivating the county's power grid. Activating the Reactor instantly turns on all of the Perk-a-Cola machines around town.

Once you arrive at the Power Station, you may need to run around a bit to look for the secret entrance into the station's underground facility. On the surface, you'll see an old, broken-down power building as well. But your first order of business is locating the entrance to the underground Reactor Core.

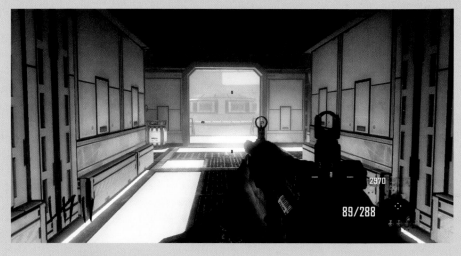

The Core

The access door costs 750 points to open. It's hidden somewhere around the ground level…you smell something? You can pick up another wall-weapon around here, so keep your eyes peeled. Once inside, you'll drop down to the underground level.

This is a good time to point out that the deeper you get into TranZit, the harder the wall-weapons are to find.

Down inside the Reactor room, you need to start building. Here's another opportunity to use your skills creating useful objects. And for *Zombies* vets reading this, you'll know the parts and their function the second you see them.

Once assembled, feel free to flip the switch, and the power-shutters blocking the stairs will open once the Reactor's power-up sequence completes, allowing you to escape. Why exit without turning on the power? Well, you'll learn the answer to that question shockingly quickly. You may just want to use this strategy on a subsequent play session.

6.022 114Xx10²³

Turning on the power is beneficial for reaching the later waves and gives you *consistent* access to Perk-a-Cola Machines. However, turning on the power may also have a *shocking* side effect.

Once the power is activated, you may notice that some of the reactor's juice has made its way up into the atmosphere. It's a pretty light show, sure. You think maybe the Mystery Box has a solution for this one? Seems to solve a lot of *other* problems.

The Destroyed Building

The remains of the upper damaged building can *only* be reached from the lower Core. So, if you want to see what's inside here, you have to find your way underground.

Now don't rush through here, guns blazing; and watch out for zombies popping up from below. Get crafty on these catwalks. You'll be thankful later, but only if you've found a source of power. Once you leave the destroyed building (that's some drop), you have to run all the way through the lower Core to get back to this area again.

THE TOWN CENTER

The fifth stop on the bus tour is the ruins of a small downtown main street. Disembark here for a pair of important Perk-a-Colas. There's quite a bit going on in this area, so have some fun.

City Streets

The Town is the largest of the five main areas in TranZit. This could be a great place for the ever-popular "Zombie Trains"—vets, you know what we're talking about.

While it is larger and does have more room to escape pursuit, it also has ██ wall-buy weapons. Yes, the Mystery Box may appear, but don't think for a ██████████ ██ means of weaponry available in this area. A little patience ████████ ████ring light to some other possibilities…

████ ██████gs from the streets, a bar with a second floor, and ████ ████. Both have blasted-out ceilings and multiple non-████ ███es to enter. So, don't assume you're safe off the ████ ████ver choreography, you can dance with the undead from ████ ██ne time.

There are two possible locations for the Mystery Box here. One location is upstairs in the bar. The other is in a small alley off the main street. This means there's a slightly greater chance for the box to teleport here after it has been exhausted elsewhere on the map.

The last locked door leads into the Bank, which has its own bevy of secrets.

The Bank Vault

The bank contains several interesting features, the Vault being target number one. After you case the joint, it's time to get your Bonnie and Clyde on.

Behind the first vault door is a safety deposit box that can be used to deposit or withdraw points in increments of 1000. There is, however, a fee. In life and un-life, someone *always* gets their cut. You can deposit points; you can withdraw points. Should you go down without being revived, and you haven't taken a swig of Tombstone, this is a good place to fill your wallet.

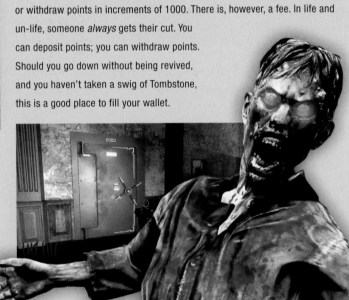

Just past the safety deposit box, there's a second Vault door that can be opened in much the same way as the first. Doing so grants access to the innermost Vault. Here you'll find another wall of deposit boxes marked with a certain symbol. Hmm. Does this symbol look vaguely familiar to you? We'll leave this one up to you to crack.

No Gear, Here

As with many of the accessible features in TranZit, the deeper you get, the more difficult they become to achieve. Consider that when looking for parts to Buildables within the boundaries of the Town Center.

Oh look: another powered door. Behind it is a stash of Semtex and maybe even a part to a Buildable. Wait a second… You've thrown the Power Switch and still the door won't budge? Look around. Did you happen to notice that the power line is severed?

Round and Round We Go

The bus makes an endless loop around each of the five stops, but there is much more lurking in the smoky haze to be discovered. All you have to do is buff up, put your head down, and double-time it into the smoke and ash. Sure, maybe you can make it to one of the uncharted clearings hidden in there. But can you make it back?

Truly adventurous explorers may even find other methods of travel around town…

WIN UNTIL YOU FAIL

You can't "win" TranZit. It's more a question of how long you can survive—and how many secrets you can unlock.

With that in mind, you should have certain goals for your team in every round:

> Upgrade your weapon   > Acquire Perk-a-Colas
> Assemble critical equipment > Turn on the Power…?

Zombies is a game with layers upon layers of challenges. Killing zombies and surviving as long as humanly possible is just the surface of the experience. How you strategize your survival will vary from game to game. You have to be ready for anything, be fluid enough to make snap decisions, and have a keen eye for scavenging and completing side-quests. Those who discover all of *Zombies'* secrets, unlock every Easter egg, and complete all of the side-quests are a very exclusive club. Do you have what it takes?

You have to deal with variables; it's the nature of the game. TranZit is filled with relatively obvious operational procedures, but they may also have *hidden* alternative methods. So keep your eyes open and look for other ways to accomplish objectives.

Check out the parts to the Buildables. From game to game, you have to check several hiding spots within each area to construct its relevant Buildable.

And because of the unpublished bus departure times, planning how long to stay at a given area (say, to exhaust the Mystery Box) borders on impossible. The bus may leave before you're ready, or it may wait longer than you want, letting the zombie wave number creep a little too high for comfort.

If you've played *Zombies*, you know there are other means of moving about the map. But digging into this process can be dangerous. You may end up separated from your team. Even worse, some of those final destinations are deep in the smoke and ash haze and *very* unsafe.

You should also consider how to organize your team. Structure your team in terms of specialization. Who's on revive duty? Who's the barricade builder? Who's carrying the Zombie Shield or any other particular Buildable? There are also times when you may have to split up and accomplish two goals at once. Teamwork and communication are absolutely essential. These are all important considerations to get to the top of the leaderboards for Highest Round Reached.

DEATHMATCH MODES

The various Deathmatch modes all have the same basic rule: Reach the target kill score and win. How you get there is a bit different in each mode. In Team Deathmatch and Multi-Team Deathmatch, your team's kill score counts. In Free For All, only your kill score counts. In Kill Confirmed, you must collect dog tags from downed targets to earn points.

FREE FOR ALL

Eliminate hostile targets at all costs.

FFA is a race to the finish line, with every player in the match competing to reach the target score first.

Kill/Death ratio is less critical in FFA than other Deathmatch modes (it is possible to win with higher deaths than in the team modes). Although playing recklessly is still a bad idea.

Aggressive or defensive play can win a match in FFA, though aggressive play is more difficult. If you plan to play aggressively, take stealthy Perks and Attachments, and be wary of campers.

Conversely, if you want to play defensively, pick an area of the map to lock down and use Equipment and Attachments that can guard your back and give you early warning of incoming enemies.

TEAM DEATHMATCH AND MULTI-TEAM DEATHMATCH

Work with your team, take down the opposition.

Team Deathmatch demands more careful play than FFA. A negative k/d ratio here is very damaging to your team, though this is more true in "regular" two-team Deathmatch than in Multi-Team.

Stick together with your team and communicate. Constantly updating your team on enemy positions is vital in TDM. You need to know both where enemies are and where they are respawning.

In Multi-Team, you have less friendlies and more enemy targets, so working together is even more critical. Similar to FFA, picking out an area of the map to lock down is viable if you work closely with your smaller team.

> **MULTI-TEAM MAYHEM!**
>
> Multi-Team Deathmatch is a new game mode variant in *Call of Duty: Black Ops II.*
>
> In Multi-Team, your team can face off against multiple opposing teams. This is a great mode to play with a small group of friends when you don't have a
>
> that can be played in Multi-Team either.
> ment with Multi-Team modes, and you can
> ny team setups you want!

KILL CONFIRMED

Team Deathmatch with dogtags; collect enemy tags to score, and deny kills by saving friendly tags.

Kill Confirmed plays out very close to TDM. The dogtags mix things up by creating hotspots and giving a chance for teammates to save tags from downed friendlies.

You can use enemy tags as bait to down more enemies as they move to recover them. Don't try to pull this stunt without team support, or you can end up giving up points unnecessarily.

Kill Confirmed demands more mobility than vanilla TDM. You *must* move out of cover to recover tags, so simply camping and locking down the enemy team at their spawn isn't enough to win.

> CUSTOMIZE YOUR CUSTOM CLASSES!

The classes here have all been built with a degree of personalization in mind. All classes in this section have one or more options for you to pick your *own* favorite weapon, and often different Perks, Equipment, or Scorestreaks. In each case, we're pointing you toward a *template* for a specific role.

You can use whatever your favorite weapon is within the same weapon class. We give you the reasoning behind our choices (or options) for the Perks, Equipment, and Scorestreaks that make up each build.

In some cases, we give you a few options that you might want to change mid-match. If you want to take advantage of that sort of flexibility, make two copies of the same class, then put in the alternate picks in the second class. Naturally, as you grow more experienced, we expect you to move on to using your own classes. But if you're unsure where to start, these classes are a great place to begin.

Because you won't have all items unlocked when you begin your *Call of Duty: Black Ops II* career, don't hesitate to substitute similar items. Look over the builds and see if you can maintain the core of the build, whether it is for offense, defense, or stealthy roaming.

DEATHMATCH CLASS SUGGESTIONS

THE PURE LONE WOLF SLAYER

PRIMARY	Full-auto AR with Suppressor and Sight, or Semi-Auto/Burst AR with Sight and Quickdraw Handle
SECONDARY	Pistol with Dual Wield
PERK 1	Ghost
PERK 2	Scavenger
PERK 3 or	Dexterity or Engineer
LETHAL	Semtex
TACTICAL	Concussion
WILDCARDS	N/A
SCORESTREAKS	UAV, Stealth Chopper, and Escort Drone or K9

Kill hoard—go for kills above all other concerns. Use Ghost and your Suppressor to flank the enemy team and pick them off, or use a long-range AR to take them down at a distance.

Scavenger keeps you loaded at all times. Dexterity brings up your weapon more quickly as you move around the map and helps you navigate any terrain quickly. If you're planning on operating in close proximity to the enemy team, consider bringing Engineer to warn you of traps.

Use your UAV to propel you to your Stealth Chopper. Once your chopper is in the air, play conservatively until you accumulate enough points to bring your Escort Drone or K9 pack online.

THE RUSHER

Primary	SMG with Suppressor and Extended Clip
Secondary	Pistol with Suppressor
PERK 1	Ghost
PERK 2	Cold Blooded
PERK 3	Dead Silence
Lethal	Semtex
Tactical	Concussion
Wildcards	N/A
Scorestreaks	UAV, Stealth Chopper, and Escort Drone, VSAT, K9, or Swarm

Aggressive and close range, this build is used to close the distance with the enemy team and engage in CQC. Ghost and Suppressor keep you off the radar. Cold Blooded makes you harder to spot. Dead Silence makes you harder to hear.

Stick tight to the enemy team and attack aggressively and relentlessly. This is a good build for training your situational awareness and your CQC skills. You need to learn to deduce enemy positions at all times to perform well with this type of build and playstyle, on top of fighting while moving fast.

THE TEAM PLAYER

Primary	AR or SMG
Secondary	Any pistol or SMAW/FHJ-18
PERK 1	Hardline
PERK 2 or	Fast Hands or Scavenger
PERK 3 or	Engineer or Awareness
Lethal	N/A
	Blackhat PDA or Sensor Grenade
	N/A
	UAV, CUAV, and Care Package, VSAT or EMP

Work with your team to win. Use Hardline to propel your Scorestreak acquisition, calling in supportive streaks that benefit your team or weaken the enemy. Stack UAVs and CUAVs to propel you into your higher streak. Take an AR or SMG, based on the size of the map, and back up your build with a pistol and Scavenger, or a launcher and Fast Hands.

Use the Blackhat if you take the pistol. Use a Sensor grenade if you take the launcher. Either way you have something to take down enemy air support and Scorestreaks.

Use Engineer to locate enemies based on their Equipment and Scorestreak positions. Make sure you constantly call out suspected enemy positions to your team. Use Awareness and your Sensor grenade for the same purpose, to warn of enemy locations and track down targets.

Communicate and coordinate to pinpoint the enemy spawn and lock them down for the win.

DOMINATION

Secure a control point for your team to earn points toward victory. Reach the score limit to win the round.

Domination puts teams into conflict over three key flags, designated A, B, and C. Controlling a flag earns your team points. Owning at least two of the three flags for the majority of the match is required to win.

To succeed in Domination, you have to work with your team to capture (or recapture) points. The goal should be to pin the enemy team at the third flag, preventing them from moving out of their spawn location or securing any flags.

The central B flag is typically the most hotly contested and exposed. If your team is locked down and you cannot quickly recapture B, you may need to perform a sneaky rear capture to flip your team out of your spawn area.

DOMINATION CLASS SUGGESTIONS

FLAG ASSAULT

Primary	SMG with Extended Clip and Laser Sight
Secondary	N/A
PERK 1	Lightweight and Flak Jacket
PERK 2	N/A
PERK 3	Extreme Conditioning and Tactical Mask
Lethal	N/A
Tactical	Smoke Grenade or Trophy System
Wildcards	Perk 1 and 3 Greed
Scorestreaks	UAV, CUAV, and Guardian, Hellstorm, Lightning Strike, or Sentry Gun

You are built to capture flags. Lightweight and Extreme Conditioning in combination with an SMG let you reach points more quickly to secure them as the round begins and as the match progresses.

Flak Jacket, Tactical Mask, and your Trophy System or Smoke grenade can protect you while you are on the flag capturing it.

Your Scorestreaks are also built to support your team and lock down flag locations once secured. Use your UAV and CUAV to give your team an information edge. Then use your high-end streak to aid in clearing or securing a flag.

POINTBREAKER

Primary	Full-Auto AR with Target Finder or Millimeter Scanner
Secondary	RPG
PERK 1	Flak Jacket
PERK 2	Scavenger
PERK 3	Engineer
Lethal	2x Frag
Tactical	Tactical Insertion
Wildcards	Danger Close
Scorestreaks	UAV, Hunter Killer, CUAV

If your team is losing and you're struggling to retake flags, pick this class and make a methodical push on one of the flag locations. Use your Target Finder or MMS to locate camping defenders and eliminate them. Your grenade battery in combination with Scavenger gives you the ability to clear out an area of any sizable enemy force.

Your UAV and CUAV are more team support. The Hunter Killer is solely there to give you another explosive weapon to eliminate more enemies guarding the flag.

THE DEFENDER

Primary	LMG with Target Finder or Dual Band or Semi-Auto/Burst AR with Target Finder or ACOG Sight
Secondary	Pistol
PERK 1	Hardline, Blind Eye
PERK 2	Toughness
PERK 3	N/A
Lethal	Bouncing Betty
Tactical	Trophy System
Wildcards	Perk 1 Greed
Scorestreaks	Guardian and any two of Stealth Chopper, Warthog, Escort Drone, or VSAT

Set up shop in a key overwatch position covering the central flag and deny any enemy attempts to recapture it. Use an LMG or long-range AR and keep your distance from the flag. This forces a long-range engagement that puts anyone with a shorter range setup at a severe disadvantage.

Blind Eye lets you ignore hostile automated Scorestreaks. Toughness helps you take glancing hits and stay on target at long range. The Betty and Trophy are there to guard your back.

Hardline helps you build toward your high-end streaks. Play conservatively, engage and eliminate enemies at a distance, back off if you are being pushed, and come back from a different angle. Once you secure your Scorestreaks, call them in to hammer the enemy team.

THE LONEWOLF

Play *around* the flags. Don't risk your life out in the open. Instead constantly seek out and eliminate the opposing team as they go for the flags, using your stealth to stay off the radar.

Primary	AR with Sight, Suppressor, and Fast Mag
Secondary	N/A
PERK 1	Ghost, Hardline
PERK 2	Scavenger
PERK 3	Dexterity, Dead Silence, or Awareness
Lethal	N/A
Tactical	N/A
Wildcards	Perk 1 Greed, Primary Gunfighter
Scorestreaks	UAV, Stealth Chopper, and Warthog or K9

If you are comfortable with the irons on your AR of choice, swap out the Reflex sight for Quickdraw to get even more of a combat edge. Use Scavenger to keep your customized weapon loaded. Hardline helps lower the cost of your high-end streaks.

Choose one of Dexterity, Dead Silence, or Awareness based on the map. If you expect to be highly mobile, take Dexterity or Dead Silence. If you anticipate lurking in a few key areas eliminating incoming foes, take Awareness.

This is a challenging build to run your Scorestreaks up. In order to benefit your team in a Domination match, you need to be eliminating enemies around the flags constantly *and* keeping yourself alive to call in your devastating high-end streaks.

DEMOLITION

Two bomb sites with the offensive team all equipped with bombs. Detonate both bomb sites or defend until the time limit expires.

Demolition is a high-action version of Search & Destroy, with respawns, and all players on offense armed with a bomb. A defender defusing does *not* end the round.

To secure a victory on offense, it's critical to target the *more* difficult of the two bomb sites first. That way the final plant and cover is easier. Once one bomb site goes up, the entire defensive team will be concentrated at the remaining location. Which site is more difficult varies from map to map. Experiment with tackling each point with all of the offensive team to see which goes more easily for your team.

It is possible to plant at both bomb sites, using the second plant as "cover" for the real plant. But be careful about splitting your team to do this. It can pay off if defense is simply too intense on your primary target. Like CTF, Tactical Insertions are very important on offense, and sometimes for defense on any map with a lengthy run to the bomb sites.

DEMOLITION CLASS SUGGESTIONS

THE PLANTER

Plant the bomb at all costs. Flak Jacket, Tactical Mask, and Smoke grenades all protect you while planting the mob. Tactical Insertion ensures you can respawn near the bomb to go for another attempt.

Primary	SMG with one Attachment
Secondary	N/A
PERK 1	Ghost, Flak Jacket
PERK 2	Cold Blooded
PERK 3	Tactical Mask
Lethal	Smoke
Tactical	Tactical Insertion
Wildcards	Perk 1 Greed, Tactician
Scorestreaks	UAV, CUAV, and one of Guardian, Hellstorm, Lightning Strike, or AGR

Ghost helps to get close undetected, and Cold Blooded makes you harder to spot once you are close (or planting!). Ghost also stays active while you are planting the bomb, even though you are stationary.

Take an SMG to maximize your movement speed, and choose your favorite Attachment to customize it. Or take a launcher secondary to help you clear out targets around the bomb. Another option is to take an Assault Shield and a pistol secondary, using the Assault Shield to give you cover while you plant the bomb.

Remember that if you use the Assault Shield, you need to move with your pistol in hand to move at full speed. Also remember that you give up any ability to take out targets reliably at a distance with this variant.

Your Scorestreaks are all built to help your team and secure the bomb site once the bomb is planted. Use your UAV and CUAV to help the team. Your higher streaks are all ideal for clearing the bomb site or locking it down once you plant.

TEAM SUPPORT

Cover the bomb site. Use your Tactical Insertion to ensure you always respawn nearby. Take FMJ to maximize your penetration against defenders hiding in cover or trying to defuse the bomb *through* the bomb target itself. Use Engineer to spot enemy Equipment and simply drill it right through the wall with your AR. You can also use FMJ to aid in quickly taking down hostile Guardian or Sentry turrets, as well as enemy UAVs or CUAVs.

Primary	AR with Sight and FMJ
Secondary	SMAW or FHJ-18
PERK 1	Lightweight
PERK 2 or	Toughness or Scavenger
PERK 3	Engineer
Lethal	EMP Grenade or Sensor Grenade
Tactical	Tactical Insertion
Wildcards	Tactician
Scorestreaks	RC-XD or Hunter Killer, UAV or CUAV, and Sentry Gun or Death Machine

Save your SMAW or FHJ-18 for difficult air support. If you take the SMAW, you can also use it to clear out hostiles around the bomb.

Lightweight improves your speed so you can keep up with SMG runners. Toughness aids in staying on target in mid-range firefights. Scavenger keeps you supplied. Choose whichever you prefer. Use your EMP to shut down enemy Equipment, or the Sensor grenade to locate enemy targets near the bomb site.

Engineer is crucial for supporting your team on offense. Call out enemy Equipment locations if you are unable to destroy it yourself so your bomb planters know what route to take. Don't hesitate to go for a plant if you see a chance.

Your streaks are all there to help eliminate enemies around the bomb site, support your team, or to cover the bomb site.

THE DEFENDER

Primary	AR with Grenade Launcher
Secondary	SMAW
PERK 1	Flak Jacket
PERK 2 or	Scavenger or Hard Wired
PERK 3 or	Engineer or Tactical Mask
Lethal	2x Semtex or Frag
Tactical	2x Concussion or Flash
Wildcards	N/A
Scorestreaks	UAV, CUAV, and one of Hellstorm, Lightning Strike, Guardian, Sentry Turret, or VSAT

Play around the bomb site and cut down incoming enemies. Use your massive loadout of explosives and grenades to launch a lethal barrage toward the bomb site if any enemy even thinks about planting. Restock with Scavenger and do it again.

Perk 3 is an important choice. Either take Engineer to spot enemy Tactical Insertions and Equipment, or take Tactical Mask to defend yourself against enemy bombardment.

For Perk 2, if enemy CUAV coverage is a serious concern, you can swap out Scavenger. Just be aware this weakens your ability to bombard continuously on one life!

Your Scorestreaks are all meant to support your team and cover the bomb site once active.

SOLO STALKER

Avoid the bomb sites, move to the edges of the map, and dig deep into the enemy team's flank. Use your Overkill and Fast Hands combination to ensure you always have the right weapon in hand for the area you are traveling through. Proactively switch to your shotgun as you approach CQC areas, and keep your AR out to tackle medium-range threats.

Primary	AR with Fast Mag and Quickdraw Handle
Secondary	Shotgun with Quickdraw and Long Barrel
PERK 1	Ghost
PERK 2	Fast Hands
PERK 3	Dexterity
Lethal	N/A
Tactical	Tactical Insertion
Wildcards	Overkill
Scorestreaks	UAV, Stealth Chopper, and one of Escort Drone, Warthog, or EMP

Use your Tactical Insertion to set a respawn point on the outskirts of the map so you can quickly re-engage the enemy team if you are taken out. Because you lack Scavenger, you may need to grab enemy weapons to maintain your ammo supplies. However, Fast Hands ensures you can quickly switch between any two weapon types.

Ghost helps to get you into a flanking position. Dexterity gives you an edge if you suddenly encounter an enemy, or if you need to traverse terrain to reach the enemy.

Note the lack of a Suppressor. You *want* the enemy team chasing you, wasting time instead of going for the bomb! Recognize that the enemy team will know where you are when you take down one of their teammates. Be prepared for a second or third enemy to appear quickly. Baiting enemies to rush into CQC situations with your shotgun is ideal! Play aggressively, but show restraint. Don't move into a direct route between the enemy spawn and the bomb sites. You want to draw them off to the sides and rack up your Scorestreaks.

HARD POINT AND HEADQUARTERS

Headquarters is a returning star. Hardpoint is a new game mode for *Call of Duty: Black Ops II*.

HARDPOINT

Lock down one of three Hardpoints to score points. The Hardpoint changes during the match.

Hardpoint is a "king of the hill" game type, where you compete with the enemy team to score points by holding one of three control areas located on the map. These control areas move around the level as the match progresses until one team hits the score limit or the time expires.

There is typically a Hardpoint near each spawn, and then a more centrally-located point. This varies depending on the map. To hold a Hardpoint, you simply need a friendly inside the Hardpoint area. If an enemy moves into the Hardpoint, it becomes contested, and neither team scores points until the Hardpoint is occupied by only one team.

The active Hardpoint can significantly change your approach to securing it. Central Hardpoints out in the open are very exposed to bombardment from enemy explosives and air support. Interior Hardpoints are best tackled with CQC weaponry.

Because a single player can hold the Hardpoint, a well-organized team can have one player hold the Hardpoint while the remainder of the team secures the immediate area. This prevents enemy players from even approaching the Hardpoint itself.

HEADQUARTERS

Secure and control random Headquarters locations to score points.

Headquarters plays out over a wider range of areas than Hardpoint. It also operates under a different set of rules for holding the points. To secure a Headquarters location, you have to move friendly players into the HQ area and hold it until the point is captured.

Once secure, the team owning the HQ *does not* respawn. This gives the attacking team a chance to pick off the defending players one by one until they can lock down the Headquarters. Each time the Headquarters moves to a new position, there is a delay before it becomes active and can be captured. Use this time to get into position and eliminate hostiles.

Because Headquarters covers all areas on the map, highly mobile builds are crucial for covering ground quickly and reaching key overwatch positions before the opposing team.

HARDPOINT AND HEADQUARTERS CLASS SUGGESTIONS

THE CAPPER

Primary	SMG with Laser Sight, Extended Clip, and Rapid Fire
Secondary	N/A
PERK 1	Flak Jacket
PERK 2	Scavenger
PERK 3	Tactical Mask
Lethal	Frag
Tactical	Trophy System
Wildcards	Primary Gunfighter
Scorestreaks	UAV, CUAV, and Guardian, Hellstorm, Lightning Strike, Deathmachine, or Warmachine

Move in quickly, clean out the enemy, and lock down the objective. Use your incredibly powerful close-range customized SMG to mow down any opposition in the objective area. Avoid long-range fights until you can grab an enemy weapon better suited for distance fighting.

Flak Jacket, Tactical Mask, and Trophy System all help to protect you from enemy bombardment. Expect to be taken down often. When you can run up your Scorestreaks, use them to support your team's push to hold the objectives.

TEAM SUPPORT

Primary	AR with Fast Mag and Quickdraw, or LMG with Quickdraw Handle, and Fore Grip or Sight
Secondary	B23R
PERK 1 or	Hardline or Lightweight
PERK 2	Scavenger
	Extreme Conditioning
	C4
	2x Shock Charge
	N/A
	UAV, Guardian or Sentry, and one of War Machine, Stealth Chopper, VSAT, Escort Drone, or EMP

Play around the objective area. Capture the point if it is safe to do so, but don't expose yourself to excessive risk. You lack the gear to survive a bombardment. Mow down any enemies that attempt to secure the objective. Take up overwatch positions that can cover the objective or the enemy team's approach to it. If you take an LMG, be sure to take Lightweight to counteract the speed penalty.

Loiter near the objective. Your role is to stay around and pick off people rushing for the point. You should obtain your streaks quickly. Use them to support your team around an objective. Your Guardian or Sentry can protect a point or block an approach. Any of your higher streaks can be used to hammer the enemy team or aid your own.

THE SOLO SNIPER

A variant on the Team Support build, this is a sniping build made to support your team. Keep your distance from the objective and pick off any enemies that attempt to capture or approach it.

Primary	Sniper Rifle with Ballistic CPU
Secondary	Pistol with Dual Wield
PERK 1	Blind Eye and Ghost
PERK 2	Fast Hands and Cold Blooded
PERK 3	Engineer
Lethal	N/A
Tactical	N/A
Wildcards	Perk 1 and 2 Greed
Scorestreaks	UAV, CUAV, Guardian or Sentry

Three of your Perks are taken to make you hard to locate. Blind Eye and Ghost protect you from enemy air support. Cold Blooded makes you harder to spot. Engineer is in place to warn both you and your team of hostile Equipment while you are keeping your distance.

Your Scorestreaks are simple and low. You may even wish to drop the Guardian or Sentry and simply loop the UAV and CUAV. Or take a Hunter Killer so that you never have to move close to the objective to place a turret.

Fast Hands gives you incredibly fast switching to your dual-wielded pistols. If you do get jumped at close range, quickswitch and take down your opponent with your strong short-range firepower. Once they're down, take their weapon if it's a shotgun, SMG, or AR suitable for close-range work.

CAPTURE THE FLAG

Capture the enemy flag. Defend your own.

Capture the Flag is played out over two rounds and one overtime round if the teams are tied. To score, grab the enemy flag and bring it to your own while it's still in your base. Victory in CTF relies on good teamwork. You need a few players covering your flag on defense, with the rest of your team on offense either running the flag or intercepting enemy players.

CTF has a respawn delay, which gives the offense a chance to break through defenders. You need to watch yourself on offense and defense. You can deprive your team of coverage if you are taken out while protecting a key route.

Flag runners should be using fast stealthy builds. Also, Tactical Insertions are very important on any sizable map. Defenders can get away with less mobile builds. However, they may not be able to chase an enemy who does get away with the flag. LMGs and sniper rifles both shine on defense on many maps, as do proximity mines (Lethal and Tactical).

CAPTURE THE FLAG CLASS SUGGESTIONS

FLAG RUNNER

Primary	SMG with Laser Sight and Long Barrel
Secondary	Pistol
PERK 1	Lightweight
PERK 2	N/A
PERK 3	Extreme Conditioning and Dexterity or Tactical Mask
Lethal	Semtex
Tactical	Tactical Insert or EMP Grenade
Wildcards	Perk 3 Greed
Scorestreaks	UAV, CUAV, Escort Drone

Run far; run fast. Grab the flag and go, go, go! Fire from the hip with your SMG and take targets down with your superior maneuverability. Then go right back to sprinting. Dexterity ensures you have absolutely minimal delay before you start spraying when running the flag. However, you may wish to take Tactical Mask to avoid being slowed by a Concussion, Flashbang, or Shock Charge.

Tactical Insert is typically a must for a flag runner. On some smaller maps, you can get away with taking an EMP grenade instead to help clear out enemy Equipment around the flag. Otherwise, use your Semtex for that task.

FLAG GUARDIAN

Primary	AR with Sight and Extended Clip
Secondary	N/A
PERK 1	Lightweight
PERK 2	Toughness
PERK 3 or	Extreme Conditioning and Engineer
Lethal	N/A
Tactical	EMP Grenade
Wildcards	Primary Gunfighter, Perk 3 Greed
Scorestreaks	UAV, CUAV, and one of Guardian, Sentry Gun, Lightning Strike, or Stealth Chopper

Support the flag runner. Move parallel to his route, take down hostiles in his path, and clear out the enemy flag defenders. Engineer and your EMP grenade help to clear the way. Engineer warns the flag runner of enemy Equipment, and your EMP grenade can be used to eliminate any around the flag. In a pinch, you can run the flag. But as long as you have a dedicated flag runner to protect, do so!

FLAG DEFENDER

Primary	AR with Millimeter Scanner and Adjustable Stock
Secondary	N/A
PERK 1	Lightweight
PERK 2 or	Toughness or Hard Wired
PERK 3	Extreme Conditioning
Lethal	2x Bouncing Betty or Claymore or C4
Tactical	2x Shock Charge or Concussion
Wildcards	N/A
Scorestreaks	UAV, CUAV, and one of Guardian, Sentry Gun, Death Machine, or War Machine

Hold down the flag. Plant your Equipment all around the flag area to kill or halt any incoming flag runners. Use Shock Charges if you want extra flag area defense, or use Concussion to stop runners in their tracks.

Lightweight and Extreme Conditioning give you the ability to chase down flag runners. You're likely to have more breath than they do, because they tend to be sprinting before they reach the flag. Take Toughness for an edge in firefights and pursuit, or Hard Wired to prevent enemy CUAVs from blinding you. Use your Millimeter Scanner and Stock combination to move at full speed while in ADS to quickly sweep the area for hostile incoming targets.

THE QUIET THREAT

Primary	SMG with Suppressor and Fast Mag or Extended Clip
Secondary	N/A
PERK 1	Ghost
PERK 2	Scavenger and Cold Blooded
PERK 3 or	Dead Silence
	Claymore
	Concussion
	Perk 2 Greed
	UAV, Lightning Strike or Hellstorm, and one of Stealth Chopper, Warthog, or Escort Drone

Roam the battlefield invisibly, picking off enemy runners and defenders. Plant Claymores to intercept runners or use Concussion grenades to stop them in their tracks. Use your stealthy setup to constantly ambush enemy players as they move across the map, or advance on the enemy flag and eliminate their defenders with a sneaky approach.

SEARCH & DESTROY

A single bomb with two targets. Teams swap offense and defense. Eliminate the opposing team, and detonate or defuse the bomb to win.

Search & Destroy is an intense Tactical mode. Two teams compete to either eliminate the opposing team, or detonate or defuse a bomb.

The offensive team is given a single bomb. To win, they can either plant the bomb and detonate it or eliminate the enemy team. For the defensive team to win, they can either eliminate the offensive team or defuse the bomb after it has been planted. Whether you choose to go for the enemy team or plant the bomb can be a team decision or an individual one. You can react to the changing situation as the round develops.

If the bomb carrier is downed, the bomb remains on the map. Be aware that the enemy team may watch the bomb if it sits for too long.

Stealth and detection Perks and Equipment are extremely important on both offense and defense in Search & Destroy. With no respawns, you have to make the most of every round. Once downed, you can no longer communicate with your teammates. Keep them updated while you're alive! Unlike Demolition, you have to defuse the bomb where it was planted. This can be important on both offense and defense. Mind the placement of the bomb.

SEARCH & DESTROY CLASS SUGGESTIONS

OFFENSE

Primary	SMG or AR (based on map size) with one Attachment
Secondary	Pistol
PERK 1	Lightweight
PERK 2	Toughness
PERK 3	Awareness and one of Dead Silence, Engineer, or Extreme Conditioning
Lethal	Semtex or Frag
Tactical	Concussion
Wildcards	Perk 3 Greed
Scorestreaks	Any three from: RCXD, UAV, CUAV, Hunter Killer, Care Package

This is a customizable build for offense. Choose your weapon and your second Perk 3 based on the map in question. For smaller maps, use Dead Silencer. For larger ones, take Extreme Conditioning. If you see heavy enemy Equipment usage, take Engineer.

Lightweight gives you the extra speed needed to reach key areas on the map quickly. Toughness gives you an edge in the critical life-or-death firefights. Any of the low score streaks can be useful. Care Package is particularly helpful in S&D, as it can net you a high-end Scorestreak.

DEFENDERS

Primary	AR or SMG (based on map size) with one Attachment
Secondary	Pistol
PERK 1	Lightweight or Flak Jacket (depending on bomb distance)
PERK 2	Toughness
PERK 3	Awareness and Dead Silence or Extreme Conditioning
Lethal	Claymore or Bouncing Betty
Tactical	Shock Charge
Wildcards	Perk 3 Greed
Scorestreaks	Any three from: RCXD, UAV, CUAV, Hunter Killer Care Package, Guardian

Post up and build a bunker. Get to the bomb site fast with Lightweight and possibly Extreme Conditioning. Place your mine around one site and a Shock Charge at the location you are covering. As with the offensive setup, your streaks are low to work with low S&D scores. If you want to take a situational variant of the build, take Ghost, Hard Wired, or a SMAW/FHJ-18 to counter enemy UAV or CUAV usage.

ERNEST

Ernest Le has his roots on YouTube, posting commentaries over *Black Ops* gameplays in early 2011. His content primarily focused on using quirky setups to achieve top scores and kills in online matches.

Later that year he moved his fanbase and was one of the first YouTubers to begin streaming *Call of Duty* on Twitch. His most notable achievement was his road to max Prestige, where he became the first player worldwide to reach the top level in *Call of Duty: Modern Warfare 3*.

Because of his streaming and YouTube accomplishments in the *Call of Duty* community, Ernest was able to obtain a job at Twitch shortly after his *Modern Warfare 3* run, where he currently works as a member of the strategic partnerships team.

> Twitter/Facebook/YouTube: **MrErnestLe**

ERNEST ON *CALL OF DUTY: BLACK OPS II*

Play the Objective

What's the purpose of your game mode? Well play it! *Call of Duty: Black Ops II*'s Scorestreak system rewards players for playing the objective more than those that just go for kills.

Kill values are much lower for players who play away from flags, domination points, and bomb spots. To maximize your scores, optimize your position around the objective while using Scorestreaks that support your team (UAV, CUAV, VSAT, EMP).

Pick Your Flavor

With the new Pick 10 and Wildcard systems, *Call of Duty: Black Ops II* allows players to truly choose what they want to use in their class setups. Take the time to test out different weapons, Attachments, Equipment, and Perk combinations that work best for *you*.

Not everyone can quickscope, jump shot, or tomahawk, so make it a point of emphasis to figure out what you are most comfortable with using. Always keep in mind the game mode that you're playing when choosing a specific loadout. For example:

> **Ghost:** An amazing perk for TDM, Kill Confirmed, FFA, and Domination. But is it really needed in the first round of Demolition or Search & Destroy?

> **Lightweight:** Speed is always a good thing, but other Perks in this tier (Ghost, Flak Jacket, Hardline, Blind Eye) may be more beneficial for particular game modes and map layouts.

Then, Pick Your Poison

Don't forget that by using what you're comfortable with, you may overlook what you may need. *Call of Duty: Black Ops II* has many counters in place for Perks, Scorestreaks, and playstyles. Here are some helpful considerations when choosing your classes and Scorestreaks:

> **Hard Wired:** This is a situational Perk. CUAVs and EMPs won't always be active, so use this Perk when needed. I recommend always having a class with Hard Wired on it. Then switch to the class (upon death, or suicide with a grenade) when you can't locate the CUAV to shoot down or when the EMP becomes too much to handle.

> **Blind Eye:** This is also a situational Perk. Switch to this Perk class when you need to destroy AI-controlled Scorestreaks for your team, or to be completely ignored by them when you're playing solo (effective against Hunter Killers, Stealth Chopper, Warthog, and Swarm).

> **Cold Blooded:** Switch to this Perk class when you need to destroy player-controlled Scorestreaks. I recommend using this more frequently than the other situational Perks.

> **Awareness:** If you have a headset (or solid speaker setup), directional sound can give you a solid advantage over your opponents. Pair Awareness with Dead Silence and you'll be able to hear everything (recommended for S&D and FFA in particular). It's almost cheating, and you'll be able to counter the silent players (Dead Silence users).

> **Counter UAV:** By blinding the enemy's radar, you force them to become more aware of their teammate's positions. Calling in a CUAV also prevents the enemy from strategically calling in Scorestreaks to specific areas of the map. I highly recommend using this against UAV heavy teams.

> **Guardian:** Having trouble defending objective points? The Guardian is a nuisance of a Scorestreak that deals minor damage (major over time) and slows your enemies. Place these on objective points or cross routes to buy yourself time back to the objective. Guardians must be shot or blown up, and your foes will be forced to take these out if they want to get on the objective.

> **EMP Grenades:** Tactically use these to take out any Claymores, C4s, Betties, and Shock Charges. Enemies that are defensive typically will run some type of proximity explosive, so keep a class with EMP grenades handy.

> **Note:** Traditionally, Concussions/Flashbangs would temporarily disable enemy Equipment for long durations. In *Call of Duty: Black Ops II*, the duration of the disables is much shorter than in previous games.

> **Trophy System:** When Flak Jacket and Tactical Mask aren't enough for the objective, equip a class with the Trophy System. It not only will nullify any grenades thrown at you, it will also save you from explosive Scorestreaks.

> **Blackhat/FHJ-18/SMAW:** Using these to get rid of Scorestreaks (Blackhat can do Equipment, too) will not only boost your score, but also help your team. UAVs and CUAVs are the easiest to destroy out of all the streaks. Consider using these to nullify your opponent's advantage and to give yourself an extra score boost.

Optimizing Your Leveling

Run low Scorestreaks and play the objective. The best way to optimize your experience flow is to present yourself some "guarantees." Guarantee is a term I coined to explain how easy it is to earn a given Scorestreak. For example, the UAV is a safer guarantee than the K9 unit, since score wise it is easier to obtain.

You are at better odds obtaining three or four UAVs before you would earn one K9 unit. Also, keep in mind that kills from your Scorestreaks in *Call of Duty: Black Ops II* typically generate far less points than gun kills, especially around objectives. It is not practical to rely on your Stealth Chopper to net you points into your Swarm.

Ernest's Favored Classes

THE OBJ (HQ/DOMINATION/HARDPOINT)	
Primary	MSMC with Extended Clip, Laser Sight
Secondary	None
Perk 1	Flak Jacket
Perk 2	Scavenger
Perk 3	Tactical Mask
Lethal	Trophy System
Tactical	Concussion, Concussion
Wildcards	Tactician (take Tactical Equipment as Lethal)
Scorestreaks	UAV, CUAV, Guardian

THE LONE WOLF SLAYER (FFA, TDM)	
Primary	M27 with Suppressor, Fast Mag
Secondary	B23R
Perk 1	Ghost
Perk 2	Scavenger
Perk 3	Dead Silence
Lethal	Semtex
Tactical	Concussion, Concussion
Wildcards	None
Scorestreaks	UAV, Stealth Chopper, K9 Unit

I highly recommend this class for the objective game modes such as Domination, Headquarters, and Hardpoint. Your purpose is to capture the objective, then play around it to rack up points. Flak Jacket, Trophy system, and Tactical Mask will save you from explosives and Tactical Equipment. Low Scorestreaks not only will be practical (you will probably die, a lot), they will also help your team locate the enemy, jam their radar, and slow them down at the objective point.

This is the ideal class for kill farming in Team Deathmatch when you play alone, or when you play Free For All. Your purpose is to constantly flank and do so quietly. You'll want Dead Silence to mask your footsteps and the Suppressor to hide your position on the minimap.

Any silenced AR or SMG works here, but I prefer the M27 for the fire r style, of course!). Your Scorestreaks lead into each other: obtain y then strategically pick off the enemies into your Chopper, then

Have Fun

Call of Duty: Black Ops II presents a new change to the franchise, allowing players to play the game how they want to play. I challenge you to figure out what drives you to play the game. Whether you're a competitive guy who will play in League matches or a pubstomper who wants to get a high kill count, I urge you to figure out what your niche is and stick to it.

Not everyone has my mindset of using wacky setups and playing to win, but everyone should know what fuels them to enjoy the game.

ERNEST'S ACKNOWLEDGMENTS

I wouldn't have had this opportunity if it weren't for YouTube, streaming, and *Call of Duty*. I want to thank the fans for all the support and for making me who I am today. Without you guys "Ernest Le" the commentator wouldn't exist! I was simply a guy who wanted to play the living heck out of *Modern Warfare 3*. Who'd have thought that a graduate school dropout's love for a game would score him a chance like this?

Secondly, I want to thank Phillip Marcus and Jason Fox for mentoring throughout this trip. Never have I seen (nor appreciated) the absurd amount of work it takes to write a complex strategy guide. You two are tremendously hard-working individuals who deserve all the credit in the world for these projects.

TmarTn and Nadeshot, thank you two for joining me on this trip. I'm glad we could butt heads and put our talents together to write something for the fans. You guys are great and you will go places with your personalities and passion for *Call of Duty*.

BradyGames! Thank you! This opportunity wouldn't have been possible if you guys didn't recognize my past accomplishments and potential. From the bottom of my heart, I thank you (Chris, Tim, Leigh), for this has been a dream come true. Also, thank you Chris and Yale from Activision for helping us make our job easier.

...are great!

...pporting me and

...Without Twitch, I wouldn't

...*Call of Duty* for all the fans

...m (Synwyn, Fuzzy, Eleine,

...ATK, djWheat). If you want

...Twitch!

MATT

OpTic NaDeSHoT has been playing *Call of Duty* at a professional level since 2008. With many major tournament wins under his belt, the Call of Duty XP 1 Million Dollar Event in 2011 was probably his most notable achievement. Nadeshot spends most of his days livestreaming, practicing, and uploading *Call of Duty* videos with the intent to help other gamers become better players.

> Twitter: OpTic_NaDeSHoT	> Facebook: NaDeSHoT	> YouTube: OpTicNaDe

MATT ON *CALL OF DUTY: BLACK OPS II*

It's All in the Hips!

The one thing that I believe separates *Call of Duty: Black Ops II* from all the past *Call of Duty* titles is definitely movement! Treyarch has decided to slow down the movement speed of your character as well as change up a few audio files, which can offer a big change compared to *Modern Warfare 3*. That is why, in my opinion, your Perk selections will make the biggest impact on your ability to play at the highest level.

Since the new Pick 10 class system is completely new, I'm going to try and explain why the new Wildcards will have the biggest impact on your classes. EVERY SINGLE ITEM in your class can now be swapped out for something else. Don't use your secondary? Get rid of it. Hate Tacticals? WHO NEEDS 'EM ANYWAYS!? The two most important Wildcards will be Perk 1 and Perk 3 Greed. Both of these allow you to double up on Perks. This will enable you to use several different combinations which will be crucial for MOVEMENT!

Matt's Favored Classes

Now that you're up to speed, here are two of my favorite classes that you can try out yourself!

THE OG H3CZ	
Primary	Ballista, Iron Sights, and Extended Mags
Secondary	B23R
Perk 1	Lightweight
Perk 2	Fast Hands
Perk 3	Extreme Conditioning, Dexterity
Lethal	Semtex
Tactical	None
Wildcards	Perk 3 Greed

THE AIMBOT	
Primary	MSMC, Extended Mags, and Laser Sight
Secondary	None
Perk 1	Lightweight, Ghost
Perk 2	Scavenger
Perk 3	Extreme Conditioning, Dexterity
Lethal	None
Tactical	None
Wildcards	Perk 1 Greed, Perk 3 Greed

As you can see with these classes, movement and power is key!

FULL-FLEDGED COMPETITION!

With the release of *Call of Duty: Black Ops II* comes the beginning of a new era in the *Call of Duty* franchise, LEAGUE PLAY! You will now be able to team up with your friends and fight your way to the top. Treyarch will be offering us a Champions League and World League, which will offer meaningful competition in *Call of Duty: Black Ops II* matchmaking. Now, I can't go as in depth as I'd like to, but I can fill you in on everything I know so far!

> 6v6

> Scorestreaks allowed

World League

A mix of Team Deathmatch and objective game modes that uses standard rules for scoring and how you respawn after dying.

Champions League

A mix of objective games that uses professional scoring and how you respawn after dying.

> 4v4 team play

> 4 placement matches

> Placement matches will determine your ability and then place you into a league that best fits your skill set

> Scorestreaks not allowed

I'm super passionate about competitive *Call of Duty* and really think league play will give you a taste of how fun competition in *Call of Duty* can be! Please try it out!

MATT'S ACKNOWLEDGMENTS

After helping with this guide, I truly saw how much work and time these guides actually take! I want to give infinite thanks to Phillip Marcus and Jason Fox who basically held my hand throughout this entire project. I'm very new to the corporate side of the gaming industry and their help really sent me in the right direction.

Secondly, I'd like to thank Ernest Le and TmarTn for working with me throughout the entirety of this guide. They made my experience so much more enjoyable and they truly are insanely hard-working and great friends.

BradyGames, you guys are awesome! This opportunity wouldn't have been possible without you. This has been a dream come true; thank you so much!

Lastly, I'd like to thank each and every one of you for supporting me throughout my entire gaming career. Without you guys, none of this would be possible. I truly humbled by the opportunities that I've gotten through just playing video games.

TREVOR

Trevor "TmarTn" Martin is an avid gamer and *Call of Duty* player. Hooked on the series since *COD4*, he has logged over 1,000 in-game hours doing everything from pub-stomping to competing to his current passion, YouTube. Trevor started posting videos in late 2010 and rapidly grew to become one of the largest gaming channels. Known for his in-depth Tips and Tricks videos, the premise behind his channel is to improve his viewers at the game in fun, entertaining, and informative ways.

> Twitter/Facebook/YouTube: **TmarTn**

TREVOR ON *CALL OF DUTY: BLACK OPS II*

Scorestreaks

Seeing that Scorestreaks build on each other, as well as reset when you earn your highest reward, they will play a very prominent role in *Call of Duty: Black Ops II*'s multiplayer. Here are some tips to maximize your killing potential:

> **New Old Favorites:** Fan-favorite rewards from previous *Call of Duty* titles are returning in *Black Ops II*, however, many have minor but key differences. For example, the Care Package no longer gives ammo, the UAV and CUAV are now visually distinguishable in the sky, and the Death Machine no longer goes away if you die or switch weapons (you keep it until you run out of ammo).

> **Use It Before You Lose It:** As stated previously, your Scorestreak resets after you earn your highest reward, allowing you to earn multiple rewards in the same life. Be careful though; rewards will not stack on each other. For example, if you earn a UAV, don't call it in and go through all your rewards to earn another UAV. You will still only have one UAV (you lose the original). Make sure to use your rewards when you earn them!

> **Play the Objective:** This may be the biggest tip I can give you regarding Scorestreaks: Play the objective! *Call of Duty: Black Ops II* does a very good job of rewarding those who are helping their team win. Whether you are actually completing the objective (planting the bomb, capping the flag, etc.), or just killing enemies NEAR the objective, you will earn many more points than you will sticking on the outskirts of the map. These points lead to more Scorestreaks, which lead to more kills, which lead to more XP. Who doesn't want to level up faster?

> **Point-Farming Rewards:** The UAV and Counter UAV Scorestreak rewards bring much more to the table in this game. Rather than simply highlighting enemies on your team's radar or blocking the enemy team's radar, they can also earn you assist points. When you call one of them in, you get bonus assist points for every kill that your team gets while it's in the air. As you can imagine, these points can rack up very quickly, dramatically increasing your chances of earning those higher rewards. Other point-farming Scorestreaks include the Guardian, Sentry Gun, Orbital VSAT, and EMP.

> **Find That Loop:** If you're going for high-scoring games, your goal should be to get in an infinite loop of Scorestreak rewards. Use one of the point farming rewards (listed above) to earn one or two of the larger, more lethal rewards (such as the Warthog, Lodestar, VTOL Warship, K9 Unit, or Swarm). If you manage to do this, and you can stay alive while the larger reward does its work, it should loop your streak back around and put you at or close to earning a large reward again. This strategy can be very destructive and lead to some high kill games.

Don't Be Scared—Experiment!

Call of Duty: Black Ops II is easily the deepest *Call of Duty* game to date. With millions of different class combinations, there are an infinite number of ways for you to play the game. Get creative and have fun with it!

Always be switching up your class combinations; you should never have a dull moment in the game. Set up Claymore-Shock Charge death traps. Run around with six Perks and just a knife. Snipe enemies with a Dual Band Crossbow that shoots a cluster of three explosive arrows. All of these things can be done in *Call of Duty: Black Ops II*, so get creative and have fun with the game!

Trevor's Favored Classes

hicom CQB with Reflex Sight and Extended Clip

and I'm so

ss

y

sion, Concussion

uardian, Stealth Chopper

The highlight of this class is its primary weapon, the Chicom CQB. This burst-fire SMG is brand new in *Call of Duty: Black Ops II* and unlike any other SMG we've seen before. The fire rate is insanely fast, allowing a good trigger finger to essentially fire full-auto at close range.

Additionally, the fact that it's a burst-fire weapon allows one to be extremely accurate at longer ranges, picking off enemies at a distance. These features combine to make a very unique and fun-to-use weapon that excels in many situations, maps, and game modes.

THE SLAYER	
Primary	M8A1 with Reflex Sight and Quickdraw
Secondary	KAP-40
Perk 1	Hardline
Perk 2	Toughness
Perk 3	Engineer and Dead Silence
Tactical	Shock Charge
Wildcards	Perk 3 Greed
Score Streaks	UAV, Warthog, Swarm

The maps in *Call of Duty: Black Ops II* tend to be on the larger end of the scale, offering many long lines of sight with head-high cover. This class takes advantage of that.

Stick to the outsides of the map, constantly flanking and picking off enemies. The goal is to stay alive in order to earn your Warthog streak. This will lead to your Swarm, which can potentially put you in a never-ending Scorestreak loop, resulting in a very high-scoring game.

TREVOR'S ACKNOWLEDGMENTS

My biggest thank you has to go to my fans; without them, I would not have been blessed with the opportunity to work on this guide. You guys, through your loyalty and support, have put me in a position in life that I never could have dreamed of. I truly appreciate it and will continue to strive to produce bigger and better content every single day.

Secondly, I would like to extend a big thank you to Phillip Marcus and Jason Fox. Being new to a project like this, I didn't know what to expect. You two made it extremely easy (and fun) to tackle such a daunting task as writing a multiplayer guide. I can't think of two other guys I would rather spend 10 hours a day in a small room with.

Ernest Le and Nadeshot, I had a great time working on the guide with you guys; thanks for making it such an enjoyable experience. Even more so, thanks for being there for me to play against in private lobbies. I needed some noobs to whoop up on. ;)

Next, I would like to thank BradyGames for giving me an opportunity like this! This has truly been a dream come true. I thoroughly enjoyed the experience and look forward to the future. Also, thank you to Activision for providing us a space to work and the resources we needed to make the best guide possible.

Finally, I would like to thank my friends and family, especially my mom, for supporting this crazy hobby/career that I have. I travel a lot and have an extremely unpredictable schedule, resulting in me not being able to be available as much as I would like. Thanks for understanding and supporting me in my endeavors.

ASSAULT RIFLES

WEAPON	LV UNLOCKED	DESCRIPTION
MTAR	4	Fully automatic assault rifle. Versatile and strong overall.
Type 25	4	Fully automatic assault rifle. High rate of fire with moderate recoil.
SWAT-556	10	3-round burst assault rifle. High damage output in each burst.
FAL DSW	22	Semi-automatic assault rifle. Light recoil with strong damage output.
M27	31	Fully automatic assault rifle. Higher mobility and reduced recoil.
SCAR-H	40	Fully automatic assault rifle. Increased damage and range.
SMR	46	Semi-automatic assault rifle. Highest damage per round in class.
M8A1	49	4-round burst assault rifle. Bursts can be fired in quick succession.
AN-94	55	Fully automatic assault rifle. The first 2 rounds of each burst are fired at a faster rate.

SMGs

WEAPON	LV UNLOCKED	DESCRIPTION
MP7	4	Fully automatic personal defense weapon. Versatile and strong overall.
PDW-57	4	Fully automatic personal defense weapon. Increased range and largest ammo capacity in its class.
Vector K10	16	Fully automatic submachine gun. Contains recoil mitigation technology.
MSMC	28	Fully automatic submachine gun. Increased range and reduced recoil.
Chicom CQB	37	3-round burst submachine gun. High cyclic fire rate allows for fast consecutive bursts.
Skorpion EVO	46	Fully automatic submachine gun. Highest rate of fire in class.

LMGs

WEAPON	LV UNLOCKED	DESCRIPTION
QBB LSW	4	Fully automatic LMG. Highest rate of fire in class.
Mk 48	4	Fully automatic LMG. Increased damage and range.
LSAT	13	Fully automatic LMG. Versatile and strong overall.
	37	Fully automatic LMG. Reduces fire rate over time, becoming more accurate.

SHOTGUNS

WEAPON	LV UNLOCKED	DESCRIPTION
R-870 MCS	4	Pump-action shotgun. Strong damage and range.
S12	4	Semi-automatic shotgun. Deadly at short range.
KSG	34	Pump action slug shotgun. Fires a single slug for high damage at longer ranges.
M1216	52	Fully automatic shotgun with a rechamber every 4 rounds.

SNIPER RIFLES

WEAPON	LV UNLOCKED	DESCRIPTION
SVU-AS	4	Semi-automatic sniper rifle. High fire rate with low recoil.
DSR 50	4	Bolt-action sniper rifle. Deadly from the waist up.
Ballista	43	Bolt action sniper rifle. Deadly from the chest up, with faster handling speeds.
XPR-50	52	Semi-automatic sniper rifle. Deadly from the chest up, with moderate recoil.

SPECIALS

WEAPON	LV UNLOCKED	DESCRIPTION
Crossbow	25	Bow-action bolt launcher. Fires explosive bolts that detonate a short time after impact.
Assault Shield	34	Ballistic-proof blunt shield weapon. Can be deployed on the ground as cover.
Ballistic Knife	49	Spring-action knife launcher. Increases melee speed and can fire blade as a projectile.

PISTOLS

WEAPON	LV UNLOCKED	DESCRIPTION
Five-Seven	4	Semi-automatic pistol. Versatile and strong overall with a large magazine.
Tac-45	4	Semi-automatic pistol. High damage at close range.
B23R	19	3-round burst pistol. High rate of fire with moderate recoil.
Executioner	31	Double-action revolver pistol. Fires 28 gauge shotgun shells.
KAP-40	43	Fully automatic pistol. Incorporates recoil-mitigation technology.

LAUNCHERS

WEAPON	LV UNLOCKED	DESCRIPTION
SMAW	4	Free-fire shoulder-fired rocket launcher. Can lock-on to vehicles and turrets
FHJ-18 AA	4	Guided shoulder-fired rocket launcher that can lock-on to vehicles and turrets.
RPG	40	Free-fire shoulder-mounted rocket launcher.

PERK 1

PERK	LV UNLOCKED	DESCRIPTION
Lightweight	4	Move faster. Take no damage when falling.
Hardline	4	Earn Scorestreaks faster.
Blind Eye	5	Undetectable by AI-controlled air support.
Flak Jacket	32	Take less explosive damage.
Ghost	55	Cannot be detected by enemy UAV's while moving, planting or defusing bombs, or while controlling Scorestreaks.

PERK 2

PERK	LV UNLOCKED	DESCRIPTION
Toughness	4	Flinch less when shot.
Cold Blooded	4	Resistant to targeting systems including: Dual Band, Target Finder, Sensor Grenade, MMS, and player-controlled aircraft.
Fast Hands	8	Swap weapons faster and use Equipment faster. Reset the fuse when throwing back Frag grenades.
Hard Wired	26	Immune to Counter-UAV and EMP.
Scavenger	44	Replenish ammo and equipment from enemies killed by non-explosive weapons.

PERK 3

PERK	LV UNLOCKED	DESCRIPTION
Dexterity	4	Aim faster after sprinting. Mantle and climb faster.
Extreme Conditioning	4	Sprint for a longer duration.
Tactical Mask	20	Reduce the effects of Flashbangs, Concussion Grenades, and Shock Charges.
Engineering	14	Show enemy Equipment in the world. Delay triggered explosives. Reroll and booby trap Care Packages.
Dead Silence	38	Move silently.
Awareness	50	Enemy movements are easier to hear.

WILDCARDS

WILDCARD	LV UNLOCKED	DESCRIPTION
Perk 1 Greed	4	Take a second perk 1.
Perk 2 Greed	10	Take a second Perk 2.
Perk 3 Greed	13	Take a second Perk 3.
Overkill	16	Take a primary weapon as your second weapon.
Secondary Gunfighter	19	Take a second Attachment for your second weapon.
Primary Gunfighter	22	Take a third Attachment for your primary weapon.
Tactician	25	Take a Tactical grenade in place of your Lethal grenade.
Danger Close	28	Take a second Lethal.

LETHALS

LETHAL	LV UNLOCKED	DESCRIPTION
Grenade	4	Produces lethal radius damage upon detonation.
Semtex	4	Grenade that sticks to surfaces before detonating.
Combat Axe	17	Retrievable axe that causes instant death on impact.
Bouncing Betty	28	Proximity mine that launches into the air before detonating. Can be avoided by crouching or going prone.
C4	41	A plastic explosive device that is detonated remotely with the clacker or by double-tapping "X."
Claymore	53	Directional anti-personnel mine that triggers a proximity-based explosion.

TACTICALS

TACTICAL	LV UNLOCKED	DESCRIPTION
Concussion	4	Slows movement, disorients targets, and temporarily disables enemy Equipment and turrets.
Smoke Grenade	4	Produces a smoke screen immediately upon impact.
Sensor Grenade	6	Detects enemy soldiers within line of sight.
EMP Grenade	11	Disables nearby enemy electronic systems.
Shock Charge	23	Electrocutes and stuns nearby enemies.
Black Hat	25	Hack Equipment and Care Packages, or disable enemy vehicles.
Flashbang	29	Blinds targets, impairs hearing, and temporarily disables enemy Equipment and turrets.
Trophy System	35	Destroys income enemy projectiles within 10 meters. Vehicle missiles have a chance to penetrate.
Tactical Insertion	47	Drop-zone beacon that allows you to place your next spawn point. Unavailable in Free For All game modes.

SCORESTREAKS

SCORESTREAKS

SCORESTREAK	LV UNLOCKED	COST	DESCRIPTION
UAV	7	350	Shows enemies on the mini-map.
RC-XD	18	450	Remote-controlled car strapped with explosives.
Hunter Killer	7	525	Infantry deployed drone that seeks out an enemy target or vehicle.
Care Package	7	550	Airdrop a Random Scorestreak.
Counter-UAV	33	600	Temporarily disables enemy mini-map.
Guardian	15	650	A placeable dish that projects a cone of microwave radiation that stuns and impairs enemies.
Hellstorm Missile	24	700	Remote controlled Hellstorm Missile with a cluster bomb payload.
Lightning Strike	7	750	Launch a coordinated Lightning Strike on three locations.
Sentry Gun	9	800	Deploy an automated Sentry Gun. Can be remote controlled.
Death Machine	36	850	Your own personal handheld minigun.
War Machine	45	900	Grenade launcher with rapid semi-automatic firing.
Dragonfire	7	975	Remote-controlled quad rotor with a lightweight machine gun.
AGR	27	1000	Airdrop an Autonomous Ground Robot that patrols for enemies. Can be remote controlled.
Stealth Chopper	21	1100	Call in a Stealth Helicopter. Does not appear on the enemy's mini-map.
Orbital VSAT	42	1200	Shows both enemy position and direction on the mini-map. Cannot be shot down.
Escort Drone	48	1250	Get personal air support from an Escort Drone.
EMP Systems	39	1300	Temporarily disables enemy electronics.
Warthog	30	1400	Jet aircraft that provides close air support (CAS) via several strafe runs.
Lodestar	12	1500	Laser missile targets remotely from the Loadstar.
VTOL Warship	7	1600	Be the gunner of a power VTOL Warship.
K9 Unit	51	1700	Attack Dogs that hunt down the enemy.
Swarm	54	1900	Call in a swarm of lethal Hunter Killer Drones.

ATTACHMENTS

ASSAULT RIFLE ATTACHMENTS

ATTACHMENT	LV UNLOCKED	XP EARNED	DESCRIPTION
Reflex Sight	2	100	Precision red dot sight.
Quickdraw	3	200	Ergonomic handle for faster aiming.
Fast Mag	4	300	Reload faster.
ACOG Sight	5	500	Enhanced zoom sight.
Fore Grip	6	600	Reduced recoil when aiming down the sights.
Adjustable Stock	7	400	Move faster when aiming.
Target Finder	8	700	Identifies enemies and notifies when an enemy is in the crosshair.
Laser Sight	9	800	Increases hipfire accuracy.
Select Fire	10	900	Switch to burst or automatic fire with Left Directional pad. Automatic fire will always have more recoil.
EOTech Sight	11	1000	Holographic sight. Provides a clearer view of the target than a red dot, but with less peripheral vision.
Suppressor	12	1100	Invisible from radar when firing, reduced muzzle flash, but less range.
FMJ	13	1200	Increased material penetration and damage against enemy Scorestreaks.
Hybrid Optic	14	1300	ACOG Sight with Reflex Sight attached on top. Press Left Control Stick while aiming down the sight to switch between optics.
Extended Clip	15	1400	More ammo in each clip.
Grenade Launcher	16	1500	Switch to an underbarrel grenade launcher with Left Directional pad.
Millimeter Scanner	17	1600	Detects lingering heat signatures from stationary enemies through materials at up to 25 meters.

SMG ATTACHMENTS

ATTACHMENT	LV UNLOCKED	XP EARNED	DESCRIPTION
Reflex Sight	2	100	Precision red dot sight.
Laser Sight	3	200	Increases hipfire accuracy.
Suppressor	4	300	Invisible from radar when firing, reduced muzzle flash, but less range.
Fast Mag	5	400	Reload faster.
EOTech Sight	6	500	Holographic sight. Provides a clearer view of the target than a red dot, but with less peripheral vision.
Fore Grip	7	600	Reduced recoil when aiming down the sights.
Quickdraw	8	700	Ergonomic handle for faster aiming.
FMJ	9	800	Increased material penetration and damage against enemy Scorestreaks.
Long Barrel	10	900	Increased range.
Target Finder	11	1000	Identifies enemies and notifies when an enemy is in the crosshair.
Adjustable Stock	12	1100	Move faster when aiming.
Extended Clip	13	1200	More ammo in each clip.
Select Fire	14	1300	Switch to burst or automatic fire with Left Directional pad. Automatic fire will always have more recoil.
Rapid Fire	15	1400	Increased rate of fire.
Millimeter Scanner	16	1500	Detects lingering heat signatures from stationary enemies through materials at up to 25 meters.

LMG ATTACHMENTS

ATTACHMENT	LV UNLOCKED	XP EARNED	DESCRIPTION
EOTech Sight	2	100	Holographic sight. Provides a clearer view of the target than a red dot, but with less peripheral vision.
Fore Grip	3	200	Reduced recoil when aiming down the sights.
FMJ	4	300	Increased material penetration and damage against enemy Scorestreaks.
Reflex Sight	5	400	Precision red dot sight.
Quickdraw	6	500	Ergonomic handle for faster aiming.
Target Finder	7	600	Identifies enemies and notifies when an enemy is in the crosshair.
Adjustable Stock	8	700	Move faster when aiming.
ACOG Sight	9	800	Enhanced zoom sight.
Laser Sight	10	900	Increases hipfire accuracy.
Suppressor	11	1000	Invisible from radar when firing, reduced muzzle flash, but less range.
Variable Zoom	12	1100	While scoped in, press the Right Control Stick to adjust between two different zoom levels.
Extended Clip	13	1200	More ammo in each clip.
Hybrid Optic	14	1300	ACOG Sight with Reflex Sight attached on top. Press Left Control Stick while aiming down the sight to switch between optics.
Rapid Fire	15	1400	Increased rate of fire.
Dual Band	16	1500	Nightvision scope with interlaced thermal overlay.

SHOTGUN ATTACHMENTS

ATTACHMENT	LV UNLOCKED	XP EARNED	DESCRIPTION
Reflex Sight	2	100	Precision red dot sight.
Long Barrel	3	200	Increased range.
Fast Mag	4	300	Reload faster.
Laser Sight	5	400	Increases hipfire accuracy.
Adjustable Stock	6	500	Move faster when aiming.
Suppressor	7	600	Invisible from radar when firing, reduced muzzle flash, but less range.
Extended Clip	8	700	More ammo in each clip.
Quickdraw	9	800	Ergonomic handle for faster aiming.
Millimeter Scanner	10	900	Detects lingering heat signatures from stationary enemies through materials at up to 25 meters.

SNIPER RIFLE ATTACHMENTS

ATTACHMENT	LV UNLOCKED	XP EARNED	DESCRIPTION
Suppressor	2	100	Invisible from radar when firing, reduced muzzle flash, but less range.
Ballistics CPU	3	200	Reduced weapon sway when aiming.
Variable Zoom	4	300	While scoped in, press the Right Control Stick to adjust between two different zoom levels.
Fast Mag	5	400	Reload faster.
FMJ	6	500	Increased material penetration and damage against enemy Scorestreaks.
ACOG Sight	7	600	Enhanced zoom sight.
Extended Clip	8	700	More ammo in each clip.
Laser Sight	9	800	Increase hipfire accuracy.
Dual Band	10	900	Nightvision scope with interlaced thermal overlay.
Iron Sights	11	1000	(Ballista Only) Rail-mounted tritium iron sights.

PISTOL ATTACHMENTS

ATTACHMENT	LV UNLOCKED	XP EARNED	DESCRIPTION
Reflex Sight	2	100	Precision red dot sight.
Extended Clip	3	200	More ammo in each clip. (Not present on Executioner)
Laser Sight	4	300	Increases hipfire accuracy.
Long Barrel	5	400	Increased range.
FMJ	6	500	Increased material penetration and damage against enemy Scorestreaks.
Fast Mag	7	600	Reload faster.
Suppressor	8	700	Invisible from radar when firing, reduced muzzle flash, but less range.
Tactical Knife	9	800	Carry a tactical knife in your off hand for faster melee attacks.
Dual Wield	10	900	Hipfire two weapons.

CROSSBOW ATTACHMENTS

ATTACHMENT	LV UNLOCKED	XP EARNED	DESCRIPTION
Reflex Sight	2	100	Precision red dot sight.
ACOG Sight	3	200	Enhanced zoom sight.
Dual Band	4	300	Nightvision scope with interlaced thermal overlay.
Tri-Bolt	6	500	Fires a bundle of 3 bolts at a time.
Variable Zoom	5	400	While scoped in, press the Right Control Stick to adjust between two different zoom levels.

ACHIEVEMENTS & TROPHIES

There are 50 Achievements/Trophies in *Black Ops II*.

SINGLE-PLAYER CAMPAIGN

> The following are earned by completing the story mode. Finish the campaign on Veteran and successfully complete the Strike Force missions to earn them all.

NAME	DESCRIPTION	POINTS
No Man Left Behind	Rescue Woods. Complete Pyrrhic Victory.	20
Gathering Storm	Investigate the jungle facility. Complete Celerium.	20
Shifting Sands	Gather Intel on Raul Menendez from Mullah Rahmaan. Complete Old Wounds.	20
Driven by Rage	Take down Menendez and his operation. Complete Time and Fate.	20
Waterlogged	Gather information on Raul Menendez's suspected terrorist plot. Complete Fallen Angel.	20
What Happens in Colossus…	Find the Karma weapon. Complete Karma.	20
False Profit	Capture Manuel Noriega and bring him to justice. Complete Suffer With Me.	20
Deep Cover	Capture Menendez. Complete Achilles' Veil.	20
Sinking Star	Interrogate Menendez. Complete Odysseus.	20
Late for the Prom	Escort the president to the secure location in downtown LA. Complete Cordis Die.	20
Death from Above	Stop Menendez once and for all. Complete Judgment Day.	50
Old Fashioned	Complete Pyrrhic Victory, Old Wounds, Time and Fate, and Suffer With Me in Veteran.	50
Futurist	Complete all future levels in Veteran.	50
Defender	Successfully defend FOB Spectre from incursion. Complete FOB Spectre Strike Force Mission.	15
Singapore Sling	Successfully neutralize the SDC freighter at Keppel Terminal. Complete Shipwreck Strike Force Mission.	15
Desert Storm	Successfully escort the VIPs to safety. Complete IED Strike Force Mission.	15
Blind Date	Successfully rescue HVI. Complete Second Chance Strike Force Mission.	15
Art of War	Successfully assassinate SDC Chairman Tian Zhao. Complete Dispatch Strike Force Mission.	25
Black Ops II Master	Complete the campaign on Hardened or Veteran difficulty.	15

> Complete challenges during the campaign and collect all of the Intel for these Achievements/Trophies.

NAME	DESCRIPTION	POINTS
Just Gettin' Started	Complete 1 challenge in any level.	10
Mission Complete	Complete all challenges in a level.	10
Giant Accomplishment	Complete all challenges in *Black Ops II*.	50
High IQ	Collect all Intel.	20

STORY

> The following Achievements/Trophies are earned during the campaign.

NAME	MISSION	DESCRIPTION	POINTS
Back in Time	Any (after completing the game)	Use a future weapon in the past. Customize your loadout with a future weapon before starting a past mission.	10
Gun Nut	Any	Complete a level with a customized loadout.	10
Ten K	All	Minimum score of 10k in every mission.	15
Man of the People	Time and Fate	Stop the brutality inflicted by the PDF. As Menendez, kill PDF troops who abuse civilians.	15
Hey Good Looking	Fallen Angel	Plastic surgery avoided. Avoid the flame when driving the SOC-T at the very end of the mission.	10
Dirty Business	Old Wounds, Time and Fate, and Suffer With Me	Listen and think before you shoot. Resist shooting Kravchenko, find the CIA file in the cocaine bunker, and let Noriega speak in the motel.	15
Family Reunion	Suffer With Me	There are two futures. Wound your target at the end of the mission.	10
Ultimate Sacrifice	Achilles' Veil	Only one can survive. Shoot at Menendez.	15
Ship Shape	Odysseus	Reinforcements on the way. Wound Admiral Briggs. China has to be an ally.	10
Showdown	Odysseus	A duel between rivals. Defalco survives Karma mission and Farid survives Achilles' Veil mission. Chloe must not be rescued.	15
Good Karma	Odysseus	Crack the Celerium worm. Karma survives through Odysseus mission.	20
Dead or Alive	Judgment Day	Jailor or executioner. Decide Menendez's fate at the end of the mission.	15

MULTIPLAYER

> These Achievements/Trophies are earned through Multiplayer play.

NAME	DESCRIPTION	POINTS
Welcome to the Club	Reach Sergeant (Level 10) in multiplayer Public Match.	10
Welcome to the Penthouse	Prestige once in multiplayer Public Match.	50
Big Leagues	Win 5 multiplayer League Play games after being placed in a division.	20
Trained Up	Win 10 multiplayer games while playing in Combat Training playlists.	10
Party Animal	Win 10 multiplayer games while playing in Party Games playlists.	10

ZOMBIES

> These Achievements/Trophies are earned by playing Zombies.

NAME	DESCRIPTION	POINTS
Tower of Babble	In TranZit, obey the voices.	75
Don't Fire Until You See	In TranZit, have all doors opened without being set on fire.	30
The Lights of Their Eyes	In Green Run, pacify at least 10 zombies with 1 EMP.	5
Undead Man's Party Bus	In TranZit, complete all additions to the bus in 1 game.	15
Dance on my Grave	In Green Run, acquire your Tombstone.	5
Standard Equipment May Vary	In TranZit, acquire 4 different equippable items in 1 game.	25
You Have No Power Over Me	In TranZit, defeat "him" without being attacked by "him."	15
I Don't Think They Exist	In TranZit, kill one of the denizens of the forest while it is latched onto you.	10
Fuel Efficient	In TranZit, use an alternative mode of transportation.	10
Happy Hour	In TranZit, buy 2 different Perks before turning on the power.	15

PLATINUM TROPHY ON PLAYSTATION 3

> PLATINUM: Earn all available Trophies.

CALL of DUTY
BLACK OPS II

Written by Phillip Marcus, Michael Owen, Kenny Sims, Jason Fox, Ernest Le, Matthew Haag, and Trevor Martin
Maps illustrated by Rich Hunsinger and Darren Strecker

DK/BradyGames, a division of Penguin Group (USA) Inc.
800 East 96th Street, 3rd Floor
Indianapolis, IN 46240

ISBN 13 EAN: 978-0-7440-1420-4

Printing Code: The rightmost double-digit number is the year of the book's printing; the rightmost single-digit number is the number of the book's printing. For example, 12-1 shows that the first printing of the book occurred in 2012.

15 14 13 12   4 3 2 1

Printed in the USA.

CREDITS

TITLE MANAGER
Tim Fitzpatrick

SENIOR DEVELOPMENT EDITOR, LE
Chris Hausermann

MANUSCRIPT EDITOR
Matt Buchanan

BOOK DESIGNER
Tim Amrhein

DESIGNER, LE
Dan Caparo

PRODUCTION DESIGNER
Tracy Wehmeyer

BRADYGAMES STAFF

GLOBAL STRATEGY GUIDE PUBLISHER
Mike Degler

EDITOR-IN-CHIEF
H. Leigh Davis

LICENSING MANAGER
Christian Sumner

MARKETING MANAGER
Katie Hemlock

DIGITAL PUBLISHING MANAGER
Tim Cox

OPERATIONS MANAGER
Stacey Beheler

ACKNOWLEDGMENTS

BradyGAMES sincerely thanks everyone at Activision and Treyarch for their support and hospitality during this project. A thousand thanks to Vickie Farmer, Yale Miller, Alicia Mandeville, John Banayan, and Jay Puryear—your time and effort made this guide possible. Very special thanks to the following folks who worked hard to ensure this guide's thoroughness and accuracy—thank you!

PMG

Chris Baggio	James Bonti	Alyssa Delhotal	Yale Miller	Shannon Wahl
John Banayan	Ben Brinkman	Jason Harris	Lisa Ohanian	

QA

Jeff Roper	Ryan Trondsen	Christian Baptiste
Kevin Yoo	Pedro Aguilar	Johnny Kim

TREYARCH

Reza Elghazi	Anthony Ruiz	Kim Park	Jay Puryear
Jimmy Zielinski	Ronnie Fazio	David Vonderhaar	Anthony Flame
Bryan Pearson	Don Oades	Dan Bunting	

Phillip Marcus: I've been writing *Call of Duty* guides for years now, and yet every year I'm still trying to find new ways to present information, new ways to share ideas with you, the player. This year was exceptionally challenging for many reasons. But despite the struggle, I think we've created something special this time. What do you think? Share your thoughts online, I'll be watching.

Rich, your maps look amazing. Ernest, Matt, Trevor, you're a great bunch of guys. And Jason, I couldn't have put these ideas in print without your help. At ATVI, my personal thanks to Yale Miller, Chris Baggio, Lisa Ohanian, and Jason Harris for their help. At Treyarch, a special thanks to David Vonderhaar for his time. And as ever, it takes a village to make a book this complex. My utmost respect to the editorial and design team at Brady; thank you for steering this ship, Tim!

Evilgamer fans, you guys rock. And finally, I love you Daphne!

Jason Fox: Over the last several years I've contributed to four separate *Call of Duty* guides, each one more detailed than the last. I hope that I have helped to properly describe the care with which the designers have crafted and iterated on the proven *Call of Duty* formula with the data analysis for *Black Ops II*.

I'd like to send thanks to our Activision hosts Chris Baggio and Yale Miller for accommodating our stay. Also, a big shout-out to the onsite Pro crew of Ernest Le, Trevor Martin, and Matt Haag for providing initial counterpoints and eventual agreement with our gameplay assessments. One day Matt will learn the true power of the prone LMG. A big thanks to Phil Marcus for bringing me along on another guide and for constantly challenging my development skills with data analysis ideas. The level of detail in the multiplayer stats section is directly attributable to hours of rumination and argument between us. Lastly, I'd like to send a special thank you to psijaka for his assistance with some remedial physics! All of my love goes out to Lindsey, Jake and Ellie!

Rich Hunsinger: I'd like to thank Leigh Davis and Tim Fitzpatrick at BradyGames for the opportunity to work on this project. Thanks to Michael, Kenny, Phil, Jason, and Darren for their help and camaraderie, and Chris Baggio and Yale Miller from Activision for their accommodations during our stay. Thanks to the Sea Snipers that held the fort down while I was on site. Special thanks to my wife for her patience and support on this project and everything else I do. She is awesome. Be jealous.

Darren Strecker: My thanks go to Leigh Davis and Tim Fitzpatrick for bringing me onto this project and showing me so much trust in representing BradyGames on the road. It was a great experience and a good chance for me to work with this fine team of human beings. Thanks also to Michael and Kenny for their help and guidance through the process. I already miss the food trucks... I also want to give a shout out to Rich, Phil, and Jason for their support, and thank everyone at Activision for their hospitality.

To Mog, thanks for the tour of the darkish side of Santa Monica, and to Naomi for cat sitting. You're special. Finally I'm grateful to have the kind of parents who would pick me up from the airport at 4:00 a.m. with